THE
CHANGING FACE
OF BATTLE

from Teutoburger Wald to Desert Storm

BRYAN PERRETT

CASSELL&CO

Cassell & Co
Wellington House, 125 Strand, London WC2R 0BB

First published 2000

British Library Cataloguing-in-Publication Data:
a catalogue record for this book is available from the
British Library

ISBN 0-304-35307-8

Distributed in the USA by Sterling Publishing Co. Inc.,
387 Park Avenue South, New York, NY 10016-8810.

Designed and edited by DAG Publications Ltd.
Designed by David Gibbons; layout by Anthony A. Evans;
edited by Michael Boxall; printed and bound in
Great Britain by The Bath Press.

CONTENTS

PREFACE

I suppose that for most boys of my generation the books of George Alfred Henty formed a normal part of growing up. There were many of them in the family's bookcases, most having been awarded to my father and uncles as school or Sunday school prizes. Some were very fine editions indeed, with title and an illustration stamped into the binding in gilt, more gilt edging the pages, tissues protecting the more important plates and a silk ribbon with which to mark one's place. The curious thing was that by the time I picked up my first Henty, the author had been dead for some forty years, yet he remained remarkably popular. Some of his books remained in print and were readily available; indeed, a few titles can still be found and a collector's market exists for the remainder.

Henty was no stranger to the sharp end of war. In 1854 he left Cambridge without a degree to serve in the Crimea with the Purveyor's Department and five years later was sent to Italy to assist in hospital organisation during the war between Piedmont and Austria. Shortly afterwards, he left government service to become a war correspondent, a career which took him to Italy again in 1866, to Abyssinia in 1867–8, to Paris during the Commune 1870–1, to West Africa with Wolseley 1873–4, to Spain during one of the Carlist Wars in 1874, and to the Balkans for the Turco–Serbian War of 1876. Gifted with immense energy, he began writing adventure stories for boys in 1868, taking as their background military or naval events as widely separated as the Punic Wars and the Second Boer War. Generally, they had rousing titles such as *The Young Buglers* or *Under Drake's Flag*, their heroes were young men caught up in great events, and they emphasised the virtues of leadership, courage,

loyalty, integrity and team spirit. The research that went into them ensured that, fictional storylines apart, they are still regarded as respectable reflections of military and naval history. Such was his output that by the time of his death in 1902, Henty had produced seventy books for boys, ten novels for adults and two volumes dealing with his personal experiences as a war correspondent. He had earned a place in *The Oxford Companion to English Literature*, but as his biographer, George Manville Fenn, was to put it, his real legacy was that he had 'taught more lasting history to boys than all the schoolmasters of his generation'. And, one might add, of several generations to come.

My own enjoyment of Henty's work was enhanced by that of A. Hilliard Atteridge, one of his younger contemporaries. Atteridge did not have such a colourful career as Henty, nor was he as prolific, but he was a respected writer of military history and a good, clear communicator. In June 1914 he completed his book *Famous Land Fights*, which was intended for the general reader but also had the juvenile market in mind. In it he traced the evolution of land warfare from the earliest times to the present, using specific battles to illustrate the influence on tactics of weapon systems, organisation and terrain.

Both Henty and Atteridge were read while a world war was in progress, and neither the former's emphasis on the heroic virtues nor the detached analysis of the latter could conceal the fact that war is the most tragic, brutal, squalid, ugly and wasteful of all mankind's activities. Unfortunately, as humanity stubbornly refuses to learn from its mistakes, war must also be regarded as one of history's primary driving forces and thus cannot be ignored. To a very large extent, the wars of the past two millennia have determined where we live, how we are governed, how we worship, whether we consider ourselves to be free or not, and even the language we speak.

My task is to examine the development of warfare over the past 2,000 years in as intelligible a manner as did Atteridge. I have, however, forsaken his purely narrative style, for he was neither the first nor the last to travel this particular road and it was not the only option. Significantly, both Sir Edward Creasy in his *Fifteen Decisive Battles of the World* and Major-General J. F. C. Fuller in his *Decisive Battles of the Western World, 480 BC–1944* decided to connect their discussions of specific battles with commentaries outlining the most important historical and military developments of the intervening period. This method, it seemed to me, offered the greater scope to examine the evolution of warfare set within its inseparable political, social and technical contexts, and I have done my best to follow it throughout.

Bryan Perrett

Picture credits

The illustrations on pages 21, 24, 26, 35, 42, 51, 55, 57, 59, 61, 69, 71, 74, 76, 77, 78, 80, 91, 93, 124, 144, 173, 208 and 238 are by courtesy of Ladybird Books Ltd. Other illustrations and photographs are individually acknowledged in the captions. Maps are by DAG Publications Ltd.

Introduction – In The Beginning ...

We tend, because we have put men on the moon and have devised the computer, to think that we are cleverer people than those who have gone before, yet all we have done is apply accumulated experience and scientific knowledge. No evidence exists to suggest that human nature has itself changed since mankind replaced the dinosaurs. To illustrate the point, a letter has survived from the days of Ancient Egypt in which the writer seeks to dissuade a younger man from abandoning his studies in order to join the army. 'You'll be mucked about until you won't know whether you're coming or going,' warns the writer. 'You'll march till you drop, you'll swelter and freeze, and you'll eat the worst food you've ever tasted. There's a real chance you'll be injured. You'll be lucky if you're paid, but even then it won't be much. All you'll end up with is a crack on the head and no thanks from anyone. Is it worth it?' Such well-intentioned letters are still written today, more often than not by those with no experience of the profession of arms or the counter-attractions it offers.

Primitive men fought one another for possession of hunting-grounds, water-holes and the best caves. It was quickly apparent that families who fought as a unit stood a greater chance of survival than those who did not. Soon, related families banded together as clans for their own protection. In time, several clans would form a minor kingdom, which would absorb or be absorbed into other kingdoms to form an empire. If threatened, that empire would field an army.

The first weapons were clubs, pointed sticks and the hunter's sling or bow. Metal workers produced more efficient spear and arrow heads, and the long knife evolved into a sword with which one could slash or stab. Suddenly, the battlefield had become a terribly dangerous place. The shield, made from wicker or hide, probably provided the warrior with his first piece of protective armour. For those who could afford it, the helmet came next, followed by body armour. War was now becoming expensive and in the developing civilisations of the Middle East it became the State, for want of a better word, that was responsible for equipping its armies, the first known example being the Chaldeans in about 3500 BC. This naturally reinforced the authority of the ruler and in return he and his provincial governors provided security by fortifying their most important cities and towns, a process which is believed to have begun between 3000 and 2500 BC.

Thus far, war had been waged by armies consisting almost entirely of infantry, although the Chaldeans did possess 'war cars' drawn by four very small horses, from which spears could be thrown or an archer could shoot. Selective breeding produced bigger, stronger horses which, though not yet large enough to carry a man, could as a team pull a light wicker or shaped wood chariot at great speed. The chariot would carry a driver, an archer and a shield bearer who would protect both. Using such weapons the Hyksos, a nomadic people, invaded Egypt in 1680 BC and completely defeated the simple militia opposed to them. Under Pharaoh Amosis, the Egyptians learned from their conquerors and, recognising that no one constituent arm is of greater importance than the whole, they raised an army in which chariot units, infantry and archers were trained to fight a mutually supportive battle under central direction. In 1600 BC the Hyksos were driven out and for the next century the Egyptians extended their rule northwards as far as the banks of the Euphrates.

It was the Egyptian army which, in 1479 BC, won the Battle of Megiddo, the first recorded battle in history. Pharaoh Thutmosis III was determined to stamp out a rebellion in Palestine by the Kings of Megiddo and Kadesh. Leading his army by night through a narrow defile in the hills to the south of the Megiddo, he achieved complete tactical surprise. Mounting a holding action against the rebels' left and centre, he threatened their right in such a manner that they believed their line of retreat to Megiddo would be cut. They immediately fled within the city gates and surrendered after a siege of three weeks.

Another interesting battle involving the Egyptians was Kadesh in 1294 BC, fought between Pharaoh Rameses II and King Muwatalis of the Hittite Empire for control of Syria. Rameses, having been tricked into believing that the Hittites had withdrawn, was advancing northwards intent on capturing Kadesh. His army consisted of four brigades, strung out across many miles of country, plus a strong flank guard to the west. Rameses, leading with the Amun brigade, established a fortified camp near Kadesh, little suspecting that the Hittites were waiting in ambush east of the town. As the second brigade, the Ra, approached the camp it was suddenly assailed in flank by swarms of Hittite chariots and routed, its survivors fleeing north towards the camp. Rameses counter-attacked with the Amun, hoping to fight his way through to the Ptah, which was approaching from the south, but was quickly encircled. Luckily for him, many of the Hittites believed that the battle was won and left to plunder the abandoned camp. At this stage the Ptah brigade arrived and the Egyptian flank guard came in from the west, with the result that the Hittites were driven off. The fourth Egyptian brigade, the Seth, was not engaged and the Hittite infantry, which remained on the eastern bank of the Orontes, took no part in the fighting. Neither commander deserved high marks for his handling of the battle, but Rameses was sufficiently pleased with himself to record the details of the action, one of the greatest chariot battles of ancient times, on the walls of the many temples he built. The Egyptian chariot was superior to the Hittite vehicle and its crews used a composite bow whose long range gave them a decided advantage over their opponents, who used short-range bows, javelins and spears during the missile phase of the engagement. Conversely, when it came to handstrokes it was the Hittites who fought at a decided advantage, having begun to use iron weapons while the Egyptians were still using bronze.

Neither the Egyptians, nor the Hittites, nor anyone else, could stand for long against the new military super-power that was emerging in the Middle East – Assyria. Centred upon what is today northern Iraq, the Assyrian state had had to fight hard for survival during its early years, and quickly recognised that by conquest and plunder it could enjoy a far higher standard of living than was to be gained by tilling its own poor soil. In many respects it bore a startling resemblance to Nazi Germany in that it was organised solely for war, crushed internal and external opposition with merciless severity, deported those of its opponents who might be useful for work in the homeland, and slaughtered the rest. Likewise, its rule was based on fear, with an efficient secret police force reporting the slightest hint of independence on the part of its functionaries.

The Assyrian army was the most formidable yet seen. It had first call upon manpower resources, employing conscription and call-out to maintain its strength, and its ranks included large numbers of subject peoples. It also had first call upon supplies of iron, absorbing the bulk of the national production. Its soldiers wore conical helmets and long mail coats made from plates stitched on to a leather undergarment. Chariots remained the prestige arm, the vehicles being enlarged to accommodate a second shield bearer. However, by about 1000 BC the horse had evolved to the point that the Assyrians became the first people to form cavalry, or, more accurately, mounted infantry units. These were of two types, spearmen and mounted archers, and it is thought that the two co-operated closely with the former providing a protective hedge when the latter dismounted to shoot. Together, chariots and mounted units softened up the enemy with a hail of arrows in preparation for the decisive infantry assault, then took up the pursuit. The infantry included units of archers, slingers and spearmen. The composite bow was used by both mounted and dismounted units, and in siege operations at least the latter troops were issued with a huge protective shield, curved back at the top, carried by another soldier. In addition, all infantrymen seem to have been equipped with a straight sword, worn on the left, and a dagger, while the spearmen were equipped with a smaller shield.

The Assyrians were experts in fortification and siegecraft. When attacking a city they employed fighting towers with which to dominate the defences on the chosen sector, and sheds housing pointed rams which were used to pick stones out of a wall until it collapsed, creating a breach. These machines were wheeled and were protected by hides, being pushed against the walls under cover of a heavy arrow storm. Another aspect of their military engineering was the use of inflated goatskins to ferry chariots across a river.

Logistics, too, were understood, provincial supply depots being established to feed armies on campaign. There was also a system of dispatch riders, and written orders ensured that local commanders knew exactly what was required of them. Whereas, however, the Third Reich did not survive its only war, the Assyrians remained the scourge of the Middle East for the better part of four centuries. No detailed accounts of their battles have survived, although carved reliefs and other archaeological sources show us the manner in which they fought. What is certain is that they sustained very few checks, and that of these some can be attributed to epidemics of various kinds. Much of their success stemmed from the fact that while their kings wielded absolute power, they were also first class field commanders and capable administrators.

Like all such empires, that of Assyria had been extended beyond safe limits and decadence had begun to rot its centre; again, the purely Assyrian element of the population had been severely diluted by the constant importation of conquered peoples into their midst. Revolts coincided with internal power struggles, and in 612 BC an alliance of Medes, Babylonians and Scythians stormed Nineveh, the capital, bringing the empire to a sudden and dramatic end.

Within sixty years of the Assyrian collapse the dominant power throughout the Middle East had become Persia, which inherited much of the Assyrian military tradition, including conscription, although rule through fear was largely replaced by benevolent despotism.

Under Cyrus the Great the division appeared as a viable military formation for the first time. Each division was 10,000 strong and contained ten battalions of 1,000 men which were further sub-divided into 100-strong companies and 10-strong sections. In action the division was deployed in ranks ten deep, the front rank being equipped with large leather and osier shields and fighting spears six feet long, and the rest with bows and curved swords. The most famous of these divisions was under the King's personal command and known as The Immortals. This élite was composed of selected Persians and contained its own élite battalion, The King's Spearbearers, selected from men of the highest social standing.

Persian infantry provided the core of the army, supplemented by divisions raised from subject races. The Persians also deployed their own chariots, but at first cavalry contingents were provided by other races. Among these the Medes were prominent, but Cyrus did not trust them entirely and decided to raise Persian cavalry regiments from among his own nobility, the most prestigious of them being known as The Kinsmen.

Cyrus died in 530 BC, having conquered half the known world. His son Cambyses added Egypt to the empire but died prematurely in 522. Following a power struggle a noble named Darius came to the throne and continued the policy of expansion until his boundaries stretched from the river Indus to the shores of Asia Minor and beyond. Such huge acquisitions of territory made immense demands on the army, which became increasingly reliant on the recruitment of mercenary troops to meet its commitments. Even so, it is not surprising that whoever occupied the throne of the Persian empire included among his titles those of Great King, King of Kings, King of Many Peopled Countries and Upholder of the World.

Up to now the major military historical events of the ancient world have been seen through a glass darkly. Generally, the history of wars tended to be written by the victors, preserved on wall reliefs and stellae or in more fragmentary form on papyri or inscribed tablets. The pictures that emerge are one-sided of course, and further distorted by the scribe's desire to earn the favour of his royal master. The size of the king's army, and especially that of his expensive chariot arm, was inflated so as to emphasise his wealth and power, as was that of the opposing army and its casualties, in order to illustrate the scale of the victory. The enormous numbers of troops sometimes quoted are suspect given the immense quantities of food that would have been required to maintain them in the field. However, once the Persian empire comes into contact with the democracies of the Hellenistic world, the mists begin to roll away as historians with no axe to grind produce more objective versions of events.

Contact with the Greeks introduced the Persians to a new kind of soldier. The city states of mainland Greece, though often bickering among themselves, belonged to a loose confederacy that was perpetuated every fourth year with a competitive athletics meeting at Olympia. Among the events were racing in armour and the Pyrrhic Dance, a team event designed to test co-ordinated movement and endurance, also performed in full armour. As rivalry between the states was fierce, great emphasis was placed on the physical education of their young men with a view to producing an overall high standard of fitness and stamina.

In theory the city states were democracies lacking an hereditary aristocracy. In time of war, therefore, the burden fell upon the middle classes, who alone could afford to provide themselves with armour and weapons. Armour consisted of a crested helmet with visor, breast and back plates, greaves to protect the lower legs and a large circular shield emblazoned with the city's emblem. The principal weapon was the fighting spear, eight feet long, plus a short sword for use in emergency; the shield, too, was used offensively and could be smashed into an opponent, knocking him to the ground or forcing him backwards. Heavy infantrymen so equipped were known as hoplites. They were formed into a phalanx eight ranks deep which would advance at a steady pace maintained by a rhythmic paean or war chant, with shields locked in a protective wall. It would crash into the enemy line with terrific momentum, the soldiers in the forefront – pushed on by those behind – stabbing over their shields at their opponents' heads, shoulders and necks until they broke. Although the clash of these opposing phalanxes inspired a 17th-century playwright's line, 'When Greeks joined Greeks, then was the tug of war', the evidence suggests that such encounters were of short duration and that fatal casualties were light on both sides – about two per cent for the victors and fifteen per cent for the losers – almost certainly because the phalanx was quite unsuited to any form of pursuit.

The phalanx had further disadvantages. Once set in motion it could either advance or withdraw, but despite complex drill movements to adjust its depth on one or both flanks, it lacked the flexibility to move in any other direction. Its flanks, furthermore, were dangerously vulnerable; the effect of swordsmen breaking into the packed ranks of spearmen, only a few of whom could use their weapons at any one time, can well be imagined. It was in this context that the city's poorer folk came into their own. They armed themselves with whatever they could afford, bows, slings, javelins, clubs, swords and light shields known as bucklers, and their principal responsibility was to act as light infantry and protect the flanks of the phalanx.

Greece being a mountainous country, horses were few in number and for all practical purposes the armies of the city states lacked any sort of mounted arm. On the other hand, not only did they have a strong territorial loyalty, but their members also fought all the harder for being in the company of their kinsmen, neighbours and friends. Such motivation, added to physical fitness, was a powerful combination, and unlike anything the Persians had encountered before.

Friction between Persia and the city states of mainland Greece became inevitable when some of the Ionian islands rebelled against the Great King and received Greek support. In 490 BC Darius decided that the Greeks must be punished. A punitive expedition was dispatched across the Aegean, landing in the Bay of Marathon. It is thought that about 20,000 troops were put ashore, including a cavalry contingent. Opposing them was an 11,000-strong army composed of Athenians and their allies under the command of Miltiades. At first the Greeks were seriously worried by the prospect of having to fight cavalry, but when a deserter informed Miltiades that the horses were being watered at springs some way to the north he decided to attack at once, having first made sure that his front equalled that of the Persians by thinning the centre of the phalanx, while maintaining a twelve-deep formation on either flank. This proved to be the key to success, for while the Median and Persian troops holding the centre of the enemy line withstood the shock and more than held their own for a time, the subject peoples on either side gave way at once. As the Greek wings wheeled inwards to complete the encirclement the remaining Persians bolted for their ships. The Greeks lost 194 killed, the Persians 6,400. News of the victory was carried to Athens by the famed runner Pheidippides, whose feat is still commemorated in the athletic event named after the battle.

If Marathon was regarded as a great victory by the Greeks, it was held to be no more than a temporary check by the Persians. Indeed the fact that it encouraged more states to resist Persian incursions merely emphasised the need to bring the Greeks under control. Ten years later the Persians returned in force and in 479 BC the climactic battle of the campaign was fought at Plataea, eleven miles south of modern Thivai. The Persian general, Mardonius, commanded an army estimated to number 120,000, including a contingent of pro-Persian Greeks and a large cavalry element.

The Greek army, led by Pausanias, Regent of Sparta, the most militaristic of the states, is said to have included 32,000 hoplites and 48,000 light infantry. Both sides held their positions for eight days without making a move. During this period, however, the Persian cavalry preyed on Pausanias' lines of communication and poisoned his water supply, causing him to begin a tactical withdrawal. Mardonius promptly launched a general attack but the phalanx, operating on favourable ground, counter-attacked and drove the Persian infantry back into its stockaded camp, which was then stormed with great slaughter. Plutarch suggests that some 1,300 of Pausanias' men were killed, but given the nature of the fighting this may refer solely to the hoplites, the total figure almost certainly being much higher. Mardonius was among the 50,000 Persians said to have been slain, a suspiciously high figure even allowing that their wounded would have been finished off. Whatever the respective body counts, the battle put an end to Persian dreams of conquering Greece.

Half a century later Greece was thrown into turmoil by the long Peloponnesian War, lasting from 431 to 401 BC, which set the city states at one another's throats. The Persian empire, too, had its internal troubles, and in 401 Cyrus, satrap of Lydia, decided to challenge his brother, Artaxerxes II, for the throne. Cyrus, knowing the fighting value of the Greek hoplites, followed the Persian tradition of hiring 13,000 of them as mercenaries to support his cause. When the two armies met at Cunaxa the Greek phalanx carried all before it. When Cyrus was killed during a huge chariot and cavalry mêlée on another part of the field, the remainder of his troops fled. After the battle Artaxerxes invited Clearchus, the Spartan commanding the mercenaries, to a feast on the pretext that no quarrel existed between them. Clearchus and his senior officers were then treacherously murdered. The junior officers declined to surrender and decided to march their men to the nearest friendly city, the Greek colony of Trapezus on the Black Sea, more than 1,000 miles away across the mountains of Armenia. For most of this journey, which took five months and is better known as 'The March of the 10,000', the Greeks had to fight their way through, living off the land; about 6,000 of them reached safety. The story, one of history's greatest epics, was recorded by Xenophon, a young Athenian officer who played a prominent role, in his *Anabasis*. It was to have an enormous influence on subsequent events, for the survivors returned to their own cities filled with contempt for the Great King and his empire, saying that Persia belonged to any man who had the courage to attack it.

The Persian empire had indeed entered the terminal phase of its cycle and was rotting at its core. The veterans' words remained in the mind of one man, King Philip II of Macedonia, a kingdom lying to the north of mainland Greece, regarded by the rest of the Hellenistic world as being semi-barbarous. Philip was an excellent strategist and a gifted organiser who produced the finest army in Greek history, adapting traditional methods to suit his own requirements. Cavalry had always formed an important element in Macedonian warfare and Philip's intention was that it should remain the arm of decision, exploiting any weakness in the enemy ranks and turning it to ruin. His troopers wore a helmet and cuirass and were armed with a lance long enough to penetrate infantry formations equipped with spears of conventional length. The *corps d'élite* of the cavalry was a unit known as 'The Companions', consisting of eight squadrons each between two and three hundred strong. There was also a similarly organised unit of Thessalians and a 600-strong light cavalry unit known as 'The Scouts'.

The bedrock upon which the Macedonian army based its tactics remained the phalanx, although this was a very different organisation from that of the city states because Macedonia lacked a middle class. The Macedonian phalangite was lightly equipped, but armed with an 18-foot-long pike, known as a sarissa, and he fought in battalions that were sixteen files wide and as many ranks deep, giving a strength of 256 men in each. As both hands were needed to handle the pike, shields could not be carried, but troops in the front rank had a small buckler strapped to their left arm. In fact, the protection afforded by rank on rank of lowered pikes was similar to that of a quickset hedge in which most missiles would be caught among the shafts; again, the length of the pikes prevented the enemy from striking directly against the phalangites themselves. As usual, the flanks of the phalanx were protected by light troops. In this context, Philip was not averse to employing units contributed by allied or subject peoples. These included Thracian light cavalry, Agrianian javelin throwers and Cretan archers.

In addition, Philip's army included 3,000 hypaspists (shield-bearers). These were regular troops, armed and equipped very similarly to conventional hoplites. Deployed in 1,000-strong battalions, their duties were various and included the provision of a hard link between the cavalry and the phalanx once battle had been joined, and the storming of fortifications. In broken or mountainous terrain where the phalanx could not operate, they played the traditional role of heavy infantry.

Philip possessed a siege train that was the wonder of the age. It consisted of towers and rams that could be broken down and carried by pack animals, and portable stone-throwing catapults and ballistae that shot darts, both powered by twisted skeins, which could be used in siege operations and in the field. The army also had an expert engineering element which took care of bridge-building, water supply and mining operations. In the opinion of Field Marshal Montgomery, the Macedonian army 'was the best balanced and most powerful army of ancient times – an army equipped to fight in any type of country and against any enemy'. As if this was not enough, Philip possessed a secret weapon. Active military operations were customarily suspended during winter and in accordance with the seasonal demands of agriculture, but Philip managed his troops' supplies so efficiently that they could campaign throughout the year.

Their opponents thus faced a stark choice between severe economic dislocation if they remained in the field, and submission if they did not.

Having made himself master of all Greece and secured a mandate from the representatives of the city states for an invasion of the Persian empire, Philip was assassinated in 336 BC. He was succeeded by his 20-year-old son Alexander, who spent the next two years ruthlessly eliminating all rivals to the throne and securing his home base before continuing with Philip's grand design. Handsome, charismatic and a natural leader, he combined a streak of cruelty with unfailing courtesy towards women and consideration for his troops. Some generals are brilliant strategists, others are masters of the tactical battle. Alexander was both and as such was admired by subsequent great commanders from Scipio Africanus to Napoleon Bonaparte.

The Macedonian army, consisting of just 4,500 cavalry and 30,000 infantry, crossed the Dardanelles into Asia Minor in 334 BC. As the veterans of Cunaxa had predicted, the Great King's army which opposed it was but a shadow of its former self and within four years the Persian empire had ceased to exist. Only three pitched battles were required, but along the way Alexander secured his flank by subduing the enemy province of Egypt and besieging walled cities loyal to the Great King. The most important of these sieges was that of almost impregnable Tyre, which had once held out against the dreaded Babylonian King Nebuchadnezzar II for thirteen years, but fell to Alexander after only seven months.

Having been defeated at Granicus in 334 and again at Issus in the following year, the Great King, Darius III, sensed impending disaster and offered Alexander a huge bribe, half his empire and the hand of his daughter in marriage. Alexander would have none of it and closed in for the kill, the two armies meeting at Gaugamela near Arbela, not far from the overgrown ruins of Nineveh on the left bank of the Tigris. Darius' host was but a ghost of that fielded by his ancestors, and although it numbered about 200,000 men its quality was uneven. The Kinsmen and other cavalry units remained formidable opponents, but among the infantry the Immortals were only a memory, their place taken by Greek mercenaries, Persians equipped as hoplites but lacking their training, and tribal levies of indifferent motivation from the four corners of the empire. Darius had selected the battlefield because it was flat and therefore suited his mobile arm; he had even levelled it further to ensure the rapid movement of the 200 scythe-armed chariots he had dug out, a branch of service that was rapidly sliding into obsolescence as cavalry absorbed its previous functions. He also had fifteen war elephants, although these do not seem to have formed a major element in his plans.

Alexander's army was the largest he ever commanded, having been reinforced by Greek mercenaries and three more cavalry units, so that its strength amounted to 7,000 cavalry and 40,000 infantry. Even so, the Persian line extended far beyond his own and as a precaution his cavalry on each wing offered a refused flank and his centre was backed by a second-line phalanx composed of Greek infantry.

During its approach march the Macedonian army inclined somewhat to its right. Darius, seeing that if this movement continued the action would be fought off the stretch of specially prepared ground, sent his left-wing cavalry to halt it. A fierce cavalry combat ensued in which the Greeks succeeded in holding their own, with difficulty. At this point Darius launched his chariots in the hope that they would throw the phalanx into disorder. Instead, they ran into the Greek light infantry screen, consisting of Agrianian javelin men and Macedonian archers. The horses, driven mad by a rain of missiles, quickly became unmanageable. Many of the crews were killed by opponents so nimble that they ran beside the horses and cut their the reins. The surviving charioteers galloped harmlessly on through lanes opened for them by the hypaspists and the battalions of the phalanx, only to be killed by the Greek second line.

15

Hardly had this drama ended than Alexander spotted the movement of a Persian cavalry unit, dispatched by Darius to join the mêlée on the Greek right. This opened the gap in the enemy centre for which Alexander had been waiting. He immediately exploited it with the Companions, the hypaspists and four battalions of the phalanx, ripping through the Persian ranks in a wedge formation. Darius quickly took flight, pursued by Alexander and the Companions, and the entire Persian centre collapsed in rout.

Simultaneously, however, the right wing Persian cavalry had charged the Thessalian cavalry on the Greek left. This was soon in such difficulty that its commander, Parmenion, sent numerous requests for assistance to Alexander. The commanders of the two left-hand battalions of the phalanx, seeing the danger, wheeled left to cover Parmenion's right flank. This had the effect of opening a gap in left-centre of the Greek line and through it galloped a large force of Indian and Persian cavalry, though their intention was neither to complete Parmenion's destruction, nor even to fight for Darius, but simply to plunder. They rode through the gaps in the reserve phalanx to the Greek camp where they overwhelmed the Thracian guards and proceeded to help themselves until chased off by phalangites from the second line.

By degrees, word of Darius' flight reached the Persian cavalry on each wing and they disengaged. Alexander, having at last learned of Parmenion's situation, was returning to his assistance when he ran into the Indians and Persians who had just looted his camp. Another fierce cavalry combat ensued, ending with the death of 60 of the Companions and most of their opponents.

The huge Persian army was now streaming away in rout. Just how many died on the battlefield and in the general pursuit is uncertain, but many more were drowned in the fast-flowing river Lycus, where the one bridge was quickly choked with panic-stricken fugitives. What is certain is that Alexander's recorded loss of 300 killed was but small fraction of the Persian casualties.

When Darius was murdered by his own satraps Alexander became ruler of the entire Middle East. Further campaigns and victories would follow, taking him as far as the Indus. In India, however, his Macedonians made it clear that they would march no farther from home and he returned to Babylon, where he died suddenly in 323 BC. His huge but short-lived empire was divided by his generals among themselves.

Meanwhile, far to the west, a new and even more impressive military power was beginning to emerge. In 340 BC Rome became leader of the Latin League and by 280 BC had become the pre-eminent city of Italy. At first the Roman army had consisted of a citizen militia of spearmen which was equipped and fought in a similar manner to the Greek phalanx. Experience, particularly against the Celts, produced a new sort of organisation, the legion, the hallmark of which was tactical flexibility. Each legion contained between four and five thousand infantry and 300 cavalry, the former being divided into tactical sub-units known as maniples. These consisted of 40 lightly armed skirmishers and three groups called principes, hastati and triarii, each commanded by a centurion. The younger principes and the hastati were each about 120 strong and armed with two heavy throwing javelins (pila), a short thrusting sword and a long oval shield. The veteran triarii, as their name suggests, formed the third rank and were additionally equipped with a thrusting spear. The legion's field officers were six tribunes, drawn from the republic's aristocratic and political classes, who took it in turn to command, and herein lay a potential source of trouble since their respective abilities and experience were bound to differ.

This was also true at the higher command levels and was to be demonstrated on several occasions, notably during Rome's second war against Carthage. At Cannae on 2 August 216 BC an army consisting of eight Roman and eight allied legions, with 80,000 infantry and 7,000 cavalry, was butchered by a Carthaginian army numbering only 40,000 infantry and

10,000 cavalry. Exercising command of the Roman army on alternate days were the Consuls Aemilius Paulus and Terentius Varro, while commanding the Carthaginians was Hannibal, who possessed a tactical genius similar to Alexander's and who had already defeated Roman armies at the Trebbia (218 BC) and Lake Trasimene (217 BC).

Varro first threw away his numerical superiority by deciding to smash through his opponent's centre using sheer mass; the doubling of his maniples' depth shortened his front until it corresponded to Hannibal's. The Carthaginian infantry was formed with the Spaniards and Gauls in a convex crescent in the centre, and African troops on either side. Both armies deployed their cavalry on the flanks. The Roman cavalry was defeated on both wings but in the centre the legions were apparently successful, pushing back the Spaniards and Gauls until their convex line had become concave. At this point Gnaius Servilius, commanding the Roman infantry, sensed victory and committed more troops to the struggle. This was exactly what Hannibal wanted and at the critical moment he ordered the hitherto lightly engaged African divisions to wheel inwards in a double envelopment. As they did so, the rallied Carthaginian cavalry fell on the Roman rear, compressing the legionaries so tightly within a pocket that many of them were unable to use their weapons. Perhaps 8,000 desperate men managed to fight their way out, but the remainder were slaughtered where they stood.

If, in the immediate aftermath of the battle, Hannibal had possessed a siege train capable of taking Rome, the subsequent history of the world might have been different, but he had no such train and his government at home did not support him. The result was that while his own army slowly wasted away, Rome recovered from the disaster and, under Publius Cornelius Scipio, concentrated on the destruction of Carthaginian power in Spain. Scipio, having learned the lessons of Cannae, abandoned the concept of mass attack and adopted instead the flexible advance of successive lines of cohorts, each of three maniples, with the object of turning his opponents' flanks; further, the spear was relegated to use as a missile and much heavier reliance was placed on the short stabbing sword for close-quarter combat. By 206 BC the Carthaginians had been driven out of Spain and the war was carried into Africa itself. In 202 BC Hannibal, recalled from Italy to defend Carthage, met Scipio at Zama, some 60 miles south-west of modern Tunis, with an army greatly inferior to that which had won his great victories, and was easily defeated.

The humbling of Carthage marked a watershed in the history of Rome in that henceforth she embarked on a career of expansion throughout the Mediterranean and beyond. This brought her into conflict with King Philip V of Macedonia. The contest between the Greek and Roman way of war was resolved at Cynoscephalae in 197 BC. This was an encounter battle in which each side sought possession of a ridge which had previously separated them. Philip's phalanx bundled the Roman left down the ridge but on the opposite flank the Macedonians, still deploying, were pushed up the hillside. At this point, acting on his own initiative, a Roman tribune led twenty maniples, probably of triarii, along the ridge and fell on the flank and rear of the phalanx, which disintegrated in confusion amid heavy loss of life.

At this time the legions were formed from conscripts who served a six-year term, but during the next century the army underwent a series of radical reforms, notably at the hands of Gaius Marius. Initially only those who owned property had been eligible to serve, but the lowering of this qualification opened a military career to a great mass of men who had hitherto been excused service on the grounds that they had no stake in the state's continuing welfare. Thus, by degrees an army of disciplined conscripts was replaced by one of professional soldiers, a process accelerated by the need for the legions to serve progressively farther from home as the Roman sphere of influence expanded. Another logical step was the standardisation and mass production of the soldier's weapons and equipment, including his sword, shield and mail shirt. Training programmes placed strong emphasis on physical fitness, which was produced by running in full equipment, route marches, some of which had to be completed at speed, and incessant sword drill. On the march the legionary carried his personal baggage, thereby reducing the size of the unit's mule train. Thus heavily burdened, the Roman soldiers of the period referred to themselves as 'Marius' Mules'.

Marius is also credited with increasing the size of the legion to a nominal strength of between 5,000 and 6,000 men and a radical reform of its internal organisation in which the original 30 maniples were formally replaced by ten cohorts each of six centuries, giving a total of 60 centuries. It was Marius, too, who introduced the Eagle as the principal standard of each legion, replacing the diverse emblems formerly carried, thereby reminding its soldiers that while they were right to take pride in their legion's seniority, history, achievements and traditions, it was to Rome that their loyalty lay. In theory the idea was respected; in practice the legionary remained loyal to his legion and his general.

The last century before the birth of Christ was marked by several important developments. In 91 BC Rome's Italian allies initiated a successful rebellion known as the Social War. This ended with all Italians living south of the river Po being granted Roman citizenship with all its rights and privileges, including eligibility to serve in the legions. The result was to increase the number of legions, while the auxiliary role previously performed by the former allies as cavalry, light infantry, slingers and archers was henceforth carried out by non-Roman units raised in the provinces.

The period was also marked by civil wars and a slave revolt led by a former gladiator, Spartacus, which was only put down with the greatest difficulty. In 60 BC three successful military commanders, Marcus Licinius Crassus, Gnaius Pompeius (Pompey) and Gaius Julius Caesar, formed an informal association known as the Triumvirate which exercised political control in Rome.

From 58 BC to 51 BC Caesar was engaged in the conquest of Gaul. During 55 BC and 54 BC he carried out two raids on southern Britain, partly intended as reconnaissances in force and partly as punitive expeditions to discourage the Britons from sending reinforcements to the Gauls. The Romans were immediately confronted with a number of problems with which they were unfamiliar, including, during the first raid, an opposed landing in tidal waters near Dover. The shoreline and dominant cliffs were crowded with the Britons' infantry, cavalry and chariots, against whom the heavily encumbered legionaries, compelled to jump into deep water from their transports, were unable to make the slightest headway. Caesar ordered his war galleys to run themselves ashore on the enemy's right, then engage the enemy with their catapults, ballistae, slingers and archers. This caused the Britons to retire up the beach out of range. The Romans, however, had been shaken and continued to hesitate until the standard-bearer of the 10th Legion led the way ashore, shouting, 'Jump down, comrades, unless you want to surrender our Eagle to the enemy! I, at any rate, mean to do my duty by my country and my general!' This had the desired result, for rather than endure the disgrace of a lost Eagle the soldiers piled ashore to fight under the nearest leader until the Britons had been driven off.

The second factor which unnerved the legionaries was the Britons' use of chariots, of which they had had no experience, these vehicles having all but disappeared from the battlefields of the classical world. Furthermore, as Caesar tells us, the Britons used them in a unique and very dangerous way.

'In chariot fighting the Britons begin by driving all over the field hurling javelins, and generally the terror inspired by the horses and the noise of the wheels is sufficient to throw their opponents' ranks into disorder. Then, after making their way between the squadrons of their own cavalry, they jump down from their chariots and fight on foot while their charioteers retire a short distance from the battle and place the chariots so that their masters, if hard pressed, have an easy means of retreat to their own lines. Thus they combine the mobility of cavalry with the staying power of infantry, and by daily training they obtain such proficiency that even on a steep slope they are able to control the horses at full gallop and to check and turn them very quickly. They can run along a chariot pole, stand on the yoke, and get back into the chariot in a trice.'

In essence, Caesar is describing the tactics of mounted infantry, an arm of service which was to disappear from the battlefield for long periods and reappear periodically to meet particular tactical demands. Even when he had cavalry at his disposal Caesar never quite found an answer to the Britons' chariots. Equally, once the Romans became used to them, the latter made little impression on the legions, since men fighting as individuals in loose open order cannot defeat those fighting as a team in close formation.

Elsewhere, Caesar's fellow triumvir Crassus had run his head into a noose. A vain, silly man, he was bitterly jealous of Caesar's success and in 54 BC, while serving as proconsul for Syria, he provoked a conflict with neighbouring Parthia in the hope of adding to his own laurels. Disregarding advice, he launched an invasion at the head of a 39,000-strong army, consisting in the main of marching legionaries. He crossed the Euphrates and entered an area of semi-desert plain near Carrhae, known today as Haran. Here the trudging column was suddenly assailed by swarms of mounted archers. As men began to drop the column halted to form square. This merely provided the enemy, circling just beyond reach, with a larger target. The Parthian general, Surenas, brought up a camel train from which his archers regularly replenished their quivers. Amid broiling heat and the tortures of thirst, the Romans' ordeal continued until, in desperation, Crassus counter-attacked with the legions' small cavalry detachments and the fittest of his infantry. The counter-attack group, 6,000 strong, was quickly swallowed up and slaughtered to a man. Next, Crassus decided to retreat, abandoning his 4,000 wounded, to whom no mercy was shown. The following day the pattern of fighting was repeated and when Crassus requested terms he was treacherously killed. Only 5,000 Romans reached safety; 10,000 more were sold into slavery, and the bones of the remainder were left to whiten in the desert. The lesson was that in this sort of environment infantry are at the mercy of an enemy who employs firepower and mobility, unless they possess comparable firepower and access to water.

In 52 BC Pompey was illegally appointed sole Consul by the Senate. Two years later Caesar declined to obey an order to disband his army and marched on Rome. During a bitter series of civil wars lasting until 30 BC the legions fought and killed one another across the Roman world. Pompey was assassinated in 48 BC. Four years later Caesar, having made himself the autocratic ruler of Rome and been accorded the title of Imperator, was also murdered. His nephew, Gaius Julius Caesar Octavian, emerged victorious from the ensuing power struggle and was also granted the title of Imperator. In 27 BC the Senate conferred on him the name Augustus and with it status approaching that of a god. The Roman Republic was dead; the Roman Empire had been born.

So far, warfare at sea has barely been mentioned, although this was of critical importance in such struggles as those between the Greek city states and the wars between Rome and Carthage. It was, in fact, regarded simply as an extension of land warfare and, given the weapons available, this is hardly surprising. The warship was the galley, driven by sail in normal circumstances but powered by banks of oars in action. Fleets of galleys were deployed like armies, with wings, a centre and a reserve. For success, individual captains relied on splintering the enemy's oars, ramming and boarding. As opposing ships converged, their catapults and ballistae would exchange projectiles; for obvious reasons, combustible materials were much favoured, including the notorious Greek fire which had some of the properties of napalm and was either thrown in frangible pots or pumped from a primitive flame-thrower. At close range, archers and slingers would start picking off the enemy crew. If boarding were necessary, it would be carried out by a complement of soldiers whose numbers formed a small percentage of the crew in relation to the number of rowers required. Boarding, however, depended upon the proximity and angle of the opposing vessel and could be difficult and dangerous. In this connection the Romans found an answer with the corvus (crow), a bridge with a large spike on its outer end. This was dropped on to the deck of the enemy ship where the spike embedded itself in the timber, holding the two vessels close-grappled while the boarders rushed across.

This type of sea warfare would continue until the middle of the 16th century, and in some navies war galleys would remain in service until the 19th century. It was the soldiers who gave the orders; the task of the seamen being simply to transport them wherever they wanted to go and handle the ship in action. This remained true even outside the Mediterranean. The medieval tubs which fought at Sluys (AD 1340) were fitted with fore- and stern-castles for use by archers, and the fighting itself resembled an infantry battle fought at sea.

From this very brief survey of the art of war until the beginnings of the Roman Empire it becomes apparent that many developments that we consider to be relatively recent were already understood very thoroughly during ancient and classical times. These included the recognition of the fact that, in one form or another, an army should include infantry, a mobile arm and a missile arm, plus adequate engineering and logistic elements, if it were to achieve all the tasks it was likely to be set; familiarity with every possible tactical manoeuvre including out-flanking, double envelopment and penetration of the centre; the uses of firepower, mobility, shock action, attrition, intelligence-gathering and surprise; and appreciation of unit *esprit de corps* and the main-

tenance of morale. These fundamentals were not to change although, as we shall see, the way they were applied would be influenced by the development of weapon systems and changing historical circumstances.

Commentary 1 – The Early Roman Empire

Our study proper begins with the Imperial Roman Army, which is very convenient because its inception coincides approximately with the start of the Christian era, the precise date of which is still a matter for discussion between theologians, plus the fact that it was an army whose basic elements are all to be found in the armies of today.

Augustus established the strength of the Roman regular army at 28 legions, each with a nominal strength of 6,000 men, producing a total of approximately 168,000, plus an equal number of auxiliaries recruited from the empire's provinces. Most authorities suggest that the actual strength of the Augustan legion was about 4,800 men. The 2nd to 10th Cohorts were all 480 strong and had 80 men in each of their six centuries. On the other hand, the 1st Cohort, including as it did the legion's administrative personnel and specialist tradesmen, consisted of six (later five) 'double centuries', giving it an approximate strength of 800 men. The legion also included a 120-strong cavalry element and its own artillery. The latter, it has been suggested, included powerful ballistae that shot heavy darts, issued on the scale of one per century and mounted on mule-drawn carts, and catapults capable of hurling large stones, issued on the scale of one per cohort. These weapons did not form a specialist sub-unit and seem to have been manned from within the centuries. On the other hand, the existence of what were obviously artillery training grounds confirms that the crews trained and carried out practice shoots in groups. In action it was logical that they should be brigaded together as appropriate, concentrating their fire on a particular sector of the enemy's battle line or defences prior to an attack. The legion, therefore, was an all-arms battle group which, because of its size, has been compared to a modern brigade group, although in contemporary terms its importance equated more with that of a division.

The legionary himself was a long-service professional who enlisted for 26 years. In theory at least, he was paid regularly and at the end of his service he received a gratuity and a grant of land. His pay was subject to a number of stoppages, including the burial fund and the annual 'camp dinner', the latter probably being held to commemorate a special event in the legion's history. He trained hard, often with heavier packs and weapons than he would use on active service. In addition to the sort of training that has already been mentioned, he would become adept at producing an entrenched camp very quickly. Every so often the legion would be subjected to the equivalent of a modern Fit For Role Inspection, during which the inspecting officer would cast a critical eye over its speed-marching, entrenching abilities, drill and weapon training; as today, this would end with an encouraging speech to the troops, any reservations being saved for private discussion with the legion's senior officers. When he was not training or on active service, the legionary could find himself employed on a wide variety of engineering tasks. Under expert guidance, he constructed long, straight roads, bridges, walled camps and frontier defences. The Roman passion for order ensured that bases and camps throughout the Empire had an almost identical internal layout whatever the size of the unit occupying them. Their entire internal area was occupied by the headquarters building, barrack blocks, storehouses and workshops, the parade and training ground being a cleared space outside the walls.

Off duty, the legionary lived with seven of his comrades in a barrack room divided in two, the outer half containing stands for armour and equipment. His major diversion was the bath house, which served as a sort of canteen and leisure centre and was located outside the walls. Wine shops, brothels and other amenities existed nearby. Because the military

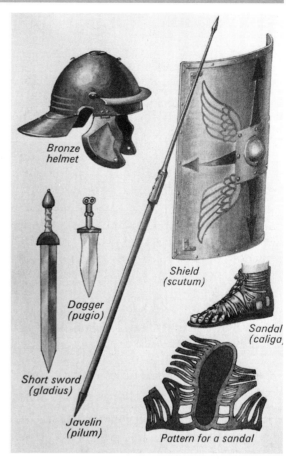

Above: Standardisation of equipment and centralised manufacture gave the Roman Army an advantage over many of its opponents.

authorities believed that bachelors made the best soldiers, the legionary was forbidden to marry until he was discharged. On the other hand, if he formed a relationship it was respected and any male offspring therefrom was styled *ex castris* and was entitled to join the legion in due course; many did.

If he showed promise the legionary would be promoted to decanus (chief of ten) and given responsibility for a section. If he continued to make satisfactory progress the next step on the promotion ladder would be optio, or second in command of a century. His promotion to centurion would be a matter for serious discussion. He was unlikely to attain the rank before he

21

was thirty because these men were the backbone of the army and set a high standard. A strict pecking order existed among them, the most recently promoted being given command of the 6th Century of the 10th Cohort, while the most senior commanded the 1st Century of the 1st Cohort. The latter, known as the Primus Pilus or First Spear, was a soldier of immense experience and accumulated wisdom whose opinions were sought and respected by the legion's senior officers. His appointment was intended to last for one year, but was sometimes extended well beyond that. The centurion has no precise parallel in a modern army, because his status clearly exceeded that of the warrant officer yet did not quite equate with commissioned rank. But it was possible for an outstanding Primus Pilus to end his career in the commissioned rank of Praefectus Castrorum, enabling him to administer and train the legion but not command it in the field.

The officers commanding the legion were still drawn from the aristocratic and senatorial classes, the slightly suspect theory being that he who rules in peace can also command in war. There was, however, one important change from the days of the Republic in that the legion now had a permanent commanding officer, known as the Legate, who was appointed directly by the Emperor. His second-in-command, usually a nobleman waiting to enter the Senate, was designated Tribunus Laticlavius. Five more tribunes completed the commissioned rank strata. In settled times the officers tended to live with their families and slaves outside the legionary base.

During this period the legionary's mail shirt was replaced by articulated plate armour, consisting of iron strips that buckled together across the chest, back and shoulders, providing the wearer with protection without restricting his freedom of movement. His helmet was improved by fitting it with a neck guard and cheek pieces. His shield has been described as the best designed of the Classical period. Oblong in shape, it had a pronounced convex curve and consisted of several layers of wood strips covered with hide and overlaid with linen on which an Imperial or legionary emblem could be painted, the whole being edged with a bronze strip and fitted with a metal boss to protect the hand grip. On approaching his opponent, the legionary hurled his pilum at him. If it struck home, well and good. If it stuck in his shield, that was also very satisfactory because the shank behind the head was deliberately left untempered so that it bent on impact; this unbalanced the shield, which would become useless if several long, bent pila were sticking in it. The legionary would next smash into his opponent with his own shield, hoping to destroy his balance, and wade in with his short stabbing sword. Enemies such as the Celts who used their longer swords as slashing weapons thus fought at a disadvantage, because in raising their arms to strike a blow they exposed the right side and armpit to thrusts delivered with trained rapidity and force. Furthermore the legion's flexible organisation enabled centuries and cohorts to relieve one another from the forefront of the battle line very rapidly, which meant of course that the enemy's tiring front ranks remained under constant pressure from fresh troops.

Before leaving the purely Roman element of the Imperial Army, it is necessary to mention one further unit. Because the legions were deployed along far-flung frontiers, the Praetorian Guard had been founded by Augustus to provide a personal bodyguard and a local force with which to maintain control of Rome itself. It consisted originally of nine 500-strong cohorts, but unlike some of history's later Guard units, it was not formed from veterans who had already distinguished themselves in the field. The Praetorians were recruited locally, enjoyed better pay and higher terminal gratuities than the legionaries, and they enlisted for only sixteen years. Occasionally part of the Guard would accompany the Emperor on campaign, but most of its time was spent amid the fleshpots of the capital. Naturally the rest of the Army disliked the Praetorians and their privileged lifestyle, although envy was far from being the only reason. In theory the Praetorians were above politics; in reality they were corruptible to the point that they influenced politics and even the succession to the throne. To this day the term Praetorian has a grubby connotation.

With so much territory to secure and a limit on the Italian manpower available, Augustus reinforced the army with auxiliary units (auxilia) recruited in the provinces, thereby doubling its size. There were various types of auxiliary unit of which the infantry cohort and the cavalry regiment (ala) were the most common. These took their name from the province in which they were raised but usually served in other parts of the Empire. So it was that the garrison of Britain included auxiliary units which had been raised in Spain, Gaul, Lower Germany, Dalmatia, Syria and elsewhere. Like the legionaries, the auxiliary soldiers were long-service professionals serving for pay. Promotion to centurion or troop leader was made from within their own ranks, though commanding officers were either Romans or exceptional men brought in from other auxiliary units. At the end of their service auxiliaries and their families were rewarded with Roman citizenship.

Most auxiliary infantry cohorts fought in the same manner as the legions. Their equipment had the look of Roman hand-me-downs, consisting of a simpler helmet, a flat oval shield and a mail shirt, although articulated plate armour does seem to have been issued to some units. The same sword was used, but the pilum was replaced by a short spear. In addition to these conventional infantry units, there were cohorts of archers recruited in the Middle East as well as slingers.

The small number of cavalrymen serving within the legions gave the auxiliary cavalry regiments an added importance. The regiment had a nominal strength of 480 and was divided into sixteen troops of 30 men, each commanded by a decurion. The trooper wore a large helmet, mail or scale body armour, and carried an oval or hexagonal shield. His weapons included a spear and a long straight sword. There were also a number of light cavalry units, including mounted archers from the Middle East. Heavy cavalry made its appearance under the Emperor Hadrian with the formation of the first of several fully armoured lancer regiments known as cataphracti, clearly intended to combine shock action with mobility.

The Empire continued the expansionist policy of its predecessor. As Dr Brian Dobson points out in *Warfare in the Ancient World*, this produced a recurring cycle of events. Easy victories over the tribal levies of frontier kings would be followed, sooner or later, by bloody rebellions that were put down with total ruthlessness. If the enemy, incapable of beating the Roman army in the field, resorted to guerrilla warfare and declined to accept terms, the policy of *vastatio* (the root of our word devastation) was applied. His farms would be laid waste, his stock driven off and his villages burned, the slightest resistance being sufficient to provoke a massacre; the survivors, men, women and children, were then dispersed or sold into slavery.

Despite this, the Roman establishment was shrewd enough to recognise that certain areas existed where such benefits as might accrue from continued occupation did not balance either the military or economic cost involved. One such, as we shall see, was Germany, where the frontier was finally set along the river barriers of the Rhine and the Danube. Another was northern Britain where, in the second century, the frontier was pushed north from Hadrian's Wall, running between the Tyne and the Solway, to the Antonine Wall, running between the Forth and the Clyde, but withdrawn to the original line after only twenty years.

THE TEUTOBURGER WALD, AD 9

During the years immediately preceding the birth of Christ, Augustus decided to extend the northern frontier of the Empire from the Rhine to the Elbe, his intention being to create a buffer province that would halt German incursions into Gaul, which had now been pacified and begun to prosper. This was achieved against ferocious resistance from the German tribes, but by AD 5 the Emperor's adopted son, Tiberius, had quelled all opposition and imposed the Roman will on the sullenly resentful population.

The following year he was recalled to put down a serious revolt in Pannonia. He was replaced by Publius Quintilius Varus, who had married into the Imperial family and until recently had been governor of Syria. Varus, described as 'a man of mild character and quiet disposition, somewhat slow in mind as he was in body, more accustomed to the leisure of the camp than actual service in war', epitomised the basic flaw in the Roman command system. The tribes seemed quiet enough and as some of their leaders had even begun to adopt Roman ways the prospect of a rising seemed remote.

Varus brought with him the sybaritic lifestyle of Syria and his self-indulgent example spread downwards and began to affect the troops. There were, too, despite appearances to the contrary, many Germans who were willing to take advantage of the fact, given an appropriate opportunity. One such was a young nobleman of the Cherusci named Arminius, who had served as an auxiliary with the Roman army and actually been elevated to equestrian rank. Despite this, he was driven by a deep hatred of Rome, equalled only by that for his pro-Roman uncle, Segestes, who had refused him his daughter's hand in marriage, a problem which was solved by an elopement.

Arminius was simultaneously planning a rising, but knowing that he could not hope to beat the legions in open combat, he organised this in a most ingenious way while still apparently remaining loyal to Varus. Such a major undertaking could hardly be kept secret and Segestes provided Varus with ample warning. The governor, however, believed that such accusations of treason were merely an extension of the family quarrel and did nothing.

In AD 9 the Roman garrison of Germany consisted of five legions, three of which, XVII, XVIII and XIX, were present with Varus in the Minden area. As a result of the softer regime permitted by the governor, the soldiers not

Above: The Legions' senior officers were patricians performing one stage of their senatorial careers. Generally they were men in their early thirties who received their appointments direct from the Emperor. Middle-ranking officers and commanders of auxiliary units were drawn from the equites (knights) who formed the municipal aristocracies of Italy and the provinces.

only had women, children and camp-followers with them, a total of 10,000 non-combatants, but also a long convoy of unwieldy baggage wagons which had taken the place of the legions' more usual mule trains.

In September or October Varus was preparing to march back to his winter quarters at Aliso (modern Haltern) on the Lippe when he received word that an apparently minor rising had taken place near the Weser. This was intended by Arminius to draw him off his route into the difficult country of the Teutoburger Wald, where the main rebel force was waiting to ambush the column. The area where the battle was fought has never been precisely identified for the very good reason that it stretched along many miles of terrain which, as quoted by Sir Edward Creasy, consisted of 'a table-land intersected by numerous deep and narrow valleys, which in some places form small plains, surrounded by steep hills and rocks only accessible by narrow defiles. All the valleys are traversed by rapid streams, shallow in the dry season, but subject to sudden swelling in autumn and winter. The vast forests which cover the summits and slopes of the hills consist chiefly of oak; there is little under-brush, and both men and horse could move with ease if the ground were not broken by gullies or rendered impractical by fallen trees.' On balance this description fits the hills in the Detmold area, particularly the Grotenburg.

Despite warnings from friendly Germans that he was heading for serious trouble, Varus decided to put down the rising. Having reached this decision, a less complacent commander would have detached the camp-followers and wagon train and sent them by the direct route to Aliso, under escort. Varus chose to keep them with him and thus multiplied his prob-lems manifold. The third factor, which would aggravate his situation still further and materi-ally assist his attackers, was incessant, drenching rain.

We do not know exactly what happened, although by piecing together the evidence of the very few survivors, escapees and others, contemporary historians have left us enough to trace the general course of events. At first, it seems that Arminius and his auxiliaries, still above suspicion, remained with the column and acted as guides; the first hint that some-thing was wrong came with their disappearance during the night.

The column had now entered the area of difficult terrain in which Arminius had laid his ambush. Next day the legionaries were fully employed in dragging wagons out of the mud, cutting a track through the wilderness and building causeways across the swollen streams, when the Germans struck. The camp-followers were slaughtered, draught animals killed, and isolated groups of soldiers cut down. Amid a rain of spears and other missiles the column fought its way slowly forward until an area of clear ground was reached. On this, with their customary speed and efficiency, the Romans constructed a fortified camp for the night.

Next morning they marched out and deployed for battle. Arminius did not oblige; nor did he have to, because he was achieving the desired results by fighting in his own way on ground of his own choosing. The column was reformed and the march continued, immediately attracting further attacks. The going, already dreadful, became even more difficult, and the Germans sought to block further progress with barricades made from felled trees. Too late, it was decided that better progress would be made if the wagons were abandoned. At this point something like a breakdown in discipline occurred as the legionaries ran to collect their belongings. Arminius promptly launched a general attack which seems to have succeeded in cutting the column into several sections. Varus, badly wounded during one attack, clearly accepted that further advance was impossible and gave the order to withdraw, hoping to break out of the forest and reach Aliso.

This merely encouraged the Germans. By nightfall it was apparent that the column, disorganised, burdened with many wounded, and under frequent attack, was trapped. One section seems to have struggled to build itself a fortified camp, but it was a small, incomplete thing, incapable of offering determined resis-tance for long.

During the night Varus and his senior offi-cers, recognising that the entire command was doomed, committed suicide rather than face capture. Leaving the troops to their fate as it did, their act was the ultimate self-indulgence. Next morning the rain intensified until it became difficult to keep a footing on the slip-pery hillsides. Under Vala Numonius, the legionary cavalry tried to break out. Their formation broken by the forest terrain, their horses floundering in the trampled mud, the troopers were hunted down and killed to a man.

Now grim-faced and silent, the legionaries responded to quiet words of command, forming defensive squares. Discipline and comradeship took hold, enabling them to beat off one attack after another. Gradually, their numbers thinned and two Eagles were lost. Perhaps some groups managed to hold out for a day or two longer.

A dreadful fate awaited those who were taken alive. In applying their policy of *vastatio* the Romans had shown no mercy to the Germans and they could expect none in return. The Germans were also in a particularly savage mood, which suggests that they had paid dearly for their victory. Some of their captives they nailed to trees, some they buried alive, and others they sacrificed to their forest gods on makeshift altars.

Arminius next led his army to besiege Aliso itself. The garrison was commanded by a very capable officer, Lucius Caedicius, whose archers beat off every attack. The Germans, lacking formal discipline, became slack in their routine and this enabled Caedicius to execute a well-planned breakout and, with the women and children, reach Vetera (Wesel) on the Rhine, where he was met by Lucius Nonius Asprenas and the two remaining legions. Arminius, having achieved his object of liberating Germany east of the great river, then retired.

Rome was severely shaken by the disaster. Augustus is said to have torn his clothes and let his hair and beard grow untended for several months in mourning; at times, he would bang his head on door-posts, crying 'Quintilius Varus, give me back my legions!' Those legions were never re-formed.

During the next five years punitive expeditions were mounted under Tiberius and Germanicus. Heavy losses were inflicted on the Germans, several standards were recovered and the pregnant wife of Arminius was captured; later, his infant son was paraded in triumph

Left: Roman legionary battle line advancing. After hurling their pila, rendering their opponents' shields unusable, the legionaries would draw their short stabbing swords and smash their way into the enemy battle line with their own shields. The tendency would then be to fight to their right-front, where an enemy who raised his arm to strike a slashing blow would immediately expose his unprotected right side and armpit. Another point of interest is that the troops are wearing braccae (pants), normally issued for campaigning in cold climates.

through the streets of Rome. At one point, however, a detachment under a subordinate commander named Caecina came close to sharing the fate of Varus and his legions, an event which almost certainly reinforced the decision to abandon Germany.

In AD 15 Germanicus, operating near the Teutoburger Wald, in which the remains of the three lost legions still lay unburied, decided to pay his last respects to them. 'The scene', wrote Tacitus, 'lived up to its horrible associations. Varus' extensive first camp, with its broad extent and headquarters marked out, testified to the whole army's labours. Then a half-ruined palisade and shallow ditch showed where the last pathetic remnant had gathered. On the open ground were whitening bones, scattered where men had fled, piled up where they had stood and fought back. Fragments of spears and horses' limbs were scattered about – also human heads, fastened to tree trunks. In groves nearby were the outlandish altars on which the Germans had sacrificed the Roman tribunes and senior centurions. Survivors of the catastrophe, who had escaped from the battle or from captivity, pointed out where the generals had fallen and where the Eagles were captured. They showed where Varus had received his first wound, and where he died by his own unhappy hand, and spoke of all the gibbets and pits for the prisoners. So, six years after the disaster, a Roman army came to this place and buried the bones of the men of the three legions. No one knew if the remains he was burying belonged to a stranger or a comrade. Germanicus shared in their grief and laid the first sod of the funeral mound as a heartfelt tribute to the dead.'

Both Creasy and Fuller regard the Teutoburger Wald as being one of the most decisive battles in world history. To quote the latter: 'Had Germany west of the Elbe been for four centuries Romanised and roaded, one culture and not two in unending conflict would have dominated the Western world. There would have been no Franco–German problem, or at least a totally different one. There would have been no Charlemagne, no Louis XIV, no Napoleon, no Kaiser Wilhelm II, and no Hitler.'

Nevertheless, as Creasy points out, if Germany had become a Roman province, the history of Britain would also have been very different. Arminius and his men were Low Germans, related to the Angles and Saxons who, in later centuries, migrated in large numbers to Britain. To these men Arminius was a dim god-like folk memory, but still revered to the extent that they named one of the Roman roads they inherited after him – Irmin Street. Without the Anglo-Saxons there would have been no England and no English language; and without the inherited energy which was to take their descendants to the far corners of the world, English would never have become a world language. Had Arminius failed, the probability is that none of this would have taken place.

THE MEDWAY, AD 43

Although almost 100 years had passed since Julius Caesar carried out his reconnaissances in force to Britain, this did not mean that Rome had lost interest in the island. Britain had valuable resources of tin and lead, and, properly governed, could become as profitable a province as Gaul. Furthermore, occupation of the island would eliminate a source of potential hostility to Rome and a refuge for her enemies. Expeditions against Britain had been planned in 34, 28 and 27 BC but had been abandoned because of events elsewhere. The same was true of an expedition planned by the Emperor Caligula in AD 39.

The most prosperous part of Britain was its south-eastern corner, peopled by tribes of Belgic origin. These included the Cantiaci of Kent, the Atrebates of Sussex and Surrey, the Trinovantes of Essex and Suffolk and the Catuvellauni of Bedfordshire and Hertfordshire. Of these the last, ably ruled by Cunobelinus (Shakespeare's Cymbelene), had become the dominant power.

Cunobelinus had established an understanding with Rome, but when he died in

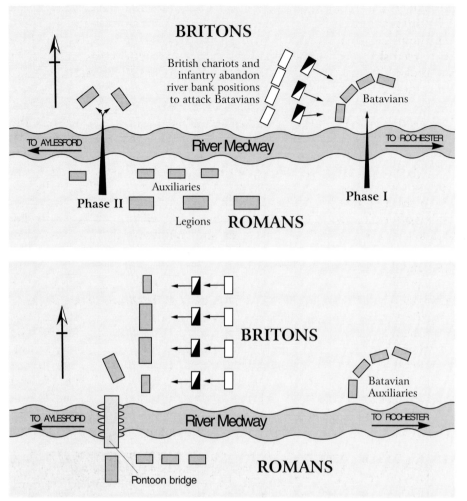

BRITONS

British chariots and infantry abandon river bank positions to attack Batavians

Batavians

TO AYLESFORD ← River Medway → TO ROCHESTER

Auxiliaries

Phase II

Legions

ROMANS

Phase I

BRITONS

TO AYLESFORD ← River Medway → TO ROCHESTER

Batavian Auxiliaries

Pontoon bridge

ROMANS

Phase I: Batavian auxiliaries swim river and establish bridgehead.

Phase II: After dark, II Augusta legion cross in boats and establish bridgehead. Engineers start work on pontoon bridge.

Phase III: Next day, the Britons abandon their attacks on the Batavians and concentrate against the main Roman crossing, only to be defeated after heavy fighting.

about AD 40 a power struggle developed between pro- and anti-Roman factions. The latter, led by his sons Caractacus and Tugodumnus, emerged victorious, but the pro-Roman faction, led by a third son, Adminius, and the king of the recently defeated Atrebates, Verica, travelled to Rome seeking help. The Emperor Claudius, perceiving a route to comparatively inexpensive military glory, sanctioned an invasion, using many of the resources previously assembled for Caligula's aborted expedition.

The troops involved consisted of four legions – II Augusta from Strasbourg, IX Hispana from Pannonia, XIV Gemina from Mainz and XX Valeria Victrix from Neuss – plus some 20,000 auxiliaries, including infantry and cavalry units. In command was one of the Empire's best generals, Aulus Plautius, until recently governor of Pannonia.

By the summer of 43 all was ready, but the troops did not like the idea and refused to embark. It was not just the well-known fact that ocean tides could sweep one over the edge of the world, but also that Britain was known to be an extremely dangerous place; even the great Julius Caesar hadn't stayed there long, because he knew what was good for him! The invasion was a disaster waiting to happen. And didn't the Druids stuff their prisoners into huge wicker figures and burn them alive? Generals always had strange ideas, but whoever thought this one up needed trepanning! The troops were not out of hand, but they were adamant – they were not going to Britain. Several weeks passed without their officers being able to make any impression on them, until at last Narcissus, a freed slave and confidant of the Emperor, broke the tension by making them laugh and then explained away their fears.

As matters transpired the mutiny had served a completely unexpected purpose. Caractacus and Tugodumnus, having been warned that an invasion was in the offing, had assembled an army with which to oppose the landing. As the weeks passed it began to seem as though the Romans were not coming after all. The army was therefore disbanded and returned home to bring in the harvest.

The historian of the campaign, Dio Cassius, records that the expedition sailed in three divisions. His account does not say that these landed separately, but given the way Aulus Plautius thought, the probability is that they did, for the Britons could not be strong everywhere and if one landing were opposed the others would have no difficulty in obtaining a beachhead. The most likely landing places are thought to have been Richborough, Dover and Lympne. To everyone's surprise, none of the landings was opposed. It seems that the Romans already had a reasonable knowledge of British geography and, once ashore, the three divisions almost certainly converged on an assembly area near Canterbury. Again, to their surprise, they encountered not the slightest opposition, the reason being that the Britons' leaders, having missed the chance to meet the invasion at the water's edge, had begun to re-assemble their army much farther inland.

From Canterbury the Romans marched west along what became known as The Pilgrims' Way until, having fought several skirmishes, they reached the vicinity of present-day Rochester and found the Britons present in strength, lining the opposite bank of the Medway.

Once again, the precise site of the ensuing battle is uncertain, but probability suggests that it took place in the area of the modern motorway bridge, because downstream the river widens into a tidal estuary, and upstream, though it narrows near Aylesford, access to the banks is difficult because of wooded and marshy approaches.

Dio's description of the battle is far from being as complete as it might be, but it does tell

Right: Legionaries crossing a pontoon bridge, as depicted on Trajan's Column. Helmets are hung from the right shoulder while shields are either slung across the back or on the left; this cannot have been either easy or comfortable as the left hand was required not only to carry the pilum but also the forked stick on which the legionary hung his personal possessions and daily rations. Nevertheless, the marching standard set was 15 miles in four hours. *Philip Haythornthwaite Collection*

Left: A similar illustration to that on page 29, but this time a romanticised Victorian view showing legionary and auxiliary standard bearers, distinguished by their head-dress made from bears, wolves and other savage animals. *Philip Haythornthwaite Collection*

us the course of the action. Plautius had several Batavian auxiliary units that were trained in river-crossing techniques. These included both cavalry and infantry and, according to Dio, they 'were trained to swim with full equipment across the swiftest of rivers'. Plautius used them to create a major diversion on the downstream flank, sending them across the river during the hours of darkness. The move was not detected and at dawn the startled Britons found the Batavians firmly established on their own bank. The tribesmen came swarming out of their camps, led by their charioteers. This was exactly what had been anticipated and the Batavians were prepared. The Britons were met with a hail of javelins and arrows, aimed not at the men but at their horses. Those not killed were maddened beyond endurance. 'In the confusion that followed,' wrote Dio, 'not even the charioteers could save themselves.' For the rest of the day the Britons seem to have contented themselves with containing the bridgehead, anticipating that the legions lining the south bank would, sooner or later, attempt to reinforce it.

After dark, however, Plautius activated the second phase of his plan. II Augusta, commanded by Flavius Vespasian, a future Emperor, crossed the river on the upstream flank, using boats and locally constructed rafts. The legion achieved complete surprise, killing those Britons who had remained in the area, and established a second bridgehead. Dio, writing long after the event, does not say as much, but the legionary engineers promptly began constructing a bridge, possibly of the pontoon type; this offers the only rational explanation for the rapid build-up which took place within the bridgehead. By dawn two legions and some auxiliary units were across and had formed a battle line facing east, under the overall command of a senior officer named Gnaeus Hosidius Geta; a third legion was crossing and the fourth was marching towards the bridge.

If, perhaps, the Britons thought that the second crossing was a feint intended to draw them away from the Batavians, daylight revealed that they had been sold a pup. Once more they swarmed to the attack, hurling themselves against the Romans with desperate fury. At one point they broke through the centre of the line and almost succeeded in capturing Geta. As more troops continued to pour into the bridgehead, however, they were forced back. Slowly the initiative passed to the Romans and, with the Batavians hovering in their rear, the Britons conceded defeat and withdrew, subsequently crossing the Thames into Essex. It seems likely that Tugodumnus was mortally wounded during the fighting. Geta, who may have been the senior legionary legate, was decorated with the *Ornamenta Triumphalia*, normally reserved for those of consular rank.

The battle had offered the Britons their best chance of defeating the invaders, a chance that was never to be repeated. Claudius, accompanied by part of the Praetorian Guard and elements of VIII Augusta, paid a brief visit to congratulate the victorious army and was hailed as Imperator. Plautius quickly consolidated his hold over southern Britain. Caractacus continued to offer resistance but was defeated and captured by the next governor, Ostorius Scapula. By AD 49 Roman rule had been extended as far north as Lincoln and Chester. In 60 Queen Boudicca of the Iceni led a serious revolt that was mercilessly put down by Suetonius Paulinus, but not before the Roman centres of London, Colchester and St Albans had been burned. During the years 74–7 Petilius Cerealis, one of the Emperor Vespasian's ablest generals, conquered the Brigantes in Yorkshire and the Silures in South Wales. In 77 Cerealis was succeeded by Gnaeus Julius Agricola who destroyed the hostile Druidic presence on Anglesey and, during a series of campaigns, some of which were supported by the fleet, advanced north into Scotland. The decisive battle was fought in 83 at Mons Graupius, believed to be the mountain known today as Bennachie, some miles north-west of Aberdeen, and resulted in the shattering defeat of an alliance of Caledonian tribes. One point of interest regarding the battle is that only the auxiliaries were engaged, the legions remaining in reserve throughout. The conquest of Britain – though not quite as complete as Tacitus, Agricola's son-in-law, would have us believe – had taken forty-one years.

MASADA, AD 73–4

Palestine in the days of the early Roman Empire was as volatile and potentially violent a place as, sadly, it is today. In AD 66 it exploded into rebellion, one result of which was that the Roman garrison was driven out of Jerusalem after sustaining heavy losses. With four legions and 25,000 auxiliaries, Vespasian restored

Right: Another scene taken from Trajan's Column, showing legionaries and auxiliaries engaged with barbarians; unfortunately, the artist's interpretation of the gladius has much in common with the potato knife! Having served a term with the Auxilia, many barbarians passed on Roman military methods to their own people with the result that the gap between the tactical abilities of the two began to close slowly but steadily. *Philip Haythornthwaite Collection*

order after three years of bitter fighting. By the beginning of 69 he had succeeded in overrunning most of the country and laid siege to Jerusalem, using no less than 340 catapults and ballistae. On his becoming Emperor later that year the siege was continued by his son Titus. When, in AD 70, the city's last defences were finally stormed amid much slaughter, the Temple was destroyed by fire.

The best account we have of these events is that written by Flavius Josephus, the Roman name adopted by Joseph ben Matthias, a Jewish politician and soldier who played a prominent part in the war. During the early stages of the rebellion he had vigorously supported his countrymen, but as soon as he realised that a Roman victory was inevitable he shamelessly deserted them during the siege of Jotapata. Thereafter he served Rome with unswerving devotion, being rewarded with Roman citizenship, a pension and the revenues from confiscated Jewish lands. Curiously, he still wished to be regarded as a loyal Jew and his book, *The Jewish War*, was partly written as a justification for his actions. This, together with his tendency wildly to inflate any sort of statistic, does not detract from a coherent and, at times, very moving narrative.

After the fall of Jerusalem there remained much mopping-up to be done, many of the Zealots having made it perfectly clear that they would never again accept Roman rule. The centre of Zealot resistance was the fortress of Masada, occupying a detached massif several hundred feet high on the western shore of the Dead Sea. Over many thousands of years the feature has crumbled so that the steep lower slopes consist of fallen rock and sand, leaving sheer cliffs above. The summit, with a perimeter of some 1,300 yards, consists of a plateau. Josephus tells us that at the time it could only be reached by two routes. The first, known as the Snake Path, was 3½ miles long, ascended from the east, and was extremely dangerous; the second, starting in the valley to the west of the massif, was much easier and shorter, but was guarded by a strong fort at its narrowest point, 500 yards below the summit.

A fortification of some sort had existed on the summit for centuries, but it was King Herod the Great, living in constant fear of his own people and his Egyptian neighbour, Queen Cleopatra, who decided to turn it into an impregnable refuge. According to Josephus: 'He enclosed the entire summit within a limestone wall eighteen feet high and twelve wide, punctuated by 37 towers, 75 feet high. As the plateau was of rich soil, the king reserved it for cultivation, so that the garrison could be fed if their external supplies were cut. He built a palace, also, on the western slope, below the fortifications; the palace wall was of great height and strongly built, with towers 90 feet high at the four corners. At various places he had great cisterns cut out of the rock to hold water, ensuring a supply as great as where spring water can be used.' Josephus also mentions well-stocked, cool, underground storerooms and an armoury which he claims was capable of equipping 10,000 men. On its own, therefore, Masada presented an extremely formidable challenge to any besieger. As if this were not enough, the surrounding area was hot, humid and contained no convenient sources of food or water.

Masada had been seized from its Roman garrison by *coup de main* during the early days of the rebellion and held by the Jews ever since. The Romans decided to complete their mopping-up operations elsewhere before tackling the fortress, but in AD 73 they closed in on it under the new procurator, Flavius Silva, who had at his disposal the Legion X Fretensis and an equivalent number of auxiliary units.

One cause of the Jews' defeat had been uncompromising and sometimes violent sectarian disputes among themselves. Most intolerant of all were the Zealots who, after the fall of Jerusalem, regarded those who had submitted to Rome as their enemies and preyed upon them without mercy. As the majority of people simply wanted to get on with their lives in peace, Silva had little difficulty in persuading them that the Zealots holding Masada were little better than a gang of self-serving brigands. Large numbers of the local population therefore supported his opera-

Right: The fortress of Masada beside the Dead Sea. The ramp constructed by the Romans during their siege is clearly visible. The figures on the path below confirm the huge scale of the operation. For over 1900 years Masada has remained a symbol of Jewish resistance. *Courtesy Israel Government Tourist Office*

tion by providing the transport and porterage necessary to bring in the huge quantities of food and water required by the troops.

Within the defences of Masada there were approximately 1,000 people, including a large number of women and children. It might, perhaps, be wondered why the might of Rome should have been deployed, at enormous expense, against this tiny group, many of whom were harmless. First, of course, it was necessary to demonstrate that there was nowhere that the writ of Rome did not run. Secondly, Eleazar, commanding the Zealots, had been one of the rebellion's most intransigent leaders and it was essential that he be killed or captured. Thirdly, Masada had to be taken in order to prevent the fortress becoming a rallying point for further subversion.

Having established themselves in their camps, the Romans' first task was to construct a wall with watch towers all round the base of the feature to prevent the Zealots' escape. This was completed in a remarkably short time. Silva, meanwhile, had decided upon his point of attack, which is described by Josephus.

'Behind the fort that guarded the road leading from the west to the palace and the summit was a rocky outcrop, quite wide and protruding a considerable distance, 450 feet below the walls; this was called the White Cliff.'

Josephus does not say whether the fort was defended by the Zealots and had to be stormed, merely that the Romans took possession of it. The outcrop was then used as the base for an enormous ramp, still visible to this day, that was pushed steadily upwards towards the walls. Thousands of tons of rock and sand were used, the huge quantities of timber required to shore up the sides having also to be brought in. Eventually the ramp reached a height of 300 feet, but its top was considered to be neither sufficiently stable nor wide enough for the next phase of the operation. Working under the protection of shields and archers, the engineers built a solid stone platform, 75 feet wide and the same height, at the head of the ramp. On this the Romans constructed a 90-foot-high siege tower, armoured with iron plates. Ballistae and stone-throwing catapults were set up on various floors of the tower and these quickly drove the defenders from the walls. Next, Silva had a large ram dragged up the ramp and used it to batter the wall until part of it collapsed, creating a breach.

In the meantime Eleazar had not been idle. Anticipating the outcome, he stripped the timber beams out of the internal buildings and built an interior, earth-filled wall with lateral bracing. Confronted with this, the Romans brought their ram through the breach in the masonry wall and began hammering at it. To their surprise each blow simply compressed the earth and rendered the construction yet more solid.

The siege now entered its final phase. Withdrawing the ram, Silva decided to destroy the inner wall by fire. Torches were thrown at it and, being tinder-dry, the timbers caught at once. As the flames began to roar the wind drove them into the faces of the attackers, creating a serious danger to their siege engines. Then the wind backed, turning the timber wall into an inferno. Delighted, the Romans began preparing for the final assault, which would be delivered next morning, 15 April 74.

During the night Eleazar made an impassioned speech to his followers, convincing them that it was more honourable to die by their own hands, as free servants of God, than to live as slaves of the Romans. According to Josephus, one man in every ten was chosen by lot to kill nine of his family and comrades and then commit suicide. When the Romans stormed the still smouldering breach they entered a grimly silent fortress. Eventually two women and five children emerged from the underground water system and told them what

had happened. Within the palace they found, lying together, the bodies of 960 men, women and children, their throats cut. Josephus says: 'They did not exult over them as enemies but admired the nobility of their resolve, having shown no hesitation and an utter contempt for death.'

The fall of Masada marked the end of rebellion, which was itself the first step along the road to the great Dispersion of the Jewish people. There would be further Jewish revolts in the years 115–17 and 132–5, the latter being provoked by the Emperor Hadrian's plan to erect a shrine to Jupiter on the site of the Temple, and ended with his harsh suppression of the practice of Judaism.

For the Roman army, the siege and capture of Masada was but one episode in its long history, albeit a triumph of sound planning, logistics and engineering skill. To Jews everywhere, however, the event retains a profound significance. Today Masada has become a place of pilgrimage and is also used by the Israeli Defence Force for induction ceremonies during which recruits are made aware of what might be demanded of them. 'Masada', goes the Israeli saying, 'will not fall again.'

Commentary 2 – The Late Roman Empire

From the year 200 onwards barbarian pressure forced the Roman Empire steadily on to the strategic defensive. As the American historians Ernest and Trevor Dupuy comment in their *Encyclopedia of Military History*, there was no common pattern of barbarian military methods and tactics. Thus, the Franks fought as infantry while the Alemanni of southern Germany, the Sarmatians, the Alans and the Ostrogoths were horsemen. The Visigoth armies, on the other hand, contained both infantry and cavalry, while the Saxons of north Germany became sea rovers and raided the coasts of Britain and Gaul.

As time went by the Empire became progressively less capable of defending itself. This was not simply the result of periodic power struggles at the highest levels. In Italy itself, the prosperity brought by the Empire had led to a movement into the towns where the population, which had long since ceased to be purely native, was kept quiescent by a 'bread and the games of the circus' dependency culture. As with many previous empires the rot had begun at the centre, where people were no longer interested in a soldier's life on distant frontiers.

More and more the legions drew their men from the provinces and even recruited barbarians, entire units of whom were enlisted. Pressure on the frontiers also led to the creation of a central strategic reserve, consisting of small additional legions each about 1,000 strong, and, because so many of the Empire's enemies were mounted, a much higher proportion of the army's strength consisted of cavalry units, either Roman, auxiliary or barbarian. Tactically, the legion was confronted with a number of problems. When fighting infantry it preserved the old, flexible open order which served as well as it had always done, but when fighting cavalry it was necessary to adopt close order for its own defence. For this reason the pilum was replaced by a throwing spear. Close

order, too, rendered the legion vulnerable to missile engines which the barbarians, having learned the Roman art of war, were bringing into the field. The Roman response was to increase the missile weapon establishment within the legion and raise more auxiliary units of slingers and archers, the latter being both foot and mounted.

The changed nature of warfare meant that commanders were required to adapt to whatever tactical situation confronted them. This demanded the highest professional standards, initiating a process in which experienced officers gradually replaced political appointees; it even became possible for senior centurions to command their legions in action. Another worthwhile step was the abolition of the politically dangerous Praetorian Guard, which had its wings clipped by the Emperor Diocletian and was disbanded by the Emperor Constantine. In its place Constantine formed a 4,000-strong personal bodyguard unit, recruited from distinguished veterans throughout the army, which had a role in the strategic reserve.

Diocletian recognised that the Empire had become too unwieldy to be administered effi-

Right: Extensive barbarian migrations overran the Roman Empire during its later years. Sometimes barbarians were permitted to settle on the condition that they served Rome; such arrangements usally ended with them taking over entire provinces.

ciently and in 285 he divided it into two portions, East and West, ruled over by emperors with equal status. Constantine reversed the process but in 330 moved the capital from Rome to Constantinople (Istanbul), which offered a more central location. In 364 the empire was again divided, with Valentinian being emperor of the West and Valens emperor of the East.

In approximately 375 there began what German historians call the *Völkerwanderung* (the Wandering of the Nations). The proximate cause was a build-up of demographic pressure which had its origins in the steppes of central Asia, whence the Huns, a fierce Mongoloid people, emigrated into Europe, overwhelming the Alans. The nomadic Huns cared nothing for the comforts of civilisation. They took their pleasures in killing, plunder and destruction, showing no mercy to anyone who opposed them, and they used the terror they inspired as a weapon. The Goths fled before them, seeking sanctuary within the boundaries of the Roman empire. The scene was now set for the greatest disaster to befall the Roman army since Cannae.

ADRIANOPLE, 9 AUGUST 378

Under the leadership of Fritigern and Alavius, perhaps as many as one million Visigoths reached the Danubian frontier during 376, seeking refuge from the dreaded Huns, and in their wake came a smaller but significant number of their Ostrogoth cousins.

Approximately 200,000 of the Visigoths were warriors. This raised serious doubts in the mind of Valens, the emperor of the East, but he reluctantly permitted them to cross into the empire on condition that they surrender their arms and that all male children be handed over as hostages. Desperate, the Visigoths agreed at once, but while they conformed to the second condition, the boys being subsequently removed to Asia Minor, they managed to retain most of their weapons by bribing the Roman officials with gold and women. When the Ostrogoths arrived and began crossing, the

same officials turned a blind eye in return for similar favours.

Soon the province of Thrace had become crowded with Gothic refugees, whom the officials began to exploit. Naturally, the Goths objected and the situation became unsettled. The following year the Romans treacherously attacked the Goths' leaders at a meeting intended to resolve these difficulties. Alavius was killed, but Fritigern managed to escape and led his people into the marshy area south of the Danube delta known today as the Dobruja. When the Romans pursued them they found that the Goths had made a fort from their wagons. A bloody but indecisive battle followed. While the Romans were preparing for a second attack, Fritigern managed to break out, ravaging most of Thrace and Moesia with an army which now not only included Visigoths and Ostrogoths, but also Alans, Sarmatians and even Huns.

Valens now had a very serious problem on his hands. He appealed for help to Gratian, his nephew and emperor of the West. Gratian had problems of his own with the Franks and Alemanni along the Rhine. In 378, however, he inflicted a shattering defeat on the latter and then marched to join his uncle.

Meanwhile the Romans had been making slow but satisfactory progress against Fritigern's army. Early in August Fritigern and his allies established a huge camp of wagon forts on a hill in a valley near Adrianople (modern Edirne). There were 50,000 infantry present, the same number of cavalry, and a large number of women and children. The Goths had now begun to regret having ravaged Thrace so thoroughly because they were dangerously short of food. Fritigern therefore sent his cavalry on a wide foraging sweep.

At this point the Roman army, commanded by Valens in person, appeared from the direction of Constantinople. Valens had 40,000 infantry and 20,000 cavalry at his disposal, and he had forced the pace throughout the hot summer morning in the hope of obtaining a great victory for himself before Gratian, approaching from the north, could join him.

Goths' Wagon fort

GOTHS

ROMANS

TO ADRIANOPLE

ADRIANOPLE, AD 378

1: Valens lanuches attack on wagon fort prematurely, before all his infantry have arrived.

2: Gothic cavalry returning from foraging.

3: Roman left-wing cavalry routed.

4: Gothic cavalry encircle most of the Roman infantry, compressing them against the defences of the wagon fort.

Fritigern dispatched urgent orders for his cavalry to return and also sent a message to Valens, offering to talk. This suited Valens very well, because it gave his men time to get their breath and deploy, but he neglected to take the elementary precaution of posting cavalry vedettes on his flanks.

The action was brought on prematurely when an auxiliary unit began shooting at the Gothic negotiating party. By now the Roman cavalry was in position on the flanks of the battle line, but the legions were still coming up to fill the centre and some were still marching in column. Nevertheless Valens gave the signal for a general attack. The cavalry charged forward against the wagon fort, but at that precise moment the Gothic horsemen arrived on the high ground over-looking the valley. Without hesitation they thundered down the slope to smash into the flank of the Roman left-wing cavalry which was utterly routed. Some of the Goths then rode across the rear of the Roman army while others galloped through the camp itself to join a counter-attack on Valens' right-wing cavalry. This, too was rapidly routed – so quickly, in fact, that the legions had still not completed their deployment. Left unsup-

ported, the legionaries were quickly surrounded as the Gothic infantry came swarming out of their wagon fort. Some 40,000 Romans, including Valens and his senior officers, died in the disaster, which marked the end of the legions' domination of the battlefield.

Under Valens' successor, Theodosius, the area was briefly pacified in 383, but the Goths retained their tenure and were soon in revolt against the empire again. Moving westwards under their leader Alaric, they ravaged Italy and in 410 sacked Rome itself. Within four years they had marched into Gaul and invaded Spain. The end of the Empire was in sight.

CHÂLONS, JUNE 451

By the fourth decade of the 5th century the Wandering of the Nations had dismembered huge areas of the Roman Empire of the West. Some provinces, like Britain, had simply been abandoned without the need for a stricken field. Others, like North Africa and much of Spain, had fallen to the barbarian hordes or simply been swamped under the tide of immigration. Apart from Italy, all that remained to Rome was Gaul and the north-eastern corner of Spain. Gaul, however, while still nominally Roman, was widely covered with barbarian settlements – Franks in the north, Burgundians in Savoy, Alemanni on the Upper Rhine, Alans at Orléans and Visigoths in the south-west. The wonder is not so much that the frontiers of the Empire collapsed so quickly, but rather that the Roman army had succeeded in holding them for as long as it did. Nevertheless it was inevitable that as the Empire shrank the strength of the army it could support had decreased proportionately, to the point where it would require barbarian assistance to repel further incursions. In this context it is not altogether appropriate to continue using the word barbarian, for many of those who had settled within the imperial boundaries were already fully conversant with the Roman way of war and had begun to absorb the benefits of Roman civilisation.

As always, beyond the eastern horizon hovered the Huns, as unpredictable as they were terrifying. By now they had established a large if ill-defined empire of their own, centred on the area of modern Hungary with Buda as its primitive capital. The Huns, however, having no interest in civilisation or formal agriculture, tended to consume everything in their path so that once an area had been stripped of its resources they were forced to move on.

The typical Hun soldier was a cavalryman of stocky, Mongoloid appearance, deliberately inured to hardship from the moment he was born. His life revolved around his horses, the quality of which had improved by the addition of Roman-bred stock. In managing his herds he often employed a lasso, which he would also use in battle to incapacitate or bring down an opponent, although his usual weapons were the horn bow and sword. On campaign he might

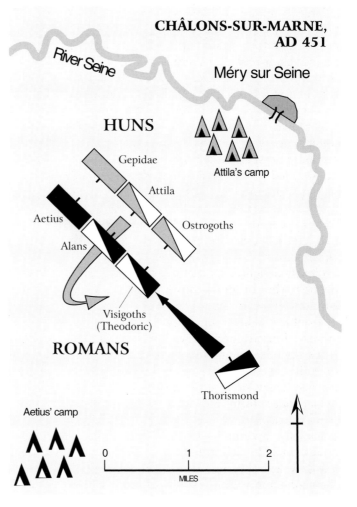

CHÂLONS-SUR-MARNE, AD 451

take a dozen or more horses with him, riding them in rotation, drinking mares' milk and, whenever necessary, eating horseflesh. Naturally, this gave the Hun armies a mobility and stamina superior to that of opponents who relied on conventional logistics. Tactically, the hallmarks of the Huns were speed, surprise, the ability to concentrate quickly, ferocity and terror. They fought only the battles they thought they could win, avoided those where the issue was dubious, and saw no disgrace in flight. Like the Goths, they made use of wagon trains for their families, forming them into makeshift forts in the presence of the enemy.

At this period the Huns were ruled by Attila, who was described by a contemporary Roman ambassador as being short, swarthy and having a large head notable for its tiny eyes, snub nose, wispy beard and greying hair; in character he was covetous, vain, superstitious, cunning, excessively arrogant and cruel, yet surprisingly simple in his tastes. Some subsequent commentators have portrayed him as an excellent tactician with limited strategic ability. Fuller does not agree, commenting that as a soldier he was no more than a plunderer, revealing no spark of constructive genius. That he revelled in his reputation for wholesale slaughter and destruction is an impression reinforced by an encounter with a Christian hermit who, apparently seeking early martyrdom, told him that he was 'The Scourge of God for the chastisement of Christians!' Attila was evidently delighted by the image, for instead of putting the hermit's head on a pole, he adopted the words as one of his titles.

Trouble had been brewing between the Huns and the Empire for a while. First, the Romans had suspended their annual payment of tribute in gold, which Attila was determined to recover. Then, he received an unsolicited offer of marriage from Honoria, the unbalanced sister of the Emperor Valentinian III, which he graciously accepted on condition that her dowry include half the empire of the West; naturally enough, Valentinian refused. Finally, the succession to the Frankish throne being in dispute, one candidate appealed to Attila for help, and the other to Valentinian, creating a situation that led to war.

In the spring of 451 Attila crossed the Rhine into Gaul. Contemporary sources claim that his army numbered half a million men, but this was a wild exaggeration stemming from the usual terror engendered by the Huns. Probably 100,000 is nearer the mark, of which about one third were Hun cavalry and the rest contingents from subject peoples including Ostrogoth cavalry and infantry provided by the Gepidae, Franks and others. In three columns, occupying a total frontage of 100 miles, the Huns began to ravage northern Gaul. Trier, Cologne, Mainz, Strasbourg and many other towns and cities were pillaged and put to the torch. Attila's own column then moved south

to Orléans, which covered a strategic crossing of the Loire. Here, the townspeople's refusal to be intimidated by his ferocious reputation ensnared him in a protracted siege.

Meanwhile the Romans had been preparing their response in the south of the country. In command was Aetius, the best Roman general of the times, whose title was Master of the Soldiers. Aetius knew Attila personally, had lived among the Huns, and more recently had hired some of them as mercenaries, so he was fully conversant with the way they conducted their campaigns. Having crossed the Alps in some haste with a token force, he picked up more troops in Gaul, but was still too weak in numbers to challenge Attila in the field. King Theodoric of the Visigoths was persuaded that his best interests lay in joining Aetius. The combined army advanced to relieve Orléans, its arrival on 14 June evidently taking the Huns by surprise. Some of the besiegers were driven into the suburbs, being hounded from street to street while the inhabitants rained stones and tiles at them from the rooftops until they were wiped out. Attila hastily raised what remained of the siege, withdrawing towards the Seine, where better cavalry country existed in Champagne, and summoned the rest of his troops to join him.

Success brings its own reward, although in this case it was thought to be of doubtful value. As Aetius and Theodoric followed up, they were joined by a strong contingent of Alans under their king, Sangibanus, whose loyalty they distrusted. Nevertheless by the end of the month Aetius had caught up with the enemy rearguard, consisting of Gepidae whom Attila was willing to sacrifice, and overwhelmed it in a night attack. Shortly afterwards the allied army came within sight of the Huns' wagon laager.

Although the subsequent battle is most frequently referred to as Châlons-sur-Marne, most authorities believe that it actually took place in the open country south-west of the little town of Méry-sur-Seine. Attila, still awaiting the rest of his horde, was aware that he was out-numbered and far from confident of success. His intention was to fight a holding action during the afternoon and continue his retreat during the night. He deployed the Gepidae and other infantry on his right, opposite Aetius' legions, his own Hun cavalry opposite the Alan cavalry in the centre, and the Ostrogoth cavalry on his left, opposite the Visigoth cavalry. He recognised that the Alans were the weakest element in the allied line and decided to direct the weight of his attack against them.

This suited Aetius and Theodoric very well. They did not trust the Alans and had deliberately placed them in the centre of the line. If they gave way, that was all to the good because this would draw the Huns away from their wagon laager. The allied plan was, in fact, to execute a double envelopment which would separate the Huns from the laager. To this end Theodoric's son Thorismond was sent with a force of cavalry to a small hill, known today as Point St Georges, situated a mile or so from Attila's left flank. This was the only feature of real tactical importance on the battlefield. Belatedly recognising the fact, Attila sent some of the Ostrogoths, reinforced with Huns from his centre, to capture the hill, but their attack was successfully beaten off.

The battle then became general. On the allied left the legions clashed with Attila's infantry in a protracted struggle. In the centre the much-maligned Alans stood up to the charge of the Hun cavalry and, although they might have given ground, they do not seem to have given way altogether. On the right the Visigoths became involved in a huge cavalry mêlée with their Ostrogoth cousins. In the course of this Theodoric, leading a charge, was either struck down or thrown from his horse and trampled to death. The incident was witnessed by Thorismond who led a thunderbolt charge down the slopes of the hill into the Ostrogoths' flank. Enraged by the death of their elderly but popular king, the Visigoths bundled their opponents across the rear of the Hun army, coming close to killing Attila himself.

On the opposite flank, the legions had begun to gain ground as they cut their way into the heart of the Gepidae. Attila, whose Huns were making progress against the Alans, saw the danger and ordered a general withdrawal to the wagon laager. The movement was confused and untidy, fighting continuing into the growing darkness as scattered parties of the Hun army tried to regain their own lines. For a while both Aetius and Thorismond were separated from their men and in some danger.

Expecting that the allies would storm the laager next morning, the Huns prepared it for defence. Their losses, however, had been enormous and few expected to survive. Attila, determined that he should neither be killed nor captured, had a pyramid made from the wooden saddles of his cavalry, placed himself, his wives and his treasure on it and gave instructions for it to be set ablaze when the enemy broke into the camp.

The carnage revealed by dawn confirmed that the legend of Hun invincibility had been shattered. Aetius, however, had even wider considerations on his mind. Thorismond had been elected king by his troops and such had been his share in the victory that Aetius was worried lest, in the aftermath of the battle, the Visigoths should begin to regard themselves as over-mighty subjects. In an avuncular sort of way, he re-assured the young king that the situation was now under control and recommended that he return to Toulouse and consolidate his hold on the levers of power. Once the Visigoths had left Aetius permitted Attila to slip back across the Rhine with the remnant of his army; such were the devious politics required to preserve the Empire in its final days.

Creasy and Fuller both regard Châlons as one of the decisive battles of the Western world, not because it was the last occasion on which the Eagles looked down upon a critical victory, but because, had the Huns won, they would have turned Gaul into a semi-desert, destroying in the process every element of the Graeco-Roman culture on which Western civilisation is based.

In 452 Attila invaded Italy but withdrew having achieved comparatively little. The reasons for his retreat may have been concern for his lines of communication, which were being threatened by Aetius, or the defeat of one of his flank columns, or a general shortage of supplies, or epidemics which had broken out among his troops, or the payment of tribute, or, according to tradition, a visit from Pope Leo I, or, more probably, a combination of all these factors. When Attila died the following year the Hun empire was torn apart as his sons fought for the throne, and when its subject tribes rebelled the Huns themselves vanished from European history.

In 454 Valentinian, jealous of Aetius, murdered him, only to fall himself to an assassin's blade the following year, which also witnessed a further sacking of Rome, this time by a Vandal fleet. The empire of the West, though it would enjoy further brief successes, no longer had the power to influence events and in fact had only a few years to go. In 476 Odoacer, a barbarian mercenary general of part Hunnish descent, seized power in Italy and deposed the last emperor, Romulus Augustulus. Odoacer did not assume the title of emperor and the event is usually accepted as marking the end of the Roman state.

Commentary 3 – The Dark Ages

Rome and the empire of the West had become a folk memory, although in time the title of Holy Roman Emperor would be resurrected. Rome may not have been popular with her subjects, but her piecemeal departure nevertheless engendered a sense of loss, for with it went a strong central authority, a common language, a common currency and a common legal system. The local kingdoms, some of them very small, which replaced Roman rule, lacked the financial resources to maintain the superb system of roads along which the empire's trade had flowed so that in many places they became overgrown and vanished beneath the soil. Commerce itself, inhibited by war and barbarian incursions, also became more localised. When established towns, cities, villas and farms were sacked, the financial resources no longer existed to rebuild them in their original form, even if the surviving inhabitants possessed the necessary skills. Despite this, the basic elements of civilisation and learning were preserved by the Christian Church through its monastic system.

The major military development of these years was the introduction of the fixed stirrup. Saddle technology was already far advanced and rope or leather toe stirrups had been in use for some time, especially among the races that had migrated westwards from central Asia. Precisely when fixed iron stirrups came into common usage is uncertain, but it may have been during the 5th or 6th centuries. The effect was revolutionary. Stirrups increased the rider's endurance by supporting the legs during long marches, they provided a lancer with real stability and, by standing in them, a swordsman was able to deliver a wider variety of cuts with all his strength.

Following the departure of the legions, the Anglo-Saxon raids on Britain escalated to the point where they became an invasion followed by settlement. Slowly but steadily the Romano-Britons were pushed westwards. By the end of the 5th century, however, they had acquired a war leader named Ambrosius Aurelianus, who is generally accepted to have been the legendary King Arthur. It seems probable that Ambrosius had a sufficiently powerful personality to persuade the remnant of the Romano-British aristocracy, plus a number of local kinglets, that their only chance of survival lay in forming a confederacy in which all were equal, hence the Round Table at which he was merely first among equals. Perhaps he emphasised the need of a regular body of heavy cavalry capable of moving from one threatened point to another and administering the final crushing blow in a pitched battle, but that is likely to remain a matter for speculation. Whatever the truth, the Britons won twelve battles in succession, the last being a crushing victory at Mount Badon, where so many Saxons were killed that 50 years were to pass

41

Left: Later, Viking raiders from Denmark, Norway and Sweden carried out raids, followed by full-scale invasions, on the coasts of England, France and Ireland. The Vikings also penetrated deep into Russia and even crossed the North Atlantic.

before their expansion was resumed. By the time it ended the Britons had been pushed back into Cornwall, Wales, Cumbria and Galloway. England had now become a patchwork of small kingdoms squabbling for supremacy. The battles between them, and between similar kingdoms in western Europe, were fought by local levies using sword, spear, axe, club and shield. In such circumstances there was little room for innovative thought, most encounters being decided by simple brute force and numbers. Such accounts as we possess were often produced by monkish chroniclers writing long after the event. Like the scribes of ancient times they tend to over-inflate the size of the armies involved and the casualties inflicted; many are unashamedly partisan. The deeds of individual heroes are recorded, but tactical detail is sparse. On the other hand there is heavy emphasis on the savagery with which these battles were fought.

Elsewhere, the Eastern or Byzantine Empire had remained in being and retained much of the later Roman military system. Under Justinian the Great it even briefly recovered some of the lost territories. But Justinian's wars left large areas devastated, his treasury empty and his subjects crippled by taxes, so that by the time they came to an end the Empire had

been fundamentally weakened and was in no condition to meet a threat that arose in Middle East with all the sudden ferocity of a tropical thunderstorm.

In about 615 the Prophet Mohammed began preaching the gospel of Islam in Mecca. The essentially benevolent concepts expressed therein fired the minds of his countrymen, especially the promise that those who died fighting for the Faith against the infidel would be rewarded with everlasting pleasure in heaven. When Mohammed died in 632 the sovereignty of Islam had been extended to the whole of the Arabian peninsula. The same militant policy was pursued by his Caliphs (successors), although this brought them into direct conflict with the Byzantine Empire and actually induced an intermittent struggle between Christian Europe and Islam that would last for a thousand years.

The ragged warriors swarming out of the desert gained one spectacular success after another, not so much because they fought with fanatical zeal, but because in many areas they were welcomed as liberators. The original armies were joined by enthusiastic converts in their thousands, bringing with them divers military skills. Within 70 years of Mohammed's death the Byzantine provinces of Syria,

Egypt and North Africa had been conquered. In 709 a Muslim army crossed the Straits of Gibraltar into Spain and within four years had overrun the country. The Crescent Moon of Islam, it seemed, was about to devour Europe, the right horn through Asia Minor and Constantinople, the left horn through the Pyrenees and northwards into France.

THE SIEGE OF CONSTANTINOPLE, 717–18

The Caliph Suleiman was determined to capture Constantinople and allocated the bulk of his resources to the task. One Arab army, commanded by his brother Maslama, was already operating in Europe and closing in on the city while another, under the Caliph's personal command, was being formed at Tarsus. A large fleet, commanded by another Suleiman, known as the General, had closed off the Dardanelles and, when the moment came, would be ordered to blockade the Bosphorus as well, thereby cutting the city's last remaining sea supply route from the outside world.

Unfortunately for the Caliph, just as his plans were coming to fruition, the throne of the Eastern Empire was seized by a very capable, wily and tough officer known as Leo the Isaurian, who persuaded its previous incumbent, Theodosius III, that what remained of his life would be better spent in a monastery.

Leo III was well aware of Arab intentions. Constantinople was built on a peninsula, flanked on the south by the Sea of Marmara and on the north by its famous harbour, the Golden Horn, the entrance to which could be closed by a great chain suspended between two towers, from which it could be raised or lowered. Across the neck of the peninsula ran an inner and an outer wall, the former built by Constantine the Great, the latter, four miles long, by Theodosius II. These Leo repaired, mounting missile engines on the towers. The defences were considered to be impregnable – and would remain so until the invention of gunpowder – but what worried him most was the possibility that the enemy would close the Bosphorus. He therefore re-stocked the granaries and arsenals in preparation for a long siege, allowing for the fact that the normal population of 500,000 had been swollen by refugees.

The Arab army arrived outside the city walls on 15 August 717. Maslama began badly by ordering an immediate assault, which was promptly repulsed with heavy casualties. He then decided to reduce the city by blockade, built himself an entrenched camp, and ordered Suleiman the General to close the Bosphorus with half his fleet.

As Suleiman's leading ships attempted to pass the Golden Horn on 3 September, they encountered the unexpectedly strong currents which sweep round Seraglio Point and lost their formation. Leo immediately ordered the chain to be lowered and sallied forth with his own galleys, destroyed 20 of the enemy's with Greek fire, captured others and withdrew before Suleiman could intervene. For the moment, the idea of closing the Bosphorus was abandoned.

Maslama next learned that his brother the Caliph, a man of voracious appetite, had died after consuming two baskets of eggs and figs, followed by a quantity of sugared marrow. Suleiman's successor, Omar II, being more interested in religion than war, simply left Maslama to get on with the siege.

The winter months were unduly severe for the region, with snow lying for 100 days. Unused to the cold, ravaged by the diseases prevalent in encampments before sanitation was properly understood, and starving to the point of cannibalism, the Muslims died in their thousands; among them was Suleiman the General.

In the spring of 718 Maslama's depleted ranks were filled out by the arrival of the reserve army from Tarsus. More ships arrived from Egypt and North Africa, enabling the Muslims to close the Bosphorus at last. Superficially, the chances of Constantinople being able to hold out had begun to dwindle. Unfortunately for Maslama, the crews of the

Egyptian vessels numbered a high proportion of Coptic Christians who deserted regularly, keeping Leo informed as to the true state of the fleet.

Once again the garrison's galleys emerged from the Golden Horn and fell on the Egyptian squadron, the Christian crews of which either mutinied or deserted. The squadron was virtually annihilated, its ships being either sunk by ramming, burned or captured. Leo used the captured vessels to transport a large force to the Asiatic side where part of Maslama's army was ambushed and cut to pieces.

Leo had been active in other areas, too. By diplomacy and promise of reward he persuaded the Bulgars to harry the Muslim rear. This they did, wiping out a strong detachment in the area of Adrianople. As a result of these continued reverses the Muslims' morale plummeted, but Leo had by no means finished with them yet. He generated terror among Maslama's troops with a rumour to the effect that huge numbers of Christian Franks – a general term used in the Middle East for western Europeans rather than specifically the inhabitants of France – were approaching Constantinople by land and sea with the intention of breaking the siege. On hearing this, Caliph Omar, who clearly regarded the siege as being prohibitively expensive as well as futile, ordered Maslama to withdraw, which he did on 15 August, exactly a year after his arrival.

Even then the wretched Maslama's cup of woe was not quite full. Having shipped the remnant of his army across the Sea of Marmara, the fleet set sail for the Dardanelles but, save for five galleys, was lost in a storm. Of the 200,000 men who had been directly engaged in the siege, only 30,000 are said to have reached Tarsus. Quite possibly these figures are the product of a joyful imagination, but whatever the true statistics the fact was, as Gibbon puts it, the Muslims had sustained an 'almost incredible disaster'.

Had Constantinople fallen the entire subsequent history of eastern Europe and the Middle East would have been different, just as it was when the city finally fell seven centuries later. As it was, Leo's victory was decisive in that it saved Christian Europe from Muslim domination. To that victory he added a post-script in 739 by defeating the Muslims again at Acroinon and forcing them to abandon the western half of Asia Minor.

TOURS, OCTOBER 732

By the year 600 the Franks had emerged as the dominant power in what had once been Gaul. For more than three centuries they had been ruled by the Merovingian dynasty, but since 639 the line had become effete and all effective power was concentrated in the hands of a succession of Mayors of the Palace, a title descended from the old Roman Master of the Soldiers. In 714, following the death of Mayor Pepin II, his natural son Charles Martel (Charles the Hammer), emerged as his successor.

Two years earlier the Muslims had begun raiding through the Pyrenees. They were successfully opposed for a while by Count Eudo of Aquitaine, who had proclaimed his independence from central authority after Pepin's death. The raids became heavier and more frequent. In 721 Eudo inflicted a serious defeat on the Muslims at Toulouse, killing Samah, the governor of Spain. Samah, however, was succeeded by the even more energetic Abd er-Rahman, whose raids struck ever deeper into Eudo's territory.

In 732 Abd er-Rahman launched another major invasion, the object of which seems to have been the acquisition of yet more plunder rather than occupation. His army, estimated to have numbered between 50,000 and 80,000, consisted almost entirely of cavalry, mainly unarmoured Moorish and Berber light horsemen. He defeated Eudo at Bordeaux and the latter, with what remained of his army, retreated northwards to join Charles Martel who had just returned from a successful campaign in southern Germany. Eudo patched up his differences with Charles by swearing fealty to him and the two began assembling a force with which to repel the invaders.

Meanwhile Abd er-Rahman's troops had swept through Aquitaine, laying siege to Poitiers and storming Tours. The early ideals of Islam seem to have been forgotten as they indulged in an orgy of killing and pillage which disgusted even the Muslim historian of the campaign. 'That army went through all places like a desolating storm,' he wrote. 'Prosperity made those warriors insatiable. Abd er-Rahman and his host attacked Tours to gain still more spoil, and they fought against it so fiercely that they stormed the city almost before the eyes of the army that came to save it; and the fury and the cruelty of the Muslims towards the inhabitants of the city were like the fury and cruelty of raging tigers. It was manifest that God's chastisement was sure to follow such excesses.'

As the chronicler suggests, the sudden appearance of the Frankish army took the Muslims by surprise. Together Charles and Eudo had about 30,000 men including a heavy cavalry element formed from the nobility. There were also some household troops but the bulk of their army consisted of levies. Most wore armour of some sort, even if it were restricted to helmet, shield and some kind of body protection, mail, leather or quilted

Abd er-Rahman was confronted with a dilemma. Even allowing for, say, 20,000 men having been detached to forage and invest Poitiers, he still had an impressive numerical superiority with which to give battle. But his army was now in such a condition that it could neither fight nor retreat. The chronicler continues: 'Abd er-Rahman and other cavaliers saw the disorder of the Muslim troops, who were loaded with spoil; but they did not venture to displease the soldiers by ordering them to abandon everything except their arms and war-horses. Abd er-Rahman trusted in the valour of his soldiers, and in the good fortune which ever attended him; but such defect of discipline is always fatal to armies.'

It seems that Abd er-Rahman decided to fall back on Poitiers, covered by a cavalry screen. The pace of the army, however, was tied to that of its convoy of booty which, being drawn by over-burdened oxen, moved very slowly

indeed. For seven days Charles followed closely, sizing up his opponents and cutting off stragglers but not launching a major attack. The conclusions he reached were that the Muslim light cavalry were effective only when attacking, being able to take ground but not hold it; that his own cavalry element was too small and too slow to compete; and that his infantry would have to fight in close order, denying the Muslim horsemen any gap in their line.

At length Abd er-Rahman, realising that he could not shake off his pursuers, decided to stand and fight in the area of Cenon. Charles dismounted his cavalry who joined the infantry in forming a phalanx along the crest of a hill. According to the Arab historian, the Muslims launched their first charge shortly after:

'The hearts of Abd er-Rahman, his captains and his men were filled with anger and pride, and they were the first to begin the fight. The Muslim horsemen dashed fiercely and frequently against the battalions of the Franks, who resisted manfully, and many fell dead on either side, until the going down of the sun.'

The Christian version of events, written by Isodorus Pacensis, tells us that: 'The men of the north stood as motionless as a wall; they were like a belt of ice frozen together and not to be dissolved, as they slew the Arabs with the sword. The Austrasians, vast of limb and iron of hand, hewed on bravely in the thick of the fight; it was they who found and cut down the Saracen king.'

Here accounts diverge, some Christian versions stating that, disheartened by the death of Abd er-Rahman, the Muslims abandoned their plunder and fled during the night. The Muslim version, however, makes it clear that heavy fighting continued next day:

'In the grey of the morning the Muslims returned to the battle. Their cavaliers had soon hewn their way into the centre of the Christian host. But many of them were fearful for the safety of the spoil which they had stored in their tents, and a false cry arose in their ranks that some of the enemy were plundering the camp; whereupon several squadrons of Muslim horsemen rode off to protect their tents. But it seemed as if they fled and all the host was troubled, and while Abd er-Rahman strove to check their panic and lead them back into the battle, the warriors of the Franks surrounded him and he was pierced through with many spears, so that he died. Then all the host fled before the enemy and many died in the flight.'

This provides a more credible alternative. The probability is that Charles and Eudo, satisfied that they had written down the Muslim strength during the first day's fighting, decided to exploit the enemy's sensitivity regarding his plunder. It seems probable that Eudo, no mean soldier in his own right, used the hours of darkness to execute a flank march with his Aquitanians then, when the Muslims launched the first charges next morning, either menaced or actually attacked the camp. During the ensuing panic Charles may well have remounted his own cavalry and launched a counter-attack into the disorganised mass, with the result already described.

The pursuit was evidently of limited duration, partly because the Muslims had the greater mobility, and partly because Charles intended them to remain a threat to Eudo and thus preserve his new-found loyalty. How much of the recovered plunder was shared among the victorious army and how much was returned to its rightful owners, remains an unanswered question. As to casualties, the wildest estimates place the Muslim loss at many times the number actually present, while Charles is said to have lost a mere 1,500 killed, an unbelievably low figure for a hard-fought, two-day action. But there seems little doubt that the Muslim loss was the heavier, and heavy enough to dissuade them from further ventures of the same kind.

Gibbon suggests that had it not been for the Battle of Tours the Koran would have formed the basis of religious education at Oxford. This overstates the case somewhat, although it was of great importance and did complement Leo III's great victory at Constantinople. Rather it represents the limit to which the Muslims were willing to extend their forays into western Europe. By 759 they had been driven out of France altogether.

Commentary 4 – Feudalism, Chivalry and the Middle Ages

In 751 Pepin the Short, who had succeeded his father Charles Martel as Mayor of the Palace, deposed the sickly Childeric III, the last Merovingian king of France, packed him off to a monastery and had himself crowned, all with papal approval. On Pepin's death in 768 he was succeeded in turn by his son Charles, better known as Charlemagne or Charles the Great.

The ambitions of Charlemagne, all of which were achieved within his lifetime, were to create a large Christian empire in western Europe, to restore within it the order which had been lost with the onset of the Dark Ages, and to encourage the revival of learning, art and literature. In due course his empire was to cover an area which included all of modern France, Belgium and Holland, western Germany, parts of Bohemia and Austria, and most of Italy.

This could only have been achieved by a leader with an efficient military machine at his disposal. The empire was sub-divided into districts, each governed by a count. Within the districts were fortified posts serving as pivots of manoeuvre for mobile forces. These consisted mainly of armoured cavalry, for which each count was required to provide shields, lances, swords, bows and daggers. The old infantry levies, armed with whatever weapons they could lay hands on, were replaced by much smaller bodies of picked men equipped with swords, spears and bows from central resources. Charlemagne also made provision for siege and supply trains in his armies.

From these roots sprang the two factors which were to dominate warfare in the Western world during the Middle Ages, namely the feudal system and the code of chivalry. Under the feudal system the king owned all land, areas of which he granted to his nobles in proportion to their importance and degree; the nobles, in their turn, allocated portions of their domains to relatives or lesser nobles. In peacetime the king would maintain a bodyguard and such troops as were required to garrison his fortresses throughout the realm. In time of war the nobles would support the king with their personal presence if possible, as well as contributing mounted knights and men-at-arms to his army in numbers appropriate to their importance. If the central authority was strong, the system worked; if it was weak, over-mighty nobles would erect their own fortresses, maintain their own armies and threaten the authority of the king, if not actually displace him.

In this secular age it is difficult for us to understand the powerful hold which the Church exercised on men's minds in medieval times. The Church accepted war as being part of man's condition and was inclined to approve heartily of wars fought for its own benefit. On the other hand, it sought to control the conduct of war by softening its worst effects. As already mentioned, the mounted arm achieved dominance in Charlemagne's time and was to retain it until the later Middle Ages. Only the nobility and men of substance could afford to equip themselves with horses and armour, and so war became primarily a matter for the upper classes. Simultaneously, the Church taught that the true Christian warrior should be devout, should offer his protection to women and children, the old, the poor and the helpless, and evince charity, mercy and courtesy to all. From this evolved the code of chivalry, an Old French word for horsemen, and with it the concept of knighthood. As the Middle Ages progressed, the ancient Arthurian legends were dusted off and translated into the chivalric terms in which they have come down to us; sadly the ideals expressed therein were seldom translated into reality.

The knight's pastimes were hunting and mock battles called tourneys, recreations which maintained the level of fitness and skill he would require in war. He possessed his own coat of arms by which he could be recognised, and a simplified version of the device was worn by his retainers on their surcoats. Yet, formidable though he might be as a fighting man, the knight remained an individual within a group rather than a member of a disciplined body with a common purpose. In battle, the capture and ransom of a wealthy opponent was always preferable to his death, a situation which naturally resulted in low casualties among the hierarchy. A later Middle Ages exception to this was provided by the Wars of the Roses, during which the nobility of England slaughtered one another without mercy.

Medieval warfare was dominated by the castle (or fortified town) and the knight, the former providing the pivot of manoeuvre for the latter. There was, of course, a need of infantry, archers and others in a medieval army, but their part was considered secondary to that of the mounted men, save in formal sieges. On balance, therefore, the burden of war was removed from the ordinary man, the effect being to consolidate the power of an unassailable aristocracy. At the beginning of the 11th century, however, the crossbow appeared. This was the best personal missile weapon yet developed, possessing range, accuracy and the power to penetrate mail. Suddenly the knight had become vulnerable and neither he nor the Church liked the idea. In 1139 the Second Lateran Council prohibited the use of the weapon against Christians as being 'hateful to God'. As technology cannot be un-invented, few paid much attention. Two hundred years later an even more terrible weapon, the English longbow, with longer range, higher rate of fire and penetrative power, caused a revolution in the armourer's art. Whereas the earlier short bows had been drawn to the chest or cheek, the 6-foot longbow was drawn to the ear with a pull of 100 pounds so that the kinetic energy stored in the arrow head was capable of penetrating four inches of oak, or nailing together a knight's thigh, saddle and horse. Overnight, the old chain mail, leather and quilted armour had become useless against such weapons unless it was augmented. It was replaced or supplemented by plate armour presenting a series of deflection surfaces, but even this did not guarantee protection because the archers then modified the design of their arrow heads. Thus, additionally encumbered, the knight soldiered on until gunpowder finally rendered him obsolete.

The formative military events of the medieval period included the Viking attacks on western Europe, the Norman Conquest of England, the Crusades, the Mongol invasion of eastern Europe and the Hundred Years War between England and France.

Vikings from Norway, Denmark and, to a lesser extent, Sweden began raiding the British Isles and the western European continent at the beginning of the 9th century. They provided incentives towards the adoption of the feudal system and the rise of the mounted arm. This was especially true of mainland Europe where the use of mobile forces was found to be an effective counter to Viking forays up river estuaries. In England, however, history followed a different course. Available resources were channelled into the building of a fleet rather than raising a mounted arm, with the result that the English continued to fight on foot. Raids were followed by invasion and settlement over much of the country. However, whereas the Saxons and Romano-Britons had not been compatible, the Danes were quickly assimilated, although they exercised effective control. In this context, therefore, the Anglo–Danish wars of the 9th, 10th and early 11th centuries can be seen as contests between northern and eastern England on the one hand, and southern and western England, led by Wessex, on the other.

In 911 Norse activity in France culminated in Charles III ceding the region of the lower Seine to the Viking leader Rolf on condition that he did homage for his lands and that he and his followers become Christians. The result was the creation of the Duchy of Normandy, reflecting the origin of the newcomers, who assimilated quickly without submerging their own positive characteristics. The Normans' drive and energy, allied with a natural sense of order and discipline, proved to be a compelling combination in every sphere of life. Once they had embraced the chivalric code, Norman soldiers were much sought after as mercenaries. In 1066, as we shall see, a comparatively small Norman army conquered England, changing the entire course of British history.

Ostensibly, the purpose of Crusades was to liberate the Holy Places of Palestine from Muslim control, a cause which generated immense enthusiasm at all levels throughout Western Christendom. In political terms, however, they were initiated by Pope Urban II to assist the embattled Byzantine empire, which remained under immense pressure from the Muslims, notably the Seljuk Turks. The First Crusade took Jerusalem in 1099, after which a number of Crusader states were established in Palestine and Syria. These included the Kingdom of Jerusalem, the Principality of Antioch, the County of Edessa and the County of Tripoli, known collectively as Outremer, or the Land Across the Sea. The varying fortunes of the Crusader states prompted further Crusades, although in due course the term was applied to any protracted drive against non-Christian people, including the reconquest of Spain and German expeditions into the Slavic lands to the east.

The original Crusades brought the West into contact with the Arab skills of applied mathematics and medicine, although the major lessons lay in the military sphere. Faced with a mobile, resourceful foe in a frequently hostile environment, the Crusaders were forced to re-learn the value of light cavalry, co-ordination between arms and the importance of logistic planning.

The greatest impact, however, was in the field of scientific fortification. In western Europe castles had either been built in unassailable places or took the form of a palisaded earthwork motte (mound) and bailey. In time, these were simply translated into stone, a keep taking the place of the motte while the bailey was surrounded by a crenellated wall entered through a strong gatehouse. Contact with Byzantine and Muslim fortifications revealed to the Crusaders the value of high curtain walls punctuated by massive towers that could deliver heavy flanking fire at an attacker, and that concentric fortification, with two or even three such walls built within one another, rendered a fortress or city almost impregnable. The result, when the Crusaders returned home, was a complete revolution in castle building.

The Crusaders had less to learn from their enemies about siegecraft. The principal missile engines, the ballista and the catapult, differed little from those used by the Romans. At about this time, however, a new and deadly missile engine entered service. The trebuchet relied not on twisted skeins for its power, but used a combination of gravity and centrifugal force. A pivoting beam was placed across a tall framework, with a heavy weight attached to its shorter forward end. Attached to the rear end was a sling into which a large stone was placed. When released, the weight fell and in rising the rear end of the beam activated the sling; at the top of its arc the sling opened, hurling the stone at the target with immense force. The damage caused was far greater than that which could be achieved by conventional catapults, which could only throw smaller stones at lower velocity. In addition, by adjusting the sling, it was possible to send balls sailing over the battlements to shatter against any hard surface within, 'the smallest part of which, striking a man, utterly spoileth him', as one chronicler put it. Incendiary material, executed prisoners, dead horses, dung and indeed anything which would make the besieged's life unpleasant would also be dispatched in this way. The principal effect of the trebuchet on fortification was that walls were made thicker and taller.

During the Crusades the Church Militant was represented by several military orders of monks, the most important being the Knights Templars, founded to escort pilgrims on their journeys between the coast and the Holy Places; the Knights Hospitalers who provided medical care; and the Teutonic Knights, who served briefly in the Holy Land but soon moved to Prussia. The military orders also held fortresses and formed a most important element within the Crusaders' field armies, their combined religious and military discipline making of them fierce, uncompromising opponents who were feared and hated by the Muslims.

Towards the end of the Crusading era Europe was menaced by the fresh and terrible danger presented by Mongol armies which, having destroyed all their Asiatic enemies, swept westwards. In some respects the Mongols resembled the Huns in that they were impervious to hardship of any kind, took spare horses on campaign with them, lived off the country and used terror as a weapon. There the similarity ended, for under successive khans, of whom Genghis Khan is the best remembered, the Mongol army had been turned into the best organised, disciplined and trained military machine of its day.

Cavalry formed the great mass of the army. The light cavalry were unarmoured and armed with a bow that was only slightly less powerful than the English longbow. The heavy cavalry wore leather or mail armour and were armed with a lance. Every trooper was equipped with a scimitar or battleaxe and wore a shirt of raw silk that an arrow would not penetrate, so the head could be drawn from the wound by pulling the fabric.

The army operated in corps-sized groups each of three divisions. Below that level it was organised in multiples of ten, 10,000 men forming a division of ten regiments each 1,000 strong, regiments in turn consisting of ten squadrons each of ten troops of ten men. Mobility, accompanied by deception and trickery, was the keynote of Mongol operations, great attention being paid to intelligence-gathering and maintaining communications between formations on the march. Therefore, once an enemy force had been located it became possible for a Mongol army commander, whose troops advanced on a very wide front, to hold it with a frontal attack and simultaneously direct one or more divisions to mount a completely unexpected assault on its flank or rear. Usually the shock generated was sufficient to break the opposing army, the survivors of which invariably exaggerated the

Mongols' numbers, so creating a legend of invincibility. Nor were fortified cities safe. If they chose to surrender, they would be subjected to a harsh but orderly occupation. If they resisted, the Mongols would bring up a portable siege train the like of which had not been seen since the days of Alexander the Great, and the city would be stormed amid fire and slaughter as a warning to others who chose to fight rather than submit.

It remains a matter of speculation as to what the outcome would have been had the Mongol hordes reached the more broken terrain of western Europe. The probability is that they would have taken it in their stride. Doubtless there would have been hard-fought battles, but in the end their ability to wage war at the higher level would have enabled them to defeat the more fragmented Western commanders whose experience was limited to the tactical battle. In 1242, however, following the death of Ogatai, son and successor of Genghis Khan, the hordes withdrew to Mongolia for the election of a new khan. They did not return to Europe, although they retained control of Russia.

Not long after this there came indications that the sun was beginning to set on the era of the knight. At Morgarten (1315), Laupen (1339) and Sempach (1386) Swiss pikemen fighting on their own terms defeated the chivalry of Austria and Burgundy, winning independence for their cantons. These lessons were emphasised during The Hundred Years War, which lasted from 1337 until 1453 and was actually a series of dynastic wars between the English and French ruling houses, allied with commercial considerations and a growing consciousness of nationhood unseen in Europe since the fall of Rome. Although the English archers repeatedly inflicted grievous loss on the French nobility, and at times the French cause seemed to be on the verge of collapse, the patriotic resurgence inspired by Joan of Arc proved so decisive that when the war ended only Calais remained in English hands.

The reasons for this were threefold. First, it was absurd to believe that England, with a population of only 2½ million, could hold down a united nation of 15 million. Secondly, the English armies were of necessity small and relied heavily on their archers' firepower. Thirdly, primitive guns had begun to appear on the battlefield in the middle of the 14th century and by now had been improved sufficiently for them to become effective anti-personnel weapons. At the battles of Formigny (1450) and Castillon (1453) they outranged the archers and played a major role in both French victories. Thereafter the energies of the English establishment became absorbed in the self-destructive Wars of the Roses. For more than two centuries the English would play little or no part in continental land warfare, pursuing instead a policy of maritime expansion.

HASTINGS, 14 OCTOBER 1066

The question of who would succeed to the crown of England on the death of Edward the Confessor was a troubled one. Edward was half-Norman, had been brought up in Normandy, relied on the advice of unpopular Norman advisers and, being childless, had promised William, Duke of Normandy, that he would inherit the throne. Later he changed his mind and nominated Harold, Earl of Wessex and scion of the powerful house of Godwin, as his heir. In the meantime Harold, during a visit to Normandy, had sworn to support William's claim to the English crown, allegedly under duress. In fact neither William nor Harold had a legitimate claim. If one followed the royal Anglo–Saxon bloodline, the real heir was the Aetheling Edgar, described by Fuller as being 'a weak, unpromising boy'. Unfortunately, England had suffered too much under earlier royal minorities and his claim was simply ignored. When Edward died on 5 January 1066 the need to install a strong monarch in his place was of paramount importance. The Witan, or Council of Nobles, conscious not only of Norman unpopularity but also that Harold was the most powerful man in England, had no hesitation in electing him king.

William, who had a genius for organisation, reacted by assembling an army and building a fleet with which to invade England. His own Normans were too few for the task, so, having obtained papal blessing to add respectability to the enterprise, he also recruited among the French and Bretons, promising to reward them with English lands once their victory was complete.

A third player now entered the game. Harald Hardrada, King of Norway, thought that he, too, had a claim to the English throne, and in this he was encouraged by Harold's brother Tostig, who had quarrelled bitterly with his new sovereign. The Norwegians entered the Humber with 300 ships in September and at Fulford on the 20th defeated the local fyrd (levies) raised by Edwin and Morcar, the Earls of Mercia and Northumbria. Harold hurried north from London with his housecarls, the only professional troops in the kingdom, picking up reinforcements on the way. The story that during a parley Harold's response to the Norwegian king's demand for territory was an offer of six feet of English earth in which to be buried is good theatre but almost certainly apocryphal. Having effected a junction with Edwin and Morcar, Harold took his enemy by surprise at Stamford Bridge on 25 September. The battle, a very sanguinary affair, lasted throughout the day, ending with the deaths of Harald Hardrada, Tostig and so many

of their men that only 20 ships were needed to carry the survivors home. The English too had suffered severely and, in view of the threatened Norman invasion, the heavy losses among the housecarls gave particular cause for concern.

A day or so later William sailed for England. He enjoyed a favourable wind and a calm sea but was also lucky in that the fleet Harold had left to guard the Channel had retired into the Thames for provisioning. He reached Pevensey on 28 September, then marched to Hastings where he built a fortified camp, and set about ravaging the surrounding countryside in the hope of provoking a battle at the earliest opportunity.

Right: Hastings, 1066. Norman cavalry and infantry, supported by archers, during one of their early attacks against the English position.

On 1 October Harold was at York celebrating his victory, when he learned that William had landed. The next day he began marching south, forcing the pace so that he reached London on 6 October. As this represents an average of 40 miles a day, he can only have been accompanied by the housecarls, who usually travelled on horseback but dismounted to fight; the fyrd contingents of Edwin and Morcar could not possibly have kept up. In London Harold was joined by his brothers Gurth and Leofwine, accompanied by their own housecarls, and by fyrd contingents from Middlesex, Surrey, Kent, Sussex and Hampshire. It was thought at the time, and by the majority of subsequent commentators, that Harold's best course would have been to complete the consolidation of his army before moving on. He was, however, possessed of an impatient, impulsive temperament, was openly derisive about the enemy and remained supremely confident of victory. On 11 October he marched out with an army representing perhaps half of his potential strength. Even then he pushed his troops hard, covering an average of nineteen miles per day, so that by the time he reached Senlac (Battle), some seven miles short of Hastings, on 13 October, one third of the army was still straggling behind. Quite possibly his intention had been to repeat his success at Stamford Bridge and surprise William in his camp. In this he was disappointed for it was soon apparent that the Normans were aware of his approach and were marching to meet him. He therefore dismounted his army and deployed it along a ridge fronting a shallow valley with a marshy bottom, using the afternoon to construct an abattis of branches and fallen trees across the front of his position. By degrees the Normans came up and occupied the slightly lower ground across the valley.

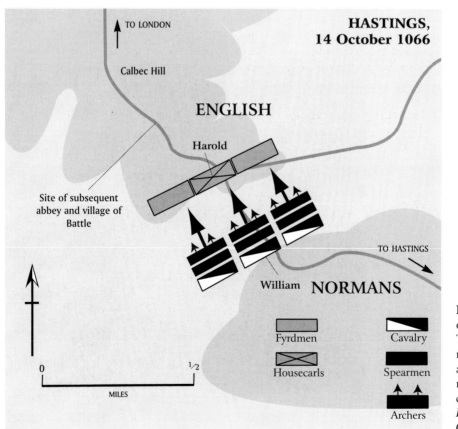

HASTINGS, 14 October 1066

TO LONDON

Calbec Hill

ENGLISH

Harold

Site of subsequent abbey and village of Battle

TO HASTINGS

William NORMANS

Fyrdmen
Housecarls
Cavalry
Spearmen
Archers

0   ½
MILES

Right: As this copy of the Bayeux Tapestry shows, many Norman attacks were repulsed with severe casualties. *Philip Haythornthwaite Collection*

Given the decisive nature and historical importance of the battle, the number of participants was surprisingly small. Harold had about 2,000 housecarls and 5,500 fyrd, a total of 7,500 infantry; William had perhaps 2,000 knights and mounted men-at-arms and 5,000 infantry, including a large contingent of archers, a total of 7,000. It is also, perhaps, surprising that the battle should have been fought with such grim determination until one remembers that both sides had everything to gain or lose by the result. The English knew that their lands had been promised to the invaders and could not afford to lose; the Normans knew that they would be richly rewarded if they won, and that few of them would see France again if they lost.

The most important elements of both armies were equipped with conical helmets, sleeved mail hauberks reaching to the knee but divided from the lower hem to the crutch to permit easy movement, and kite-shaped shields. In the Norman army the knights fought with lances, spears, two-edged swords, maces or battleaxes; the Norman infantry fought mainly with the sword but were less well-protected, although most had helmets, mail shirts or leather jerkins and shields, either kite-shaped or round. The Saxon housecarls were similarly equipped to the Norman knights and fought with spears, broad-bladed slashing swords or the terrible two-handed axe, which had a foot-wide cutting edge and a three-foot handle, enabling enormous power to be generated. The fyrd, long considered to have been an ill-armed levy of peasants, was actually well-organised on a county basis and drawn mostly from what would become the yeoman class. Its members were similarly equipped to the Norman infantry and armed with a variety of weapons including throwing or stabbing spears, axes, swords and hunting bows.

Because of the presence of the enemy's cavalry, Harold was forced to deploy his purely infantry army in close order along the crest, behind the abattis and the traditional English shield wall. He almost certainly believed that he was capable of standing off William's attack and writing down the strength of the Normans until fresh English troops arrived, enabling him to drive the invaders back to their ships. However, instead of the arrival of reinforcements, William of Malmesbury, writing some fifty years after the battle, tells us that desertions took place from the army, giving the reason as being Harold's failure to give the troops a share in the captured Norwegian treasure after Stamford Bridge. The likelihood is

that the deserters were Danish mercenaries who declined to fight another battle until they had been paid for the last one.

Harold may have been an energetic and, in his way, an able commander, but William was the better general. At the strategic level he had dragged Harold the length of the country, forcing him to give battle with an unexpectedly small, tired and apparently grumpy army against his own fresh troops. Tactically, the possession of an all-arms army gave him numerous options, whereas Harold was restricted to static defence. The initiative had therefore passed to William before the first blow was struck, enabling him to dictate the course of the battle from the outset.

On the morning of 14 October he drew up his army in three lines, the archers in front, the infantry in the middle and the knights behind, sub-divided into three divisions, the right commanded by Roger de Montgomery, the centre by William himself, and the left by the Count of Brittany. William's intention was that the archers would first soften up the English, after which the infantry would go in, clearing the abattis and creating gaps in the shield wall through which the knights would make their final decisive charge.

The battle began at about 9.30 a.m. The archers advanced to within 50 yards of the English line and opened fire. Most of their arrows thudded harmlessly into the shield wall or, because they were shooting uphill, passed overhead. Having themselves sustained casualties from the English bowmen and slingers, the archers withdrew to replenish their quivers and the Norman infantry passed through to begin their assault. They advanced into a fierce barrage of javelins, spears, arrows, slingshot and rocks tied to pieces of wood. The front ranks were felled at once and those behind who came to handstrokes quickly discovered to their horror that their armour offered little defence against the English two-handed axes and broadswords. Skulls were cloven, heads severed and limbs lopped with horrifying ease. Seeing his infantry falter, William immediately sent in his knights, but they fared no better. Unable to penetrate the close English array, they found themselves confronted by an unbelievably tough enemy who could bring down their horses with a single axe blow to the neck.

Left: A copy of another section of the Bayeux Tapestry. The original has a superscription HAROLD: REX: INTERFECTUS: EST (King Harold is killed). For many years the figure on the left was believed to be Harold. However, careful examination of the stitching shows the arrow protruding from the man's helmet rather than his eye and the figure on the right is understood to be the king. *Philip Haythornthwaite Collection*

On the left, the knights recoiled, carrying away the infantry with them. The movement spread to the centre and finally the whole Norman line was pouring down the ridge in headlong retreat. In the confusion William was unhorsed. A cry arose that he was dead, but he found another horse and, removing his helmet, managed to suppress the panic.

Fuller believes that at this moment Harold had victory in his grasp. If a general counter-attack had been ordered the probability is indeed that the Norman infantry and archers would have been annihilated. The knights, still in disarray, would not have been able to affect the issue, though many would have been able to escape to their fortified camp at Hastings. If Harold chose to give them terms, these would have included the personal surrender of William and his principal followers, who would then have been executed. Some discussion to this effect almost certainly did take place on the ridge, but Harold declined to give the necessary order. Despite this, Gurth and Leofwine seem to have taken matters into their own hands and, with their own housecarls and some troops from the right wing, launched an unsupported local counter-attack. The numbers involved were too few, and the moment had certainly passed. Rallied, the Norman knights cut off and killed many of the attackers, including Gurth and Leofwine. While the casualties incurred, especially the loss of the king's brothers, was regrettable, the event was not the disaster sometimes claimed for it. Many of the English regained the ridge and to the Normans their number seemed 'scarcely diminished'.

A pause now ensued during which Harold probably reinforced his right and William re-planned the battle. His infantry was so severely shaken that he kept it out of the fighting for a while. For several hours groups of knights probed unsuccessfully for a weak spot in the shield wall. Casualties began to mount for no appreciable gain. At length William resorted to the stratagem of a feigned flight opposite the English left. The ruse worked,

Above: A modern reconstruction of the same scene as that shown on the opposite page, allowing for both possibilities.

drawing out a large body of the fyrd. Their pursuit was allowed to continue across the valley to a point where they were beyond assistance, then the knights wheeled and slaughtered them to a man.

It was now about 4 p.m., yet still the shield wall stood unbroken. William, who had led by personal example, having had two horses killed under him during the day, was conscious that he must win in the short period of autumn daylight left. A drawn battle would be tantamount to a defeat, as the English would receive reinforcements and his own badly mauled army would not. He decided to combine shock action with firepower, the attacks of the knights, supported now by the infantry, alternating with his archers firing a high-angle rain

Left: A Victorian representation showing the last stand of Harold's housecarls on Senlac Hill. *Philip Haythornthwaite Collection*

of arrows that fell on those behind the shields. Very slowly the Normans began to make progress. The trampled abattis was no longer an obstacle. Gaps appeared in the shield wall into which a knight would spur and cut down a man or two before being cut down in turn, but gradually the English were pushed up the ridge by sheer weight of numbers. Harold was killed at about this time. The Bayeux Tapestry suggests that an arrow penetrated his eye, but there is some doubt that the man depicted is Harold; again, an analysis of the original stitch marks show that the arrow is protruding from his helmet. However he died, his body was evidently so badly battered that only his mistress could identify it.

The English fought on, but the light was fading and the battle clearly lost. Those on the already weakened left gave way first and then the whole line shredded into the darkness. One body of the royal housecarls, having decided to sacrifice themselves by acting as rearguard, died around their two standards, 'The Fighting Man' and 'The Dragon of Wessex'; another, having reached the forest behind the ridge, wiped out the Norman pursuit force in a ravine subsequently and appropriately named the Malfosse.

Each side probably sustained the loss of between two and three thousand men. The Saxons simply dispersed to their homes and it took William a week to get his much-reduced army moving again. He could not afford to fight another such battle, but he was clearly well versed in English politics and knew that, following the destruction of the house of Godwin, there were no others with the ability or inclination to resist him. He was not strong enough to besiege London, but having sent a detachment to burn Southwark as a warning to its citizens, he marched in a great arc around the city, ravaging the countryside. At Little Berkhamstead he was met by the earls Edwin and Morcar, bringing with them the Aetheling Edgar, the principal churchmen of England and the most important citizens of London, from whom he accepted the crown after a suitable display of modesty.

Unlike previous invaders, the Normans remained a small minority within a hostile or indifferent population. They retained control by building motte and bailey castles at every strategic location, by taking hostages, by devastating rebellious areas, and by rigid application of the feudal system. In due course they too would become assimilated and English would become their first language.

In the broader sphere, the events of 1066 saw England drawn away from her connections with Scandinavia and restored to the mainstream of western European life. The immediate results of Hastings were that, as Fuller puts it: 'In the place of a loosely knit and undisciplined country was substituted a unified and compact kingdom under a firm and hereditary central authority.' The American historians Ernest and Trevor Dupuy offer a wider, longer-term view of the consequences, describing the battle as: 'The initiation of a series of events which would lead a revitalised Anglo–Saxon– Norman people to a world leadership more extensive even than that of ancient Rome.'

ARSUF, 7 SEPTEMBER 1191

Despite the common purpose which had brought it into being, Outremer was a hotbed of rivalry and intrigue. The Crusader states plotted against the Military Orders and one another, the Military Orders plotted against one another and the Crusader states, and from time to time unlikely allies were sought, even among the Muslims, including the Brother-hood of Assassins, led by Rashid al-Din Sinan, the Old Man of the Mountains. At a time when unity was needed most to combat the rising star of Islam, Salah-al-Din Yusuf ibn-Ayub (Saladin), it was sadly lacking.

A Kurd of Turkish descent, Saladin had come to power in Egypt, but between 1183 and 1187 he extended his dominions until they encircled the Crusader states. His disciplined, well-trained army included, among others, Egyptians, Sudanese, Turks and Arabs, known collectively to the Crusaders as Saracens, and featured a large element of mounted archers as well as armoured heavy cavalry.

Friction between Saladin and the Crusaders came to a head in 1187 when, the latter having broken two truces, he declared a *jihad* or holy war against them. In June he invaded Palestine with 20,000 men and besieged Tiberias. Under Guy, King of Jerusalem, the Crusaders assembled a force of comparable size and marched to its relief. Ignoring advice, Guy led his troops along a hot, arid, waterless route until, near the Horns of Hattin, the Crusaders were sur-

Right: Crusading knights of the late 12th century. By now flat-topped helmets were in fashion, but the Crusaders quickly adapted to local condi-tions and often preferred to dispense with facial protection, wrapping a turban around the helmet to keep the sun off the metal, as well as a light surcoat.

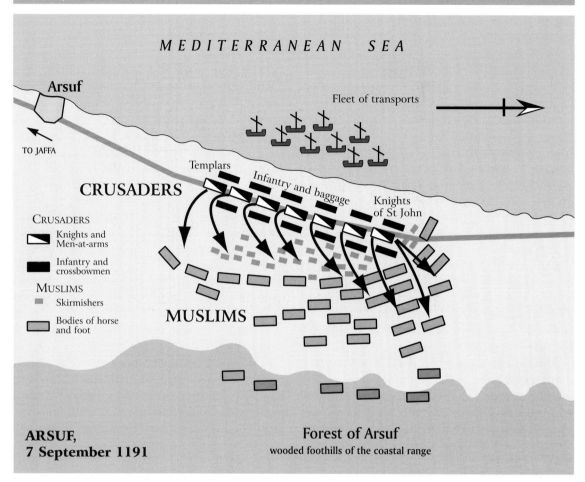

**ARSUF,
7 September 1191**

MEDITERRANEAN SEA

Arsuf

TO JAFFA

Fleet of transports

Templars

CRUSADERS

Infantry and baggage

Knights
of St John

CRUSADERS

Knights and
Men-at-arms

Infantry and
crossbowmen

MUSLIMS

Skirmishers

Bodies of horse
and foot

MUSLIMS

Forest of Arsuf
wooded foothills of the coastal range

rounded by swarms of mounted archers and subjected to the same sort of ordeal Crassus and his legionaries had endured at Carrhae twelve centuries earlier. Night brought no relief because the Muslims set fire to the scrub surrounding the Crusaders' camp, adding to the torture of thirst. Next morning, 4 July, Saladin's attacks drove the Christians, now reduced to a thirst-crazed mob, up one of the Horns, where they were cut to pieces and forced to surrendered. Guy and his more important nobles were held for ransom, but 200 Templar and Hospitaler Knights, regarded by the Saracens as the most formidable element of the Crusader armies, were decapitated on the spot. The remaining survivors were marched to Damascus in chains and sold into slavery. So numerous were they that the bottom dropped out of the market; one Muslim gladly exchanged his pris-

oner for a pair of sandals, thereby relieving himself of the expense of feeding him!

Having destroyed the Crusader army, Saladin went on to capture Tiberias, Acre, Ascalon and, on 2 October, Jerusalem itself. Had not a small reinforcement reached Tyre by sea, enabling it to hold out, all of Outremer would have fallen to him. As it was, the Crusaders were able to hold on by the skin of their teeth while Pope Clement III proclaimed the Third Crusade to restore the situation.

Among those who responded to Clement's call were Richard Coeur de Lion, King of England, Philip Augustus, King of France, and Frederick Barbarossa, Emperor of Germany. Starting in 1189, the Germans marched overland across Europe and Asia Minor. The English and French set off the following year, travelling first by sea to Sicily. Philip Augustus

Right: Saracen light cavalry, especially mounted archers, were particularly dangerous to the Crusaders' marching columns. When counter-attacked they would simply disperse and return to torment their opponents once the immediate threat had passed.

then sailed direct to Acre, while Richard broke his journey to secure a base in Cyprus.

Since 1189 the situation at Acre had been complex. The Crusaders, commanded by Guy and Conrad de Montferrat, were besieging the Muslim garrison, but were in turn besieged by Saladin's army, although the presence of the Genoese fleet offshore enabled them to receive reinforcements and supplies. The arrival of Richard's and Philip's fresh troops proved decisive. Saladin's relief army was driven off, and on 12 July 1191 the siege was brought to a successful conclusion.

It says much for the power of Richard's personality that his leadership was accepted not only by the diverse national contingents, but also by the squabbling factions of Outremer itself. Philip Augustus, who disagreed with Richard on almost every point, went home in disgust. Richard not only possessed drive and energy but was also, unlike many commanders of the chivalric era, gifted with a natural understanding of staff work and logistics. He understood, for example, that there was a connection between dirt and disease, the scourge that decimated every army, and recruited a contingent of laundresses to wash the troops' clothing regularly.

Having knocked the disparate elements of his army into shape, Richard set off for Jerusalem, the first phase of his march being made in easy stages along the coast southwards towards Ascalon, the fleet keeping pace offshore. The order of march consisted of three parallel columns: the transport wagons escorted by infantry nearest the sea; the centre column led by the Templars, followed by the Angevins, Poitevins, English and Normans with the remainder of the Crusaders' mounted troops and the Hospitalers forming the rearguard; and the third column made up of infantry who covered the inland flank.

The reason for this defensive formation was that the Saracen horse archers were often unable to penetrate the knights' mail and made the horses their target instead, reckoning that a dismounted knight would quickly become vulnerable. The Crusaders were familiar with this tactic and, on the march, protected the horses with the infantry, who were therefore a valuable component of their armies. Obviously the infantry in turn required greater protection, so in addition to their shields they wore leather, felt or quilted jackets over their mail. These must have been unbearably hot but they were efficient; indeed, Muslim accounts speak of Crusader infantry continuing to trudge

59

along looking like hedgehogs because of the number of arrows protruding from their shields and jackets. Not that such engagements were anything like one-sided; a proportion of the infantry were always armed with crossbows, which outranged and were more accurate than the short bows of the Muslim light horsemen, whose saddles were regularly emptied, for all their speed and daring.

Saladin, having failed to relieve Acre, believed that he could destroy the Crusaders on the march, just as he had done at Hattin. He laid an ambush to the north of Arsuf, concealing his heavy cavalry among the low, rolling wooded hills that flanked the narrow coastal plain. During the morning of 7 September the Crusader army emerged from an area of dunes and, having forded a shallow stream, entered the plain. Saladin immediately loosed his light horsemen to harry it but kept his heavy cavalry concealed until the moment had come for the decisive attack.

Flights of arrows flew into the Crusader ranks, answered by volleys of bolts from the infantry's crossbows. Both sides sustained casualties, but gradually the Muslims closed in until the knights, galled by their fire, became restive. Richard, however, resolutely forbade them to counter-attack until they heard his trumpeters sound six blasts. This was a stern test for any troops, but it was necessary. Too often in the past Crusader knights had mounted charges only to see the enemy light horsemen disperse before them, then become isolated and have to cut their way out when the Saracens closed in behind. Such tactics were wasteful, tiring and had contributed to the disaster at Hattin. Richard intended to wait until Saladin deployed his main force and then launch a thunderbolt response with all his knights simultaneously.

Slowly the Crusader army was brought to a standstill by the galloping bowmen. Pressure on the Hospitalers and the infantry at the rear became intense as Saladin committed some of his own infantry and heavy cavalry against them. 'First came the trumpeters and drummers,' wrote a Crusader eye-witness named Ambroise, 'sounding their instruments and yelling so loudly that God himself would not have been heard. Then they moved away and wave after wave of Sudanese and Arab infantry raced forward, shooting their arrows and hurling their lances. They threw the first line of our infantry into disorder but made no impression on the men of iron behind them. Then the Turkish cavalry, their axes and scimitars flashing in the sunlight, charged the Knights Hospitaler, hoping to turn our left flank, and you could see nothing in the turmoil of dust, shrieking horses and shouting men.'

The attack was narrowly beaten off but the Hospitalers' Grand Master, worried that his men were at a disadvantage when fighting defensively, rode up to Richard and requested permission to counter-attack. Richard, who had already observed Saladin's main body debouching from the hills, replied that a few minutes' delay would be to everyone's advantage. Just then, the Hospitalers, followed by the rest of the knights, took matters into their own hands. The Arab chronicler Bohadin, riding beside Saladin, recounts how intervals suddenly appeared in the wall of Crusader infantry and the knights, brandishing their lances and shouting war cries, rode out to charge.

Ambroise continues: 'The Hospitalers charged in good order, and were followed by Count Henry of Champagne and his brave followers, and Count James of Avesnes and his followers. Count Robert of Dreux and the Bishop of Beauvais charged together. Also charged Count Robert of Leicester with all his men, and there were no cowards among them. Then all the army was charging – the Angevins, the Poitevins, the Bretons, the Manceaux, the Normans, English and all the other divisions. Oh, the brave knights! They attacked the Saracens with such vigour that each one found his man, planted his lance in his entrails and hurled him from the stirrups. When King Richard saw that the charge had begun without waiting for his command, he clapped his heels into his horse's flanks and launched himself at full speed against the enemy. And such was his prowess that September day before Arsuf that

Left: The Crusaders' successful counter-attack at Arsuf routed Saladin's army.

all around him I saw the bodies of Saracens with their bearded heads planted like cabbages in the field.'

Richard retained a tight grip on the battle. The Saracens on the Crusader left, packed too tightly to fight or flee, went down in heaps before the Hospitalers. The rest of the Saracen light cavalry, seeing the mass of knights bearing down on them at speed, lance points gleaming, simply bolted. Well aware of the dangers inherent in a disorganised pursuit, Richard had the Recall sounded and the knights, having worked off their frustration, responded.

The Muslim light horsemen, rallied by their emirs, could be seen reforming beside their heavy brethren. Satisfied with the order of his own line, Richard ordered his trumpeters to blow the Charge. Again the mailed line thun-dered across the plain. Now unstoppable, it smashed through light and heavy cavalry alike. This time Richard allowed the pursuit to continue for almost a mile, during which it also broke Saladin's reserve, before the Recall rang out. There was no point in squandering men in chasing even a badly beaten enemy into broken, wooded country, and the march to Ascalon was resumed.

At Arsuf each side deployed approximately 25,000 men. The Crusaders' loss was put at 700, the most conservative estimate of Saladin's being ten times that figure. Saladin, recognising an extremely dangerous opponent, never again sought to bring Richard to battle.

After spending the winter at Ascalon, the Crusaders advanced inland against Jerusalem, only to find that Saladin had retired before them, systematically destroying crops and grazing land over a wide area, as well as poisoning the wells. In such circumstances it was impossible to mount a siege. Richard withdrew to the coast, and concluded a treaty with Saladin which granted special rights and privileges to pilgrims visiting Jerusalem.

Arsuf had gone some way to avenging the disaster of Hattin, but despite this and the death of Saladin in 1193 the fortunes of the Crusader states continued to decline. Notwithstanding the mounting of further Crusades in their support and the negotiated repossession of Jerusalem from 1229 to 1244, they were now firmly on the strategic defensive and throughout the next century fought hard but unsuccessfully to retain their possessions. Acre, the last Christian stronghold in the Holy Land, fell after a long and bloody siege in 1291, the event signalling the end of the Crusading era in the Middle East.

LIEGNITZ (WAHLSTATT), 9 APRIL, AND RIVER SAJO (MOHI), 11 APRIL, 1241

In 1237 Ogatai Khan, son and successor of Genghis Khan, dispatched an army of fifteen divisions, about 150,000 men, to invade eastern Europe. By December 1240 his field commander, Subotai, had overrun all of Russia and was poised to advance into central Europe. With the usual Mongol thoroughness, his intelligence-gathering system provided him with a detailed briefing on the political, economic and social conditions in Europe, pointing out that Poland, Silesia, Hungary and Bohemia were all capable of raising armies of comparable size to his own and that he would probably have to fight two or more of them together. Of the more distant states, including the Holy Roman Empire, France and England, it was felt that mutual rivalries would prevent their intervention until the eastern European powers had been dealt with. Nevertheless speed was essential.

Subotai set Budapest, the capital of Hungary, as his principal objective. Leaving three divisions to maintain his lines of communication, he divided the rest into four corps, each three divisions strong. The task of the northern corps, commanded by Ogatai's grandson Kaidu, was to protect the right flank of the advance; the southern corps, under Ogatai's son Kadan, was to protect the left flank; the two centre corps, under Batu, another grandson of Genghis Khan's, and Subotai himself, were to fight their way independently through the Carpathian passes and rendezvous on the Hungarian plain within striking distance of Budapest. To deceive the Europeans as to the real objective, Kaidu's northern corps was to leave in February, somewhat ahead of the others.

Kaidu detached one of his divisions to cover his own right flank. Moving at the Mongols' usual breathtaking pace, this swung north into Lithuania and East Prussia, then west along the Baltic coast. Although his own strength had been reduced to some 20,000 men, Kaidu swept across Poland with fire and sword, routing the army of King Boleslaw V at Krakow on 3 March. Terrified refugees fled westward in droves, magnifying the size of the Mongol corps until its strength was put at 200,000 men. While in one way this suited Kaidu very well, in another it was counter-productive because Henry the Pious, Duke of Silesia, and Wenceslas, King of Bohemia, decided to fight the invaders together. Henry's army, which numbered approximately 40,000 men, contained his own troops, a contingent of Teutonic Knights under their Grand Master, and the remnant of Boleslaw's Polish army. Wenceslas raised 50,000 men and agreed to join Henry at Liegnitz.

As always, Kaidu's scouts brought him accurate information. Henry, they told him, had already reached Liegnitz, but Wenceslas was still two days' march short of the concentration area. Kaidu decided to attack the former at once. Of Henry's army, very few men capable of recording their experiences survived the subsequent battle, so that we are left with only a general impression of the course of events. What is certain is that the recently raised Silesian army lacked cohesion and organisation. The Mongols, on the other hand, though far fewer in numbers, were professionals, trained and disciplined to the highest levels, and their sub-units were well used to working together. We can imagine the frustration created by their galloping horse archers, the feigned retreats that enticed groups of knights to their death, the confusion created by the totally unexpected attacks of the Mongol heavy cavalry into the European flank and rear. It was all too much for Henry. He fled the field only to be cut down by the fleeter Asiatic horsemen. As his army broke, too, the final act in the tragedy ended with a courageous last stand by the Teutonic Knights and the nobles, from which none emerged alive. It would be many years before the Silesian aristocracy recovered from the effects of the battle; for example, the von Strachwitz family, which would later give generations of service to the Prussian and

German armies, lost no fewer than ten of its members at Liegnitz. Henry's head was displayed on a spear before the walls of Liegnitz as a warning to the defenders of what would happen to them if they did not surrender. Again terror was counter-productive; they decided to hold out and, as events transpired, their decision was correct.

Some terror-stricken fugitives from the battle reached Wenceslas, who declined to try conclusions with what he believed to be a much stronger Mongol army. Instead he turned away to the north-west, intent on joining the forces which German nobles, now thoroughly alarmed, were hastily assembling. Kaidu did not pursue, and the reason sometimes suggested for this is that he had himself sustained severe casualties at Liegnitz. Given the size of his corps, the victory cannot have been cheap, but the real reason was that he had completed the task he had been set, namely the strategic protection of Subotai's right, by defeating in turn the Poles and the Silesians and forcing the Bohemians to withdraw out of harm's way. Calling in the detached division from the Baltic, he turned south to rejoin the main Mongol army in Hungary.

On the central front, the corps of Batu and Subotai had broken through the Carpathian passes on 12 March and effected a junction beyond. The Hungarian king, Bela IV, assembled an army which is said to have numbered 100,000 – certainly it was large enough to impress the Mongols whose screening force fell back before it when it advanced from Budapest.

During the afternoon of 10 April, at Mohi (modern Miskolc) on the river Sajo, some 90 miles north-east of his capital, Bela achieved the rare distinction of surprising a Mongol detachment and capturing a bridge. He pushed a strong force across the river to secure the bridgehead and, as the rest of his army came up, formed a fortified camp with his wagons which were chained together. This, however, was to be his last taste of success for Subotai reacted with bewildering speed.

At dawn on 11 April the bridgehead force came under a fierce bombardment from catapults and ballistae hurling stones, bolts and pots of blazing naphtha, accompanied by 'thundrous noise and flashes of fire'. This curious passage is usually taken to indicate the presence of gunpowder in the Mongol arsenal, though not, of course, of guns. Gunpowder is believed to have originated in China and the Mongols would have been familiar with some of its properties if not its application as an artillery propellant. The probability is that their missiles were accompanied by large firecrackers, the explosion of which would have induced terror and confusion among those who had never experienced them before. Panic-stricken, the Hungarians bolted across the bridge with the Mongols hard on their heels.

Bela's army, woken by the tumult, swarmed out of camp and was soon engaged in a fierce battle. It must soon have become apparent that they were confronting a much smaller force, and at this stage Bela can have had few misgivings. In fact his attackers were Batu's corps, just half the Mongol army, and their task was simply to pin his troops down in a holding action. In the pre-dawn darkness Sabutai had led his own corps southward for several miles then forded the river and was now trotting north towards the battle. Achieving complete surprise, he fell on the Hungarians' right flank and rear with two of his three divisions, putting them to headlong flight in the direction of their camp.

By 7 a.m., about an hour after fighting had begun, the shaken Hungarians were effectively penned inside their perimeter of wagons. Soon afterwards the Mongols brought their missile engines across the bridge and opened a bombardment of the camp. Amid burning tents and wagons, inexplicable explosions and flights of arrows from galloping horsemen, the defenders held out for several hours but with waning hopes. Then it was noticed that the enemy encirclement had left a large gap uncovered on the western side of the defences, although it occurred to no one that the Mongols always had excellent reasons for everything they did or did not do. A few men managed to make their escape but as Batu and Subotai intensified their attacks on the perimeter the trickle became a stream and ultimately a flood of fugitives who cast away their arms and armour in their desperation to escape. It was at this point that the Hungarians discovered to their horror that they had fallen into a deadly trap. Subotai's third division, it will be recalled, had taken no part in the battle; instead, he had designated it as his pursuit force and it was lying concealed some distance to the west of the camp. It now fell on the terrified men, hounding them through burning villages and into swamps, and cutting them down in a savage pursuit that continued throughout the rest of the day. Bela managed to escape, but his army was annihilated, estimates of the Hungarian dead varying between 40,000 and 70,000.

The Mongols were now masters of all eastern Europe between the Baltic and the Danube. During the summer Subotai consolidated his control over Hungary, made good his losses and planned the next year's campaign, which would have seen further advances into Germany and across Austria into Italy. By December his patrols had begun to range down the Danube towards Vienna. Then, as mentioned earlier, there came the news of Ogatai Khan's death. As the Mongols withdrew into Asia, never to venture so far west again, Europe heaved a collective sigh of relief.

Thousands had died, huge areas of land had been laid waste, and all apparently to no purpose. Just as the Mongols contributed little save their military system to the world's cultural heritage, so too their incursion into Europe left no tangible result save the memory of one of history's most brilliantly executed campaigns. In four months Subotai had defeated European armies totalling five times his own strength at a cost which he evidently did not regard as excessive. His grasp of strategy was faultless, his corps commanders were masters of battles fought at hitherto undreamed of operative levels, and the speed with which events unfolded left his opponents stupefied. Yet this legacy was also to vanish

along with the Mongols and their way of war. Five and a half centuries would pass before European armies began conducting operations at the corps level, and nearly seven before these achieved a pace that Subotai would have found acceptable.

CRÉCY, 26 AUGUST 1346

For its size, the English army of the 14th and early 15th centuries was the most efficient in Europe. There were four reasons for this. First, successive kings had modified the military aspects of the feudal system by paying their vassals to provide standing contingents of troops who, in time of war, served in the field or garrisoned the royal fortresses. This not only avoided the need to call out the militia, but also had the effect of turning the troops so raised into disciplined, professional soldiers whose loyalty lay directly to the king rather than their own feudal landlords.

Secondly, the longbow, believed to be of Welsh origin, had proved its worth during the hard-fought wars against the Scots. It had, in fact, become so much a national weapon that regular practice at the butts was mandatory for all males of military age. Indeed, many surnames in use today, including Bowyer, Stringer, Arrowsmith and Fletcher, are descended directly from the ancient trades associated with the use of the weapon.

Thirdly, the growing sense of nationality was itself strengthened by the English way of fighting. In battle, the nobility and knights, comparatively few in number, would fight on foot alongside the archers, only mounting their horses to carry out a pursuit when the issue was decided. Thus the shared dangers generated a fellow feeling between them which came to be reflected in civil life. In sharp contrast, the more numerous aristocracy of England's continental neighbours despised their infantry, who were either hastily raised levies or mercenaries.

Fourthly, while the English might choose to fight set-piece defensive battles on foot, they also employed mobility to effect in France, mounting fast, deep-penetration raids which left the French cavalry standing. These raids, known as *chevauchées* because the entire force, knights, men-at-arms and archers, was mounted, caused widespread devastation and reflected the apparent inability of the French king to protect his subjects.

The first major land battle of the Hundred Years War may have been induced by a naval mutiny. In July 1346 King Edward III of England landed near Cherbourg with an army consisting of 5,500 archers, 1,000 Welsh infantry, 2,500 knights and men-at-arms, and a small number of very primitive guns. What his intention may have been remains unclear, but when the crews of his ships chose to return home in defiance of their orders, his only alternative was to march north and join his Flemish allies who had laid siege to Béthune. This was easier said than done, because it involved crossing the Seine and the Somme. Anticipating such a move, the French king, Philip IV, had most of the bridges destroyed and Edward was forced to march up the Seine as far as Poissy before he found a repairable bridge. This took him uncomfortably close to Paris where Philip was known to be assembling a large army. With the French now closing in behind him, Edward marched hard for the Somme, which he was only able to cross by a tidal ford at Blanchetaque, ten miles below Abbeville. The crossing was made during a rising tide, enabling the French to snap up several supply wagons, but not those carrying the English army's arrow supply. The same tide enabled Edward to put a day's march between himself and his pursuers, who crossed the river at Abbeville where the bridge had been denied to the English by the town's fortifications rather than destroyed.

Edward used the time to find a position where he could turn and give battle and chose a gentle slope overlooking the route which the French would have to take from Abbeville. The right flank rested on the village of Crécy-en-Ponthieu and was protected by the little river Maye; the left flank extended to the village of Wadicourt, covered by trees and some ditches dug by the infantry. The king divided his army into three 'battles' or divisions of equal strength. The right division was nominally commanded by the Prince of Wales, later known as the Black Prince, under the guidance of the veteran Earl of Warwick. The left division was commanded by the Earls of Arundel and Northampton, and the reserve division, some way to the rear, was under the king's personal command. Edward stationed himself between the forward and reserve divisions, at a windmill from which the entire battlefield could be overseen.

The centre of each division consisted of dismounted knights and men-at-arms, flanked by archers echeloned forward at an angle from which they could shoot obliquely across the battlefield. In the centre the archers of the right and left divisions met in a 'V' pointed at the enemy. Behind each division was a small mounted reserve whose task was to deliver local counter-attacks if the French broke through. The position was consolidated by the digging of a large number of small holes on the forward slope intended to trip and bring down the enemy's horses.

During the late afternoon of 26 August the impressively large French army began to arrive from the direction of Abbeville. It numbered about 6,000 professional and mercenary infantry, including a large contingent of Genoese crossbowmen, considered to be the best in the business, 10,000 knights and men-at-arms, and about 14,000 feudal militia.

When Philip sighted the English his army was strung out along many miles of road and he decided to wait until all arms were concentrated and give battle on the morrow. A better alternative, and one which would instinctively have been chosen by any commander other than one with a chivalric background, would have been to leave his leading elements as a holding force in front of the English and pass the rest of the army through Estrées to an old Roman road that by-passed Wadicourt to the east. The effect would have been to render the English position untenable and force Edward to decamp hurriedly during the night. This was

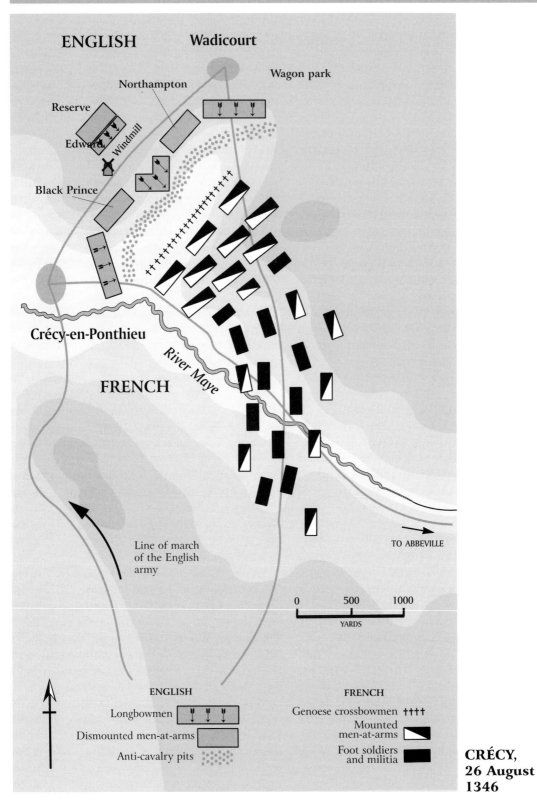

ENGLISH

Wadicourt

Wagon park

Northampton

Reserve

Edward

Windmill

Black Prince

Crécy-en-Ponthieu

River Maye

FRENCH

Line of march
of the English
army

TO ABBEVILLE

0   500   1000

YARDS

ENGLISH

Longbowmen

Dismounted men-at-arms

Anti-cavalry pits

FRENCH

Genoese crossbowmen ††††

Mounted
men-at-arms

Foot soldiers
and militia

**CRÉCY,
26 August
1346**

not even considered; even the idea that the army should be allowed to close up was dismissed out of hand by Philip's brother, the count d'Alençon, commanding the leading division of knights. Seeing the small dismounted force to their front, nothing less would satisfy the impatient French nobles than the chance to get at the English and perform heroic deeds. Philip agreed to attack, provided the Genoese went in first to soften up the enemy line. The Genoese, however, were at pains to point out that they had just completed a long march in rain and needed to rest; more importantly, their bowstrings were wet and must be allowed to dry out if good results were to be achieved. Alençon passed some scornful comments on their courage and, stung by these, the Genoese deployed.

They advanced across the valley performing some sort of routine that involved whoops and waving of arms, clearly intended to bolster their own morale or intimidate the enemy. In contrast, the English line remained ominously silent and immobile. The Genoese halted 150 yards from the line, gave three shouts and loosed a volley. Because the rain had reduced the tension of their strings most of their bolts pattered harmlessly into the ground, yards short of the target. The longbowmen, on the other hand, suffered no such disadvantage, it being their custom to unstring their bows in wet weather, keep the string dry under their helmets, and restring only when going into action.

Now, while the Genoese were cranking up their crossbows, the setting sun appeared, shining straight into their eyes. Suddenly they could hear sharp words of command cracking out:

'Make ready!' Each bowman took a pace forward with his left foot, fitting a long cloth-yard shaft to his string.

'Mark your target!' The bows came up and every archer's face became a study of intense concentration.

'Shoot!' The air became black with whispering death. Thousands of arrows slashed into the Genoese ranks, skewering bodies,

arms and legs. Men were going down in heaps, but still the arrows flew like murderous sleet. Bravely some of the Genoese tried to close the range, releasing a second ragged volley. Flashes, bangs and clouds of white smoke marked the discharge of Edward's cannon; here and there a ball ploughed a bloody furrow through the ranks, but it was the blizzard of clothyard shafts that the Genoese found unbearable. As they retired in disorder Alençon, coming up behind with the first of the French mounted divisions, suspected treachery and shouted, 'Slay me those rascals! They do but hinder and trouble us without reason!' The Genoese, frustrated, bitter and angry, responded by shooting several of their employers out of their saddles, much to English amusement.

Spurring forward through the wretched crossbowmen, Alençon led his division on to the killing-ground. Knights and horses went down, hindering the rest, uncontrollable pain-maddened horses adding to the confusion, but still the French pressed forward. Significantly they ignored the archers and made for the dismounted knights and men-at-arms as being the only foemen worthy of their steel. Some reached the Prince of Wales's division where so furious a fight raged that Edward was asked for reinforcements. The king declined with the comment, 'Let the boy win his spurs,' and indeed within minutes the division's mounted detachment had restored the situation with a local counter-attack.

As each French mounted division reached the battlefield it was senselessly committed to yet another charge across the same ground. Fighting had begun at about 4 p.m., and most authorities agree that during the next five hours fifteen charges surged across the killing-ground, each made more difficult than the last by the growing heaps of dead horses and riders. Among those who charged was John, the blind king of Bohemia, riding between two of his knights with his bridle buckled to theirs; none of the three survived. Between charges the more agile Welsh infantry sallied forth to bring down and kill lumbering unhorsed knights and dispatch the

Right: The Black Prince leading an English counter-attack at Crécy. *Philip Haythorn-thwaite Collection.*

enemy's wounded with a dagger thrust between the joints of their armour; in what had become a fight to the death the chivalric concept of ransom no longer applied. Edward was principally concerned in maintaining his archers' supply of arrows, fresh bundles being brought forward continuously from the wagon and horse lines to the rear. At length Philip, who had been wounded, was restrained from leading his remaining 60 knights in one last charge and led them from the field to seek shelter for the night in the castle of Labroye. His substantial infantry levies had played no part in the battle and, having witnessed the discomfiture of their masters, had already set off for their homes.

English casualties totalled two knights and about 100 others killed. Next morning Edward sent his heralds and clerks to examine and enumerate the grisly tangle littering the slopes. Among the slain the heralds were able to recognise from their arms the bodies of the king of Bohemia, the counts Alençon and Blois, all the army's principal officers and more than 1,500 members of the French nobility and orders of chivalry. Altogether, in what is still called the Val-des-Clercs, the bodies of 10,000 Frenchmen and Genoese were counted.

The body of King John of Bohemia was treated with the respect due to the courageous old man and sent to his son for burial. There is a story to the effect that Edward presented three ostrich feather plumes from the dead king's helmet to the Prince of Wales in recognition of his part in the battle and that the latter, as an expression of his own admiration for John, also adopted the motto *Ich Dien* (I Serve) from the device on his shield. The story can neither be proved nor disproved. What is certain is that in the illustrated manuscripts of Froissart's *Chronicles* the Black Prince is always depicted with three feathers in his helmet, and that the feathers and motto have remained part of the Prince of Wales's insignia ever since.

Crécy signalled the end of the mounted knight's domination of the battlefield. It was the knight who had sustained the feudal system unchallenged save by his own kind, and

Right: A formation of English longbowmen could produce a dense and sustained hail of arrows capable of stopping any attack in its tracks. For added defence against cavalry their position was usually fronted with sharpened stakes. This bowman is wearing a quilted surcoat over a mail shirt and has protected his left forearm against the whip of the bowstring by wrapping several layers of cloth around it. To obtain maximum power, the bow was drawn as far as the ear.

now the flower of French chivalry had been laid low by a much smaller infantry army composed mainly of commoners. Such were the social implications that the battle's outcome sent shockwaves across Europe. True, the Swiss pikemen had inflicted similar defeats, but it could be argued that Switzerland was a special case; Crécy, on the other hand, had conformed to the normal rules of engagement and been fought on good cavalry terrain. When the French aristocracy set about analysing the causes of their defeat, they refused to accept that the English archers had been largely responsible, assisted in no small measure by their own stupid élitism. The socially acceptable conclusion was that the English knights' decision to fight on foot had been the critical factor. This failed to recognise that the knights had simply been providing a firm base not only for the archers' firepower but also for their own counter-attack force. If the French nobles' analysis strayed far from reality, their plans for the future beggared belief. Should a similar situation arise, their knights would also fight on foot, wearing heavier armour, allegedly proof against arrows.

POITIERS, 19 SEPTEMBER 1356

A similar situation did arise, ten years later. In September 1356 the Black Prince, as he had now become, was returning from a *chevauchée* to his base at Bordeaux. With him he had 2,000 archers and 4,000 men-at-arms, many of whom had been recruited in the English dominion of Aquitaine. Heavily laden with booty, the raiding force was making such slow progress that an avenging army, commanded by King John II of France, was closing in rapidly on its rear.

On 18 September the Black Prince turned to give battle at a point some four miles south of

Poitiers. The position he chose was similar to that at Crécy, lying along a plateau fronted by a hedge and approached from the enemy side by two sunken lanes; the left flank was anchored on the marshy valley of the Moisson stream and the right was reinforced with a wagon laager. As at Crécy, the army was deployed with two divisions forward and one in reserve with the archers on the flanks of each division.

John's army consisted of 3,000 cross-bowmen and some 17,500 knights and men-at-arms. Once again, no attempt was made by the French to manoeuvre the English out of their position. Instead John approved a plan in which the army would mount a frontal attack in a column of four divisions. The first division, led by Marshals Clermont and Audrehem, would be spearheaded by two mounted detachments each of 250 knights who, covered by the fire of the crossbowmen, would charge up the sunken lanes and break into the English line while the rest of the division advanced on foot. The second, third and fourth divisions, commanded respectively by the Dauphin, a survivor of Crécy, John's brother the Duke of Orléans, and King John himself, would then attack in succession. Apart from the two mounted detachments in the van, all the knights and men-at-arms would fight on foot, protected by a combination of mail and plate armour in which they no doubt felt secure.

Following negotiations which neither side expected to succeed, the French attacked on the morning of 19 September. From the outset things began to go wrong for them. In its advance the vanguard division masked the fire of the crossbowmen. A few of the mounted men and their infantry support succeeded in reaching the hedge line, but the attack was shot to tatters as a large party of archers deployed on its flank in the marsh. During a series of sharp local fights Clermont and Gautier de Brienne, the Constable of France, were killed and Audrehem was captured. The assault ebbed away.

Next to come up was the Dauphin's division. It took severe casualties from the arrow storm

as it trudged up the slope, heads bowed, but the French came bravely on until they were at hand strokes with the two forward divisions of the English line. The fighting was so fierce that the Prince repeatedly sent forward reinforcements from his reserve division to prevent them breaking through until he was left with just 400 men. It was during this period that the English sustained their heaviest casualties, but their opponents, galled continuously by flanking fire from the archers, suffered the greater loss. Finally the French fell back, defeated but by no means routed.

Orléans' division, which should have been next into action, had been completely unnerved by the repulse of the vanguard and the Dauphin's men. Instead of advancing up the now body-strewn slope, it turned and fled in a blind panic. John's division, some distance behind, halted to form a rallying point for those survivors of the Dauphin's troops who had not been swept away.

It was now about 10 a.m. and a lull ensued. John had become so dubious of victory that he ordered three of his sons, the Dauphin and the Dukes of Anjou and Berry, off the field, although he allowed his youngest son, Philip, to remain. On the other hand, almost half his army remained, and as this still outnumbered the English by a wide margin he decided to risk all on one last attack. The division began marching towards the enemy ridge, a mile distant.

The archers used the lull to retrieve as many arrows as possible, but in their leaders' opinion they had only sufficient ammunition in hand for a few minutes' serious fighting. Some of the weary knights and men-at-arms were also seriously alarmed by the sight of the French mass coming on yet again in splendid array beneath its banners. There was a moment of keen apprehension, calmed personally by the Prince. Aware of the effect of the unexpected, he detailed one of his Gascon officers, Captal de Buch, to take 60 men-at-arms and 100 archers, all mounted, and to circle round a hillock, known today as La Masse des Anglais, on the right, ensuring that they were not seen by the

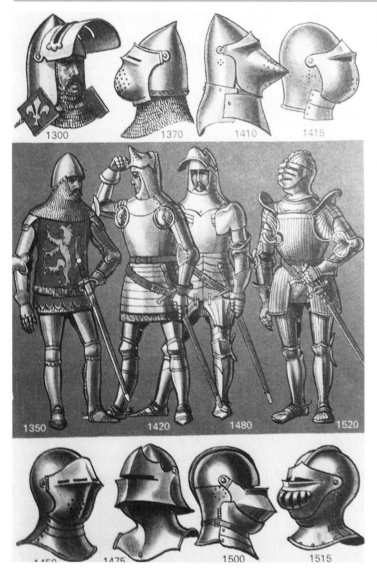

Left: The development of plate armour and visored helmets from the 14th to the 16th centuries.

down the slope. The French withstood the impact very well, despite the fact that, unexpectedly, they were fighting on foot while the English were mounted. For a few minutes the two sides were locked in deadly personal combat. Then Captal's force smashed into the French rear. Most of John's men, believing themselves to be surrounded, began to seek safety in flight. Some few remained to fight beside their king but gradually exhaustion took its toll and most, including John and his son, surrendered.

The English casualties at Poitiers have been estimated as being in excess of 1,000 killed and wounded; French losses included 2,500 killed, a larger number wounded and more than 2,000 taken prisoner. Many French noblemen and knights were quickly overtaken and captured as they tried to escape to Poitiers on foot. Archers, grinning from ear to ear, brought in four, five or even six prisoners apiece, according to Froissart. The object, of course, was ransom money of which there was plenty to go round. The Prince, as good a businessman as he was a field commander, personally bought all the prisoners at a price below that of their ransom value, paroling the less important to present themselves at Bordeaux before Christmas with the full amount. The others, including King John, who was sent to England, enjoyed a free and easy captivity until their ransoms could be raised.

French. Once they had reached a position from which they could attack the enemy's flank and rear, they were to display the banner of St George.

As soon as Captal's detachment had left the Prince had the rest of the horses brought forward and ordered everyone to mount. Just as the French started up the slope and had begun to labour inside their heavy armour, Captal's signal was observed. The timing could not have been better. The Prince gave the order to charge and the entire English line, knights, men-at-arms and archers alike, thundered

France, left leaderless, lapsed into anarchy for a while and was only saved from collapse by

71

her able Constable, Bertrand du Guesclin, who declined to meet the English in the field but instead embarked on an effective policy of picking off isolated detachments and garrisons. Du Guesclin, however, died in 1380 and during the decades that followed much of what he had taught was forgotten.

AGINCOURT, 25 OCTOBER 1415

In October 1415, having captured the town of Harfleur, a small English army under King Henry V was retreating northwards to Calais. The overall situation was very similar to that which had faced Edward III prior to Crécy, in that it involved a difficult crossing of the Somme under pressure from a much larger French army under Charles d'Albret, Constable of France. On this occasion, however, once north of the river it was the French who marched the faster, so that on 24 October Henry found d'Albret's entire army deployed across the Calais road near the village of Azincourt. The French position was a strong one, with its flanks resting on the forests of Azincourt, to the west, and Tramcourt, to the east. Henry took up a similar position about a mile to the south.

The French army consisted of 3,000 crossbowmen, 7,000 mounted and 15,000 dismounted knights and men-at-arms, a total of 25,000, and a few guns. It was supremely confident that it could destroy the puny English force to its front, which consisted only of 4,950 archers and 750 men-at-arms, a total of 5,700. Furthermore, it was the intention of d'Albret, who was aware that the English were weary, half-starved and soaked to the skin after several days' rain, that they should attack him, with predictable consequences. To achieve this, all he had to do was remain where he was and hunger would do the rest.

Henry, however, was an inspiring leader. At dawn the following day he rode along his line whipping up the men's fighting spirit with a speech that cannot have been very different from that attributed to him by William Shakespeare:

'For he to-day that sheds his blood with me
Shall be my brother ...
And gentlemen in England, now a-bed,
Shall think themselves accurs'd they were not
here,
And hold their manhoods cheap while any
speaks
That fought with us upon Saint Crispin's day.'

Whatever was said, the English were not intimidated by the serried ranks of their distant opponents. At 11 a.m. Henry ordered the entire line to advance. He halted it at a point where the gap between the two forests narrowed to 940 yards, still a quarter of a mile from the French. As usual the dismounted men-at-arms were deployed in blocks with the archers on their flanks. Those archers in the centre of the line formed two wedges and began hammering specially prepared stakes into the ground; those on the outer flanks began infiltrating forward through the trees for 100 yards and more. The front of the position, consisting of heavy ploughed land, had now become a killing-ground.

D'Albret's army occupied a frontage of 1,200 yards. On each flank was a detachment of 600 mounted knights. The centre consisted of three divisions, one behind the other. The first two consisted of dismounted knights and men-at-arms, the third remained mounted. The crossbowmen and guns seem to have been squeezed out of the first line and found themselves positioned between the first and second divisions where, their fire being masked, they could do little or no good.

The early advance of the English army must have given d'Albret grounds for satisfaction, followed by disappointment when it came to a standstill and began consolidating its position. Shortly after, however, the archers in the trees began sniping at the mounted detachments on his flanks, dropping some horses and rendering others uncontrollable in their pain. Preposterous as it may seem, the hot-headed nobility of France had learned absolutely nothing from previous experience and soon their clamour to attack could not be gainsaid.

AGINCOURT, 25 October 1415

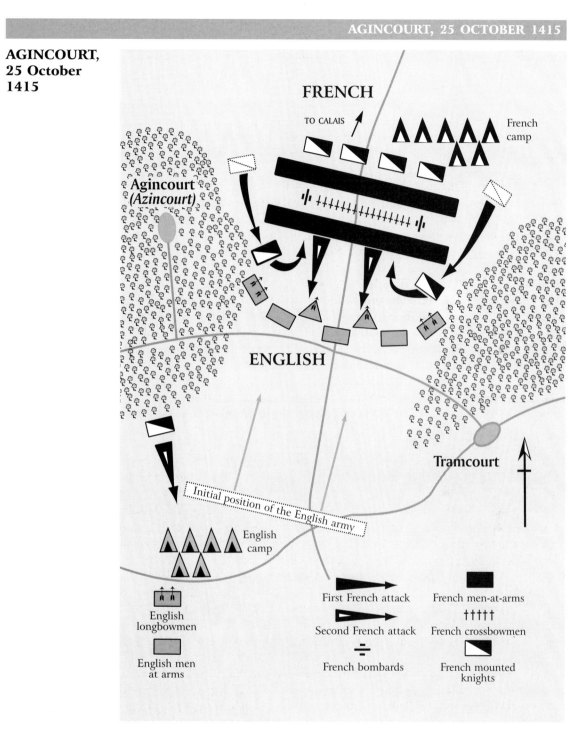

FRENCH

TO CALAIS

French camp

Agincourt (Azincourt)

ENGLISH

Tramcourt

Initial position of the English army

English camp

English longbowmen

English men at arms

First French attack

Second French attack

French bombards

French men-at-arms

French crossbowmen

French mounted knights

Led by the mounted detachments, the first division lumbered forward, followed at a distance by the second division. The mounted knights rode straight into an arrow storm that cut into their ranks from three sides. At short range helmets and visors offered no protection against the deadly marksmen, many of the riders being shot through the head. Those few that reached the English line were quickly dispatched. The survivors turned tail, the uncontrollable kicking and plunging of their wounded mounts causing chaos in the ranks of the advancing first division. In fact the first division already had enough problems of its own. Its armour, now consisting mainly of plate, was even heavier than at Poitiers, and its clattering progress through the clinging mud of the ploughland was both difficult and exhausting. As if this were not bad enough, it was trying to funnel its 1,200-yard frontage into the 940-yard gap between the two forests. Consequently the pressure on those in the centre was such that they were unable to use their weapons. However, they could not be accused of lacking courage for, disregarding their numerous casualties, they came steadily on to close with the English men-at-arms. Without pause the archers, knowing that their comrades were too few to handle the situation, swarmed out of the woods and from behind their stakes to batter the exhausted, encumbered French with swords, axes and clubs. If a

knight went down, he died either from a dagger thrust or was suffocated when more of his fellows fell on top of him. In what amounted to little more than butchery the arrival of the French second division simply added to the dreadful heaps of slain that were growing across the battlefield. The killing stopped only when there were no more Frenchmen within reach.

Two-thirds of d'Albret's army had been destroyed in about thirty minutes. Henry sent

Below left: Henry V encouraging his men at Agincourt.

Below: Special arrows were produced to penetrate plate armour. After a while, the tangle of dead and wounded men and horses in itself brought the attack to a standstill. The density of the arrow storm has not been exaggerated.

Right: After an attack had been defeated the English longbowmen, men-at-arms and nobility would counter-attack together. The enemy's nobility and knights were worth taking alive for the ransoms they would bring; lesser folk, as shown on the left, received much shorter shrift. *Philip Haythornthwaite Collection*

a herald across to the French third division, which still outnumbered his own troops, telling them that unless they left the field at once they would receive no quarter. They rode slowly off, leaving the English to pull living noblemen out of the ghastly heaps for the ransoms they would bring. At this point a report was received that the French had attacked the English camp, a mile to the rear. With the enemy's third division still in sight, Henry reluctantly gave the order to kill the prisoners, but countermanded this when it was learned that the attackers were a crowd of plundering peasants who were easily driven off.

English casualties at Agincourt included the Duke of York, smothered in his armour, 400

Right: Henry V gives thanks for his victory at Agincourt. *Philip Haythornthwaite Collection*

killed and twice that number wounded. The French lost about 8,000 killed, including d'Albret, three dukes, 90 nobles and 1,560 knights, and 2,000 captured.

Although they had won other notable victories, and would continue to do so, it is Crécy, Poitiers and Agincourt that spring to mind first when one thinks of the terrible bowmen of England who, for several generations, struck terror into the hearts of all who opposed them. In the end, it was the growing use of the new battlefield medium, gunpowder, that finally drove them and the last of their chivalric opponents into history. But that is another story.

Commentary 5 – The Gunpowder Revolution

The introduction of gunpowder was to have a greater impact upon every aspect of land and sea warfare than anything that had gone before. It is generally accepted that gunpowder was first produced in China and, as we have seen, it may well have been used by the Mongols at the Battle of the River Sajo in 1241, though not as a propellant. At about the same time an English friar and alchemist, Roger Bacon, is known to have been carrying out experiments with controlled explosions. No one knows who invented the gun, for although the credit is sometimes given to a German monk, the

mysterious Berthold Schwarz, a manuscript dated 1325 shows a primitive cannon firing at the defences of La Rochelle, pre-dating the period in which he is supposed to have worked. Edward III's guns at Crécy provide the first documented evidence of their use in the field but, again, there were probably earlier instances.

The Church did not like guns any more than it had liked crossbows, warning those involved in their development that they were meddling in the Black Arts. The first guns were indeed a menace to everyone around them. They would burst without warning and there were frightful accidents with improperly handled powder. Early in the 15th century someone produced a more stable version of gunpowder by mixing the ingredients in a wet state, then allowing the result to dry before passing it through a sieve. The end product, known as corned powder, was more powerful, travelled well and resisted damp. Its introduction was a slow process,

Right: Examples of early cannon showing the method of shrinking hoops around the longtitudinal iron bars forming the barrel. Top left, a siege piece fitted with a primitive elevating device; the gunner's evident reservation about the weapon's safety is understandable! Top right, an early mortar. Centre, Mons Meg, now at Edinburgh Castle, is believed to have been built between 1461 and 1483; it has a 20-inch calibre and, charged with 105lb of powder, could fire a 330lb stone ball to a range of 2,876 yards. Other monsters of the time could fire 800lb projectiles at the rate of seven rounds per day. Bottom, an early breech-loader or petraria. The breech, pre-loaded with charge and wadding, was inserted into the barrel and secured against the carriage by a wooden wedge.

partly because it was very expensive and partly because the older guns could not withstand the increased pressures it generated.

The earliest guns owed much to the cooper's art, hence the name barrel. They were constructed by arranging red-hot iron bars around a mandrel and hammering to weld them together. White-hot iron hoops were then shrunk onto the tube so formed to give it strength. Because of the difficulty involved in sealing the breech end of the barrel, most guns were breech-loaders, the breech consisting of a removable powder chamber closed at one end, secured by hammering a wedge between it and the rear of the gun cradle. The major disadvantage of the system was that much of the propellant's power was lost in the inevitable back-blast of gas and flame. For this reason, large-calibre siege guns were muzzle-loaders, the chamber being fitted into the rear of the barrel by a screw or lug mechanism. During the second quarter of the 15th century muzzle-loaders were being cast in one piece using bronze. From this it was but a short step to casting trunnions with the barrel, enabling the gun to be secured to its carriage by cap-squares. This not only improved the general mobility of artillery, but also enabled the gunners to elevate or depress the barrel to achieve variation in range. The next step forward was provided by the blast furnace, which produced higher temperatures enabling less expensive yet more robust guns to be cast in iron. Breech loading was abandoned and the gun assumed the form it was to retain for the next 400 years. By 1600 the number of guns in service was rising dramatically. At first they were classified by size and given names such as saker, cannon and culverin, but by the end of the 17th century they were beginning to be classified by their weight of shot. The short-barrelled mortar, capable of high-angle fire, was introduced during this period and was joined in the 18th century by another high-angle weapon, the howitzer. The difference between the two was that the mortar was fixed and variations in range were obtained by adjusting the charge, whereas the howitzer's charge was fixed and its elevation could be altered. Mortars and

Above: Matchlock musketeers firing from rest and ramming the charge. Both men are wearing bandoliers supporting measured ready-use charges. Below, an early pistol.

howitzers both fired spherical shells filled with powder, fused to burst within or above enemy lines. They were difficult to manufacture and consequently very expensive, the early examples consisting of two half-spheres welded together with a small aperture left for the fuse tube.

At first, rather than putting themselves to the prodigious expense of establishing their own artillery park, kings would hire guns, gunners, horse teams and ammunition wagons from private contractors as and when they were needed, much as a modern construction company hires in its plant. However, when the

Left: Various pole arms including linstocks, to which a length of slow-match could be fitted and which also provided artillerymen with a means of personal defence.
Below: pikemen prepare to receive a cavalry attack. Normally pikemen were flanked by bodies of musketeers who, in these circumstances, would retire behind or under the pikes.

The first guns offered little improvement on the trebuchet, but they improved in size and range to the point where, unless it were situated on an inaccessible crag or surrounded by a wide body of water, no medieval fortress could hope to survive a siege conducted with artillery support. The castle, once the pivot of the feudal system, had had its day. To emphasise the point, in 1453 the artillery of Sultan Mahommet II, consisting of 56 small guns and fourteen heavy cannon, one of which fired a stone shot weighing 1,500 pounds, experienced no difficulty in creating breaches in the once formidable walls of Constantinople, so bringing to an end the ancient Byzantine empire. Conversely, an army using medieval siege methods against a fortress equipped with cannon would have its wooden engines knocked to pieces very quickly.

feudal system was replaced by strong central administrations towards the end of the 15th century, national rather than private funds became available. The possession of artillery therefore began to reflect the status of monarchs and it was thus entirely logical that responsibility for it should rest with professional corps of artillerymen, administered by their own master gunners.

Guns had their most immediate effect on the opposed sciences of fortification and siegecraft. The fortress builders therefore found it necessary to sink most of their defences into the ground, leaving only the fighting parapets and gun embrasures visible. Henry VIII built a series of artillery forts along the south coast of England, specifically designed for all-round defence by guns, the basic format being a circular keep surrounded by interconnected semi-circular bastions encircled by a wide ditch. The problem with circular bastions was that, while less vulnerable to cannon fire, they left areas of dead ground which could be exploited by an enemy. On the other hand, a fortress consisting of mutually supporting wedge-shaped bastions connected by curtain walls, covered every possible approach. In plan such fortresses resembled a star. The outer edge of their permanent defences consisted of a sloped glacis, counterscarp, ditch, scarp and ramparts. Gateways and vulnerable sections of the curtain were further protected by ravelins and other outworks, each with its own glacis, counterscarp, ditch and scarp. The parapets were covered with a deep layer of earth intended to cushion the impact of cannon-balls, and as this grassed over very quickly an attacker saw very few details of the defences until he came to close quarters.

A direct assault on such a fortress without adequate preparation was tantamount to suicide, only a scientific approach being likely to guarantee success. The besiegers' guns would be concentrated against what was considered to be the most vulnerable sector of the defences, then progressively pushed closer to the walls by means of a trench system known as parallels. Once the enemy's fire had been silenced and a breach battered in the walls, terms would be offered to the garrison, who could legitimately claim to have resisted to the limit of their abilities. If terms were accepted the garrison might be permitted to march out with the Honours of War, flags flying and drums beating; if they were not, the breach would be stormed with heavy loss of life and few of the defenders were likely to be spared.

The undoubted master of this type of warfare was Sebastien le Prestre de Vauban who in 1687 became the French Army's Director of Engineering. Under Vauban fortification and siegecraft took the form of a mathematical science in which, taking all the factors into account, it became possible to predict accurately the time it would take to penetrate any given set of defences. The science, however, was complex and its practice led to the creation of permanent bodies of military engineers whose tasks involved not simply the design and destruction of defence works but also the construction of roads and bridges capable of supporting the transportation of artillery. This, in turn, led to more sophisticated surveying techniques and more accurate maps.

It was inevitable that smaller versions of the gun would be produced as personal weapons, the result being that infantry tactics went into the melting-pot. The arquebus, developed from a light anti-personnel gun mounted on the walls of fortifications, was first fired from an inclined rest with the butt tucked under the right arm; later and somewhat smaller models were held against the chest and gripped with both hands. From the arquebus the musket evolved, a more convenient weapon which could be fired from the shoulder, although at first a rest was still needed to support its 25-pound weight. Normally, musketeers fought in ranks ten deep, the front rank firing and then filing to the rear, where they reloaded as they made their way forward by rotation, a system which enabled a continuous if narrow fire front to be maintained. They were, however, vulnerable to attack and therefore co-operated closely with units of pikemen. The system adopted by the Spanish, and copied by most European powers, was to form integrated units known as *tercios* in which the arquebusiers or musketeers operated in front or on the flanks of the pikemen, supporting their advance or retiring under the pikes if attacked. Pikes therefore became longer until the pike element of a *tercio* resembled the Macedonian phalanx. In due course musketeers discarded armour altogether, although pikemen continued to wear helmet, breast- and back-plates and, for a while, tassets to protect the thigh.

The infantry element of late medieval armies had consisted of archers, pikemen and halberdiers, the halberd being a spear fitted with an axe blade and sometimes a hook for dragging an opponent out of his ranks. Save for ceremonial purposes, the halberdier soon disappeared because his weapon was too short for the changing conditions. The disappearance of the archer is more difficult to explain because he could get off many more shots to the minute, and with far greater accuracy, than the musketeer. There were two principal reasons for this. First, the longbow represented the ultimate development of the archer's craft and could not be improved further, while the musket was in its infancy and could be improved in many ways,

notably with regard to firing mechanisms and range. Secondly, the arrow had become less effective against the latest plate armour, whereas the kinetic energy stored in a musketball, which was much larger and heavier than a modern small-arms round, enabled the projectile to penetrate plate with ease and fell a man or horse by its impact alone.

The pikeman soldiered on until the middle of the 17th century. Tradition has it that during the siege of Bayonne in 1640 there were insufficient pikemen present to protect the musketeers and the latter resolved their difficulty by plugging long knives into the muzzles of their weapons, so creating the bayonet. By 1660 the plug bayonet was in widespread use, but its obvious disadvantage was that the musket could not be fired while it was fixed. Vauban pioneered the socket bayonet, which first appeared in 1678, and its use quickly became general. The pikeman had therefore become redundant and with him went the last vestige of infantry armour, which would not reappear until the 20th century.

A 17th century Wheel-lock Musket

A 17th century Flint-lock Pistol

Left: English Civil Wars. A cheerful Royalist surrenders to a pair of gloomy Roundheads. Despite the bandolier of powder charges, which he would use in his pistols, spurs indicate that the Royalist is a cavalryman. The Roundheads, too, are wearing spurs. The man in the centre is evidently a dragoon, a new type of soldier who rode to battle and fought on foot armed with a short musket known as a dragon, while the heavy cavalryman on the right is one of Cromwell's formidable Ironsides. Below are examples of mid-17th century firearms.

As one type of infantry soldier left the battlefield, another entered it. This was the grenadier, whose function was to hurl small grenades, which then consisted of small spheres filled with powder fused by a length of slow match. Because wide-brimmed hats interfered with the swing of the arm, grenadiers wore a distinctive cap which evolved into a mitre. As the work was undertaken by the strongest and tallest men, grenadiers came to be regarded as an élite and each battalion had a grenadier company.

The demise of the knight, already apparent, became a reality with the introduction of gunpowder. Armour continued to be worn by heavy cavalry, known as cuirassiers, but was gradually reduced to helmet, breast- and back-plates, being last used operationally during the early stages of the First World War. The essence of the cavalryman's problem was that he was unable to perform his traditional role of shock action against infantry, being simultaneously vulnerable to the fire of musketeers and kept beyond striking distance by the serried ranks of pikemen. By the end of the 16th century, therefore, the lance had been discarded, save in eastern Europe. The development of the pistol, however, seemed to present a solution. Armed with two or three pistols apiece, cavalrymen would attack at a walk in ranks ten-deep. The front rank would fire at close range, then wheel to the rear to re-load and move forward in rotation, like the musketeers. Once gaps began to appear in the enemy ranks, the troopers would attempt to close with the sword. This movement, known as the *caracole*, became something of a ritual and, once the pistol had been accepted as the principal cavalry weapon, was also employed against enemy cavalry. The result was a sort of heresy in which the concept of shock action disappeared altogether, except in pursuit of an already beaten enemy. The cavalry's contribution to the battles of the 16th and early 17th centuries was thus only decisive on rare occasions.

It was Gustavus Adolphus, King of Sweden, who applied a common-sense solution to the problem. Each of his cavalry regiments was supported by a 200-strong company of musketeers and several light guns which created gaps in the enemy ranks. The cavalry, expressly forbidden to perform the *caracole*, attacked at a fast trot in four ranks. The two leading ranks, having fired their pistols, closed immediately with the sword, followed by the rest, who reserved their fire for the mêlée. Naturally such radical tactics were devastating in their immediate effect and restored the cavalry's ability to perform shock action.

At about the same time a new kind of mounted soldier made his appearance. This was the dragoon, a mounted infantryman who rode to the battle, usually on a second-rate horse, but fought on foot, armed with a short musket known as a *dragon*, bayonet and sword. Properly used, the dragoon possessed a tactical flexibility which could be employed to great advantage. A cousin of the dragoon was the carabineer, who was armed with a short musket known as a carbine, pistols and sword.

In general, therefore, while cavalry apparently lost its purpose during the first 150 years of the gunpowder revolution, it recovered to the extent that once again it was able to perform many of its traditional roles, though in the future it was rarely to achieve its former dominance and now, of necessity, was forced to co-operate with other arms to achieve success. For this reason the ratio of cavalry to other troops continued to fall.

Faced with a completely new technology, commanders often found difficulty in applying it to the best advantage. At first even the deployment of the battle line was a slow and complex process, requiring as it did the disposition of pikemen and musketeers for the mutual benefit of both, emplacing the artillery in a favourable position and deciding how the cavalry should be used. Consequently battles tended to be slow motion, almost ritual, affairs. They generally began with an artillery duel lasting an hour or two before the contending armies came to grips. The musketeers would fire in ranks by rotation, the pikemen would close with their opposite numbers and the cavalry would perform the *caracole* until one side or the other broke and the engagement ended in a general pursuit. Even so, these battles were fiercely contested, for the period included the bitter wars of religion in which large areas of northern and western Europe removed themselves from papal influence. Sometimes quarter was neither asked nor given and atrocities were frequent. France was ravaged by wars between the Huguenot and Catholic factions, the Spanish sought to suppress Protestantism in the Low Countries and even the English Civil War, fought to decide whether the supreme authority rested with king or parliament, had strong religious undertones. Most terrible of these religious conflicts was the Thirty Years War which left huge tracts of Germany devastated for the next generation.

Armies tended to be small, and although they might be nominally French, Spanish, Dutch or Imperialist, their ranks were filled out with contingents hired from other countries and bands of professional mercenaries. Some mercenaries, notably the Swiss, earned their pay honestly, but others had fewer scruples; the German *Landsknecht* would remain loyal to their employers only so long as they could deliver pay and plunder, while the Italian *Condottiere* often had no intention of fighting at all and would change sides to avoid it. Since living off the land was only a short-term proposition, commanders setting out on campaign usually employed civilian contractors to keep their men fed. During the winter months, when even the best roads degenerated into mud wallows impassable to supply wagons, armies dispersed into billets until the spring.

At sea, battles continued to be fought as an extension of land warfare for some time after the introduction of guns. In 1571 a fleet of Christian galleys under Don John of Austria decisively defeated a similar Turkish fleet off Lepanto. Both sides mounted guns and, for the first time, ships were sunk by gunfire, but ramming, disabling and boarding remained the principal tactics.

The Mediterranean galley, however, with much of its narrow beam occupied by oarsmen, could mount very few guns, whereas the carrack, designed to cope with the heavier Atlantic weather, had a beam that equated to half its length and could therefore provide a wider, more stable gun platform. The invention of the hinged port in about the beginning of the 16th century enabled guns to be mounted broadside in the hull. Thereafter warship design followed two diverging schools of thought. The first took advantage of the existing forward and after castles of fighting carracks to produce a floating fortress which used her guns as a preparation for boarding. The result was the galleon, which was adopted mainly by the Spanish. The second, favoured by such redoubtable Elizabethan seamen as Sir John Hawkins and Sir Francis Drake, saw the warship as a weapon complete in itself, capable of disabling and sinking opponents with its own gunfire. It produced slimmer vessels with trim lines and a better sail plan than the galleons, their superior sailing qualities enabling them to fight at ranges of their own choosing. Whenever the two concepts were opposed, as they were during the defeat of the Spanish Armada, it was the second which emerged the victor. In these changed conditions it was the skill of the seaman which rightly counted for most, while that of the soldier became of secondary importance.

Designers of the new warships faced formidable problems. The tremendous weight of the guns, coupled with soaring top hamper, made it essential to preserve a low centre of gravity, especially in heavy weather or strong beam winds. Failure to allow for these factors resulted in the loss of the *Mary Rose* in 1545 and the Swedish *Vasa* in 1629. The storage of tons of dangerous gunpowder within highly combustible wooden hulls also presented serious difficulties. Then there was the question of how the guns were to be fought in the confined space available. The answer was to mount them on small four-wheeled trucks which rolled inboard on recoil, giving the crew sufficient room to use their sponges and rammers; once re-loaded, the guns were run out again by means of tackles.

The flimsy galley stood little chance against one of the new warships, unless the latter were becalmed. Nevertheless galleys had their enthusiasts who produced an intermediate design known as the galleass, which combined oars with sail and mounted broadside guns. The concept, while ingenious, was inherently flawed because, on the one hand, if heavy guns were mounted deep in the hull the oars had to shipped before they could open fire, and, on the other, if lighter guns were mounted above the oars the weight of metal thrown was far less effective. Nevertheless galleys continued to serve in the Mediterranean and, later, in the Baltic, until the 19th century.

Following the discovery of the New World, the Pope divided it between Spain and Portugal. The English, who were keen to take advantage of the new trading opportunities and had severed their formal links with the papacy, ignored the decree and by 1600 the nature of modern sea power had become clearly apparent. It could be used to prey on an enemy's mercantile interests, as England did upon Spain's, to blockade an enemy in his ports, to mount heavy and destructive raids, and to intercept neutral vessels seeking to trade with the enemy. The three Anglo–Dutch wars between 1652 and 1673 also stemmed from trade rivalry and were fought entirely at sea, producing the first major fleet actions since the Armada. They set the pattern of naval warfare for the next 150 years. Before an engagement commenced, both sides sought to put themselves up-wind of the enemy, as possession of the weather gauge enabled them to manoeuvre as they wished. Whenever possible the English sought to break the enemy's battle line, separating his ships into small groups which could be overwhelmed in turn.

War, both on land and at sea, had now become a matter for professionals at every level, with officers and men needing to be trained in tactics and the most efficient use of weapons.

CERIGNOLA, 26 APRIL, AND THE GARIGLIANO, 29 DECEMBER, 1503

In 1501 the armies of King Louis XII of France and King Ferdinand II of Aragon overran the Kingdom of the Two Sicilies, known today as Sicily and Naples. The two divided the country between them but soon quarrelled and came to blows. During the subsequent war the Spanish army was commanded by Hernandez Gonzalo de Córdoba, who was to earn such fame that he became known to his own and subsequent generations as El Gran Capitán.

Córdoba was one of those rare commanders who was able to adapt very quickly to new technology. Sent to southern Italy to defend the Spanish cause, he recognised that the key to success on the modern battlefield lay with his arquebusiers. He greatly increased their numbers, equipping them with the latest weapons, ball pouches, lengths of slow match, a bandolier from which hung small tubes containing measured charges of powder, and a sword for close protection, although their armour was restricted to a helmet. The arquebusiers also received the immediate backing of pikemen, who would be reinforced from a central reserve when the moment came to counter-attack. In place of heavy cavalry used for shock action, Córdoba preferred to use light cavalry known as genitors who performed such roles as screening, scouting and harassing the enemy.

At first the campaign did not go well for him. His small army, about 4,000 strong, was opposed by a much larger force under the Duke of Nemours and was forced to withdraw to the seaport of Barletta in Apulia, leaving most of Naples in French hands. There it was subjected to a gentlemanly sort of blockade throughout the winter of 1502/3, during which both sides competed in tournaments.

In the spring Córdoba received 2,000 reinforcements, enabling him to offer a reasonable challenge to Nemours, who had approximately 10,000 men under command. On 26 April the Spaniards marched out of Barletta, deploying on a hillside behind a long ditch reinforced

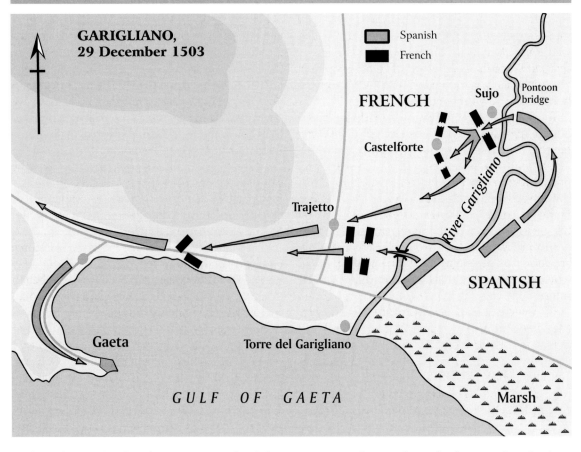

GARIGLIANO, 29 December 1503

Spanish
French

FRENCH

Sujo
Pontoon bridge

Castelforte

River Garigliano

Trajetto

SPANISH

Gaeta

Torre del Garigliano

GULF OF GAETA

Marsh

with a thin palisade of vine props. Córdoba, having stationed his arquebusiers in this protected fire position, was confident that they could break up any attack the French might launch, just as the English bowmen had in former years. Close behind the arquebusiers were the ranked pikemen, ready to intervene if necessary.

The battle began with a ponderous, slow-motion duel between the opposing artillery. This ended very quickly when, probably because of a handling accident, all too common at the time, the powder supply for the Spanish guns exploded in a deafening roar. Encouraged, the French gunners began knocking holes in the palisade, causing casualties among the pikemen beyond but barely touching the arquebusiers crouched in the ditch.

Córdoba wanted the French to attack and sent out his genitors to provoke them. Very probably, this would have been their intention anyway. Once they had completed their deployment, they came on confidently, heavy cavalry echeloned with arquebusiers, cross-bowmen and mercenary Swiss pikemen. Not until they were within thirty yards of the palisade did Córdoba's arquebusiers open a spluttering but sustained fire. The front ranks went down, as did those who pushed forward to take their place. A few reached the edge of the ditch to die by bullet or pike thrust, and then the attack faded away. Re-formed, the French came on again and again but, unable to close, were repulsed every time. Nemours himself was shot dead and in the resultant confusion Córdoba launched his pikemen in a counter-attack which swept the enemy off the field with the genitors in hot pursuit.

The battle of Cerignola was small in scale and its outcome was not decisive to the outcome of the war. Conversely it marks a major turning-point in the history of warfare in that it was the first engagement won by infantrymen armed with personal gunpowder weapons. Because of it enthusiasts have dubbed Córdoba the Father of Trench Warfare although, as we shall see, he was equally at home in a war of movement.

By the middle of May he had recovered Naples and in June he laid siege to Gaeta. The French, however, were pouring in reinforcements and in October, once again seriously outnumbered, he decided to withdraw behind the lower reaches of the river Garigliano. The French, now 23,000 strong, followed hard on his heels and actually managed to put in a pontoon bridge, but were driven back by artillery and arquebus fire. Thereafter, amid worsening weather, they seemed to lose interest.

The winter was unusually wet and cold. Morale slumped among the French, whose officers took themselves off to drier quarters in the nearest towns; even their veteran commander, Gonzago, Marquis of Mantua, a man of some reputation, having developed a convenient chill, handed over his responsibilities to another Italian officer, the Marquis of Saluzzo, who was neither liked nor trusted by his French subordinates. Set such examples, the troops were reluctant to perform duties along the muddy river bank. In contrast, Córdoba lived in a hut just behind his entrenchments, and paid daily visits to those manning the front line. He also maintained his army's morale by mounting a series of successful small-scale raids across the river. As these were never pressed too far, the impression formed by Saluzzo was that the Spaniards were unlikely to launch a general assault during the winter months. For his part Córdoba, having noted the general slackness in the enemy's lines and having received reinforcements which brought his strength up to 15,000 men, decided to do just that. Far behind the front he had a portable pontoon bridge built under the supervision of his chief engineer, Pedro Navarro. The bridge was light enough to be broken down into mule-sized loads and could be rapidly assembled on a suitable launching site. Unobtrusive reconnaissance discovered such a site opposite Sujo, some seven miles upstream from the opposing lines, where the river was narrower and the banks firmer.

Christmas was marked by a two-day truce during which the two armies fraternised. On 27 December the Spaniards returned to duty, but the French clearly indicated that they intended prolonging their festivities until the New Year. That night Córdoba began moving his pontoon train and assault force towards the crossing point, leaving a covering force in the trenches with instructions that it, too, should cross the river if the assault succeeded.

Throughout 28 December the assault force lay concealed, but when the short winter day drew to its close the engineers began converging on the bridge site. Córdoba had timed his attack to start at dawn next day and, just as the first grey streaks began to appear in the eastern sky, the last pontoons were slid into place, secured, and decked. The Spanish advance guard, consisting of genitors, arquebusiers and pikemen, rushed across and captured the French garrison of Sujo before they knew what was happening. The arquebusiers and pikemen of the main body, under Córdoba's personal command, followed at once. Before Saluzzo could mount a coherent defence the Spaniards were sweeping down the right bank of the river, driving the French from the villages of Castelforte and Trajetto. As the sound of fighting drew closer, the commander of the covering force in the trench lines launched his own attack across the southern bridge, completing the enemy's rout. The rearguard of Saluzzo's shattered army attempted to hold the Formia defile, where the road ran between the sea and steep hills, but was dislodged after an hour's fighting. Shedding prisoners, guns and baggage, the French sought refuge in Gaeta but surrendered on 1 January and were evacuated by sea.

The battle of the Garigliano forced Louis to abandon his claim to Naples, of which Córdoba became the Spanish viceroy. This was far from being the end of the French wars in Italy, but Córdoba, recalled in 1507, did not take part in them. He died in 1515, having held no further command. The lessons of Cerignola, however, were emphasised on a larger scale at the Battle of Bicocca in 1522, when the Spanish commander, Prosper Colonna, deployed arquebusiers four deep behind a sunken lane, backed by units of pikemen. On this occasion the Swiss pikemen in French service launched a premature attack as a result of which some 3,000 of them were shot dead or speared within the space of thirty minutes. Córdoba's system of fighting evolved into the *tercio* in which musketeers and pikemen provided mutual support for one another on a permanent basis. The system, backed by a strong exchequer supported in turn by bullion shipments from Spanish colonies in the New World, made Spain the pre-eminent military power on land in western Europe for the next century and more.

THE SPANISH ARMADA, 29 JULY TO 9 AUGUST 1588

Two factors rendered war between England and Spain inevitable. First, the papal decree granting Spain a virtual monopoly in the New World was fiercely resented in England and resulted in attacks on Spanish shipping and settlements there, notably by Sir Francis Drake. Secondly, although Queen Elizabeth was careful to avoid outright war, her support for the rebellious Protestants in the Spanish Netherlands was equally resented in Spain. By 1586, however, the patience of Philip II of Spain was exhausted and, acting upon the recommendation of Admiral the Marquis de Santa Cruz, he began planning a naval expedition against England. This would involve Santa Cruz's fleet sailing north from Spain and embarking the Duke of Parma's veteran army from The Netherlands for the short passage across the North Sea. Once landed, it was anticipated that Parma's professionals would not encounter much serious resistance from the English levies that would oppose them

Details of the extensive Spanish preparations could not be kept secret and were soon known in England. During the spring of 1587 a spoiling attack was mounted by Drake. On 19 April he sailed into Cadiz harbour with 23 ships and sank or disabled 37 Spanish vessels of various types, subsequently referring to the attack as 'singeing the King of Spain's beard'. Nothing if not thorough, he also raided the harbour at Lisbon, disrupted shipping along Spain's Atlantic coast and captured a treasure galleon from the New World. Such was the terror his name inspired that Spanish mothers would use it as a threat to unruly children.

The Cadiz raid, while useful in that it gained time for England to put her defences into order, merely hardened Philip's resolve. Furthermore, Elizabeth's execution of Mary, Queen of Scots, a staunch Catholic, on 8 February that year, gave what had become known as The Enterprise of England the status of a crusade with papal blessing, attracting an influx of volunteers from all over Philip's Catholic domains. The capable Santa Cruz diligently set about repairing the damage, but died on 30 January 1588. In his place Philip appointed Don Alonso Pérez de Gusmán, Duke of Medina Sidonia, a man of courage, charm and administrative ability, but with little interest or experience in naval and military affairs. The Duke did not want the job, but Philip insisted that he take it on the grounds that his diplomatic skill would form a vital element in ensuring co-operation between the various leaders of the Enterprise. His responsibilities would end when the expedition reached The Netherlands and Parma assumed overall command; in the meantime, the experienced Admiral Diego Flores de Valdez would serve under Medina Sidonia as his second in command.

Elizabeth, too, had been busy. Lord Howard of Effingham was appointed Lord Admiral of the English fleet with Drake as his vice-admiral. In March 1588 she declined to sanction another spoiling attack against the Spanish harbours, but set about raising a 60,000-strong army at Tilbury, had invasion beacons set across the country and arrested the more suspect members of prominent Catholic families.

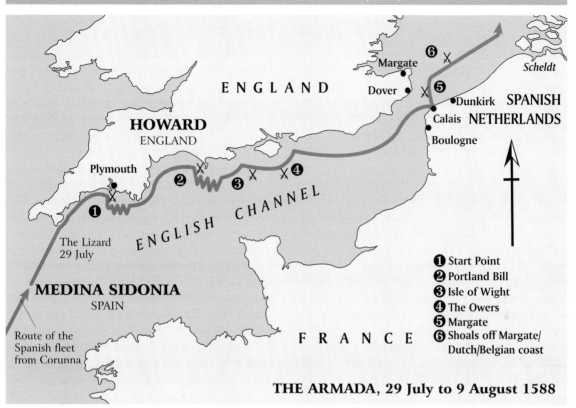

THE ARMADA, 29 July to 9 August 1588

❶ Start Point
❷ Portland Bill
❸ Isle of Wight
❹ The Owers
❺ Margate
❻ Shoals off Margate/
   Dutch/Belgian coast

The Spanish fleet, or Armada as it has generally become known, began leaving the Tagus on 9 May. It consisted of 20 galleons, 44 large armed merchantmen, four galleasses, four galleys, 23 transports and a large number of pinnaces. These mounted a total of 2,431 guns of which more than half were light anti-personnel weapons of little use save at the shortest range. Of the all-important larger guns, 489 were in the cannon class, firing a heavy ball from short to medium range, and 635 were long-range culverins, firing balls of from 4 to 17 pounds in weight. In addition to the 8,050 seamen and 2,088 oarsmen, 18,973 soldiers and 1,545 volunteers were embarked, giving a total of 30,656 men

Howard's English fleet presented a totally opposed operational concept. At Plymouth and further up-Channel he had his own and Drake's squadrons, plus a squadron fitted out by the City of London; off the Flemish coast was a squadron commanded by Lord Henry Seymour. Altogether, 197 ships were available to meet the Armada, of which only 34 were purpose-built warships belonging to the Queen's Navy Royal, as it was then called. A similar number were converted merchantmen of comparable size, but the balance was made up of small supply vessels and volunteers mounting a few guns which would willingly put out of harbour to have a crack at the Dons. As mentioned earlier, the English ships, having been designed as a weapon system complete in themselves, were trimmer and handier than the Spanish, but the nature of their armament also tells its own story. The English gunmakers of the time were among the best in Europe and of the 1,972 guns shipped, only 5 per cent were of the cannon type, the rest being long-range culverins, including no less than 1,377 4- and 5-pounders. Likewise, the crewing of the English ships with 14,385 seamen but only 1,540 soldiers reflected confidence in the long-range gunnery battle.

No doubt there were some sailing with the Armada who, encouraged by blaring trumpets, rolling drums and unfurled banners, were confident of an easy victory, but those professionals who had already fought the English at sea had serious reservations. When the papal representative at Lisbon privately asked one of the Armada's senior officers, possibly Juan de Recalde, whether he expected it to defeat the English fleet in the Channel, he received a reply heavy with sarcasm.

'Of course. It is well known that we fight in God's cause. So when we meet the English, God will surely arrange matters so that we can grapple and board them, either by sending some strange freak of weather or, more probably, by simply depriving the English of their wits. If we can come to close quarters, Spanish valour and Spanish steel, and the great masses of soldiers we have on board, will make our victory certain. But unless God helps us by a miracle the English, who have faster and handier ships than ours, and many more long-range guns, and who know their advantage just as well as we do, will never close with us at all, but stand aloof and knock us to pieces with their culverins, without our being able to do them any serious hurt. So, we are sailing against England in the confident hope of a miracle!'

From the beginning Nature dealt unkindly with the Enterprise of England. Adverse winds prevented the great mass of shipping from clearing the Tagus until 30 May, then pushed it steadily south. Two weeks later the Armada had begun to move northwards but some of its ships had sustained gale damage which required repairs and all were running short of water and provisions. These shortages stemmed directly from Drake's raid the previous year, during which enormous quantities of barrel staves had been burned. The loss had not been made good and in consequence the Armada lacked sufficient storage barrels for a long voyage. On 19 June, therefore, it was compelled to put in at Corunna and make up its deficiencies. Informed of the diversion, Howard and Drake set off to attack Medina Sidonia in his home waters but were in turn forced to return to Plymouth by contrary winds and a shortage of provisions.

The Armada did not leave Corunna until 21 July. Because Medina Sidonia's speed was restricted to that of his slowest ship, his fleet's passage north-by-east across the Bay of Biscay took more than a week, and the four galleys, unable to cope with the Atlantic swell, were forced to return to harbour.

During the afternoon of 29 July the *Golden Hind*, commanded by Captain Thomas Fleming, arrived in Plymouth harbour. She had been on watch in the area of the Lizard and had sighted part of the Armada turning east-north-east into the Channel. The story has it that Fleming found Howard and Drake playing bowls on Plymouth Hoe. On hearing the news some of their officers were for immediate action, but Drake is said to have calmly remarked, 'We have time to finish the game and beat the Spaniards, too.' This has the ring of truth about it, for to meet the Armada head-on would simply be playing into the enemy's hands, whereas the intention of Howard and Drake was to harry the lumbering Spanish vessels from the rear and break up their formation; in the circumstances, therefore, the appropriate course was to allow the Spaniards to sail by. There was, too, another practical consideration – an ebb tide was required to get all the English fleet out of harbour at once, and that was not due until the evening. Once out, the fleet anchored in the lee of Rame Head and waited.

At this point it is necessary to comment on the spirit with which the subsequent battle was fought. For the English this was no mere squabble between monarchs, but a war to the death. Everyone knew of the brutal treatment handed out to captured English seamen, of the persecution of Protestants and Jews in Spain's European territories, of the forcible conversion of Indians in the New World, and of the tortures inflicted by the Inquisition before its victims were finally burned at the stake. The short reign of Elizabeth's half-sister, known as Bloody Mary, still fresh in popular memory, had provided a taste of what life might be like under a restored Catholic rule, and now Mary's former husband, Philip II of Spain, had sworn to restore Catholicism in England. The mood of the country was very similar to that which existed nearly four centuries later, following the Dunkirk evacuation, with Philip, the Catholic Church and the Inquisition being regarded much as would be Adolf Hitler, the Nazi Party and the Gestapo.

On 30 July the Armada was sighted, an immense array of sails moving very slowly eastwards like an army at sea, with a vanguard, main body and right and left wings, the whole deployed in a vast defensive crescent several miles offshore. Closer inspection showed the *urcas* (store-ships) and pinnaces safely tucked in among the larger ships, while the flash of oars revealed that the galleasses were operating with the vanguard. To lay eyes it must have seemed invincible.

Although Medina Sidonia's primary objective was to rendezvous with Parma, he was hugging the English rather than the French coast because he intended to make a diversionary landing on the Isle of Wight. During the night Howard put to sea, a westerly wind having given him the weather gauge. At about 9 a.m. on 31 July he led his squadron roughly

in line ahead against the Armada's northern wing while Drake, accompanied by John Hawkins, Martin Frobisher and others, attacked the southern or seaward wing. English and Spanish ships had, of course, fought individual duels before, but this was to be the first fleet action of its kind in history. Obviously, no tactical manual existed and therefore commanders had everything to learn about formation, control, signalling and effective ranges.

All things are relative, and although to modern eyes, or indeed those of Nelson's era, the English attacks might seem to have been painfully slow in developing, the Spanish captains, locked within their own clumsy array with little room for manoeuvre, must have found Howard's and Drake's ships falling on them with the speed and ferocity of ravening wolves. Very quickly the Spanish gunners, watching their cannon-shots splash into the sea

Below: The Spanish Armada proceeds up-Channel in a huge crescent, harried from the rear by the English fleet, which retains possession of the wind. In the left foreground a Spanish galleon, probably the *Rosario*, has been cut off and is on the point of surrendering. In the right foreground is one of the Spanish galleasses. *Philip Haythornthwaite Collection*

short of the target, found their work impeded by the press of useless soldiers aboard. Much of the English fire was absorbed by the thick sides of the galleons, but shots which penetrated the thinner stern timbers raked their way through the crowded space between decks, striking down all in their path. Some English captains ordered their gunners to fire on the upward roll into the enemy's rigging, but special munitions for this task had not yet been fully developed and little serious damage was done. The principal result of these ranging attacks was to cause serious alarm aboard the rearmost Spanish vessels, some of which put on more sail, seeking to escape into the mass of shipping ahead. In an attempt to protect the rear several galleons of the van, including Medina Sidonia's *San Martin*, beat upwind round the entire Armada but failed to bring the English to close quarters.

At 1 o'clock there was a lull in the fighting which probably led Medina Sidonia to think that he had temporarily disposed of the threat, but at about 4 o'clock the galleon *San Salvador* was all but blown apart by a terrific explosion, much to the delight of the English who believed this to be a belated result of their own gunfire. In fact, it was an act of sabotage. The ship's master gunner, who was either a German or a Fleming, had been given a physical thrashing by the ship's captain because of his allegedly poor performance and, in revenge, he had set a port-fire to burn in a powder barrel. The explosion blew out most of the sterncastle and stern, killed 200 men and started a serious fire. As the *San Salvador* was carrying the Spanish Paymaster-General and the Armada's pay chest, Medina Sidonia at once went to her assistance with several more galleons. He managed to put out the fire and take off the money, but abandoned the now useless hulk during the night. Howard and Drake promptly took advantage of the confusion to renew their attacks, leaving Recalde's squadron flagship *San Juan* half-crippled with a tottering foremast and shot-up rigging. Even worse, when another galleon, *Nuestra Señora del Rosario*, the flagship of the Andalusian squadron, tried to help, she

was involved in a heavy collision with a third Spanish vessel in the hurly-burly, emerging minus her bowsprit and with her fallen foremast entangled with the mainmast. In such a condition she was so unmanageable that Medina Sidonia was forced to abandon her too.

The day's fighting had left the Spaniards shaken, but the English were disappointed that they had not been able to break up their close formation. During the night Drake was given the task of shadowing the Armada closely, the rest of the English fleet using his stern lantern as a marker. Spotting sails far to seaward, he extinguished his lantern and gave chase in the belief that some of the Spanish ships were trying for the weather gauge. In the event, the strangers proved to be neutral German merchantmen, but first light found him close by the drifting *Rosario*, which quickly surrendered. Both she and the gutted *San Salvador* were sent into English ports where they were stripped of their remaining guns, powder and ammunition. Meanwhile Howard, having followed what he believed to be Drake's stern lantern, suddenly found himself within shot of the Armada and narrowly avoided capture. Understandably he was less than pleased by his vice-admiral's unexpected diversion but accepted the reasons for it.

On 1 August light winds inhibited the chances for action and both fleets more or less floated eastwards along the Devon and Dorset coast. During the fighting on the 2nd, however, the English put their knowledge of local tides and winds to good use. The day began with a north-easterly offshore breeze which, for the first time, gave the Spaniards the weather gauge. Frobisher, in the *Triumph*, followed by several more ships, strove to recover it by slipping between the Armada and Portland Bill. His progress up-wind must have fuelled Spanish suspicions that the English were indeed in league with the devil, but he was simply riding the inshore tidal currents. Howard and the rest of the fleet, unable to follow through the narrowing gap, turned to seaward in the hope of recovering the wind by rounding the slow moving Armada, a manoeuvre that was fraught with risk and would take many hours to complete. Meanwhile it appeared that Frobisher and his ships were penned between the Spaniards and the coast with scant sea-room in which to manoeuvre. Medina Sidonia, believing he had a chance to destroy part of the English fleet, sent Don Hugo de Moncada with the four galleasses against them, followed by several of the galleons. Frobisher was apparently in a tight spot. The *Triumph*, nevertheless, though older and slower than some of the English ships, was still handy enough to stay out of trouble and was the most heavily armed vessel on either side, mounting 44 guns which included seven cannon and 31 culverins. In

theory the galleasses should have closed the gap easily, but Frobisher directed his gunners to fire at their rowing decks. The combination of casualties and splintered sweeps rendered the galleasses so unmanageable that the oars were withdrawn and sails hoisted. In this mode Moncada's ships were even slower than the galleons, but Frobisher was not yet out of danger.

Old Channel hands knew that an early morning offshore wind often backed during the day, and so it did on this occasion. By noon the wind was veering to the south-east, then south, and finally settled in the south-west. Immediately Howard and Drake launched a joint attack from seaward, forcing Medina Sidonia to abandon his attempt to trap Frobisher and concentrate his galleons for defence. The action was fought at closer quarters than before and ammunition expenditure on both sides was heavy. The *San Martin* was heavily engaged, losing no fewer than 50 killed and, presumably, twice that number wounded.

The day's fighting produced no tangible result for either side, although Medina Sidonia could at least claim that, without losing any more ships, he had moved a little closer to his objective. Howard, alarmed by the prodigal rate of ammunition consumption, sent pinnaces scurrying to the shore for fresh supplies. During the next few days sufficient was brought out to him for the fleet to remain in action, but only because he had carried out a drastic re-organisation. Hitherto captains had been taking their ships into action under whichever commander they favoured, with no

Left: Sir Francis Drake receiving the surrender of Don Pedro de Valdez of the *Rosario*. In the foregound is a breech-loading petraria.

central control. Now Howard divided the fleet into four squadrons, that under Frobisher being closest to the coast, his own and Hawkins' in the centre and Drake's to seaward. Captains would henceforth remain with their squadron commanders and thus a degree of control was established, one immediate effect being that ammunition expenditure was dramatically reduced.

In this formation the fleet followed the Armada eastwards throughout 3 August, the winds again being too light for action. By evening the Isle of Wight was coming up to port, but Medina Sidonia avoided the Needles Passage, then considered too dangerous for shipping, and decided to enter the Solent from the east before landing troops on the island. At dawn the next day a light offshore breeze was blowing, giving the Spaniards the advantage once more. Hawkins, in the *Victory*, spotted the transport *Santa Ana*, escorted by the Portuguese galleon *San Luis*, straggling astern of the enemy. He closed in to snap them up, whereupon Medina Sidonia dispatched three of the galleasses to their assistance, supported by another galleon. Howard, leading his squadron in the fleet flagship, *Ark Royal*, also closed in and a partial action developed. This ended with the Spaniards rescuing the stragglers, but in the process their over-worked hybrids were badly knocked about and *Santa Ana* was so damaged that, unable to maintain station, she drifted off southwards and eventually piled herself up on the French coast near Le Havre.

Elsewhere, the battle bore a remarkable resemblance to the fight off Portland. Once again Frobisher's *Triumph* swept between the Spaniards and the shore, but this time she was alone. Her size (she displaced 1,100 tons) and flagship status suggested to the Spaniards that she was Howard's ship and, the light breeze having veered to the south-south-west, they excitedly clapped on all sail in the hope of grappling and boarding her. Frobisher, suddenly becalmed, dropped eleven boats which struggled to tow her out of danger. Then the breeze reached him, freshening as it came. Gathering

way, *Triumph* forged through her boats, leaving her pursuers standing. It had been too close run a thing for comfort, but it had also provided a startling display of the superiority of English ship design which further depressed the Spaniards.

This was the moment when all of Medina Sidonia's attention should having been directed into getting his unwieldy fleet into the Solent, rather than indulging in the more prestigious pastime of chasing fellow admirals. It was also the moment that the squadrons of Hawkins and Drake mounted the most ferocious attack yet on the Armada's seaward wing. The defence crumpled at once and soon the mass of ships was being bundled north towards the treacherous Ower Banks. In the nick of time Medina Sidonia spotted the danger and ordered them to turn east while the galleons covered them. The Solent now lay astern and with it any chance he might have had of effecting a landing on the Isle of Wight. His only alternative now was to continue up-Channel to his rendezvous with Parma.

On 6 August he dropped anchor in Calais Roads, only to be told by the sympathetic but neutral French governor that the anchorage was dangerous. Some of his ships had sustained serious casualties and morale among all the crews was uniformly low. It was all very well for the optimists to point out that the Armada was virtually intact, having lost only three ships as a direct result of enemy action. The fact was that it no longer possessed a fighting capacity, for although there was plenty of gunpowder left from the additional supplies he had been carrying for the army, almost all his cannon and culverin shot had been expended.

The reason Medina Sidonia had chosen to anchor off Calais was that he was still awaiting word from Parma, to whom he had dispatched pinnaces daily, reporting his progress on the passage up-Channel. The Armada was supposed to embark Parma's army off Dunkirk, Nieuport and Ostend, but there was no sign of him or his troops. Instead a depressing message arrived from the Duke's headquarters at Bruges to the effect that he had too few barges, not enough seamen, insufficient provisions and that it would be madness to attempt an embarkation at sea while Seymour's squadron remained in the offing and the shallow waters off the ports were swarming with the merciless Dutch Sea Beggars in their fast flyboats; it would, he said, be at least two weeks before he was ready; and he regretted that he was unable to supply the Armada with the munitions which had been requested.

The unfortunate Medina Sidonia had much to worry about besides Parma's problems, for Howard's fleet had dropped anchor a short mile to seaward. It was in good heart, believing that it now had the measure of the Spaniards, and Howard used the occasion to confer knighthoods on several captains who had distinguished themselves, including Hawkins and Frobisher. Some munitions were arriving from Dover and, best of all, Seymour's squadron joined the fleet with full ammunition lockers.

A word used extensively by both sides that Saturday was 'Hell-burner', the Spaniards with mortal dread and the English with something akin to glee. The Hell-burner was the brainchild of an Italian named Giambelli, now resident in England. It consisted of a fireship in which three tons of gunpowder were compressed in brick-built chambers to increase the blast effect and detonated by a slow match attached to a clockwork fuse. It had first been employed by the Dutch against Parma during his siege of Antwerp, sent drifting on a rising tide against a heavy wooden bridge forming part

Right: The arrival of English fireships in Calais Roads created such confusion that the Armada lost its cohesion for several vital days.

of the siegeworks. The resulting explosion demolished the bridge, killed 800 Spaniards and injured many more; Parma himself was felled by a baulk of timber. Now the Armada's crews firmly believed that the English intended using similar infernal devices against them in their vulnerable anchorage. Such a thought was indeed passing through English minds, although there was insufficient time to prepare proper Hell-burners. Instead, eight small vessels were stuffed with combustible materials, their guns being double-shotted and fused to fire when the flames reached them. During the early hours of Sunday 7 August they were

93

set ablaze and the prevailing wind and tide did the rest.

The result was pandemonium. The Armada's guard pinnaces managed to intercept two of the fireships, but the rest, their guns banging intermittently, ploughed on through the crowded anchorage to burn themselves out on the shore. Long before that, however, Medina Sidonia had ordered his ships to cut their cables and, anticipating a series of fearful explosions by the minute, they headed for open water in a disorderly stampede; behind them, in the muddy bottom of Calais Roads, they left 150 anchors of which, in due course, they would have desperate need.

In the confusion the flagship of the galleasses, Moncada's *San Lorenzo*, fouled the cable of an auxiliary and lost her rudder. Moncada ran her so hard ashore under the guns of Calais Castle that she slewed onto her beam ends. The boats of Howard's squadron, ignoring French neutrality, closed in to board successfully, killing Moncada in the process, When the wretched rowing slaves were released from their benches it is quite possible that there were a number of captive English seamen among them.

During its untidy escape from Calais the Armada had lost its close formation and with it its best defence. Now simply a large straggle of ships, it was carried through the Straits of Dover past Gravelines. Medina Sidonia and his senior officers struggled courageously to form a rearguard with a few galleons, but the English squadrons were in full cry, sweeping past to savage their respective prey. Evaluation of the previous actions had revealed that at long range the culverin-shot would penetrate the Spaniards' upperworks but not their stouter hull timbers. At closer range their hulls could be penetrated, and the lesson for the future was that the Navy required guns which combined range with much heavier hitting power. On the other hand, the Spanish gunnery had been almost completely ineffective. For these reasons, therefore, the English decided to fight at closer ranges yet during the fight off Gravelines. The result was that, difficult though it

was to sink wooden warships of the type with gunfire, several Spanish vessels were lost in this way. The galleon *San Felipe*, riddled and water-logged to the point of immobility, grounded between Nieuport and Ostend. Her crew were taken off in pinnaces and eventually the Dutch patched her up, pumped her out and got her into Flushing. Another galleon in a similar state, the *San Mateo*, grounded farther east between Ostend and Sluys. She was promptly surrounded by Sea Beggars and forced to surrender after a 2-hour fight. Her captain was spared for the ransom he would bring, but none of his crew survived. She too was patched up and taken into Flushing. A third ship, the auxiliary *Maria Juan*, went to the bottom with 275 men still aboard. Medina Sidonia's *San Martin* only remained afloat because two divers were working non-stop to plug shot holes in the hull with tow and lead plates. Many other ships sustained damage which was to prove fatal when they ran into heavy weather. Once it became clear that the Spaniards had exhausted their ammunition, some of the English ships closed the range to within a point-blank 100 yards.

After dusk on Monday 8 August a steady north-westerly wind began pushing the Armada towards the dangerous shoaling banks of the Dutch coast, where hungry knives were eager to be slitting Spanish throats. Howard's ships, aware of the danger, had disengaged and given themselves plenty of sea-room as the drama unfolded. For a while it seemed to Medina Sidonia and his senior officers that the entire Armada was doomed. Then, quite suddenly, the wind veered to the south-west, enabling the Spaniards to claw themselves away from the fearful lines of breakers and resume their close formation.

At first there was talk of returning to pick up Parma and his army when conditions permitted, but aboard the shot-battered ships with empty magazines few took the idea seriously. Instead Medina Sidonia allowed his ships to be pushed steadily northwards by the prevailing winds, his intention being to return to Spain by sailing right round the British Isles.

Howard, having detached Seymour to watch Parma, shadowed the Armada as far north as Berwick, then returned to harbour to replenish his own ammunition and provisions. The largest, longest and most important sea battle in history was over, having changed the face of sea warfare for ever.

The subsequent voyage of the Armada was an epic tragedy the details of which do not form part of this study. Scattered by gales, ships vanished without trace or left their bones littering the rocky west coasts of Scotland and Ireland, some, which would certainly have been saved had they retained their anchors, being driven onto lee shores and pounded to bits by huge Atlantic rollers. From the end of August the remnant of the Armada began straggling into the ports of northern Spain and Portugal, its crews ravaged by disease, starvation and thirst. Finally, when it became apparent that no more ships would be arriving, the cost could be counted. Michael Lewis's detailed analysis gives the Spanish loss, from all causes, as being four galleons, eighteen auxiliaries, eleven trans-

Below: During the voyage home many of the Armada's ships were wrecked on the storm-lashed western coasts of Scotland and Ireland. *Philip Haythornthwaite Collection*

ports, fifteen smaller vessels, two galleasses and one galley. Of those who had sailed with the Armada, about 20,000 died in the fighting, in shipwrecks, from starvation or from disease. As the majority were obviously soldiers, the result equated to a major defeat on land as well as at sea, especially as some of the lost ships are known to have stowed quantities of field artillery and other equipment necessary for a land campaign. Philip accepted the disaster philosophically and, to his credit, looked after the survivors rather better than Elizabeth cared for the welfare of her own victorious seamen.

No English vessels were lost other than those voluntarily expended as fireships, nor was any major damage recorded. About 100 men are estimated to have died as a direct result of the fighting, and more probably died from diseases contracted from the insanitary conditions prevailing within the hulls of Tudor warships.

Throughout Protestant Europe the defeat of the Spanish Armada was welcomed joyously, not simply as proof that Spain was far from invincible, but also that the Almighty favoured the Protestant cause. Significantly, the famous Armada medal, inscribed 'FLAVIT JEHOVAH ET DISSIPATI SUNT' (God Blew and They Were Scattered), was struck not in England, as one might expect, but in Holland.

FIRST BATTLE OF BREITENFELD, 17 SEPTEMBER 1631

The Thirty Years War, which broke out in 1618, was ostensibly an extension of the previous century's religious wars, the conflict on this occasion being between the Catholic princes of the Holy Roman Empire (Austria) and southern Germany on the one hand and the Protestant princes of northern Germany, Denmark and Sweden on the other. However, complex political influences were at work as well, notably the intention of the French Bourbon monarchs to curb the expanding power of the Habsburg dynasty, a process which eventually would bring largely Catholic France into the war on the side of the Protestants.

It was, in fact, subsidies offered by Cardinal Richelieu that led King Gustavus Adolphus of Sweden to take an active part in hostilities. When Gustavus came to the throne in 1611, aged only 17, he was immediately engaged in a series of local wars whose outcome made Sweden the major military power in the Baltic. As the country was poor and had limited manpower resources, the standing army which he had created had compensated for these factors with above average efficiency. Raised by selective conscription, it was clothed in uniforms that reflected its national character and enhanced unit *esprit de corps*, was humanely disciplined, paid regularly and trained thoroughly. Above all, Gustavus was an innovator who, recognising that he must tailor his coat according to his cloth, broke the formal tactical moulds of his day.

Some earlier mention has been made of his attitude to the absurd *caracole* and his insistence that the cavalry charge home with the sword, riding knee to knee. Each cavalry regiment had the support of a musketeer company and light field guns which would be employed prior to and between the cavalry charges. His impact on the rest of the army was equally dramatic. Recognising that improved weapons were the key to better tactics, he reduced the

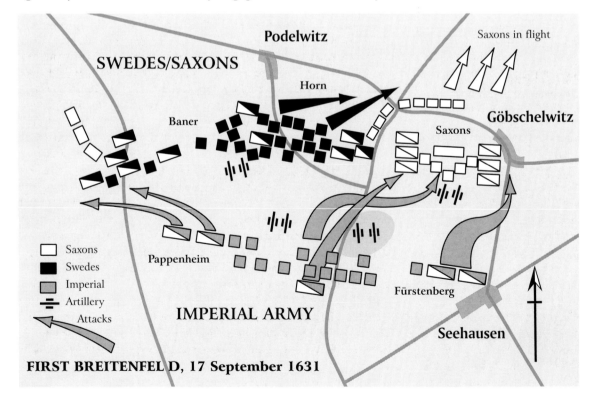

FIRST BREITENFELD, 17 September 1631

weight of the musket so that it could be fired from the shoulder without need of a clumsy rest, replaced the matchlock and its smouldering length of slow match with an efficient wheel-lock that could strike flint sparks into the priming pan even in wet weather, and introduced a combined powder and ball cartridge. As a result the musketeers' rate of fire increased sufficiently for the number of their ranks to be reduced from ten to six, and the ratio of musketeers to pikemen within an infantry company was increased. Under Gustavus, a Swedish infantry company consisted of 72 musketeers and 54 pikemen. Four companies formed a battalion, eight battalions a regiment; two or more regiments formed a brigade. In the sphere of artillery Gustavus introduced the regimental gun, issued on the scale of one or two to each infantry and cavalry regiment. These 4-pounder guns were light enough to be handled by their own crews and had a rate of fire about one-third faster than that of the musketeers. They were employed in the anti-personnel role, firing grape or canister ammunition, the former consisting of musket-balls in a bag or net and the latter musket-balls or scrap housed in a container, the effect of both being similar to that of a large shotgun. These reforms made the Swedish army a balanced force combining shock action with firepower and flexibility, and the lessons it taught on the battlefield were quickly absorbed by armies throughout Europe.

Sweden entered the war in 1630, but the full potential of her army did not become apparent until the following year. In August 1631 an Imperialist army under the veteran Count Johann Tilly marched into Saxony, laying waste the countryside. John George, Elector of Saxony, was unable to halt the invasion with the slender resources at his disposal and Gustavus marched to his assistance. On 15 September Tilly took Leipzig. Meanwhile the Swedish and Saxon armies had effected a junction at Düben and begun marching south to recapture the city. Urged by his subordinate, Count Gottfried zu Pappenheim, Tilly decided

to offer battle at Breitenfeld, some five miles to the north of Leipzig, in open rolling country lacking tactical features of any importance. His army, 21,000 infantry, 11,000 cavalry and 30 guns, was entirely conventional in its organisation and training, with the infantry formed into *tercio* units in the Spanish manner and the cavalry relying on the *caracole*. The infantry, fronted by the artillery, were deployed in fourteen *tercio* blocks in the centre with the cavalry on each flank. Tilly retained personal command of the centre and right and Pappenheim was given responsibility for the left wing.

John George had agreed to serve under Gustavus' command, and the combined Swedish/Saxon Protestant army was approximately 40,000 strong, including 248 infantry companies, 170 cavalry squadrons and 60–70 guns, a majority of these being the small regimental type. As the army deployed during the morning of 17 September it was agreed that the Saxon contingent, numbering 16,000 and organised in a similar manner to the Imperialists opposite, would cover the left. The smaller Swedish units were drawn up with two lines of musketeers supporting the cavalry on their flanks, and the infantry had the immediate support of 42 small regimental guns, the heavier artillery pieces being positioned to the front.

The battle began at noon with the usual protracted artillery exchange. Having fewer heavy weapons, the Swedes had rather the worst of this, enabling Tilly to plan a double-envelopment of the Protestant army. At about 2 o'clock Pappenheim's cavalry advanced with the object of turning the Swedish right but was balked when the Swedes simply shifted units from elsewhere in their line to extend the threatened flank, then counter-attacked with their own cavalry. Now came the first surprise of the action. The Imperialist troopers had expected the Swedes to execute the usual gentlemanly wheel to the rear after firing their pistols, but instead they spurred forward, slashing and thrusting at everything in sight, shattering the well-ordered ranks required for the *caracole*.

Both sides rallied after the first shock. While the Swedish squadrons were able to restore their ranks undisturbed, their musketeers and light guns came forward to harry the enemy. Used hitherto to a more leisurely, formal conduct of operations, Pappenheim and his men probably felt, correctly, that the Swedes were not playing the game according to the established rules. Nevertheless they were tough, battle-hardened veterans and it took three hours of Swedish counter-charges, alternating with musketry volleys, before Pappenheim was driven from the field in disorder.

Meanwhile Tilly had identified the Saxons as the weaker brethren and directed his *tercios* to advance obliquely to the right against them, covered on both flanks by cavalry. By 4 o'clock the Saxons were in full flight, leaving the Swedish left exposed. Tilly now believed that the battle was won and began re-organising the *tercios* for the decisive assault that would roll up Gustavus' line. Unfortunately for him the Swedes' inherent tactical flexibility resolved the crisis with totally unexpected speed. Gustaf Horn, commanding the Swedish left wing, launched an immediate counter-attack which bundled some of the Imperialist cavalry back into the *tercios* which, like the phalanx of old, required time to change direction. While the confused tangle was being sorted out the Swedes once again brought units from the safer sectors of their line to extend the threatened flank.

It must now have become clear to Tilly that he was engaged with an entirely new kind of enemy. He had also lost the initiative for as soon as their re-deployment was complete the Swedes launched a series of counter-attacks, combining infantry firepower with cavalry shock action. Forced steadily back, the ranks of the *tercios* became so compressed that the pikemen were unable to use their weapons. The Saxon artillery was recaptured, then Tilly's own guns were overrun as the tide of battle moved southwards, and both were turned on the struggling Imperialist infantry. At about 6 p.m. the *coup de grâce* was administered by Gustavus himself, leading his victorious right-wing cavalry in a charge which finally swept the remnant of the Catholic army off the field. The pursuit lasted until nightfall when the fugitives reached comparative safety behind a screen formed by Pappenheim's rallied cavalry.

Tilly's losses at Breitenfeld included 7,000 killed and wounded, 6,000 captured and a further 8,000 who subsequently surrendered in Leipzig. Swedish/Saxon casualties totalled 4,000 killed and wounded. The outcome of the battle ensured the continuance of the Protestant cause in Germany, which had begun to waver. Tilly survived his defeat by only eight months, being mortally wounded when Gustavus' troops stormed his entrenched camp on the Lech.

Gustavus sustained only one reverse during his subsequent career, significantly on rough, scrub-covered terrain where the Swedish tactical system was unable to operate to advantage. He was killed on 16 November 1632 while leading a counter-attack during the Battle of Lützen. He had made an indelible impression on the course of military history, laying the foundations of the conduct of warfare for the next three centuries. Had it not been for the pikemen and their residual body armour his army would have had a recognisably modern appearance; within a generation the introduction of the bayonet and improved firearms technology would ensure the disappearance of both from the infantry battle.

Commentary 6 – All-Arms Warfare in the Age of Elegance

The reforms of Gustavus Adolphus and the introduction of the bayonet together consolidated the effects of the Gunpowder Revolution into a recognisable format. Except in heavy cavalry regiments, personal armour disappeared, being replaced by uniforms in the national colour which, by and large, reflected the civilian dress of the day. Most infantry uniforms consisted of a tricorne hat bearing a royal cockade, a long coat with collar, cuffs, lapels and skirt turnbacks of regimental pattern, gaiters, stout shoes, cartridge box and haversack. Although in most respects the uniform was comfortable, the soldier was required to wear a leather stock intended to keep his chin up, and to have his hair pulled tightly back into a *queue* secured by a bow; it was said that unless a man closed his eyes during the latter process he would not be able to close them again! Officers wore a small quarter-moon gorget, and when on duty carried a light pike known as a spontoon. Sergeants were equipped with a scaled-down halberd, used to adjust the dressing of the ranks. A further survival of an earlier age, worn by officers and sergeants, was the sash which, unrolled, could be used as a simple stretcher to help the wearer off the field if he were wounded.

In addition to its line companies, the establishment of an infantry regiment provided for a grenadier and a light company. Earlier reference has been made to the grenadiers, who were the regiment's tallest and best soldiers, their height enhanced by distinctive mitre caps, replaced halfway through the 18th century by tall fur caps known as 'armchairs'. The light company consisted of soldiers of proven initiative who were also good shots, additionally trained for skirmishing and scouting. In the field regiments tended to lose their grenadier and light companies which were brigaded with those from other regiments to form élite units.

In the cavalry, breast and back plates continued to be worn by cuirassier regiments intended to perform the heaviest shock action. In some armies, the French being a notable exception, dragoons lost their useful mounted infantry role and simply became another branch of the heavy cavalry. The need for light cavalry to perform the reconnaissance and screening roles resulted in a fashion for hussars, originating in Hungary. In the British Army this need was met by the formation of light dragoon regiments which were capable of fighting mounted or dismounted and were probably the most versatile troops on the battlefield. Some lancer regiments existed, although the weapon had fallen into disrepute and was mainly to be found in eastern Euro-

pean armies. The trooper's primary weapon was the sword, the carbine and pistol playing a secondary role. Towards the end of the 18th century there was a gradual acceptance that the tricorne was unsuited to the mêlée, leading to a partial re-appearance of the helmet in various forms. Of these the most elegant was the fur-crested Tarleton helmet, named after the British cavalry leader of the American Revolutionary War, worn by British light dragoon regiments and, later, the Royal Horse Artillery.

It had now become the custom to classify guns by the weight of their projectiles. Regimental guns remained in use for much of the period, but as improvements in gun manufacture and carriage construction rendered artillery more mobile the older, heavier pieces were withdrawn from field armies. In their place guns of the same calibre were grouped permanently together in batteries and manned by professional artillerymen, although the inefficient practice of hiring civilian drivers and horses continued for many years. The increasing professionalism and complexities of the artilleryman's domain meant that it was now administered through central bodies which were responsible, among other things, for gun and ammunition procurement, training and tactics. Likewise, similar bodies were required to administer the growing engineering arm.

The 18th century was the golden era of the regimental proprietary system, under which the sovereign authorised a trusted officer to raise a regiment on his behalf. The officer then became colonel of the regiment, in which he could grant commissions, and was paid an annual sum of money by the government to cover its running costs. The system was open to abuse in many ways, one of which was to claim expenses for the number of men on the regimental rolls, which could well exceed the total actually present. Officers purchased their commissions and every step of their promotion within the regiment, the theory being that they were men of substance who therefore had a personal interest in preserving the status quo.

The idea has sometimes been expressed that the purchase system produced an officer class recruited from the nobility, but that is untrue nor was it ever the intention. Although some noblemen of military age could indeed be found in guards or select cavalry regiments, the aristocracies were too small to extend far beyond this. Most officers tended to be the sons of officers, or of the middling gentry of their counties, or, in smaller numbers, of the rising professional class of lawyers, doctors and merchants. On campaign, the system was a little fairer in that vacancy and merit played a part in promotion. Thus an officer's commission was a valuable asset which he could sell on leaving the army, the exceptions being artillery and engineer officers who received their commissions without the need to purchase and were promoted by seniority. By degrees the abuses of the proprietorial and commission by purchase systems were brought under government control and finally lapsed. Curiously, though it was logically indefensible and did sometimes produce unsuitable individuals, the purchase system served the British Army remarkably well and survived until 1871.

The rank and file of 18th-century armies were a very mixed lot, including genuine volunteers, criminals who chose the army as an alternative to imprisonment, mercenaries, and men who, for various reasons, sought anonymity. By far the greatest proportion, however, were men so down on their luck that they had nowhere else to turn, despite the fact that 'going for a soldier' was considered to be a social disgrace. Lack of recruits forced some states to adopt selective conscription to fill the ranks of their regiments. Such men had to be ruled with an iron discipline, not simply because of their disparate backgrounds, but because the battles of the day were fought in tight linear formation at murderously close range. Taking cover, save in defence of a fortified position, was never an option. The damage inflicted on arm or leg bones by heavy musket balls was such that amputation in truly gruesome conditions was often the only treatment. Other penetrative wounds might be probed and patched up, but

the danger of sepsis was always present. Whether a man survived a visit to the dressing station depended entirely on the strength of his constitution. Small wonder, then, that strict discipline was necessary to keep a soldier in the line. This was imposed in a number of ways, endless drill being the most obvious. Drill was the quickest method of instilling discipline and teaching a man to think of himself as part of a group, but it was also useful in that it provided a controlled means of movement on the battlefield. Punishments could be savage. Flogging is usually quoted in this context, but it was not a peculiarly military punishment and civilian criminals were regularly flogged as well, if not to the same degree. The most repressive discipline of all was imposed by the Prussian Army to achieve robotic obedience in its soldiers, who were subjected to a variety of savage punishments if they defaulted. Understandably many soldiers of all armies took advantage of the confusion inherent in battle to escape the harsh realities of a soldier's life by deserting. Ironically, many men hitherto rejected by society discovered comradeship amid the shared discomforts and dangers, engendering *esprit de corps* and fierce pride in their regiment's achievements.

The armies of the period tended to be small and professional in their outlook. The battles they fought were part of dynastic quarrels between the royal houses of Europe, lacking the bitterness which had marked the religious wars of the previous two centuries. Co-operation between the three arms had become the norm with each realising that it had its limitations. For example, infantry deployed in the usual two- or three-deep firing line were at the mercy of hostile cavalry. Infantry, however, could effectively defend themselves against cavalry if they formed squares, presenting the enemy horsemen with an impenetrable hedge of bayonets. Firepower now lay at the heart of the infantry battle. Firing was by volleys, which could be regimental, grand divisional (two companies), platoon or by ranks in succession, producing an average of 2–3 rounds per man per minute. Bayonets were used, but in the open field their effect was more moral than physical, for although the armoured pikeman had not hesitated in coming to grips with his opposite number, the new infantryman, possessing no protection whatever, had understandable reservations on the subject. Generally, bayonet charges were only ordered against an enemy line that was seen to be crumbling, the charge itself being sufficient to drive it off the field without bayonets being actually crossed. Artillery continued to play a supporting role for infantry and cavalry alike, although its new mobility enabled it to keep pace with the fighting and its use became increasingly aggressive.

While this study is concerned with the evolution of method, there were occasions when the tactical manuals counted for nothing in the face of sheer fighting spirit and high morale. For example, at Minden on 1 August 1759, six British and two Hanoverian regiments mistakenly advanced on the French centre in response to a misunderstood order. First, they had to endure the concentrated fire of the enemy artillery. Their ranks were shredded but they continued to march forward, closing the gaps and dressing their line as they went. Next, the French cavalry charged them, believing confidently that it could ride straight over infantry in line. The British and Hanoverians, however, shared not only a monarch and the same colour uniforms, but also training methods. Shortly before the battle their musketry techniques had undergone a radical change in that aim was not simply taken at the enemy line, as before, but directed at individuals within it. When fire was opened at 30 yards' range, it seemed as though the French had ridden into a plate-glass wall, with men and horses sent tumbling in thrashing heaps. A second wave of cavalry sought to avenge the disaster but now the ground was encumbered and it met a similar fate. So did a third wave, which consisted of the last cavalry units available to the French commander. As if this were not enough, the French sent their infantry and that of their Saxon allies against these unbelievable soldiers. Calmly, the regiments changed front to meet the new attack and, after a stiff firefight, sent their new opponents hurrying to the rear. The incredible feat of these eight regiments defies logical explanation and has never been surpassed.

Another area where the usual tactical rules did not apply was North America, where the wars between the United Kingdom and France had spilled over into their respective colonies. At first the French proved to be the better at recruiting Indian allies and developing forest fighting techniques, but once the British had adopted a similarly flexible approach they began to make progress and eventually succeeded in bringing Canada under their control. Two new units were formed to deal with the problem. The first of these was the 60th (Royal American) Regiment, four battalions strong, raised at Governor's Island, New York, under the command of a Swiss officer, Colonel Henry Bouquet, with the object of 'combining the qualities of the scout with the discipline of the trained soldier'. Its men were drilled in open order, both in quick and double time, taught to load and fire quickly in the standing, kneeling or prone positions, instructed in swimming, survival, self-sufficiency and elementary field fortification, and generally required to use their initiative. Training included a period of several weeks spent in the woods during which, apart from a small ration of flour, recruits lived entirely on whatever game and fish they could shoot or catch. Such was the regiment's success in action that it earned itself a permanent place in the British Army, where it subsequently became known as the King's Royal Rifle Corps, now part of the Royal Green Jackets. The second unit was raised from colonists in New Hampshire under the command of Captain Robert Rogers, a native of Massachusetts who had lived the life of a frontiersman in his youth. Rogers' Rangers were specialists in the art of providing advance and rear guards, intelligence-gathering, deep penetration patrols, raiding and sabotage. Their exploits were legendary but, being an irregular unit, they were disbanded when the French and Indian

Wars ended. Not surprisingly, when the United States Army decided to form its own commando units during the Second World War, it chose to call them Rangers.

The 18th century, therefore, was the period in which, once the lessons of the Gunpowder Revolution had been thoroughly absorbed, the foundations of land warfare as we know it today were laid. Regular, paid and uniformed standing armies became an established part of national life for the first time since the Roman Empire. The functions of cavalry, infantry, artillery and engineers were recognised as being interdependent within the army as a whole, and the need for what we call special forces to operate in appropriate circumstances was recognised. Indeed, were a modern soldier to be transported back to a battlefield of the time he would not feel altogether out of place, once he got used to the clouds of powder smoke and the fact that everyone – friend and foe – remained in full view throughout the engagement.

BLENHEIM, 13 AUGUST 1704

The War of the Spanish Succession (1701–14) saw the Grand Alliance of England, Holland, Denmark, the Austrian Empire and a number of German states pitted against France, Spain and Bavaria. For the first time since the days of the English longbowmen it necessitated the deployment of considerable numbers of British troops to the mainland of continental Europe under a British commander.

John, Duke of Marlborough, was born in 1650. As a junior officer he had seen active service in Tangier and at sea during the Dutch Wars, and served for a while in the French Army. He was also responsible for defeating the Duke of Monmouth's rebellion in 1685. On the outbreak of war William III had appointed him Commander-in-Chief of the Allied armies and ambassador to the Dutch United Provinces. When Anne succeeded to the British throne in the following year she added the appointment of Captain-General to that of Master General of the Ordnance, which he already held, and made him a duke.

Marlborough was gifted equally as a strategist and as a tactician. The hallmark of his victories was an unfailing ability to detect any weakness in his opponents' dispositions and concentrate overwhelming force against it. His cavalry charges were delivered at a controlled canter and pressed home to achieve deep penetration but were always followed by a prompt rally. He personally supervised the deployment of his artillery, massing guns on a critical sector and pushing them forward aggressively to provide close support during a general advance. On occasion he would personally sight individual guns. Above all he was an inspiring leader who, recognising that most men were soldiers only because they had no alternative, insisted that their welfare be his officers' first concern. The men therefore liked and trusted him, conferring on him the affectionate nickname of 'Corporal John.'

In 1704 the war was going badly for the Grand Alliance. It seemed possible that Vienna would fall to a Franco–Bavarian army and if that happened the probability was that the Alliance would collapse. Marlborough, leaving some 60,000 troops to protect Holland, embarked upon a remarkable strategic march from the Netherlands to the upper reaches of the Danube in an attempt to retrieve the situation. With him he had some 21,000 men of whom half were British and the rest German allies in British pay. The long march was remarkable on two counts. First, by a series of feints and deceptions Marlborough confused the French as to his intended destination until it was too late for them to co-ordinate a response. Secondly, every aspect of the 250-mile march had been thoroughly pre-planned. It was obviously important that the troops arrive in good fighting order, so they marched in 12-mile daily stages, partly by night, and rested every fifth day. At the end of each march they found their camp sites laid out ready for them. To maintain mobility Marlborough brought with him only his lighter guns, having been assured by the Austrians that heavier weapons would be provided when he reached their operational area. Heavy four-wheeled baggage wagons were replaced by two-wheeled carts. Supplies were purchased in advance for gold, which ensured that there were never any shortages. For example, at Heidelberg, just over half-way along the route, stocks of new shoes were immediately available to replace those that had worn out. Having started from Bedburg on 20 May, the 'scarlet caterpillar' was joined by 19,000 reinforcements along the way, including 5,000 Hanoverians at Koblenz and 14,000 Danes and Germans at Mainz.

On 2 July Marlborough stormed the Schellenberg Heights, overlooking Donauwörth, taking the town and its bridges at the not inconsiderable cost of 10,000 casualties. Next he began to ravage Bavaria, burning more than 300 villages in the hope that this would persuade the Elector Maximilian to abandon his alliance with France. It failed to do so, but it did induce the French to dispatch an army from Strasbourg to his assistance. This, commanded by Marshal Tallard, joined a Franco–Bavarian army commanded by Marshal de Marsin and the Elector at Augsburg on 5 August. With the combined force Tallard crossed the Danube and marched east towards Donauwörth in the hope of trapping Marlborough south of the river. The evening of 12 August found his army camped along the line of the river Nebel, a tributary of the Danube, between the villages of Blindheim and Lützingen. At his disposal he had 79 infantry battalions, 140 cavalry squadrons

and 90 guns, totalling 56,000 men. Tallard did not expect to be attacked; he had been fed false information by 'deserters' who told him that the Allied army was actually retreating towards Nördlingen to protect its lines of communication.

In fact, Marlborough had joined forces with an Imperial army commanded by Prince Eugène of Savoy and was advancing westwards intent on bringing Tallard to battle. His combined army now numbered 52,000 men, including 65 infantry battalions, 160 cavalry squadrons and 66 guns, and was thus only slightly smaller than the Franco–Bavarian army. During 12 August Marlborough personally surveyed the enemy position from the tower of the village church at Tapfheim. He noted that both flanks were strongly secured, with Blindheim at the confluence of the Nebel with the Danube, and Lützingen protected by

Right: John Churchill, Duke of Marlborough. Although by now full armour was never worn in action, the contemporary convention was that one should have one's portrait painted wearing it. Marlborough insisted that his officers should make themselves responsible for the welfare of their men; the soldiers' affectionate nickname for him was 'Corporal John'. *Katz Pictures Ltd*

103

BLENHEIM, 13 August 1704

thick woods. The remainder of the front sloped gently through water meadows to the Nebel which in some places formed an obstacle because its banks were marshy. The villages, which were surrounded by walled and well-fenced gardens, had been prepared for defence and in many places the ground was intersected by open ditches and hedges.

At 1 a.m. on 13 August Marlborough had his troops roused and in the warm, misty night they began marching towards the French in nine parallel columns; the British on the extreme left, the rest of Marlborough's troops in the centre and Eugène's Imperial regiments on the right.

At about 8 o'clock the mist lifted, revealing to Tallard the bulk of Marlborough's troops forming their line of battle just beyond cannon-shot on the far bank of the Nebel. He promptly summoned Marsin and the Elector to the church tower in Blindheim for a last-minute council of war, the details of which are

recorded in a contemporary English account quoted by A. Hilliard Atteridge:

'The Elector and Marsin were for drawing up the army as close to the marshy ground they had in their front as possible, and not to suffer a man over but on the points of their bayonets; but Tallard (a haughty, proud Frenchman) was of a different opinion, and said that would be no more than making a drawn battle of it; that the only way to get a complete victory would be to draw up their army at some small distance from the morass, and suffer us to come over, and the more there came over the more they were sure to kill. Neither the Elector nor Marsin could persuade him out of this notion; they were both very much dissatisfied, and dreading the consequence, left him and went to their posts.'

In the event they all apparently decided to follow their own counsel. By 8.30 their troops had marched out of camp to take up their positions as follows: the front between Blindheim and the Danube was held by several squadrons of dismounted dragoons; Blindheim village was held by nine battalions under the Marquis de Clérambault, with eighteen more battalions in reserve immediately behind them; between Blindheim and Oberglau, the next village upstream, Tallard deployed 64 squadrons of cavalry along the crest of the slope, some 600 yards from the Nebel, but unwisely chose to support them with only nine newly raised infantry battalions; Oberglau itself was held by fourteen battalions under General de Blainville; to their left the line was prolonged by the Elector and Marsin's troops, with 67 squadrons deployed close to the river and, to their left-rear, sixteen Bavarian infantry battalions in and around Lützingen.

From the outset Tallard surrendered the initiative to Marlborough. The latter made no immediate major move because he was waiting for Eugène's Imperial troops to come up on his left through some difficult country which was delaying their progress. He did, however, send parties with bundles of straw and brushwood to prepare crossing-points at the Nebel. He also arranged for rations to be issued and for the regimental chaplains to recite Morning Service. When the French heavy guns opened fire at long range he simply ordered the men to lie down amid the corn, while he surveyed the enemy position and noted Tallard's mistake in leaving his centre only lightly defended. At about 12.30 a galloper arrived from Eugène to say that the Imperial troops were now in position.

Marlborough's plan was to capture or contain the villages of Blindheim and Oberglau and then break through the enemy centre. At 1 o'clock he ordered Lord Cutts, commanding his left wing, to mount an infantry attack on Blindheim. Cutts, nicknamed 'Salamander' because he loved to be amid the heat of battle, ordered his British and Hanoverian battalions to advance with their muskets loaded, but added that not a shot was to be fired until the officers had touched the enemy palisade with their sword points. It was a severe test for the regiments as they advanced through heavy musketry and cannon-fire but they reached the defences and poured a withering fire of their own into the village. The attack failed but was repeated with equal determination, only to be beaten back again. To the north of the village the French sent in nine squadrons of their crack *Gendarmes* to relieve the pressure on the garrison. They were vigorously counter-charged

Right: Blenheim. Lord Cutts' British and Hanoverian infantry commence their attack on the village. Though repulsed, it was was repeated twice with such determination that ultimately no less than 27 French battalions were committed to its defence, being crammed uselessly between the houses. *Philip Haythornthwaite Collection*

Left: Marlborough personally brings up his reserve cavalry to repel a French counter-attack. *Philip Haythornthwaite Collection*

by five squadrons of the Royal Dragoons and the Grey Dragoons (later the Royal Scots Greys) and routed. Cutts mounted a third infantry attack but this was also repulsed. Clérambault, however, had been so shaken by the ferocity of Cutts' assaults that he had withdrawn all eighteen reserve battalions into the village, without warning Tallard of the fact. Thus, no fewer than 27 French battalions were uselessly compressed shoulder-to-shoulder within the streets and gardens of Blindheim so that only those actually manning the defences could use their muskets. At this point Marlborough, well satisfied, ordered Cutts to abandon his attacks and simply contain the village with fire.

In the centre meanwhile, German infantry under the Prince of Holstein–Beck had launched a similar attack on Oberglau. The village was held by 'Wild Geese', that is, Irish Catholic immigrant regiments in the French service, wearing red (not scarlet) uniforms. The Irish not only repulsed the attack but sallied forth with the bayonet and pursued the Germans across the river, being repulsed in their turn when Marlborough personally brought up fresh troops from his reserve. Their ranks now seriously depleted, the Irish retired to Oberglau, which was also contained with

fire, including that from eight guns which had been dragged across the river. Elsewhere, Eugène's troops were making little headway against the Franco–Bavarians holding the line between Oberglau and Lützingen.

Marlborough, however, satisfied that Blindheim and Oberglau had been neutralised, decided that the moment had come to launch the decisive attack against Tallard's centre. At about 3 o'clock his own centre, commanded by his brother, General Charles Churchill, began fording the Nebel. It consisted of seventeen battalions in the front line, then 72 cavalry squadrons in two lines, and eleven more infantry battalions bringing up the rear. Having splashed ashore, the troops had begun to form up on dry ground beyond the marshy bank when their right flank was subjected to a sudden and unexpected counter-attack by cavalry. Marsin, evidently more wide-awake than Tallard, had watched the Allied threat develop and, perceiving its full implications, had sent the disengaged element of his own cavalry round the back of Oberglau to deal with it, although it lay outside his own sector. If the French and Bavarian horsemen had concentrated on shock action instead of banging away with their firearms before closing their impact would have been much greater.

Right: Blenheim. In the immediate aftermath of the battle, Marlborough rides past captured French colours and senior officers. *Philip Haythornthwaite Collection*

Even so they forced Churchill's men back towards the river in some confusion. At this moment, had Tallard launched his own squadrons in support of Marsin's troopers the outcome of the battle could well have been different. As it was, the opportunity was fleeting, for Marlborough had already dispatched a galloper to Eugène requesting urgent assistance. The partnership of Marlborough and Eugène was remarkable for its mutual understanding and support. Without hesitation, Eugène dispatched his sole remaining cavalry reserve, Brigadier General Fugger's cuirassier brigade. Fugger's troopers, big men on big horses, smashed into the flank of Marsin's squadrons as they were rallying for another charge, and drove them back whence they had come.

This local crisis having been resolved, Churchill brought his own cavalry forward and advanced at the trot up the long slope. Tallard could claim that this was the moment for which he had been waiting; just as the Allied cavalry was reaching the crest he launched all his squadrons in a thundering downhill charge. The Allied horsemen had the worst of it and were bundled back to rally on the flanks of the nearest infantry formations, which in turn repulsed the French with disciplined volleys.

Tallard had played his ace and it had failed to take the trick. Now the odds were lengthening steadily against him as more and more of Marlborough's troops crossed the Nebel. At his immediate disposal he had only 60 squadrons and nine recruit battalions to oppose 80 squadrons, 23 battalions and a growing number of guns. In desperation he looked for infantry to shore up his line, but Clérambault had already stuffed his entire reserve into Blindheim and the Elector, threatened by Danish troops working their way round behind Lützingen, refused to send any. When the Allied attack was resumed, therefore, it resulted in a fierce but brief mêlée which ended with the French cavalry routed and in full flight. The nine recruit battalions performed unexpectedly well, dying where they stood in a fruitless attempt to cover their comrades' withdrawal.

By 5.30 the battle was over, although there remained some tidying up to do. Marsin and the Elector managed to extricate most of their troops and retreated in the direction of Höchstädt, pursued by Eugène and the Imperialists. Tallard was captured trying to make his way into Blindheim. Many of the French drowned while attempting to escape across the Danube; among them was Clérambault, who had deserted his troops. Now surrounded and choking amid the smoke of burning thatches, the 11,000 men in Blindheim surrendered at about 11 o'clock. Most had not fired a single shot throughout the day. Such was their shame that many officers were reduced to tears as the Colours of proud regiments were burned to prevent capture. Franco–Bavarian casualties totalled 20,000 killed and wounded, 14,000 captured, 6,000 desertions and 60 guns lost; further trophies included 34 cavalry standards and 128 Colours. Two-thirds of the combined army had been destroyed in this, the worst reverse sustained by French arms for 50 years.

The Allies' casualties totalled 12,000 killed and wounded. Marlborough's great victory, therefore, had not been cheap, but given what had been achieved it was not exorbitant. The threat to Vienna had been removed at a stroke and the Grand Alliance was preserved. British military prestige soared to levels it had not reached since the Hundred Years War.

Marlborough wrote a brief note to his wife on the field of battle:

'I have not time to say more but to beg you will give my duty to the Queen and let her know her army has had a glorious victory. Mons. Tallard and other generals are in my coach and I am following the rest. The bearer, my aide-de-camp, Colonel Parkes will give her an account of what has passed.'

In those days to be the bearer of glad tidings was a rewarding experience. When Parkes reported to Queen Anne at Windsor on 21 August she gave him a miniature of herself and the considerable sum of 1,000 guineas.

The continuing partnership of Marlborough and Eugène was to bring enormous benefit to the Grand Alliance. Marlborough was to win further great victories at Ramillies in 1706, Oudenarde in 1708, Malplaquet in 1709 and in forcing the allegedly impregnable 'Ne Plus Ultra' lines in 1711. But Blindheim (sometimes spelled Plentheim), or Blenheim in its Anglicised form, remains his greatest monument and was the name conferred on the Oxfordshire palace presented to him by a grateful nation.

LEUTHEN, 5 DECEMBER 1757

At the time of Blenheim the kingdom of Prussia was a minor German state owing allegiance to the Habsburg emperors in Vienna, yet within 50 years, under the dynamic leadership of Frederick the Great, she had become the fourth greatest military power in Europe.

Frederick's father, Frederick William I, was a parsimonious, boorish, cruel man whose principal pleasure lay in inspecting and drilling his troops. Under his rule Prussian discipline became a by-word for harshly enforced robotic obedience and because of this he has been called a crowned sergeant-major, which is a little unfair to sergeants-major in general. His greatest joy was a regiment of giant grenadiers known as the Potsdam Blues. None of them was under six feet tall, and some towered to over seven feet. His agents scoured Europe from Ireland to Russia for such men, sometimes kidnapping them if they would not enlist voluntarily. For all their height, many were of feeble constitution so the regiment had little military value, but because it looked well during reviews its members were treated as pets, being required to perform for the king's guests at all hours of the day and night. Frederick William was far too mean to squander his precious money fighting wars on his own account, but he was prepared to hire out officers and soldiers to other rulers for their princely squabbles and in this way considerable experience was absorbed by the army as a whole. One officer with wide experience of warfare was the Prince of Anhalt–Dessau, who invented the iron musket ramrod. Previously all armies had employed wooden ramrods which were inclined to bend, warp or break. The issue of iron ramrods to the Prussian infantry enabled them to fire three shots to their opponents' two until eventually everyone adopted the idea.

Frederick William hated his son and everything about him, especially his flute playing, his liking for literature and his correspondence

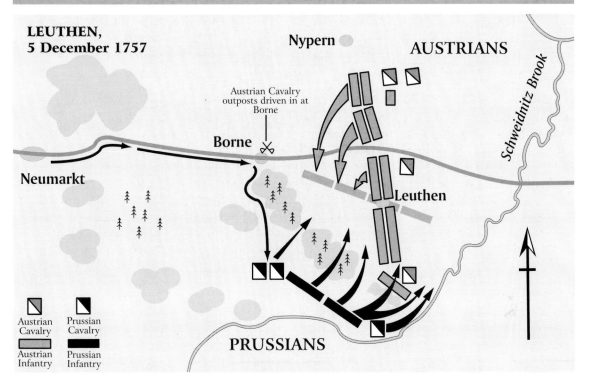

**LEUTHEN,
5 December 1757**

Nypern

AUSTRIANS

Austrian Cavalry
outposts driven in at
Borne

Borne

Neumarkt

Leuthen

Schweidnitz Brook

Austrian
Cavalry

Prussian
Cavalry

Austrian
Infantry

Prussian
Infantry

PRUSSIANS

with French philosophers. He believed that when young Frederick inherited the crown he would ruin the army and squander the national treasury on frivolities. At one stage he sentenced him to death by strangulation, but relented under pressure from his nobility and the diplomatic corps.

When Frederick came to the throne in 1740 he inherited an efficient army of 80,000 men and a fortune of 9,000,000 thalers. His was a complex and sometimes contradictory personality; the dilettante suddenly became a soldier who exercised the same ruthless discipline as his father, yet in the field he would tolerate a degree of frank speaking from his rank and file. Personally a courteous man of honour, as a monarch he was devious and dishonest.

During the War of the Austrian Succession (1740–8) and the Seven Years War (1756–63) he fought no less than 22 battles. He did not win them all, but those that he did win were of critical importance to Prussia and the advance of military science, earning him the title of 'the Great'.

Frederick's first victory, at Mollwitz on 10 April 1741, was so close to a defeat that he had ridden off the field with his routed cavalry, leaving the unshaken Prussian infantry to save the day with its sustained fire. Thereafter he resolved to bring his cavalry and artillery up to the same standard. The cavalrymen were absolutely forbidden to use firearms and were trained to drive home their charges in the manner of Marlborough and Eugène, but over much longer distances and at a faster pace. Their operations, too, were supported by the introduction of horse artillery batteries, a startling innovation quickly copied by other armies. In the artillery he also followed Marlborough's example by concentrating guns against a particular point of the enemy line, but he employed many more howitzers because they were more mobile than field guns and their high trajectory enabled them to get at enemy reserves positioned behind hills, woods and villages.

Underlying Frederick's thinking was the fact that Prussia was surrounded by enemies. Her army, therefore, would invariably fight at a

Above: Frederick the Great briefing his senior officers shortly before the battle, evidently with some vigour. His plan worked perfectly. *Philip Haythornthwaite Collection*

numerical disadvantage. The answer, he saw, lay in greater mobility, concentration of firepower and speed in deployment during the approach to and early stages of a battle. The essence of Frederick's tactics was to hold the enemy's attention frontally with part of his army, then overwhelm one of the opposing flanks by bringing an oblique concentration of force against it with the remainder. The attack on the chosen flank was made by marching diagonally across it in column, then turning into line once it had been enveloped. Success depended upon the company columns of each regiment maintaining the appropriate spacing between them so that when ordered to turn they would wheel to the left or right and bring the entire regiment into a three-deep fighting line. In this context Frederick regarded the endless drill, not as an end in itself as had his father, but as an essential preparation and conditioning for battle.

The most notable example of Fredrician tactics took place at Leuthen, a village some ten miles west of Wroclaw (Breslau) in Silesia. On 5 November 1757 Frederick had inflicted a crushing defeat on a French army at Rossbach, near Leipzig and this had enabled him to turn about and attempt to restore his fortunes in Silesia, which had been invaded by a large Austrian army. With only 13,000 men he force-marched 170 miles in twelve days, joining forces with the remnant of his Silesian army at Liegnitz. He then marched east towards Wroclaw with the intention of bringing the Austrians to battle.

The Austrian army, commanded by Prince Charles of Lorraine and Marshal Leopold von Daun, consisted of 84 infantry battalions, 144 cavalry squadrons and 65 field guns, a total of 60,000 men. Charles, aware of Frederick's approach, deployed his troops on a five-mile frontage across the Liegnitz–Neumarkt–Wroclaw road, centred approximately on the village of Leuthen. The right of the line was protected by marshland fronting another village named Nypern, and the left rested in pine covered hills above more marshes fringing the river Schweidnitz. Charles was well aware of Frederick's fondness for the flank attack and therefore refused his extreme left, which was angled back and partially covered by entrenchments. More earthwork redoubts and abattis entanglements were constructed at suitable points along the line and the villages were put into a state of defence. Finally, Charles threw out a screen of cavalry vedettes as far as Borne, half-way along the road from Leuthen to Neumarkt, to give advance warning of the Prussians' approach and line of advance. For Frederick, who had much the smaller army and was not yet fully aware of the difficulties he would face, the prospect of victory seemed so remote that, as he retired on the night of 4 December, he remarked to his senior officers: 'Tomorrow, gentlemen, we shall beat the Austrians or we shall never see each other again.'

The following day dawned misty and bitterly cold, with a covering of snow on the ground. The Prussian army, consisting of 48 infantry battalions, 129 cavalry squadrons and 71 field guns, a total of 35,000 men, tramped through Neumarkt, the breath of men and horses steaming in the frozen air. As the column approached Borne there were shouts and trumpet calls as the cavalry of the advance guard, commanded by General Hans von Ziethen, charged the Austrian vedettes, capturing some and driving the rest in upon their main body, where they reported to Charles that the Prussians were advancing straight down the road.

As the mist began to lift there was a pause while Frederick carried out a personal recon-naissance from higher ground. In the distance the Austrian line could be seen stretching away to the right and left. He knew his enemy well enough to know that he would passively await attack. He also observed a line of low hills stretching away from Borne to the south-east, under cover of which he could march unseen by the Austrians to a position from which he could launch an assault on the left of their line. To divert their attention he began pushing troops forward from Borne as though he planned to attack them between Leuthen and Nypern. Charles responded by shifting men and guns from left to right.

The main body of the Prussian army was now coming up in four parallel columns, the inner pair being infantry and the outer two cavalry. Shortly after 11 o'clock Frederick ordered the cavalry column on the left to join the demonstration against the enemy's right centre while that on the right turned off the line of march to follow the line of low hills. In two halves the infantry columns also wheeled half-right behind the cavalry to form two new columns which, when they halted and turned left, would become two parallel firing lines with the cavalry on their right. In this way the main body of Frederick's troops was already

Right: Leuthen. Prussian grenadiers advancing against the Austrian flank. Hopelessly outnumbered at the point of contact, the Austrians strove to form a new line but were driven out of this after hard fighting. *Philip Haythornthwaite Collection*

111

deployed in the order in which it would fight, long before it was in direct contact with the enemy.

In Leuthen, Charles and Daun were left to ponder the situation, unaware of what was taking place behind the hills and uncertain as to what was happening to their immediate front because their vedettes had been driven in. Meanwhile, the Prussian columns trudged steadily on; cavalry, infantry and light 6-pounder battalion guns. With them trundled ten long 12-pounders which Frederick had stripped from the fortress of Glogau during his march eastwards. They were heavier weapons than he cared to use with his field artillery, but they were to give an excellent account of themselves.

At about 1 o'clock the Prussians were within sight of the frozen Schweidnitz. To the left Frederick observed Kiepern Hill, a low, round-topped feature protected by an abattis, marking the extreme left of the Austrian position. The leading battalions halted, turned left and began to advance in line through the trees.

Everything seemed to happen at once. The white-coated Austrians holding the hill were not expecting trouble but now they found themselves being attacked in strength. Nevertheless, they reacted quickly and the summit blazed with musketry and cannon-fire. Ziethen led his cavalry round the shoulder of the hill but was counter-charged by the Austrian reserve cavalry and driven back. His troopers rallied behind the nearest infantry battalions whose fire dispersed the enemy horsemen. Frederick ordered Ziethen to try again, this time with infantry support, and the Prussian cavalry quickly penetrated the Austrian rear. Simultaneously the battery of long 12-pounders was smashing the abattis to matchwood in short order and battalion after battalion was coming up to attack in echelon. The plain truth was that the 5,000 or so Austrians on Kiepern Hill had about 20,000 blue-coated Prussians on their hands, and as more of Frederick's battalions began marching across what had been their rear they gave way. All the Prussians had to do was keep rolling up the enemy line from the south.

Charles and Daun never recovered from the disaster which had so suddenly overtaken them. With their left wing gone and their fortified line hopelessly compromised, they struggled to form a new line facing south with troops taken from their right and centre. The pivot of this was to have been Leuthen, in which the church, churchyard and two windmills had been fortified. All were stormed with the bayonet in savage fighting, and the additional battalions that had been rushed into the village to reinforce the garrison, very much in the manner of Blindheim, were torn to pieces by case shot in the narrow streets. In a desperate attempt to retrieve the situation, Charles committed his right-wing cavalry in a charge against the left flank of Frederick's advancing infantry. Frederick, however, had left a considerable body of his own cavalry under General Driesen as part of his deception force. This was now standing concealed in a hollow and, just as the Austrians came under fire from the Prussian infantry, Driesen scattered them with counter-charges from front and flank.

With Leuthen gone, Charles and Daun sought to establish yet another line, but the Austrian battalions, lacking their opponents' fluidity of manoeuvre, were beaten in detail as soon as they came up, so it was never fully formed. The northward advance of the Prussians continued until dusk put an end to the fighting, whereupon the remnant of Charles' disintegrating army vanished into the darkness.

The Austrians' losses totalled 6,750 killed and wounded, 12,000 men taken prisoner, a large number of deserters, most of their artillery and 51 Colours captured. In no condition to fight another battle, they abandoned Wroclaw and evacuated Silesia. Prussian casualties were on a comparable scale, amounting to 6,400 killed and wounded.

Writing of Leuthen, Napoleon described the battle as: 'A masterpiece of movements, manoeuvres and resolution. Alone it is sufficient to immortalise Frederick and place him in the ranks of the greatest generals.'

When Frederick died in 1786 the fire of his tactical genius was extinguished in the Prussian Army, which lived on the reputation of Leuthen and other battles but was still considered to be the oracle in all matters military. Prussian drill and discipline were copied by many of Europe's armies and once again came to be regarded as an end complete in themselves. When confronted with the completely new style of warfare waged by armies fiercely motivated by revolutionary fervour, they were to prove woefully inadequate.

Commentary 7 – The Napoleonic Era

The 20-year period spanned by the French Revolutionary and Napoleonic Wars saw the weapon systems, tactics and military theories that had evolved since the Gunpowder Revolution reach the limit of their potential. As the American military historians Ernest and Trevor Dupuy stated in their *Encyclopedia of Military History*: 'The congruence of weapons, tactics and doctrine was bound to come during this half-century as a logical result of earlier developments. But the achievement was probably hastened, and certainly made more significant, through the genius of one man: Napoleon Bonaparte. No man has more indelibly stamped his personality on an era than did Napoleon. In his own time and for more than a century to come, military theory and practice were measured against his standards and related to his concepts of warmaking.' It was also the era in which the concept of dynastic struggles gave way, in France at least, to that of a nation in arms fighting for its survival.

Despite its savage excesses, to many Frenchmen the Revolution which began in 1789 conferred hitherto undreamed of freedoms which were worth defending. Naturally, the monarchies of Europe, alarmed by the revolutionaries' promise to export their creed, attempted to crush the new regime, but almost everywhere their badly led regular troops were unexpectedly worsted by ragged, barely disciplined but highly motivated French armies which fought in an entirely unconventional manner.

The infantry and cavalry regiments which the new Republic inherited from the Bourbons were led largely by promoted NCOs and junior officers, most of their former officers having either perished during the Revolution or emigrated; the artillery and engineers were less seriously affected. When the demands of the war led to the introduction of universal compulsory conscription, termed the *levée en masse*, the overall quality of the French Army dropped even further. This was partially corrected when the war minister, Lazare Carnot, decreed that each infantry regiment would consist of one former royal regular battalion and two volunteer or conscript battalions, thereby combining disciplined firepower with revolutionary fervour.

On its own, however, this was not sufficient to guarantee success against regular troops employing Fredrician linear tactics. The answer was provided by a combination of light infantry and columnar attack, with artillery support. In the past the Austrian Army had employed Croatian troops to perform its skirmishing and, as we have seen, the British developed an efficient light infantry force as a result of their experience in North America, but the efficiency of both had been allowed to decline and the lessons would have to be re-learned. Elsewhere the Prussian and Russian armies placed a lower emphasis on the value of light infantry. The French, on the other hand, recognising that motivation could be used to supplement incomplete training, employed dense swarms of skirmishers, known as *tirailleurs*, which hugged the opposing line, taking advantage of every scrap of cover. In these circumstances return volley fire was of little use and, if counter-attacked, the skirmishers simply melted away, re-formed and came back. They could of course be ridden over by cavalry, but the latter would then come under fire from the French main line and could also be countercharged.

Once a chosen sector of the enemy line had been sufficiently softened up by the *tirailleurs* or concentrated artillery fire, it was assaulted by columns. These usually consisted of battalions in linear formation but deployed in depth, one behind another. Columns were a useful means of moving semi-trained masses of men across the battlefield; they could be formed straight off the line of march, they could as quickly assume linear formation if a firefight were required, and they also provided an attack with great physical and psychological weight. An enemy line, it was quickly discovered, was unwilling to withstand the shock of a dense column bearing down upon it through the mass of *tirailleurs*. The column, however, did have its disadvantages. It made an excellent target for opposing artillery and musketry fire, its own firepower was restricted to the leading two or three ranks, and those in front were well aware that they would become early casualties.

The success of these tactics, coupled with an overall improvement in the quality of the new Republic's army stemming from the experience gained, led to them being adopted as standard operational procedures. As a result, although some French regiments were designated 'light' and specialised in the skirmishing role, all French infantry were capable of fighting either in open order as *tirailleurs* or performing columnar tactics. With the exception of the British, the system was adopted by all European armies. Nevertheless the French had a further ace up their sleeve in that they possessed far greater mobility. Lacking an efficient supply organisation, they simply lived off the land, as the Mongols had done, and while this made them few friends it enabled them to cover far greater distances than could their opponents in the same period. Later, supply trains did follow the army, but as the rations they carried were issued only in an emergency, foraging remained the order of the day.

History confirms that successful revolutionaries, only too aware of the dangers posed by their former comrades, turn on one another until only the most ruthless survive. In France the story was the same, and as the country was almost continuously at war it was inevitable that a military man should emerge at the top of the pile. Napoleon Bonaparte, a Corsican by birth, had entered the former royal army and

been commissioned into the artillery. Good fortune had sometimes placed him in the right place at the right time, but he also showed himself to be one of the republic's most successful and charismatic field commanders. A brilliant strategist, tactician, administrator and organiser, he was driven by such burning desire for personal advancement that in 1804 he crowned himself Emperor of the French and was gladly accepted by his subjects as such.

In the field of military organisation Napoleon introduced the corps, a large formation the size of which had not been seen since the Mongol era. The brigade, consisting of two or more regiments, had existed in the 18th century as, to a lesser extent, had the division, consisting of two or more brigades, plus artillery. In 1794 Carnot introduced a divisional organisation consisting of two to three infantry brigades, each of three regiments, two artillery batteries, a cavalry unit for reconnaissance, and divisional services. The division thus became an all-arms battlegroup capable of independent action if need arose. The corps introduced by Napoleon was an extension of the idea, consisting of two to four infantry divisions, a brigade or division of cavalry, artillery, engineers and supporting services. Cavalry divisions and corps were also formed with the respective proportions of infantry to cavalry being reversed. Divisions and corps each had their own staffs, thereby contributing to the overall efficiency of the army. The system was copied by the Austrian, Prussian and Russian armies, but once again did not find favour with the British, who continued to operate in brigades until they formed divisions during the Peninsular War (1807–14).

The corps was fundamental to Napoleon's strategy. He was adept at concentrating his corps on the battlefield at the critical moment, even if they had marched from widely separated starting-points. Once in contact, one or more corps would be deployed to fix an enemy army in position; the remainder, by virtue of his troops' mobility would manoeuvre against the enemy's flank or rear to occupy a strong position straddling his lines of communication, so forcing him either to fight at a disadvantage or capitulate. When faced with the converging advance of two enemy armies, as was frequently the case, he would take a central position between them, using one corps to fight a holding action against the first while he concentrated superior numbers to defeat the second; then, detaching a corps to pursue the latter, he would march with the remainder to overwhelm the first. In this way many of his battles were won before they had begun. With him, the pursuit after a victory was a strategic rather than a tactical operation, to be carried on until the enemy army had been harried to the verge of extinction.

Tactically, Napoleon was not a great innovator, being content to use the tools he had inherited from the previous century. For example, despite the panoramic view they gave across the entire battlefield, he had little time for hot-air observation balloons because they took so long to prepare. In addition to its traditional roles of reconnaissance and shock action, his cavalry was used in battle to attack the enemy infantry, forcing it to form square, thereby not only reducing its frontal firepower but also making it a better target for his artillery; to exploit any gap in the enemy line by pouring through it *en masse* to complete the rout; and to carry out a relentless pursuit. With his artillery he would sometimes form Grand Batteries, massing guns to concentrate their fire on the sector of the enemy line chosen for his decisive attack.

Prior to Waterloo, Napoleon had a very limited experience of fighting the British and he could not understand why his Marshals were so frequently worsted by them. In fact, during the early phases of the war against Revolutionary France, the British had fared no better than their continental allies, largely because the armed services had, as usual, been criminally neglected in time of peace. Reforms instituted by the Duke of York set much to rights, and under the able and far-sighted General Sir John Moore the light infantry tactics learned in North America were revived and adopted by a number of regiments who would distinguish themselves, including the green-clad 95th Regiment, later the Rifle Brigade, equipped with the efficient Baker rifle. More rifle and light infantry units were formed from the exiles serving with the King's German Legion and from the allied Portuguese Army whose training became a British responsibility. During the Peninsular War in Portugal, Spain and southern France, Wellington reinforced each infantry brigade's three light companies with an additional rifle company and, together, these proved to be more than a match for the French *tirailleurs*.

The British infantry relied on firepower and to maximise its effect they adopted a two-deep firing line. Wellington frequently positioned this just behind a crest on a reverse slope to shelter his men from the worst of the French artillery fire. Thus when an attacking French column reached the crest after advancing blindly up the forward slope because its skirmishers had been unable to make headway, it found itself unexpectedly confronting long scarlet ranks. A series of crisp volleys would blow away the column's head and one or more battalions might wheel out of the British line to rake its flanks. As soon as the French showed signs of wavering the British would cheer and attack with the bayonet, driving them down the slope in disorder. The pursuit would be maintained for about 100 yards, after which the British would return to their position.

Serving as a regimental officer with the French in the Peninsula was the future Marshal Bugeaud, who was later to win fame during France's campaigns in North Africa, and to him we owe the following frequently quoted account of such an attack:

'The men would get restless and excited; they exchanged ideas with each other; their march began to be somewhat precipitate and was already growing a little disorderly. Meanwhile the English, silent and impassive, with grounded arms, loomed like a long red wall; their aspect was imposing – it impressed novices not a little. Soon the distance began to grow shorter; cries of "*Vive l'Empereur! En avant! A la baïonnette!*" broke from our mass. Some

115

men hoisted their shakos on their muskets. The quick step became a run; the ranks began to be mixed up; the men's agitation became tumultuous; many soldiers began to fire as they ran. And all the while the red English line, still silent and motionless even when we were only 300 yards away, seemed to take no notice of the storm which was about to beat upon it. The contrast was striking. More than one among us began to reflect that the enemy's fire, so long reserved, would be very unpleasant when it did break forth. Our ardour began to cool; the moral influence – irresistible in action – of a calm which seems undisturbed as opposed to disorder, which strives to make up by noise what it lacks in firmness, weighed heavily on our hearts.

'At this moment of painful expectation the English line would make a quarter turn. The muskets were going up to the "ready". An indefinable sensation nailed to the spot many of our men, who halted and opened a wavering fire. The enemy's return, a volley of simultaneous precision and deadly effect, crashed in among us like a thunderbolt. Decimated by it, we reeled together, staggering under the blow, and trying to recover our equilibrium. The three formidable "Hurrahs!" ended the long silence of our adversaries. With the third they were down upon us, pressing us into a disorderly retreat. But they did not pursue their advantage for more than some hundred yards, and went back with calm to their former lines to await a further attack."

History never repeats itself in quite the same way, but in these battles it is possible to see the shades of the English longbowmen.

In the Peninsula the French were also confronted by another type of opponent with whom they were unable to deal effectively. The Spanish Army, of mixed quality and poorly led, rarely provided serious opposition, but the Spanish people bitterly resented French occupation and waged an effective partisan warfare from which sprang the word 'guerrilla'. They preyed constantly upon convoys and isolated detachments with the result that thousands of French troops had to be detached from the field armies to guard their lines of communication. As might be expected, when regular troops were opposed by armed civilians not bound by the conventions of war, both sides acted with increasing savagery in the cycle of atrocity and reprisal.

Although the tools of land warfare had altered little from Fredrician times, they had been improved. As a result of Napoleon's experience in eastern Europe, lancer regiments were re-introduced in some western armies, notably the French. Lancers were deadly when employed against broken troops or in a pursuit, but they were of little use against an unbroken infantry square and, after the first shock, their weapons were actually a handicap in a close cavalry mêlée. Nevertheless the fad for them would continue until cavalry itself finally disappeared. It was the artillery which benefited most from these improvements. In 1765 a French officer, Jean-Baptiste de Gribeauval, had begun to rationalise the arm. In addition to categorising guns for horse, field and heavy batteries, he reduced the weight of the pieces, strengthened their carriages, introduced limbers and caissons and provided elevating screws to increase accurate laying. Under Gribeauval, the drivers whose teams hauled the guns became soldiers rather than, as hitherto, civilians hired for the job. Draught horses were harnessed in double files instead of in tandem. These reforms increased the artillery's mobility to the point where the infantry's little battalion guns became superfluous. By the Napoleonic era all first-rate armies had adopted Gribeauval's system in one form or another. Further improvements included prefabricated cartridges to raise the rate of fire and more precisely cast shot to increase accuracy. In 1784 Lieutenant Henry Shrapnel of the Royal Artillery invented the type of ammunition which still bears his name, consisting of a hollow shell filled with balls surrounding a fused bursting charge; the fuse was calculated to explode the charge short of and above the target, breaking open the shell, and the balls continued along their original trajectory at a slightly increased velocity that ensured most would hit the target. In 1804 Colonel Sir William Congreve began developing the rocket for military use. His rockets were of different sizes and carried a variety of warheads including shot, shell, shrapnel and incendiary. Their comparatively long range was offset by chronic inaccuracy, but they were very useful when it came to bombarding area targets. During the later phases of the Napoleonic Wars rockets were used by the British Army and to a greater extent by the Royal Navy.

Naval warfare had changed little since Drake established the warship as a sailing gun-platform. Since the defeat of the Spanish Armada the warship had simply evolved as a result of experience, so that by the Napoleonic era it was difficult to see how hulls and sail plans could be further improved. The line-of-battle ships were vessels with two or three gundecks, the heavier guns being mounted lowest within the hull and the lightest on the upper deck. They were classified by the number of guns they carried, which varied from a 50-gun 'fourth-rate' to a 'first-rate' with 110 or more guns. The ammunition fired included round-shot, grape and canister, and chain or bar shot for tearing through an enemy's rigging. Fleet engagements usually consisted of the opposing lines running parallel and battering each other at close range. In this respect the Royal Navy operated at a distinct advantage after the introduction of the carronade during the War of American Independence. The carronade was a stubby, short-range gun which threw a heavy ball, and was mounted on a sliding carriage that absorbed much of the recoil. It therefore required a smaller crew than a conventional cannon and had a higher rate of fire. Such was the damage caused by these weapons that they became known as 'smashers'. But while warships' sides were constructed to absorb a great deal of punishment, catastrophic damage could be caused by firing broadsides through an opponent's less protected bow or stern, a process known as raking. Because of this, the Royal Navy always sought to obtain the weather gauge and engage from the enemy's windward side, enabling ships to turn towards

and break through their opponents' line, which would be given a severe raking in the process.

Since the Armada, the Royal Navy had fought the Dutch, the Spanish and others, but mostly the French. Save for a few brief periods, it had established control over the oceans of the world. Under its protection an empire based on trade had developed and the United Kingdom had prospered. Despite the debt owed to the Navy, and the fact that it was by far the more popular of the two armed services, few men were willing to volunteer for the harsh life aboard a warship in time of war. Consequently, to man their ships captains employed entirely legal press gangs to impress merchant seamen and others ashore, while at sea they were not averse to picking up a man or two from passing merchant vessels. Pressed men were subject to naval discipline and remained with their ship until it was paid off. Once they had accepted the situation, they fought as hard and well as the volunteers and took as much pride in their ship's achievements. They could be rewarded with prize money from their captures which, under an enterprising captain, could amount to a considerable sum. Even so, desertion was so constant a problem that only trusted men were allowed ashore.

As a result of the Revolution the French Navy lost most of its professional class of officers who were replaced by men drawn from the merchant service. The new arrivals were competent enough seamen, but they were inexperienced in such matters as naval administration, gunnery and tactics. Furthermore, the navy being considered of less importance than the army, its claims upon resources and manpower had a lower priority, and, because its ships were frequently blockaded in harbour for long periods by the British, the efficiency of their crews' seamanship and gunnery inevitably declined. For example, constant practice might enable a British gun crew to get off ten rounds to the French crew's six or seven. Naturally, the cumulative effect was such that the British emerged the victors in the majority of fleet actions and single-ship duels. Having completed whatever mission they had been set,

117

therefore, the priority for French commanders was to return to harbour and so preserve their fleet in being. If intercepted, they tended to fire on the upward roll in the hope of so damaging their opponent's rigging that they would be able to make good their escape; the British, on the other hand, directed the weight of their fire into the French hull so as to cause the maximum damage and casualties.

In addition to ships-of-the-line, the navies of the period also employed frigates and sloops. The frigates, which nominally mounted 28–40 guns, had excellent sailing qualities which enabled them to act as the eyes of the fleet, although they were regularly employed on detached duties. Sloops were smaller and carried a variety of rig. They mounted fewer guns than the frigates, though never less than ten, and acted as maids of all work, providing convoy escorts and carrying out independent patrols. Specialist ships employed by the Royal Navy during this period included bomb vessels, mounting one or two heavy mortars, which were used for inshore bombardment, joined latterly by rocket ships. These were the only classes of warship to fire explosive projectiles, the storage of which within wooden hulls naturally required special precautions.

Just as the figures of Napoleon and Wellington bestrode the war on land, so did that of Admiral Horatio Nelson dominate the war at sea. Nelson had entered the Royal Navy as a boy and had risen to command of a ship-of-the-line when the Revolutionary Wars began. As we have seen, fleet actions had hitherto begun with the opposing battle lines running parallel to each other, in accordance with the Admiralty's 'Fighting Instructions'. Nelson took the sensible view that these instructions represented advice rather than inviolable doctrine and that tactics should be dictated by circumstances. He was not the first to do so, but at the Battle of Cape St Vincent (1797) he took the revolutionary step of turning his ship out of the line to prevent the escape of a major part of the Spanish fleet, thereby inducing a mêlée, his decision being promptly supported by the fleet commander,

Admiral Sir John Jervis, later Lord St Vincent. In 1798 Nelson wrecked Napoleon's Middle Eastern strategy by destroying the French fleet at the Battle of the Nile. In 1801 he destroyed the potentially hostile Danish fleet at Copenhagen, affecting not to see the signal to withdraw hoisted by his immediate superior at the height of this bitterly contested action. It was Nelson's conviction that in any mêlée superior British ship handling and gunnery, assisted by the improved flag signalling system recently introduced, would always win the day. The truth of this was demonstrated off Cape Trafalgar on 21 October 1805 by the destruction of the Combined Franco–Spanish fleet. Nelson was killed in the battle, but, as we shall see, his work was complete.

TRAFALGAR, 21 OCTOBER 1805

Following the collapse of the short-lived Peace of Amiens, Napoleon made extensive preparations for the invasion of England, concentrating his *Grande Armée* at Boulogne and assembling the necessary shipping at the mouths of the Rhine. Only a score or so of miles separated him from the south coast of England, but obtaining control of this narrow strip of water for the period of the crossing was a problem which he was no closer to solving than had been Philip II of Spain. As the distinguished American naval historian Alfred T. Mahan says in his *Influence of Sea Power upon the French Revolution and Empire*: 'Those far distant, storm-beaten ships (of the Royal Navy), upon which the Great Army never looked, stood between it and the domination of the world.'

Napoleon's genius did not extend to sea power, but he understood enough about the subject to recognise that if an attempt were made to wrest control of the Channel by direct force the chances of success were remote. On the other hand, if the Channel Fleet and other British naval resources could be decoyed away from the area for long enough, it would be possible for the combined French and Spanish fleets to achieve the local superiority necessary to cover the passage of the invasion force.

Right: Vice Admiral Viscount Horatio Nelson. *Katz Pictures Ltd*

He therefore put together a plan, the first phase of which called for Vice-Admiral Pierre Villeneuve to break through the British blockade off Toulon, cross the Atlantic to reinforce France's West Indian garrisons, then sail back to attack the blockading vessels off Ferrol and Rochefort. Simultaneously, an 18,000-strong military force would be shipped to Ireland in the hope of distracting the British to the extent that Admiral Honoré Ganteaume's squadron would be able to break out of Brest. Together Villeneuve and Ganteaume would have some 40 ships of the line at their disposal, more than enough to convoy the army to England and fend off any attempted intervention by the Royal Navy. The plan, evolved on the map table without due consideration of the practicalities involved, was overcomplicated, absurdly ambitious and relied heavily on luck.

Nevertheless its early phases were successful. On 25 March 1805 Villeneuve wrong-footed Nelson's Mediterranean Fleet off Toulon with eleven ships of the line, seven frigates and a number of troop transports. After passing through the Straits of Gibraltar, he was joined by several Spanish ships off Cadiz and headed out into the Atlantic; on 14 May he reached Martinique where he received further reinforcements. Nelson, with ten ships, had followed as soon as he was able to verify Villeneuve's destination, but no sooner had he reached the West Indies than the French admiral set off back across the Atlantic.

Meanwhile Napoleon's master plan was beginning to come unstuck. The Irish diversion came to naught and, although the Rochefort squadron broke out, Ganteaume declined to fight his way out of Brest until Villeneuve put in an appearance. Worse still, an 18-strong British squadron under Rear-Admiral Sir Robert Calder, which was positioned off Cape Finisterre, intercepted Villeneuve's Franco–Spanish combined fleet on 22 July and captured two of the ships. While Calder was criticised by those at home for not doing better, his action effectively destroyed whatever remaining chance of success the plan might have had, at least in Villeneuve's opinion. The Combined Fleet took refuge in Ferrol and then moved south to Cadiz where it was reinforced to a total of 33 ships of the line.

On his return to European waters Nelson took his fleet into Gibraltar and, leaving his second in command, Vice-Admiral Cuthbert Collingwood, to watch Villeneuve in Cadiz, left for a month's leave in England. Napoleon's plan had failed, but even if it had succeeded it is debatable whether he would have mounted an invasion because other matters now claimed his urgent attention. Austria, Russia and Sweden had joined England to form the Third Coalition and the *Grande Armée* was required elsewhere. On 31 August the troops began to quit the invasion-camps around Boulogne in secrecy and headed eastwards, to the scenes of their greatest victories.

Despite this the Combined Fleet posed too great a threat to be neglected. Collingwood had been steadily reinforced and when Nelson rejoined off Cadiz he brought with him a plan for the destruction of Villeneuve's command. The facilities at Cadiz, he knew, could not support a force the size of the Combined Fleet for long; sooner or later it would either have to put to sea or cease to exist as a fighting entity. When Villeneuve did come out, Nelson intended to break his line with two columns which would penetrate its centre and rear, inducing a mêlée. This would offset his opponents' numerical superiority because it would isolate the van which would have to reverse course before it could join the action. Even with a favourable wind this would take invaluable time during which immense damage could be inflicted. Nelson briefed his captains carefully on what would be required of them, but, well aware that confusion was the norm in battle, added a rider to his orders: 'In case signals can neither be seen nor perfectly understood, no captain can do very wrong if he places his ship alongside that of an enemy.'

All that remained now was to wait. To conceal the strength of his own fleet Nelson remained out of sight of land but deployed his frigates inshore where they could observe and signal the enemy's movements.

Villeneuve was not a happy man. The transatlantic passages had revealed deficiencies in crew training that could not be corrected in the short term. His Spanish allies were unhelpful and reluctant to supply him. His failure to comply with the final part of the plan had incurred Napoleon's wrath and would result in an accusation of cowardice. At length he received orders to take the Combined Fleet into the Mediterranean where the 4,000 troops aboard were to be landed in southern Italy in support of Marshal Masséna's operations. To make matters worse the commander of these troops, General Alexandre Lauriston, an honorary aide-de-camp of Napoleon's, conspired against him in his own flagship, writing frequent critical letters direct to the Emperor. Finally, having been warned that he was to be dismissed, Villeneuve decided to put to sea before his replacement arrived.

During the afternoon of 19 October Nelson's frigates reported that the Combined Fleet was coming out. Next day they signalled that it had turned south towards the Straits of Gibraltar and Nelson conformed. At about 4 a.m. on the 21st the British line turned east to intercept. First light revealed the enemy some ten miles' distant, still heading south. At 7 o'clock Nelson signalled his ships to form two columns in accordance with the earlier briefing. An hour later Villeneuve ordered his fleet to reverse course to a northerly heading. This decision was taken to prevent the faint-hearted escaping through the open waters of the Straits of Gibraltar; instead, they were now confronted with the dangerous shoals off Cape Trafalgar to leeward, a situation which virtually guaranteed their continued presence in the battle line. The day was grey, the wind light from west-north-west and there was a swell that presaged a storm.

Nelson had 27 ships of the line at his disposal. He personally led the eleven-strong port column in the 100-gun *Victory*; Collingwood led the starboard column of fifteen ships in *Royal Sovereign*, also of 100 guns; one ship, the small 64-gun *Africa*, had become separated during the night and was some way to the north, beyond the line of frigates and smaller vessels running to port of Nelson's column.

Because of the light wind the approach was slow, the ships slopping along at between two and three knots. During such hours the mind becomes concentrated and perhaps Nelson had a premonition of his own death. He amended his will and wrote a short prayer requesting that an honourable victory should be followed by humanity on the part of his fleet; when repeatedly asked to remove the glittering orders from his uniform as these would instantly identify him to every enemy marksman, he refused; and as the captain of the frigate *Euryalus* left *Victory* to return to his own ship Nelson shook his hand, saying 'God bless you, Blackwood, I shall never speak to

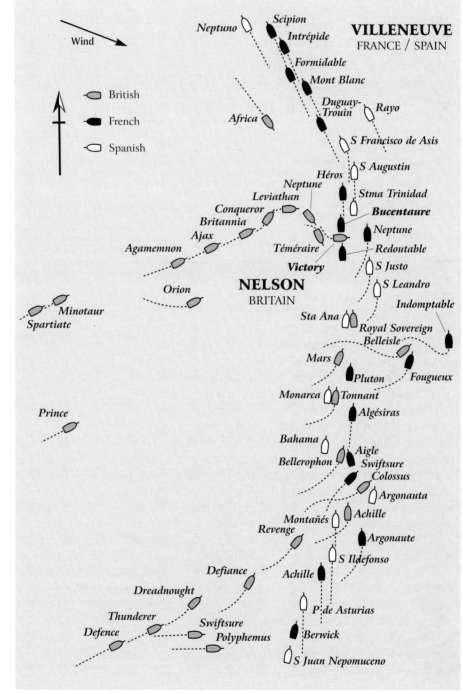

Wind

British

French

Spanish

Neptuno
Scipion
Intrépide
VILLENEUVE
FRANCE / SPAIN
Formidable
Mont Blanc
Duguay-Trouin
Rayo
Africa
S Francisco de Asis
S Augustin
Héros
Stma Trinidad
Neptune
Leviathan
Bucentaure
Conqueror
Neptune
Britannia
Ajax
Redoutable
Agamemnon
Téméraire
S Justo
Victory
S Leandro
Orion
NELSON
Indomptable
BRITAIN
Sta Ana
Minotaur
Royal Sovereign
Spartiate
Belleisle
Mars
Pluton
Fougueux
Monarca
Tonnant
Bahama
Algésiras
Prince
Aigle
Bellerophon
Swiftsure
Colossus
Argonauta
Achille
Montañés
Argonaute
Revenge
S Ildefonso
Defiance
Achille
Dreadnought
P de Asturias
Thunderer
Swiftsure
Defence
Polyphemus
Berwick
S Juan Nepomuceno

TRAFALGAR, 21 October 1805 at approximately 13.00 hours
(after Warner)

Left: Trafalgar. By breaking the enemy line in two places Nelson induced the sort of mêlée in which he knew British close-quarter gunnery would prove superior. *Philip Haythornthwaite Collecton*

you again.' At 11.40 a.m. he hoisted the signal 'ENGLAND EXPECTS THAT EVERY MAN WILL DO HIS DUTY', which was greeted with cheering throughout the fleet.

Nelson's column preserved its line-ahead formation, but Collingwood ordered his ships to form a line of bearing, that is, echeloned to the right so that they would strike the Franco–Spanish line in different places in succession. The grey of early morning had been replaced by brilliant sunshine as the two columns closed on the Combined Fleet's line, which straggled five miles from van to rear. At about noon the nearest enemy ships opened a heavy fire on *Victory* and *Royal Sovereign*. Nelson promptly hoisted the signal 'ENGAGE THE ENEMY MORE CLOSELY.'

Collingwood was the first to break the opposing line. At 12.10 *Royal Sovereign* passed between *Santa Ana* and *Fougueux*, raking both with double-shotted broadsides which caused some 400 casualties. Unconcernedly munching an apple, Collingwood tidily tossed the core through *Santa Ana*'s shattered stern windows as his quarterdeck slid slowly past. *Royal Sovereign* then turned to port and laid herself alongside *Santa Ana*. For the next fifteen minutes she fought a furious battle alone against *Santa Ana*, *Fougueux*, *Indomptable*, *San Justo* and *San*

Leandro. In their excitement the allies' fire was causing as much damage to one another as to *Royal Sovereign*, and with the arrival of *Bellisle*, the second ship in Collingwood's column, they sheered off.

A little to the north, *Victory* had taken fearful punishment during her approach. She had come under fire at 12.20 and this had increased steadily in its intensity. Her wheel had been smashed so that she had to be steered by the huge tiller in the gunroom, her mizzen topmast had been cut in two, her foremast studding-sail booms were shot away and every one of her sails was riddled with holes. Her intention was to break the enemy line astern of Villeneuve's flagship *Bucentaure*, but when he observed that the gap was rapidly being closed by *Redoutable*, Captain Thomas Hardy, commanding *Victory*, warned Nelson that a collision with one or both enemy ships was inevitable; the Admiral left the choice to him. At 12.59 *Victory*'s double- and treble-shotted port-side guns began raking *Bucentaure*'s stern, causing 400 casualties and overturning 20 guns. Simultaneously, *Victory* received a raking from the French *Neptune*, dead ahead, though its effects were by no means as serious. *Redoutable* had put her helm to starboard but at 1.10 *Victory* ploughed into her. The rigging of

Right: Trafalgar. W. L. Wyllie's painting showing (left) HMS *Temeraire* closely engaged with all-but dismasted French *Redoutable* (centre) and (right) wreckage from the Spanish *Santissima Trinidad*. In the background the rear of the British line closes in on the action.

the two ships became entangled and they swung together.

The 74-gun *Redoutable* was commanded by Captain Jean-Jacques Lucas, the French Navy's smallest captain and probably its fiercest. He had little faith in his crew's ability to match British gunnery, but had given them extensive training in musketry and boarding techniques. They immediately opened such a heavy fire, augmented by hand-grenades and two small brass guns firing scrap iron from the main and foretops, that *Victory*'s upper deck gunners were forced to seek cover. At 1.25 Nelson, who had continued to pace the quarterdeck beside Hardy, fell to a marksman positioned in *Redoutable*'s mizzen top. He was immediately carried below but the wound was mortal. The soldier who fired the shot was almost certainly killed by Midshipman John Pollard, who seized a musket and began systematically picking off the men in the enemy tops until none remained.

Only minutes after Nelson was hit Lucas ordered his boarders away. Some ran to *Redoutable*'s gangways, where they were swept away by *Victory*'s starboard 68-pounder

Right: Trafalgar. On the *Victory*'s quarterdeck Nelson is mortally wounded by a sharpshooter in the tops of the adjacent *Redoutable. Philip Haythornthwaite Collection*

123

carronade firing grape; others ran forward, their rush being matched by that of *Victory*'s marines and seamen, but were prevented from boarding partly because of the latter's fire and partly because of the gap presented by the two ships' inward sloping upper hulls, known as the tumble-home. Simultaneously, the gun crews on *Victory*'s lower decks were directing a savage fire into *Redoutable*'s hull and also engaging *Bucentaure* to port. Nevertheless Lucas persisted in his attempts to board and ordered his main yard to be lowered so that it would form a bridge between the two ships, but before this could be done there was a jarring impact and a further explosion of gunfire to starboard. *Téméraire*, the second ship in Nelson's column, had passed through the allied line at about 1.40, taking severe punishment from the French *Neptune* as she did so, and come alongside *Redoutable*. Shortly afterwards, Lucas, who had fought his ship to the limit, made an honourable surrender. He had a fire aboard which his captors helped bring under control, and of the 643 officers and men forming his crew 490 had been killed and 81 wounded. *Victory*'s casualties totalled 57 killed and 102 wounded.

The Combined Fleet's line had been broken in two places and, as Nelson intended, a mêlée ensued. The remainder of the battle, therefore, becomes the story of each individual ship's part in it. The British ships, approaching the maelstrom of powder smoke and gunfire at a slow walking pace, initially found themselves engaged with two or even three opponents, as had *Royal Sovereign* and *Victory*, but as more ships arrived and enemy vessels began striking their Colours the odds began to tilt steadily in favour of the British. By the time the last British ship got into action, at about 3.30, the issue had been decided. An exception to the general experience was that of *Africa*, which sailed down the length of the allied van exchanging broadsides with much larger opponents. Pausing alongside the huge *Santissima Trinidad* which, with 130 guns, had more than twice her firepower, she impertinently sent a lieutenant across to ask whether the Spaniard had surrendered. She had not, so *Africa* continued on her way to duel with *Intrépide* (74) which was eventually subdued with the help of *Orion*.

Shortly before 2 o'clock Villeneuve had hoisted a signal for those allied ships not yet engaged to converge on the mêlée. Not all his commanders, however, were as belligerent as Lucas. Some of them put up a terrific fight but

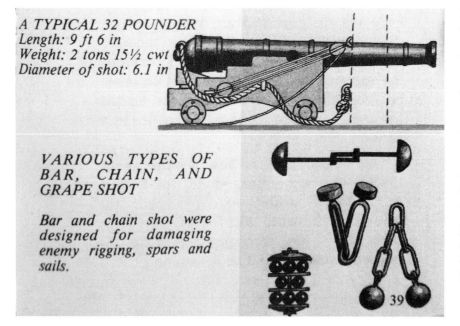

A TYPICAL 32 POUNDER
Length: 9 ft 6 in
Weight: 2 tons 15½ cwt
Diameter of shot: 6.1 in

VARIOUS TYPES OF BAR, CHAIN, AND GRAPE SHOT

Bar and chain shot were designed for damaging enemy rigging, spars and sails.

Left: Naval gun and carriage of the period showing tackle used to haul the weapon in and out of the gunport and breech-ropes to contain the recoil. Normal ammunition was a sold ball but, as shown, various types of shot could be employed against an enemy's rigging; grape shot was a close-quarter anti-personnel round producing an effect like a large shotgun.

others were less interested. Any chance of retrieving the situation rested with Rear-Admiral Dumanoir Le Pelley in *Formidable*, who commanded the allied van. Apart from the passing attentions of *Africa*, the van had remained unmolested while Nelson and Collingwood's columns were savaging the centre and rear. However, the light wind made it so difficult for his ships to go about that some of them used their boats to tow their heads round; others ignored the order and headed for the safety of Cadiz. At length Dumanoir, with four other ships, was in a position from which he might have intervened, but by then *Bucentaure* had struck and, her boats having been knocked to pieces, Villeneuve, unable to transfer his flag, was a prisoner aboard her. Furthermore, although Dumanoir was unaware of the fact, Admiral Gravina, commanding the allied rear, had been mortally wounded and his flagship, *Principe de Asturias*, could be seen leading eleven survivors from the centre and rear towards Cadiz. Prudently, Dumanoir skirted the dying battle and disappeared to the south, but not before the Spanish *Neptuno* had been cut off and forced to surrender at 5.10 p.m. by *Minotaur* and *Spartiate*.

Before he died Nelson was informed that he had won a great victory. Seventeen badly battered French and Spanish ships had surrendered and another, the French *Achille*, had caught fire and exploded. Franco–Spanish casualties included perhaps 8,000 killed and wounded and some 20,000 prisoners. British casualties totalled 437 killed and 1,242 wounded. About half the British fleet was in a severely damaged condition, some ships being wholly or partially dismasted.

There were several sequels to the battle which really form part of the story. During the night the expected gale sprang up and lasted throughout the following day. Every effort was made to save the French wounded and crew aboard *Redoutable*, but more lives were lost when she foundered, and when *Fougueux* was driven ashore only 25 men survived the wreck. Struggling short-handed against the sea, the exhausted prize crews in *Algéciras* and *Bucentaure* had to call on their prisoners for assistance and inevitably the two ships changed hands again, the former to escape into Cadiz while the latter piled herself up on the Puercos rocks.

On the morning of 23 October, with the gale still blowing, Commodore Cosmao-Kerjulien, the senior French naval officer at Cadiz, put to sea with a view to recovering more of the prizes. With him he had the most seaworthy vessels left to the Combined Fleet, including five ships of the line (*Pluton*, 74, *Indomptable*, 80, *Neptune*, 84, *Rayo*, 100, and *San Francisco de Asis*, 74), five frigates and two brigs. At about noon he found himself confronted by ten British ships and declined an engagement, although his frigates succeeded in recapturing *Neptuno* and *Santa Ana* from their prize crews. Ultimately, however, the sortie proved a complete disaster. On the 24th *Indomptable* ran aground off Rota and was pounded to wreckage by the Atlantic rollers; *San Francisco* also grounded in Cadiz Bay and when, to avoid the fate of her consorts, *Rayo* dropped anchor off San Lucar, she rolled her masts out and was forced to surrender to the newly arrived *Donegal*; two days later she too ran aground and was wrecked. The 24th also saw *Santissima Trinidad* scuttled at Collingwood's order and that night *Monarca* sank. The following night *Aigle* was wrecked off Puerto Santa Maria. Subsequently, *Intrépide*, *San Augustin* and *Argonauta* were considered to be not worth saving and were either burned or scuttled, and *Berwick* was wrecked off San Lucar. Collingwood was therefore left with only four prizes: *San Ildefonso*, the French *Swiftsure*, *Bahama* and *San Juan de Nepomuceno*. Having dispatched the schooner *Pickle* home with news of the victory, he offered to send the allied wounded into Cadiz, thereby relieving the fleet's surgeons of an immense burden. The offer was gratefully accepted and accompanied by the return of the British prize crews.

There remained a little tidying up to do. It will be recalled that in the closing stages of the battle Rear-Admiral Dumanoir had escaped to the south with four ships: *Duguay-Trouin*, 74, *Formidable*, 65, *Mont Blanc*, 74, and *Scipion*, 74. His first thought had been to make for Toulon, but knowing that a British squadron was operating near the Straits of Gibraltar he decided to try for one of the French Atlantic ports. It was his misfortune that the Rochefort squadron was still at sea and substantial British naval forces were searching for it, directly in his path. On 2 November he was spotted by the frigate *Phoenix*, to which he gave chase, only to find that he was being led straight into the arms of a British squadron commanded by Captain Sir Richard Strachan, cruising off Ferrol. This consisted of five ships of the line (*Caesar*, 80, *Hero*, 74, *Courageux*, 74, *Namur*, 74, and *Bellona*, 74) plus several frigates. Dumanoir reversed course and a protracted pursuit ensued, lasting throughout the night and the following day and night, during which the slow *Bellona* was left far behind. At noon on 4 November Dumanoir accepted battle. Once again British gunnery inflicted terrible punishment and at 3.35 p.m. the last of his ships struck her Colours. French losses totalled 750 killed and wounded, Dumanoir being among the latter; the British had 24 men killed and 111 wounded. The four prizes were taken into Plymouth and were later accepted for service with the Royal Navy. The Combined Fleet had virtually ceased to exist, its sad remnant continuing to rot in Cadiz harbour until Spain rebelled against Napoleon in 1808.

Of the protagonists at Trafalgar, Nelson received a hero's funeral; the government ignored his request to take care of Lady Hamilton but a later administration did provide some discreet support for their daughter Horatia. The unfortunate Villeneuve was taken to England but was repatriated on parole the following spring. Only days after his arrival in France he met a violent end in a hotel room at Rennes. Officially, he took his own life, but the presence of five stab wounds suggests otherwise and the Emperor's name became associated with his death.

Trafalgar marked the end of Spain as a first-class naval power. It also rendered dubious any further plans Napoleon might have conceived for the invasion of England, although he continued to build up the French Navy. Rather than risk further fleet actions, however, the Emperor preferred to prey upon British commerce, using naval vessels as well as privateers. He also sought to inflict further economic damage with his Continental System, which attempted to exclude British merchandise from mainland Europe. The system leaked like a sieve, partly because of widespread smuggling and partly because many people chose to ignore it. Ultimately, it was to provide one of the primary causes of the Peninsular War which Napoleon himself was to call 'the Spanish ulcer'. Most of all, Trafalgar was to emphasise British dominance at sea in both the naval and mercantile spheres, a position that was to be retained for the next 140 years.

AUSTERLITZ, 2 DECEMBER 1805

On paper, the plans of the Third Coalition were impressive. Hanover was to be liberated by a joint British, Swedish and Russian operation. France's ally, Bavaria, was to be occupied by an 85,000-strong Austrian army under Quartermaster General Mack and Archduke Ferdinand, to be reinforced with 85,000 Russians under General Mikhail Kutusov. In northern Italy, which was incorrectly believed to loom large in Napoleon's plans, were 100,000 men under Archduke Charles, Austria's most gifted commander. In the Tyrol another 25,000 Austrians under Archduke John were available to support either Mack or Charles as the situation demanded. Farther afield, British, Russian and Sicilian troops were to reconquer southern Italy then march north to join Charles. Simultaneously, the British were to raid the French and Dutch coasts and support a planned royalist rising in Brittany. If co-ordinated, these various ventures might have produced substantial dividends, but therein lay numerous difficulties which were largely ignored, not least the Russians' use of the old-style calendar with its 12-day difference. Even more unfortunate was the fact that French intelligence was aware of Allied intentions and Napoleon was planning a pre-emptive offensive of his own.

The *Grande Armée* had begun marching eastwards from Boulogne at the end of August, its time on the Channel coast having been spent on training, honing co-operation between arms and developing an *esprit de corps* that owed much to the troops' devotion to the Emperor. At this time it was probably the finest army that France had ever produced.

The armies it was to fight were of lesser quality and had still not fully completed the transition from 18th-century warfare. The Imperial and Royal Austrian Army in particular suffered from a number of disadvantages stemming from its innate conservatism. For example, it still employed the proprietary regimental system; its infantry still delivered volley fire in linear ranks three deep, supplemented by small regimental guns; having failed to adopt the Gribeauval artillery system, its cannon were heavier than those of the French, and the horse teams were still hired from civilians. As a whole, the artillery was under-recruited to the extent that without drafts from the infantry it was unable to man its guns. Further disadvantages stemmed from the army's being recruited from the Empire's many races in central Europe, the Balkans

and Italy, as well as an over-complicated bureaucratic administration

As Chief of Staff, Mack had striven, with limited success, to reform the army in the teeth of strong opposition. The series of unsuccessful wars against France had left the country all but insolvent, and the halving of military expenditure in 1804 had helped him not at all; nor did the constant meddling of his princely masters in the internal organisation of formations. Since the cavalry was relatively efficient, his principal efforts were directed at reconstructing the infantry and artillery, but his revised regulations were not introduced until June 1805

Right: The Emperor
Napoleon I. *Katz Pictures Ltd*

and had only been partially implemented when the new war began. One such, induced by the disbandment of the supply trains as an economy measure, was that on campaign the army should live off the country in the French manner; the result was that the troops often went hungry, and military supplies went undelivered because of the shortage of horse teams.

The Imperial Russian Army was similar to that of Austria in that it had not altogether thrown off the Prussian influence. It too had its share of conservative commanders who found the new ways difficult to accept. Most of its rank and file were peasants recruited by selective conscription to serve for 25 years. They were tough, stoical, loyal, deeply religious and possessed a fatalistic courage. Lacking any form of education, they behaved like animals if they got out of hand and, if a situation seemed irretrievably lost, could succumb to collective despair. Taken as a whole, their officers had the reputation of being the worst in Europe. Recruited from the minor gentry upwards, their promotion prospects were restricted by their limited abilities, although a capable minority could rise in their profession. The primary concerns of most Russian officers were drink and the social life, and the higher up the social scale they were the more devoted to these pastimes they seemed to be. As a consequence the army relied upon large numbers of foreign officers who were cordially disliked by the Russians but without whom it could not have functioned.

The cavalry was well mounted and of reasonable efficiency. In addition to its regular regiments, it employed irregular Cossack units raised only in time of war. They performed the light cavalry role well and were expert in harrying a retreating enemy. Their reputation as plundering savages made them feared throughout eastern and central Europe, but when confronted with steady regular troops they were less formidable. On occasion the Russians would also employ mounted archers recruited from Asiatic tribes!

The artillery had adopted the Gribeauval system and was probably the most efficient arm of service. To some extent the infantry's adherence to Prussian linear tactics and volley firing had been challenged in recent years by Suvarov's fondness for attacking with the bayonet, and under Kutusov open-order skirmishing and columnar attacks would be encouraged. By far the least efficient branch was the commissariat which had neither sufficient transport for rations nor the funds to purchase them locally. During the present campaign the Austrians had been expected to provide whatever was necessary, but since they were in little better case the Russians simply ate their way across the landscape, which did not endear them to their allies.

In a class of its own was the Russian Imperial Guard, which contained four infantry regiments, a rifle battalion, several cavalry regiments and an engineer company. The Guard infantry regiments consisted of carefully selected men whose height was enhanced by their brass-fronted mitres, and in the cavalry the Chevalier Guard recruited only members of Russia's most noble houses. The Guard's senior officers were selected for their ability, experience, courage and social standing.

Perhaps no period of warfare has ever been quite so colourful as the Napoleonic era, in which vast sums were spent on decorative uniforms. By and large the line infantry and some branches of service stuck to their national colour, the French in blue, the Austrians in white and the Russians in green. There were, however, exceptions, particularly among the cavalry, which could and did cause confusion amid the smoke and turmoil of battle. What a few weeks' campaigning in all weathers did to these fine uniforms can well be imagined, although the convention among contemporary war artists was to depict them in the same spruce condition they were issued. The average infantryman of the day, with his tunic buttoned to the throat and various straps constricting his chest, was rather less comfortable on the march than his grandfather had been.

On 2 September the Austrians under Mack invaded Bavaria and marched on Ulm. Meanwhile, Napoleon's corps, advancing on a broad front by pre-determined routes, were making steady progress towards the Rhine. On 26 September, while Mack's attention was held with a feint into the Black Forest by the cavalry of Marshal Prince Murat, Napoleon's brother-in-law, they began crossing and made a concentric wheel southwards, reaching the Danube on 6 October. Detaching corps to prevent interference from the east and south, Napoleon crossed the river and closed in on Mack's rear. Mack suddenly found his communications cut and was faced with the possibility of having to fight his way out across several river lines. Archduke Ferdinand managed to break free of the trap by riding hard to the north-east with his cavalry, hotly pursued by Murat, but for the remainder of the army there was no escape. As the noose tightened Mack made an abortive attempt to break out at Elchingen on 16 October. Believing that Kutusov's Russian army was approaching, he opened negotiations with Napoleon in the hope of gaining time, though promising to surrender on the 25th. Unfortunately failure to allow for calendrical differences meant that Kutusov was still far to the east and unable to intervene. Once he had been convinced of this, Mack capitulated on 20 October. At Ulm some 27,000 men surrendered and a similar number were rounded up throughout Bavaria, leaving the French with nearly 60,000 prisoners, 80 Colours and 200 guns. Battle casualties totalled 4,000 Austrians and 2,000 French, giving rise to the jest within the *Grande Armée* that 'the Emperor has invented a new way of making war; he makes it more with our legs than our arms!' The 'unfortunate General Mack', as he introduced himself to Napoleon, was subsequently court-martialled and sentenced to 20 years' imprisonment.

Having detached sufficient troops to protect his lines of communication, Napoleon marched east into Austria. Kutusov had 36,000 Russians and 22,000 Austrians under command, but having been told of the disaster at Ulm, he decided to fall back on another Russian force commanded by General Friedrich Buxhöwden

as this would add a further 30,000 men to his army. In addition to fighting successful delaying actions at Durrenstein and Schöngraben, he achieved his object, but was unable to prevent the French occupying Vienna. With Murat's cavalry and two corps Napoleon followed up his withdrawal northwards to Brunn (now Brno) in Moravia.

Napoleon was aware that he was becoming dangerously over-extended. The corps he had detached to the south were successfully holding Archdukes Charles and John in check, but to the north Archduke Ferdinand was reported to be marching southwards towards his flank with 18,000 men. Most serious of all, Kutusov's army, now 86,000 strong, was consolidating at Olmütz, 30 miles north-east of Brunn, and he had only some 53,000 troops with which to oppose it. A decisive battle must be fought soon, preferably one in which the Allies would launch an ill-conceived attack against a position of his own choosing.

That position was discovered seven miles along the road from Brunn to Olmütz. Beside the road was a small hill surmounted by a chapel, known locally as the Bosenitz Berg but subsequently known to the French as Le Santon. To the south lay a high, wide plateau bounded to the east and west by valleys through which ran streams; in the centre of the plateau was a village named Pratzen from which the little town of Austerlitz could be seen to the east. The valley on the eastern side of the plateau did not interest Napoleon unduly save that its marshy bottom would tend to channel troops advancing from the north and east up on to the Pratzen plateau. The western valley, through which the fordable stream of the Goldbach ran, was a different matter. From north to south it featured a number of villages including Puntowitz, Kobelnitz, Sokolnitz with its castle and walled pheasantry, and Telnitz. More significantly, it was well wooded and therefore suitable for concealing large numbers of troops, while at its southern end, where the Pratzen plateau fell away, the stream flowed through an area of marshland

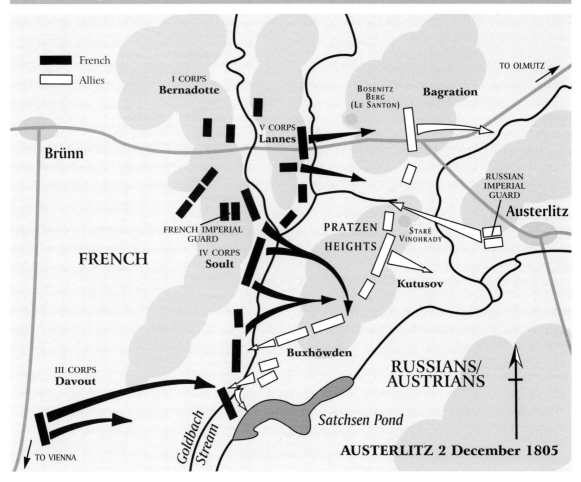

French

Allies

I CORPS
Bernadotte

Brünn

V CORPS
Lannes

BOSENITZ
BERG
(LE SANTON)

Bagration

TO OLMUTZ

RUSSIAN
IMPERIAL
GUARD

Austerlitz

FRENCH IMPERIAL
GUARD

FRENCH

IV CORPS
Soult

**PRATZEN
HEIGHTS**

STARÉ
VINOHRADY

Kutusov

Buxhöwden

III CORPS
Davout

**RUSSIANS/
AUSTRIANS**

Satchsen Pond

AUSTERLITZ 2 December 1805

Goldbach Stream

TO VIENNA

and large meres. This terrain suggested a plan to Napoleon. He would anchor his left on Le Santon, which would be fortified; his right, which would deliberately convey an impression of weakness, would rest in the area of Telnitz, suggesting to the enemy an opportunity to break through to the Brunn–Vienna road and thus sever the French line of retreat; the remainder of the army would remain concealed in the valley of the Goldbach. The enemy, having been decoyed on to the Pratzen plateau, would immediately spot the apparent weakness of the French right and attack in strength. This, however, would seriously weaken their centre, and when the moment came Napoleon intended to mount a counter-attack which would drive straight through it, then wheel to the right and take the Austro–Russian columns in rear, effectively

trapping the major part of Kutusov's army; equally, a wheel to the left would entrap the Allied right wing. When some of his staff expressed reservations about abandoning the Pratzen plateau, the Emperor tersely responded that he intended winning not just a battle but a crushing victory.

The question was, how could the Allies be persuaded to accept the bait? Napoleon pushed out his corps in the direction of Olmütz, occupying Austerlitz and the Pratzen plateau, taking care to expose their numerical inferiority. Interested, the Allies opened negotiations directly with Napoleon, ostensibly with a view to an armistice, but actually to assess the condition of the French army. The impression fostered by the Emperor was one of weakness.

Although Kutusov was nominally commander of the Allied army, Tsar Alexander I of

Russia and Emperor Francis I of Austria were also present and this complicated his position. Aged 60, he was experienced and canny enough to suspect Napoleon's motives and counsel against a counter-offensive. Alexander, however, was surrounded by rich young aides-de-camp who were dismissive of the older man's opinions. Prominent among this group was Count Dolgorouki, a young man with opinions on everything and experience of nothing who persuaded the Tsar that the moment had come to take the offensive. Francis, aged 37, was inclined to support Kutusov, but he was now the junior partner and his own Austrian generals were burning to expunge the disgrace of Ulm. The upshot of these discussions was that the Allies began advancing during the last week of November. Under orders which some senior commanders, notably Soult, were at a loss to understand, the French gave ground, abandoning Austerlitz and the Pratzen plateau, which were promptly occupied by the Allies. In the meantime Napoleon had summoned Bernadotte's I Corps from Iglau, 50 miles to the north-west, and Davout's III Corps from Vienna, some 70 miles away.

Having taken possession of the Pratzen plateau on 1 December, the Allies reacted precisely as Napoleon had hoped they would. It seemed to them that he had made a serious error of judgement in abandoning this vital ground; furthermore, the apparently yawning gap on the French right demanded exploitation. Altogether they had available 85,400 men and 278 guns, of which the bulk, amounting to some 59,000 men, would be deployed in attack columns under General Buxhöwden against the French right while 13,000 men under General Peter Bagration, supported by Prince Lichtenstein's 4,600 cavalry, would pin down Napoleon's left. Once the French right had been turned, most of Buxhöwden's troops would wheel north to roll up the enemy line while the rest would continue westwards to cut the Brünn–Vienna road. The result was adjudged to be such a foregone conclusion that it was considered unlikely that the 8,500-strong Russian Imperial Guard, positioned just west of Austerlitz, would get into action at all.

On the evening of 1 December, Napoleon, satisfied that the Allies had taken his bait, deployed his army. The right flank was to be covered by Davout's III Corps, which had made an astonishing march of 70 miles in 48 hours, suitably reinforced because some of its units were still on the road; along the lower reaches of the Goldbach was Soult's IV Corps which was to initiate the counter-stroke on the Pratzen plateau; on the upper reaches of the stream and its tributary the Bosenitz was Bernadotte's I Corps, which had remained concealed since its arrival during the day and would also take part in the counter-stroke; covering the Le Santon feature and with Murat's cavalry on its right was Lannes' V Corps; Marshal Jean Bessières' 5,500-strong French Imperial Guard, together with the 5,700 men of General Nicolas Oudinot's veteran Grenadier Division, formed the army's reserve and was positioned to the west of a feature known as the Zurlan Height, on which the Emperor had established his headquarters. Thanks to Napoleon's ability to concentrate his corps quickly, he now had more than 73,000 men available, and the Allies were blissfully ignorant of the fact.

The night was bitterly cold with a hard frost. While on a personal reconnaissance Napoleon narrowly avoided capture. He walked back to his headquarters through the troops' bivouac areas, the paths between campfires crammed with cheering men who improvised torches from twisted bundles of straw to light his way. Few slept more than an hour or two during that freezing night, and in the morning the landscape was shrouded in fog. This lay heaviest in the valleys, further concealing from the Allies the hidden menace lining the Goldbach.

Up on the plateau the Austro–Russian columns had begun to form before first light. Soon a steady procession of infantry, cavalry and guns was marching south-eastwards and descending the slopes to engage Davout's men in a fierce struggle during which the villages of Telnitz and Sokolnitz, together with the latter's castle and pheasantry, changed hands several times. Hour by hour the pressure on Davout grew and might have become insupportable save for a stroke of Austro–Russian *schlamperei*. The previous evening Lichtenstein's cavalry had camped in the wrong place, on the southern shoulder of the plateau. Now, having been told that they were needed closer to the Allied right wing to counter-balance Murat's horsemen, his trotting squadrons caused a monumental tangle as they demanded right of way along the army's front. The result was that the second assault column was brought to a standstill and the third and fourth columns piled up behind. A priceless hour was lost before these even began to get into action, and by then fresh reinforcements had reached Davout. Nevertheless, it seemed to the Tsar, Emperor Francis and Kutusov, watching the battle develop from the summit of Staré Vinohrady, a hill to the east of Pratzen, that their plan was taking effect.

Down in the valley of the Goldbach, where the fog was thickened by smoke from hundreds of campfires, Marshal Nicolas Soult could hear the roar of battle rising to a crescendo on his right and was impatient to be off. Napoleon, anxious that as many Allied troops as possible should march into the trap, delayed giving the order until 9 a.m. At that moment the sun emerged so dramatically above the mist that for years to come those present would recall it as 'the sun of Austerlitz'.

Played into action by their regimental bands, the divisions of General Louis de Sainte-Hilaire on the right and General Dominique Vandamme on the left began to climb the slopes of the plateau. It was the drifting strains of martial music that first alerted Kutusov to the fact that something totally unexpected was happening. Breasting the last slope, the heads of the French columns suddenly emerged from the mist and, bayonets levelled, smashed through the thin screen of troops protecting the now vacant Allied centre to storm their way through the undefended village of Pratzen.

Kutusov was shaken, but by no means did he consider the battle to be lost at this stage. Aides were sent galloping to Prince Lichtenstein with orders for a mass intervention by cavalry from the north, and to Lieutenant-General Miloradovitch, commander of the last Allied column to leave the plateau, to return immediately and re-occupy the centre. Lichtenstein, however, was so heavily engaged in the holding attack against the French left that he could only spare four regiments. Miloradovitch conformed willingly enough, although his Austrian and Russian regiments returned breathless and piecemeal without any clear idea of the developing situation which lay ahead of them. By now the French had their divisional artillery in action and were sweeping the confused new arrivals before them to the east and south with canister, musketry and the bayonet. Allied batteries were overrun and the Staré Vinohrady feature was taken, causing the Imperial retinue to gallop for a safer position to the south. By 11 a.m. Soult's corps was in effective control of the Pratzen plateau. Fully aware at last of the dangers inherent in the situation, Kutusov ordered the Russian Imperial Guard, commanded by the Tsar's brother, the Grand Duke Constantine, to counter-attack and recover the lost ground.

As this would take some time to implement, it is possible to examine what was taking place elsewhere on the field. To the south, fierce fighting continued around the villages of Telnitz and Sokolnitz. To the north Bagration's holding attack against Lannes' corps and Murat's cavalry could be said to have achieved its object for a while, but did not affect Napoleon's plans. The Allied cavalry charged Lannes' two infantry divisions but was repulsed with heavy loss by the latter's musketry and canister, one lancer regiment being virtually destroyed, and was then counter-charged by the French cavalry. As Lichtenstein and Murat each fed more units into the battle, charge was followed by counter-charge, the French rallying neatly behind their own infantry. Once Murat had committed his heavy cavalry brigades, consisting of carabiniers and cuirassiers, the fight began to go his way. By noon Lannes' infantry had taken the village of Bosenitz on their right and were pushing forward everywhere, despite local counter-attacks. On the left General Louis Suchet's division followed up a successful attack by a cuirassier formation that had forced the enemy infantry into defensive squares. When the cuirassiers drew off, Suchet's regiments engaged the squares with volley fire then charged home and shattered them. This one excellent example of tactical co-operation between arms resulted in 2,000 Russian casualties and the capture of sixteen guns. By 1 o'clock Bagration had been pushed back four miles, his command being saved from complete disintegration by a newly arrived concentration of Austrian guns which halted the French advance. Lannes had, in any event, fulfilled his task and was now concerned that his right flank was exposed to a possible Allied attack from the south.

During this time decisive events were taking place on the Pratzen plateau. At about noon Napoleon had transferred his headquarters to the Staré Vinohrady, ordering the Imperial Guard, Oudinot's Grenadier Division and Bernadotte's I Corps forward to join Soult. On the plateau Sainte-Hilaire's division had wheeled to the right and was confronting those of Buxhöwden's units which were still trying to fight their way back to the summit. To the north Vandamme's division had established itself on the Staré Vinohrady. Between the two lay Pratzen through which the Imperial Guard and Bernadotte's corps were coming forward.

Now the massed cavalry, infantry and artillery of the Russian Imperial Guard could be seen approaching the eastern slopes of plateau. At 1 o'clock the real crisis of the battle began with an attack by 3,000 grenadiers against Vandamme's position. The Russians were repulsed but rallied quickly, and Constantine put in simultaneous converging attacks with the grenadiers and the Guard cavalry, leaving the most exposed battalion of the French 4th Line Infantry uncertain whether to remain in line or form square. When its

commander opted for the latter the Russian horsemen wheeled aside to unmask a horse artillery battery. Riddled with canister, the square was simply ridden over and the regiment's Eagle was lost. Vandamme sent the 24th Light Infantry to retrieve the situation but this too was ridden over and reduced to a mob of panic-stricken fugitives. Napoleon ordered Marshal Bessières, commanding his own Guard, to send in his cavalry. Three squadrons each of *Chasseurs-à-Cheval* and Horse Grenadiers, supported by a battery of horse artillery, counter-charged and a fierce mêlée ensued. Onto one flank of this Constantine committed the Chevalier Guard and the Guard Cossacks, while from the other the grenadiers of the Semenovsky and Preobrazjensky Life Guards closed in to pour volleys into the French ranks. The French lost heavily and things would have gone very badly for them if, at that moment, General Drouet d'Erlon's division, the leading formation of Bernadotte's I Corps, had not arrived to fill the gap, providing a firm base through which the battered squadrons could retire and rally while the pursuing Russians were held off with musketry.

During the lull Napoleon ordered General Jean Rapp, his senior aide, to launch a fresh charge with the 250-strong Mamelukes of the Guard and two squadrons of *Chasseurs-à-Cheval*. Despite the Mamelukes' ferocity, this proved indecisive until Napoleon committed a squadron of the huge Horse Grenadiers, who broke the ranks of the Chevalier Guard and did fearful execution with their long swords. Now, the Semenovsky and Preobrazjensky grenadiers were unable to fire into the wheeling, stabbing, slashing mass of horsemen for fear of hitting their own people. Within fifteen minutes the Russian Imperial Guard was in full retreat down the eastern slopes, with all the fight apparently knocked out of it. If Bernadotte, whose second division had arrived, had chosen to pursue, this retreat might have been turned into a rout, but instead the French I Corps halted at the edge of the plateau. Meanwhile some 200 of the Chevalier Guard's *jeunesse dorée*, including their

Left: Austerlitz. The Mamelukes and Chasseurs of the Guard counter-attack the Russian Imperial Guard on the Pratzen Plateau. *Philip Haythornthwaite Collection*

commanding officer, Prince Repnine, were paraded before Napoleon, who commented wryly that it was a sad day for the fine ladies of St Petersburg.

At 2 o'clock Napoleon gave orders for Soult's IV Corps to wheel southwards along the plateau, followed by the Imperial Guard and Oudinot's grenadiers. This in effect would shut a door behind Buxhöwden, trapping him against Davout, who would simultaneously go over to the offensive. By 2.30 the French artillery was established in strength on the southern slopes and Vandamme had cut the Allies' best line of retreat. Some Russian batteries attempted to hold open a corridor until they were overwhelmed, and in the villages Austrian and Russian units courageously sacrificed themselves so that their comrades could escape. By 3 o'clock, however, Buxhöwden's withdrawal had disintegrated into a disorderly panic as his troops fled to the south and south-east. Many of the fugitives sought safety by fleeing across the frozen ponds while the artillery galloped along the narrow causeway separating the Satschan and Menitz meres. When the latter was blocked by the explosion of an ammunition wagon, the gun teams also took to the ice, which either gave way beneath their weight or was shattered

by the fire of the French guns. In this way several hundred men and 130 horses plunged into the icy water to drown or die of shock; subsequently 38 guns were recovered from the ponds. By 4 o'clock, as heavy snow accompanied the winter dusk, fighting ceased and the French began marshalling their droves of prisoners. The Battle of the Three Emperors was over.

Bagration's battered command, Lichtenstein's cavalry, the Russian Imperial Guard and 2,000 survivors of Buxhöwden's force streamed away to the south-east, so disorganised that for the moment they could scarcely be called an army. They had sustained 15,000 killed and wounded and 12,000 of their comrades had been captured. They had lost 186 guns, 45 Colours, most of their artillery ammunition and all their heavy baggage. The French had lost 1,300 killed, 7,000 wounded and 573 men taken prisoner, but were too exhausted to mount an effective pursuit.

That night Prince Lichtenstein arrived at the French outpost line with a request from Francis for a meeting with Napoleon. The two Emperors met on 4 December and concluded an armistice which was followed by the Peace of Pressburg under the terms of which Austria withdrew from the war and was compelled to

Right: Austerlitz. Russian artillery and infantry attempt to escape across the frozen Satschen Mere. Guns and horses were lost when the ice gave way but the mere was shallow and comparatively few men were drowned. *Philip Haythornthwaite Collection*

surrender yet more of her territory. The Tsar sent Napoleon a congratulatory note, but declined to conclude peace.

Austerlitz is widely regarded as being Napoleon's greatest tactical masterpiece. In French eyes it went far to counter-balance the disaster at Trafalgar, and it brought the British architect of the Third Coalition, Prime Minister William Pitt, to the edge of despair. Prior to the battle Prussia had declined to join the Coalition, but in 1806, thoroughly alarmed by French domination of central and southern Germany, she began mobilising in secret and was joined by Saxony.

Once again Napoleon received ample warning and decided on a pre-emptive strike. On 8 October, having concentrated the *Grande Armée* in secret, he marched north and within days had shattered the once-proud Prussian Army at the linked battles of Jena and Auerstadt (14 October). He pursued its remnant into Poland, winning a narrow victory over a combined Russo–Prussian army at Eylau on 8 February 1807. Four months later he inflicted a crushing defeat on the Allies at Friedland (14 June). The subsequent Treaty of Tilsit imposed punitive terms on Prussia and resulted in the final collapse of the Third Coalition. Napoleon now stood at the pinnacle of his achievements,

despite his inability to bring the Peninsular War to a satisfactory conclusion. How long he would have remained there had he not chosen to invade Russia in 1812 is a matter for conjecture.

WATERLOO, 18 JUNE 1815

The catastrophic campaign in Russia and the months of fighting against odds in its aftermath had so exhausted French resources that in April 1814 Napoleon abdicated and was confined to the island of Elba. Yet such was the resilience of France and the charisma of her Emperor that when he escaped eleven months later men flocked to his Eagles. Once again, all Europe mobilised against him. In Belgium there was an Anglo–Dutch army under the Duke of Wellington and a Prussian army under Field Marshal Prince Gebhard Liberecht von Blücher; one large Austrian army had begun assembling along the Rhine and a second was active in northern Italy; and in central Germany a Russian army was marching westwards. Calculating that the Allies would be unable to mount their planned concentric advance into France before July, Napoleon decided to defeat them in detail, dealing first with Wellington and Blücher. He concentrated

135

Left: The Duke of Wellington. *Katz Pictures Ltd*

his Army of the North in secret and on 15 June seized Charleroi. Neither of the Allied armies was far away and he intended to prevent them joining forces by inflicting a severe defeat on one, forcing it to retreat, then turning upon the other.

Although the campaigns of 1813 and 1814 had revealed flashes of the Emperor's old brilliance, nearly ten years had passed since Austerlitz. Most historians agree that by now his abilities had begun to decline. It was not simply that flexibility had been replaced by fixed ideas on a number of subjects; Napoleon was no longer well. In particular, he suffered from the discomfort caused by piles and from cystitis which induced bouts of feverishness and lethargy. Consequently he was often irritable and his decisions could be erratic. Ably supported by his Marshals, however, he was still a formidable opponent and was still worshipped by his men, many of whom were veterans of earlier campaigns. Altogether the

Army of the North was 124,000-men strong, consisting of the Imperial Guard, five corps, four cavalry corps and 286 guns.

The Duke of Wellington was the same age as Napoleon but had lost none of his vigour. A master of the defensive battle, he had maintained an unbroken record of victory throughout the Peninsular War. His troops respected him and were appreciative of his efforts to keep casualties to a minimum. He was altogether too haughty a figure for them to entertain any warmer feeling for him, but they liked him well enough to call him 'Beaky' (because of his nose) or 'Arthur' when he was out of earshot, and were uneasy when he was not about. His army numbered approximately 78,000 men and 174 guns but had not adopted the corps system, the higher formations being the division for infantry and the brigade for cavalry. His principal concern was about its mixed composition. Some 22,000 were Dutch or Belgians, numbers of whom had only recently served in the *Grande Armée* and whose loyalty remained questionable. There were also 13,000 Hanoverians, 6,000 Brunswickers and 7,000 Nassauers of unknown quality. The only troops upon whom he could rely implicitly were the 26,000 British and 6,000 King's German Legion, the latter consisting of German exiles fighting in the British service. Even so, there were comparatively few of his Peninsula veterans present with the British contingent, most having been shipped across the Atlantic to fight the Americans.

Born in 1742, Prince Blücher was by far the oldest of the three commanders and had actually served under Frederick the Great. Despite his 73 years, he possessed such determination and drive that his nickname was '*Alt Vorwärts*' (Old Forwards). Following Prussia's humiliating defeat in 1806, he had assisted Major-General Gerhard von Scharnhorst and Count Augustus von Gneisenau in their reconstruction and modernisation of the army, during which the manpower ceiling imposed by Napoleon was circumvented by training short-term conscripts who could be recalled to the Colours as required. Possessed of an intense hatred for the French, he promised to co-operate closely with Wellington whatever happened.

On 16 June Napoleon struck. Detaching Marshal Michel Ney with one-third of the army to drive in Wellington's advance guard at Quatre Bras, he attacked Blücher at Ligny with the remainder. The Prussians resisted so doggedly that Napoleon considered committing his Guard against them, but delayed doing so until he had established the identity of a large body of troops on his left flank; it turned out to be Drouet d'Erlon's I Corps which, having been subjected to order and counter-order, marched uselessly about between Ligny and Quatre Bras without contributing to either battle. Finally, however, Blücher's centre gave way during the evening.

Prussian casualties amounted to 16,000 killed, wounded and captured, plus a further 8,000 deserters. Nevertheless, the French had sustained 11,500 casualties and Napoleon had won only a partial victory. Blücher's horse had been killed under him while he was leading a cavalry charge during the closing stages of the battle and for a while he had remained pinned under it. The old man had been so badly shaken by the experience that for a while his second in command, Gneisenau, assumed control of the army. Gneisenau decided to withdraw northwards to Wavre rather than eastwards along his lines of communication through Namur. The effect of the decision not only preserved the Prussian army in being, but enabled it to maintain contact with the Anglo–Dutch army to the west. Having recovered sufficiently to resume command, Blücher promised Wellington that he would join him at Waterloo. Another important consequence of Gneisenau's decision would become apparent very shortly. On the morning after the battle, Napoleon detached Marshal Emmanuel de Grouchy with III and IV Corps plus I and II Cavalry Corps, a total of 33,000 men and 104 guns, to pursue and destroy the Prussians. Unfortunately Grouchy misinterpreted the flood of Prussian deserters streaming towards Namur, the obvious route to Germany, and he

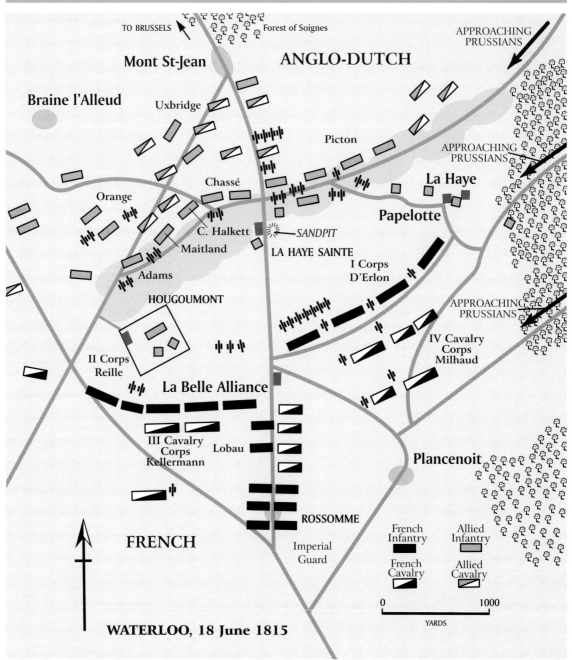

TO BRUSSELS

Forest of Soignes

Mont St-Jean

ANGLO-DUTCH

Braine l'Alleud

Uxbridge

APPROACHING PRUSSIANS

Picton

APPROACHING PRUSSIANS

La Haye

Chassé

Orange

Papelotte

C. Halkett

SANDPIT

Maitland

LA HAYE SAINTE

I Corps D'Erlon

Adams

HOUGOUMONT

IV Cavalry Corps Milhaud

II Corps Reille

La Belle Alliance

III Cavalry Corps Kellermann

Lobau

Plancenoit

ROSSOMME

FRENCH

Imperial Guard

French Infantry

Allied Infantry

French Cavalry

Allied Cavalry

0   1000

YARDS

WATERLOO, 18 June 1815

set off in the wrong direction. Not until late on the 17th did he discover his mistake and by then the lost time could not be made up. Consequently he never succeeded in engaging more than the Prussian rearguard, which covered the rest of Blücher's army when it advanced from Wavre to Waterloo on 18 June.

At Quatre Bras on 16 June Ney had fought an inconclusive battle against Wellington's advance guard. He may have been overawed by the Duke's reputation and, suspecting a trap, wasted opportunities during the early stages of the battle. By the time he had settled down Allied reinforcements had arrived and the moment had passed. Each side sustained losses in excess of 4,000 men. The Allies remained in the position overnight, but next morning Wellington, recognising that he must conform to Blücher's movements, ordered a withdrawal. This was neatly executed, its later stages being marked by a heavy thunderstorm and torrential rain.

The position where Wellington elected to stand had been reconnoitred previously and was well suited to his style of fighting. Lying ten miles south of Brussels and two miles south of the village of Waterloo in the Forest of Soignes, it was bisected by the Brussels–Charleroi road and consisted of a shallow, gently sloping ridge about four miles long, running roughly from east to west. While the Allied army deployed along this Wellington, determined to dominate no man's land, also established two strong advance posts. One, the farm of La Haye Sainte, lay beside the Brussels–Charleroi road; the second, consisting of the chateau, farm buildings, gardens and woodlands of the Hougoumont estate, lay just east of the Brussels–Nivelles road, covering his right. Allowing for the casualties already incurred and detached units, his army on 18 June would consist of 50,000 infantry, 12,500 cavalry and 156 guns. If Blücher arrived in time, he might contribute as many as 30,000 infantry, 5,000 cavalry and 100 guns.

By degrees the French came up and occupied a parallel ridge approximately one mile to the south. To the east of the main road was d'Erlon's I Corps with Milhaud's IV Cavalry Corps just behind; to the west of the road was Reille's II Corps and Kellermann's III Cavalry Corps; to the rear of these two and in a central position was Lobau's VI Corps and two cavalry divisions; farther to the rear the Imperial Guard lay in reserve. Together, these formations numbered 49,000 infantry, 15,750 cavalry and 246 guns, giving a grand total of approximately 72,000 men.

Torrential rain continued for much of the night, few men on either side finding any kind of shelter. By dawn it had ceased but the ground was so waterlogged that several hours would be required for it to dry out sufficiently to permit the passage of artillery. Napoleon therefore breakfasted as late as 8 o'clock at Le Caillou farmhouse with his senior officers, to whom he issued orders for the day's fighting. These were unfortunately based upon two faulty assumptions, the first being that Grouchy was successfully containing Blücher, and the second that Wellington was unduly sensitive about his communications with the coast and would retire in that direction if defeated, thereby widening still further the gap between the Allied army and the Prussians. The French would therefore begin the battle with a strong feint against Hougoumont by Reille's corps. This would cause Wellington to reinforce his right at the expense of his centre. Once the Allied centre had been sufficiently weakened by this and heavy artillery preparation, d'Erlon's corps would smash through it. The Allied army would disintegrate, Wellington would withdraw the remnant out of harm's way, and Napoleon would enter Brussels in triumph. Not everyone agreed with this optimistic projection. Soult, now serving as Chief of Staff, had been roughly handled on several occasions during the Peninsular War, and he recommended the recall of some at least of Grouchy's troops. Napoleon responded tartly: 'Because you have been beaten by Wellington, you consider him a great general. And now I tell you that he is a bad general, that the English are bad troops, and that this affair is nothing more serious than eating one's breakfast!' At that moment Reille, another Peninsula veteran, entered the room accompanied by the Emperor's brother Jérôme, who commanded one of his divisions. Asked for his opinion, Reille said that Wellington had posted his army well, and that any frontal attack on British infantry was doomed to failure with heavy loss; on the other hand, the British were less flexible and could be beaten by manoeuvre rather than direct assault. This too was brushed aside, but within 24 hours Napoleon was to pass another remark clearly indicating that he knew Soult and Reille had been right.

Left: Waterloo. Closing the gates at Hougoumont. *Courtesy The Coldstream Guards*

Jérôme also produced a piece of disconcerting intelligence. The previous evening he had dined at the inn where Wellington and his staff had breakfasted during the morning. The waiter who served them had overheard a remark that the Prussians intended joining them at the Forest of Soignes, which suggested that Blücher was already marching west. Again, Napoleon was dismissive, commenting that any such junction was impossible for two days. Several more senior officers supported the idea of recalling Grouchy but remained silent because the Emperor had clearly made up his mind.

After breakfast Napoleon with his staff reviewed the army, passing along the front of Reille and d'Erlon's corps to thunderous cheers and shouts of '*Vive l'Empereur!*' He then set up his headquarters on a mound near the inn at Rossomme, where he sat slumped in an armchair with his head in his hands as though the effort had been too much for him. Sunshine began to dry out the ground, but he took little pleasure in it. Across the valley a Prussian officer reached the cavalry outposts on the Allied left flank with the news that Blücher was approaching.

A grand battery of 74 guns had been assembled in front of the French centre. At 11.20 it opened fire and the Allied artillery began to reply. Shortly after this Reille's corps began its diversionary attack on Hougoumont, but the château had been thoroughly prepared for defence and it was thrown back. Reille tried again, with similar results, and kept trying until what had been intended as no more than a feint became a battle within a battle, sucking in all of II Corps. From then until 6 o'clock Reille mounted no fewer than seven major attacks, piling up casualties around the walls. On one occasion a particularly determined party of attackers broke through the north gate but were killed in fierce hand-to-hand fighting while the gate was closed by main force and secured. The French brought up a howitzer battery which turned the buildings into an inferno, but not even collapsing roofs and floors could dislodge the remarkable garrison which included detachments from all three British Guards regiments (Grenadier, Coldstream and 3rd (later Scots) Guards), the King's German Legion, Hanoverians, Brunswickers and Nassauers, under various commanders. When ammunition began to run low an incredibly brave soldier named Brewer or Brewster, disregarding both the fire of the French and the danger posed by the burning buildings, drove a powder wagon from the main position down the ridge and into the defences. Wellington kept a very careful eye on developments at the château throughout the day and he did reinforce the position, but with troops drawn from his right and not his centre, as Napoleon had hoped. Of the 3,500 men who played some part in the defence of Hougoumont, about 1,500 were killed or wounded. They had successfully tied down the entire left wing of the French army, approximately 15,000 men, and inflicted some 5,000 casualties in their turn. Why Reille, a capable officer, should have allowed a situation to develop which was quite contrary to the Emperor's stated intention is curious. It seems probable that he was heavily influenced by his nominal subordinate Jérôme Bonaparte, who claimed that at about 1 o'clock he had been told by the Emperor in a private conversation that unless Hougoumont were taken or Grouchy rejoined, the battle was lost. This was about the time that the Prussians first became visible to the east and it seems that Jérôme was privy to information that was being deliberately kept from the rest of the army.

Wellington had so deployed his British and King's German Legion troops along his front as to provide a stiffening, hoping thereby to encourage the Dutch–Belgian and German contingents. Wherever possible advantage was taken of the cover afforded by the crest, so that while the Allied light infantry and artillery could be seen by the French little else was visible. The fire of the French artillery was having some effect, but rather less than had been anticipated. The solid shot, for example, instead of bouncing to continue its career of destruction beyond the first graze, simply ploughed into the mud, while the shells buried themselves in inches of earth, markedly reducing their effectiveness.

At about 1.30 d'Erlon's I Corps, 17,000 strong, began its assault in four dense columns, covered on its left by cuirassiers. The grand battery ceased firing as the infantry passed through the intervals between the guns. The drummers began beating the *pas de charge*, a sound familiar to every Peninsula veteran. The defenders of La Haye Sainte were driven out of their orchard and into the farm buildings whence they continued to fire into the mass of infantry and cavalry. Cannon shot slashed through the packed ranks, bowling men over like skittles, but still the French came on. In their path was a Dutch–Belgian brigade who had fought well at Quatre Bras but whose commander had obstinately chosen to deploy on the forward slope. Consequently, his men had suffered more than most from the prolonged bombardment and all their senior officers were down. Apparently alone and confronted by the mass of d'Erlon's cheering columns, the survivors bolted. The French passed over the crest and found themselves confronted by the main Allied line. A furious firefight ensued in which 4,000 British infantry shot away the columns' head but suffered severely in the process. For a few minutes the issue hung in the balance until, with a blare of trumpets and the thunder of hooves, Wellington's counter-attack went in. It consisted of the Household Brigade (1st and 2nd Life Guards, Royal Horse Guards and 1st (King's) Dragoon Guards) on the right and the Union Brigade (1st (Royal) Dragoons, 2nd (Royal North British (later Royal Scots Greys)) Dragoons, and 6th (Inniskilling) Dragoons) on the left. The Household Brigade came in obliquely across the main road above La Haye Sainte, smashing into d'Erlon's flanking cuirassiers and routing them for all their longer swords and breastplates, then set about riding over everything in sight. The Union Brigade came at the French infantry head-on, shattering their columns, which burst apart and fled back down the slope. In the fury and excitement of the moment, many of the Gordon Highlanders grasped the Greys' stirrups and joined them in the charge. 'It was fearful to see the carnage that took place,' wrote a sergeant of the former. 'The dragoons were lopping off heads at every stroke, while

141

Above: Waterloo. French artillerymen struggle to limber-up as the charge of the Union Brigade reaches Napoleon's grand battery. Unfortunately, the brigade had over-reached itself and sustained heavy casualties when it was counter-charged by French cavalry. *Philip Haythornthwaite Collection*

the French were calling for quarter. We were also among them busy with the bayonet and what the cavalry did not execute we completed.' Two Eagles were taken, that of the 45th Line by Sergeant Ewart of the Greys and that of the 105th Line by Captain Kennedy Clark of the 1st Royal Dragoons. It was unfortunate that the British cavalry's reputation for reckless courage was matched by an habitual tendency to overreach itself. The word rally seemed to have no place in its vocabulary so that when members of both brigades found themselves within striking distance of the grand battery they continued their charge until they were among the guns and cutting down the gunners. In this way between 20 and 30 guns were put out of action, but it was foolish to imagine that the French would not react. Suddenly the British troopers found themselves being counter-charged and cut off by two

regiments of cuirassiers and one of lancers. With blown horses labouring in the clinging mud, they took severe casualties. Indeed very few would have returned to the ridge if the 4th Cavalry Brigade (11th, 12th and 16th Light Dragoons) had not ridden to their rescue, causing the French to retire.

The Household and Union Brigades had lost half their horses and one-third of their men. Wellington was satisfied with the result of their counter-attack, although it had effectively cost him his heavy cavalry. Three of d'Erlon's divisions had been shattered and the fourth, which had penetrated Smohain, withdrew in some haste. More than 2,000 prisoners had been taken and severe casualties inflicted. Napoleon's plan had failed, for although d'Erlon rallied a few battalions and put in a fresh attack, this was easily beaten off and it would be several hours before his corps could be re-organised sufficiently to mount another blow at the Allied line. Nor could Lobau's VI Corps provide assistance since it was now required elsewhere.

Shortly before 1 o'clock a captured warrant officer from a Prussian hussar regiment was brought to Napoleon. He had been carrying a letter from Gneisenau to Müffling, the Prussian liaison officer serving with Wellington's army, stating that General Count Bülow's IV Corps was advancing to attack the French right. The Prussians' leading elements could, in fact, be discerned to the east and the prisoner confirmed that the rest of Blücher's army was following Bülow. Lobau's corps and two cavalry divisions were therefore moved to protect the right flank and Napoleon scribbled a hasty note to Grouchy telling him to rejoin as quickly as possible. Grouchy, however, had conformed to earlier orders and advanced to Wavre, where he had become heavily engaged against Baron von Thielmann's III Corps, the Prussian rearguard. Grouchy did not receive these fresh orders until 6 o'clock and by then it was far too late to do anything.

Only ten miles separated Wavre from the Waterloo battlefield, but covering that distance on good going is a very different matter from marching through clinging ankle-deep mud, as the Prussians were doing. Blücher rode along the trudging columns, encouraging his men with repeated urgings: 'Vorwärts! It must be done! I have given my word to my comrade Wellington! You would not have me break my word?' The muddy valley of the little river Lasnes, reached about noon, caused some anxious moments because the horse teams were unable to move their guns without the assistance of tired infantry hauling on drag ropes. The crossing was not defended, but Gneisenau insisted on a halt to allow the floundering columns to catch up. The advance was resumed at 2 o'clock and by 4.30 von Bülow's infantry was ready to commence its attack on Plancenoit.

Save for the renewed fire of the grand battery and the continuing struggle for Hougoumont, a lull ensued in Wellington's sector. This the Duke used to pull back some of his units a little further from the crest so that they would be better protected from the French artillery. The movement was noted by Napoleon and his staff, who took it to mean that the Allies had had enough and were beginning to withdraw, an impression reinforced by

a steady stream of men heading rearwards towards the forest of Soignes. In fact, what they had seen were wounded men being helped towards the dressing-stations, prisoners under escort and empty ammunition wagons leaving the line. It was proposed, therefore, that the ample French cavalry be used to turn the supposed Allied withdrawal into a rout while the infantry remained to deal with the Prussians. After all, a similar attack by massed cavalry had unlocked the strong Russian position at Borodino, three years earlier. On the other hand, to achieve success cavalry required the close support of infantry and horse artillery, in the manner already described in the chapter on Austerlitz. Tactical control of the operation rested with Ney, but Reille, d'Erlon and Lobau had no infantry to give him; likewise, Napoleon, who remained torpid throughout the afternoon, declined to allocate any from the Imperial Guard, although he did order the Guard's heavy cavalry regiments forward.

While Ney was deploying his regiments Wellington began making preparations to receive the attack. His batteries, still on the forward slope, were ordered to maintain their fire until the last minute then, having removed one wheel from each gun, the gunners would retire into the nearest infantry square with their rammers and staves; the infantry regiments would form four-deep squares in a chequer-board pattern so that, in so far as it was possible, their fire did not cause casualties among neighbouring units.

Ney decided to advance between La Haye Sainte and Hougoumont, which gave him a frontage 1,000-men wide. At about 4 p.m. his first attack went in at a canter. The Allied artillery fired until the range was almost point-blank, carving lanes through the horsemen, then finished with a devastating salvo of case shot over ball, after which the gunners ran back to join the infantry. The latter were suddenly confronted by an apparently unstoppable tidal wave of glittering steel sweeping over the crest towards them. The French, having been told that they faced an army on the verge of disintegration, were just as shocked to encounter a series of squares bristling with bayonets. Then came the first of regular volleys blanketing the scene in powder smoke. Some squares aimed at the riders, emptying saddles by the score; one officer recalled the sound of balls hitting the cuirassiers' breastplates as being like hail striking a window. Others aimed at the horses, bringing down whole ranks at a time, and thereby impeding the ranks behind them. The charge burst around the squares, receiving further volleys as it passed between them. In vain did the troopers strive to hack or stab their way through the bayonets, though here and there, mainly at the corners, some infantrymen were speared, cut down or shot dead with pistols and carbines. Now thoroughly disorganised, the French were suddenly counter-charged by the less numerous Allied cavalry and driven off the ridge, to be sped on

Left: Waterloo. French cuirassiers charging a Highland square. It was said that the sound of musket balls striking their breast-plates resembled hail on a window.

Above: Waterloo. Lady Butler's painting of a British regimental square under attack, this time by lancers. The regiment's colours and commanding officer can be seen in the centre of the square. *Philip Haythornthwaite Collection*

their way by gunners who ran out to their batteries.

From 4 o'clock until 5.30 Ney was to mount twelve such charges, each more difficult to execute than the last as the entire area was so horribly strewn with dead men and horses. Between the charges the French artillery renewed its fire. Because the ground had now drained somewhat, the balls skipped over the crest to plough into the crowded ranks of the squares. Despite the troops having been told to lie down, casualties were so severe that many men looked forward to a renewal of the cavalry attacks as a relief from the ordeal. By the end of this phase of the battle some squares seemed to consist only of the dead, but Napoleon's magnificent cuirassier, carabinier, lancer, hussar and dragoon regiments had been virtually destroyed. Curiously, though the Allied guns had been overrun a dozen times, no one had

thought to spike them, an omission which gave rise to the saying that a bag of nails could have decided the battle; this was, of course, a wild over-statement, although the consequences of such neglect were clearly very serious.

By now Napoleon had been forced to take a more active interest in the conduct of the battle. At about 5 o'clock Bülow's corps had driven Lobau's troops out of Plancenoit, bringing the main Brussels–Charleroi road within range of the Prussian guns. Two battalions of the Young Guard were sent to restore the situation. This reinforcement proved insufficient, but when two battalions of the Old Guard were committed they drove the Prussians out of the village at the point of the bayonet.

Still believing that there was yet time to defeat Wellington, the Emperor ordered Ney to take La Haye Sainte. The farm had been held against all comers throughout the day by 360 men of the 2nd Light Battalion, King's German Legion, under Major Lewis Baring. During the afternoon ammunition had begun run low and, despite repeated requests, no fresh supplies had arrived. Fifty per cent of Baring's men had been killed or wounded, but their pouches yielded four rounds apiece for the remainder. Ney's attack force, consisting of the 13th Light Infantry and d'Erlon's engineer company, approximately 1,000 men, was held off until it was clear that the garrison had expended its ammunition, then broke into the defences. Baring ordered his men to abandon the position and make their escape through the rear door of the house into the garden, but most of them were unable to do so and only 40 of them succeeded in rallying on the ridge.

For both sides the effect of the French success was cumulative. Ney brought up a horse artillery battery which opened fire on the Allied line, only 300 yards away, while the survivors of d'Erlon's corps pressed on up the slope in skirmish order, inhibiting the work of the Allied gunners and galling the infantry. Wellington's second in command, the young Prince of Orange, immediately recognised the gravity of the situation but disregarded advice that a cuirassier unit had arrived in the lee of La Haye Sainte. He ordered another Legion battalion to advance in line and disperse the skirmishers. It succeeded, briefly, and was then ridden over and wiped out in less than a minute when the cuirassiers charged. The sight was too much for some of the Allied units. A Hanoverian brigade withdrew out of range and a Nassau brigade fled. The Cumberland Hussars, a Hanoverian regiment named after a son of George II, wheeled about and rode all the way to Brussels, telling everyone they met that the battle was lost. There was now a yawning gap around the crossroads which marked the centre of the Allied line.

Neither side was prepared for what had taken place. Ney was desperate to exploit the situation but the cavalry had been squandered during the afternoon's attacks and the right wing of d'Erlon's battered corps was starting to come under pressure from the Prussians. One possible source of troops was the Imperial Guard, which had been created with just such a role in mind. Ney dispatched a middle-ranking staff officer to Napoleon with his request for reinforcements, but the Emperor responded with dismissive sarcasm: 'Troops! Where do you want me to get them? Do you want me to make them?' At this moment his entire attention was focused on the crisis which had developed at Plancenoit.

For the last hour or more, Wellington had believed the battle to be won, and the loss of La Haye Sainte was most unwelcome. But by methodically drawing units from his right and left wings he slowly closed the gap in the Allied centre. The newly arrived units drove off d'Erlon's skirmishers, the guns resumed firing and the French horse artillery battery at La Haye Sainte was silenced. Furthermore, Blücher's Prussians were closing in with every minute that passed. True, Bülow had been repulsed at Plancenoit, but Pirch's II Corps was coming into action and Ziethen's I Corps was approaching his own left. Ziethen, in fact, was so seriously alarmed by the flood of fugitives and wounded heading for the rear that at first he declined to prolong Wellington's line, as agreed, but eventually did so when persuaded by the efficient Müffling that the situation was in hand. By now, too, the French line had been bent back into a right angle as a result of Blücher's arrival.

As soon as the recapture of Plancenoit temporarily eased the pressure on his immediate right, Napoleon sent an officer along the line at the gallop to say that the fighting on that flank resulted from Grouchy's arrival rather than Blücher's. The morale of his tired, dispirited troops soared, for now they felt certain of victory. Ney arrived in person to urge exploitation of the situation which existed at La Haye Sainte and this time there could be no denying the justice of his request. At 7 o'clock the French could have driven through Wellington's centre, but at 7.30, when Napoleon personally led forward six battalions of the Middle Guard and three of the Old Guard, the moment had passed. Nevertheless the sight of the Guard going in sent another thrill of excitement through the army. The Guard had never been beaten, men reminded one another, and the Guard always delivered the *coup-de-grâce*! For Napoleon it was the last throw of the dice. If the Guard did finally succeed in breaking Wellington's army, he could probably hold off the Prussians and possibly beat them on the morrow; if the Guard failed, the battle was lost and with it his political ambitions and his throne.

The Guard halted just short of La Haye Sainte. The assault was to be led by five battalions of the Middle Guard, with the sixth forming a firm base; the three Old Guard battalions would remain with Napoleon and be committed as a second wave if necessary. Curiously, the axis of the assault would not follow the relatively unencumbered route past the farm and up the road to the vital crossroads. Instead, it would wheel half-left and mount the slope already littered with the debris of the failed cavalry attacks, exposing its left to enfilade fire from Hougoumont. Furthermore, the nature of the going meant that the battalion columns, marching with two horse artillery guns in the intervals between them, would reach the Allied line piecemeal, greatly reducing their cumulative effect.

The Allied infantry, lying down beyond the crest as the French artillery redoubled its fire, could see very little although what they heard clearly indicated yet another impending trial of strength. Their own guns were being fired as fast as the gunners could load them and through the clouds of powder smoke came the steady beat of scores of drums beating the *pas de charge*, accompanied by cheers and yells of '*Vive l'Empereur!*'

So difficult was the going that two battalion columns of the Guard, the 1st/ and 2nd/3rd Chasseurs, had converged and were coming on with a combined frontage some 60 files wide. They had taken severe casualties from the Allied roundshot and canister but their ardour was undiminished. As they passed through the now deserted gun line and breasted the rise all they could see was a small group of mounted officers, watching them impassively. It was Wellington and his staff, who had positioned themselves to the rear of Major-General Peregrine Maitland's 1st Brigade, consisting of the 2nd and 3rd Battalions 1st Foot (later Grenadier) Guards.

The brigade was concealed behind a bank running along the lateral track and, because Wellington believed that the French attack would be supported by cavalry, it had adopted a compromise, four-deep linear formation. When the chasseurs were only 40 yards away, Wellington called, 'Now, Maitland! Now's your time!' This was followed by a shout of 'Up, Guards!' Suddenly the French were confronted by a solid rising wall of scarlet. For the next terrible minute they endured a succession of precise, point-blank volleys and 300 chasseurs went down. Those at the rear of the column tried to return fire, but then, with bayonets levelled, the British line charged and the chasseurs broke in headlong flight.

To Maitland's left was Major-General Sir Colin Halkett's 5th Brigade, which had suffered so severely during the afternoon that it was effectively reduced to two weak battalions of the 33rd (West Riding) and the 69th (South Lincolnshire) Regiments. These confronted the two columns formed by 1st/3rd and 4th Grenadiers, which they halted with their volleys. However, when the French horse artillery began firing canister into the British line, Halkett ordered his men back beyond the crest. In the process he was wounded, the battalions became mingled and confusion ensued until a member of Wellington's staff restored order. The French, chastened a little, resumed their advance and came on behind a ragged fire. As soon as their bearskins crossed the crest their leading ranks were again shot away. Worse still, on their right, Captain Krahmer de Binche's battery, of Lieutenant-General de Chassé's 3rd Netherlands Division, one of the formations with which Wellington had closed the gap in his centre, began firing canister into their flank from a range of only 100 yards. Finally, when Chassé launched one of his infantry brigades in a bayonet charge from the same direction, both French columns disintegrated in flight.

Maitland's brigade returned to the ridge from its pursuit in time to see the Middle Guard's last column, consisting of the 4th

Chasseurs, joined by fugitives from the defeated 3rd Chasseurs, closing in on Major-General Sir Frederick Adams' 3rd (Light) Brigade to their right. One of Adams' battalions, the 1st/52nd (Oxfordshire) Regiment, overlapped the French frontage and its commander, Colonel Sir John Colborne, having obtained Adams' permission, wheeled it out of line until it was parallel with the flank of the enemy column and opened fire. The ensuing firefight was severe, but the chasseurs were also taking heavy punishment from their front and when Colborne ordered a bayonet charge they fled in the direction of La Haye Sainte with the 52nd in hot pursuit.

From the remainder of the French army there came a collective cry of disbelief and despair: *'La Garde recule!'* The unbelievable had happened. If the Guard had been beaten, what hope was there for anyone else? Yet even if had won, its efforts would have been for nothing. At the apex of the French line Ziethen's artillery was simultaneously firing into the rear of Lobau's and d'Erlon's corps, and once again Bülow was advancing on Plancenoit. Even as the fugitives from the Guard's failed attack were streaming away, one of Ziethen's brigades smashed through the vulnerable angle. The breach quickly became a chasm as more troops streamed through. From the ridge, Wellington signalled a general advance. The Allied army poured down the slope, rolling over any opposition in its path. The French, realising that they were in danger of being trapped between Wellington and Blücher, abandoned their positions *en masse* and dissolved into an undisciplined, panic-stricken mob fleeing southwards along the Charleroi road.

At La Haye Sainte Napoleon formed the three Old Guard battalions into squares which provided a temporary refuge for him until they had withdrawn far enough for the remnant of the Guard cavalry to hurry him off the field. These three battalions – 1st/2nd Grenadiers, 2nd/1st and 2nd/2nd Chasseurs – made an epic fighting retreat until they were destroyed near La Belle Alliance. Two more battalions of the Old Guard, 1st/2nd Chasseurs and 2nd/2nd Grenadiers, died where they fought at Plancenoit. At Rossomme responsibility for the Emperor's safety was assumed by the two battalions of the 1st Grenadiers, the élite of the élite, joined by the 1st/1st Chasseurs at Le Caillou. These units alone preserved the honour of the French Army, for when Napoleon reached Genappe, where he hoped to make a stand along the little river Dyle, he found a fear-crazed mob fighting to cross the single bridge and killing one another in the process; the water below was just ten feet wide and three feet deep. By-passing the village, the Guard forded the stream and escorted the Emperor to safety.

By chance, Wellington and Blücher met at La Belle Alliance. Both were hardened to the horrors of the battlefield, but that of Waterloo, measuring only six miles by four, was so thickly strewn with dead and wounded men, the carcasses of horses, smashed guns, abandoned wagons and discarded equipment, was beyond their experience. Blücher tried to express his feelings in French but could only manage a single phrase – *'Quelle affaire!'* Wellington asked him to continue the pursuit because his own army was exhausted. He agreed and Gneisenau, mounting a drummer on a horse and having his trumpeters blow the Charge on every possible occasion, unleashed his hussars into the gathering darkness. They showed little mercy, least of all in Genappe.

Although Wellington had remained coolly efficient throughout the battle, the strain had been tremendous. He was to comment: 'In all my life I have not experienced such anxiety, for I must confess that I have never been so close to defeat. Never did I see such a pounding match. It was the nearest run thing you ever saw in your life.' When the casualty list was shown to him it contained the names of so many friends that he wept. His own army's losses totalled 15,000 killed and wounded, the British share being to two-thirds of this; the Prussians lost approximately 7,000 men; the French lost 25,000 killed and wounded, 8,000 prisoners and 220 guns captured.

On 22 June Napoleon abdicated for the second time; four months later he reached the remote island of St Helena, where he would remain in exile until his death in 1821. As Fuller comments in his *Decisive Battles of the Western World*, during the two generations which followed Waterloo a period of stability, peace and prosperity descended upon Europe, despite the revolutions of 1830 and 1848. If Trafalgar had consolidated England's supremacy at sea, Waterloo confirmed her status as a world power. Harnessed energetically to the industrial and agricultural revolutions, these factors made her the world's workshop and financial centre, generating immense wealth. In Europe, she strove successfully to preserve a balance of power, and elsewhere she was able to enforce what became known as the *Pax Britannica*.

In military terms, the last word on Waterloo should, perhaps, be left to Napoleon himself, since they indicate a radically different perspective from that which he had expressed to Soult and Reille at breakfast. During his flight to Paris his old friend Count Flahaut asked whether he was surprised by the outcome of the battle. 'No,' replied the Emperor, with a shrug. 'It has been the same thing since Crécy.'

Commentary 8 – The Birth of Industrialised Warfare

Steam engines had been in use for some time before the Napoleonic Wars ended, but their real impact only began to make itself felt in the decades which followed. They provided the power source for factories and the motive power for ships and land transport systems. The introduction of railways meant that larger armies could not only be transported very quickly to a war zone but could also be supplied regularly. Railways thus became strategic and logistic assets that were vital in planning a campaign. As their operation depended upon precise schedules, railway clocks were synchronised, so initiating common national times; from this followed synchronisation of watches on the battlefield to ensure that operational phases were activated in accordance with the master plan, first recorded during the French assault on the Malakoff redoubt at Sebastopol during the Crimean War.

In the maritime sphere, steam at first played an auxiliary role to sail and was derided by some ship owners on the grounds that wind was cheaper than coal. They quickly changed their minds when their rivals began operating predictable, frequent and therefore profitable sailings. Navies could not afford to ignore the trend and, although ever bigger ships were built with greater endurance provided by larger coal bunkers, the growing need for naval and mercantile coaling stations around the world provided a further spur to imperial ambitions. At first steamships were powered by external paddle wheels which were dangerously vulnerable, but in 1843 the exponents of the propeller or screw won the day when the paddle-wheeled *Alecto* was towed astern in a tug-of-war by the screw-fitted *Rattler*, both vessels being of similar size and power and going full ahead.

Concurrently with the spread of railways and steamships, the electric telegraph was developed, rapidly becoming international in its operation. It enabled field commanders to communicate quickly with their distant formations and depots, thereby increasing the overall efficiency of armies. It was, however, a two-edged sword on two counts. First, it permitted long-range political interference in the conduct of operations, sometimes with unfortunate results. Secondly, increased literacy had led to a popular press, and with it the accreditation of professional war correspondents. For the first time, commanders' shortcomings were ruthlessly exposed to the public, often producing a political backlash. The dispatches of William Howard Russell from the Crimea, published in *The Times*, brought down the government of the day. These, and the first photographs of conditions at the dirty end of war, radically altered for the better the public's perception of the ordinary soldier.

As a result of the industrial revolution, iron production soared. Even more significant was Henry Bessemer's conversion process of 1856, which produced high-quality machinable steel for all manner of military and civilian purposes, including machine tools which could be used to generate mass production. Together, these developments were applied by armaments industries to transform the concept of firepower, in terms of accuracy, rapidity and range, by improving both guns and ammunition.

For the infantryman the change began in the second quarter of the 19th century. First, the old flintlock firing mechanism gave way to the more efficient all-weather percussion cap. Next, the problems encountered when loading a rifled barrel with a tight-fitting round were solved by Captain Claude Minié of the French Musketry School at Vincennes. In 1841 he introduced a conical bullet which, being slightly sub-calibre, could easily be dropped into the barrel base first. The bullet's base featured a hollow which expanded to grip the rifling when the charge exploded. The effect was dramatic, for whereas troops had entered the killing zone of the old smoothbore musket at 200 yards' range or less, with the Minié rifle they entered it at 1,000 to 800 yards. At a stroke the old musket was rendered obsolete and armies hastened to re-equip with the new system. A notable exception was the Prussian Army which, during the 1840s, adopted the Dreyse 'needle gun', a breech-loading rifle in which the firing needle penetrated a paper cartridge to detonate a primer. The Dreyse was sighted to 800 yards, but lacked a gas-tight breech and its accuracy suffered in consequence. In 1866 the French took the lead again with a breech-loading rifle of their own, designed by Antoine Chassepot, who reduced gas leakage by sealing the breech with a rubber ring; significantly, the Chassepot was sighted to 1,600 yards. The introduction of breech-loading rifles enabled the infantry, for the first time, to maintain a high rate of fire while lying prone behind cover; it also meant that artillery batteries were at serious risk if, as formerly, they were deployed in or in front of the firing line.

The artillerymen, however, were not to be left behind by these developments. Rifled iron guns with increased range and power were constructed with reinforcing bands shrunk onto them in the areas where internal pressures were greatest, producing an ugly but serviceable result. In 1854 William Armstrong, a Tyneside civil engineer, produced such a gun with an added advantage in that it could be loaded from the breech. This was adopted by the British Army in two versions: the 12-pounder for field batteries and the 9-pounder for horse artillery. Its performance, both as to range and accuracy, was impressive, although difficulties were encountered with the breech mechanism. This consisted of a removable vent piece which had to be screwed tight against the chamber from the rear. On active service it was found that the vent piece could crack or even blow out because the joint was not gas-proof and for a while the Royal Artillery reverted to rifled muzzle-loading guns.

At first many artillerymen had strong reservations about steel as a gun-making material. Until manufacturing techniques had been refined to eliminate flaws in the material, steel guns could explode without warning, whereas those made from iron merely cracked. In 1851, however, the German manufacturer Alfred Krupp produced a steel gun which gave a superior performance. The problem of obtaining a gas-tight breech was solved by Krupp with an integral sliding block; later, a French engineer named de Bagne would introduce a hinged breech which was locked in place by an interrupted-screw mechanism.

As with guns, so with ammunition. Rifled guns had twice the range of their smoothbore counterparts. Solid ball shot became a thing of the past when it was discovered that elongated, ballistically shaped projectiles not only produced better results in terms of range, but could also be designed to carry an explosive payload detonated either by impact or time fuses. To eliminate windage between shell and barrel various devices were employed in turn.

One method was to use shells fitted with studs which engaged the grooves of the rifling; another was a gas-check consisting of a *papier mâché* cup loaded between the projectile and the charge; a third, and ultimately successful, method was to fit the shell with a copper driving band. From about 1860 limbered ammunition commonly in use included explosive shells, shrapnel shells and canister, carried in the proportions considered relevant to the engagement in hand. Instead of siting their batteries in close proximity to the infantry, artillerymen began to take advantage of the increased ranges available and deploying them on elevated ground to the rear, from which they could dominate the battlefield.

During the American Civil War an altogether new class of weapon system made its debut. This was the machine-gun, although at this stage the term 'manually operated rapid fire system' would be more apposite. In October 1861 the Federal government purchased a number of Ager or Union Repeating Guns which were used to guard bridges and defiles. Better remembered is the Gatling gun, named after its inventor, Dr Richard Gatling, which, though it did not appear until the later stages of the war, was taken into service by the US Army and continued to serve with several other armies and navies during the following decades. It consisted of six barrels which revolved around a central axis when a crank was turned, each barrel being loaded in turn when it reached the magazine and fired in succession. Nearly as well remembered is the Mitrailleuse, the invention of a Belgian officer, Captain Fafschamps, which was adopted by the French Army. This consisted of a tube containing twenty-five 13mm barrels which were loaded simultaneously with rounds contained in a steel plate, behind which the breech block was closed. Using a crank, the barrels could all be fired at once or singly in rotation. The weapon had a range of 2,000 yards and, using several pre-loaded plates, could fire up to 150 rounds a minute. The problem was that conservative military administrations could not decide whether the new weapons belonged to the infantry or the artillery, but since they were heavy enough to require transportation on a field carriage they tended to favour the latter.

Cavalry was now entering the period of its terminal decline. It could still perform the tasks of reconnaissance, raiding, mounted infantry and shock action against its own kind, but to attempt shock action with the sword or lance against unshaken infantry and artillery armed with breech-loading weapons was tantamount to suicide; in fact, when confronted with cavalry, infantry no longer found it necessary to form the defensive square. All of this was quickly absorbed by both sides during the American Civil War, but European armies, still heavily influenced by social tradition, found it difficult to accept the change and still fielded large and hugely expensive cavalry formations. As always, there were exceptions to the general rule such as the successful charge of Major-General Friedrich von Bredow's 12th Cavalry Brigade at Mars-la-Tour during the Franco–Prussian War, which was often cited as a justification for the retention of cavalry. This somewhat begged the questions that for much of its approach the brigade enjoyed the protection of dead ground, and that it was virtually destroyed during its attack.

The science of fortress engineering also began to decline. The production of ever-larger siege guns and more powerful explosives spelled the death of the old Vauban-style fortresses which could very quickly be reduced to rubble. Many continental cities levelled their ramparts, which became pleasant, tree-lined walks, and relied instead on a ring of mutually supporting forts sited on tactically important features well beyond the suburbs. The new forts were reinforced with concrete, sometimes in two layers with a 'burster' course of sand between to absorb the impact of exploding shells, and their guns were protected by armoured cupolas. In the long term it was a losing battle in that however hard the fortress engineers tried, the designers of siege artillery always seemed to have an answer.

Consideration of war at the higher levels was stimulated by several writers including Antoine Jomini, a Swiss who served in both the French and Russian armies. Jomini emphasised the benefit of interior lines and the importance of applying maximum force at the right time and place. While expressing a preference for small, well-trained regular forces, he predicted that ultimately the Industrial Revolution would result in massed armies equipped with terrible weapons. Karl von Clausewitz, who had served as Chief of Staff of Thielmann's corps during the Waterloo campaign, was less popular in his own day but ultimately more influential. Clausewitz saw war as an extension of politics by other means, its object being the destruction of the enemy's means and will to fight. This he foresaw would involve harnessing a nation's entire effort, political, military and economic, if it was to succeed. As an experienced soldier he was able to comment that 'Everything in war is very simple, but the most simple thing is very difficult,' since war is the realm of uncertainty, fear, physical effort and other factors which inhibit the smooth functioning of armies. Such sources of internal friction could, he said, be reduced by sound training, high morale, experience and a study of the lessons provided by military history. One officer greatly influenced by Clausewitz was Field Marshal Helmuth von Moltke, Chief of the Prussian Great General Staff from 1857 until 1888. Moltke relied on a fast and efficient mobilisation involving the rapid transport of troops to the frontier by rail. Once in the war zone, they would march separately but, controlled by the electric telegraph, would converge to fight the decisive battle, just as Blücher's army had converged to join Wellington at Waterloo. In fact, although Waterloo did provide an example of the genre, Moltke's thoughts were centred upon recreating Cannae, the crushing battle of annihilation. This was reflected in his strategic planning and was brought to dramatic fruition against the Austrians at Königgratz (Sadowa) in 1866 and against the French at Sedan in 1870. Understandably, under Moltke the Railway Section was regarded as embodying the cream of the Greater General Staff's intellect.

Inevitably, tactics lagged some way behind technical innovation, with weight, mass and speed being considered essential elements in the attack, notwithstanding the fact that the attackers would enter the killing zone much earlier than before and sustain higher losses in proportion. Thus, while the battles of the Crimean War bore some resemblance to those of the Napoleonic era, those of France's war against Austria in Italy, fought only four years later, were markedly different; the horrific casualties at Solferino caused widespread revulsion and were a major factor in the founding of the Red Cross organisation. The trend was further emphasised during the American Civil War, the Austro–Prussian War of 1866 and the Franco–Prussian War. Despite this, the manpower resources of the contending nations were not seriously affected because, with the exception of France, the European birth rate was rising rapidly while, thanks to the advance of medical science, the death rate was declining. As a result the continental powers found no difficulty in filling the ranks of their expanding armies by means of conscription, while the British and United States armies were able to rely on voluntary enlistment.

At sea, the implications of steam propulsion had barely been digested when navies were confronted by a fresh series of technical innovations. At Sinope on 30 November 1853 the Russian Navy destroyed a Turkish flotilla, the most significant aspect of the engagement being the Russian use of explosive shells that inflicted crippling damage on the Turks' wooden hulls. During the subsequent Crimean War naval operations took place in the Black Sea and the Baltic, where British and French bombardments of coastal fortifications met a similar response. Napoleon III ordered the construction of several floating batteries protected by 4-inch iron plates overlaid on thick wooden hulls and, despite being hit regularly, these proved a complete success. In 1859 the French Navy exploited the advance by launching the first ironclad warship, *Gloire*, a similarly constructed screw-driven frigate with auxiliary sails, armed with 36 rifled 50-pounder guns firing explosive shells. Seriously alarmed, in 1861 the Royal Navy responded with the armoured, iron-hulled *Warrior*, which was faster, more seaworthy and armed with a mix of 68- and 110-pounder guns with superior penetrative performance. In their turn, designers of naval ammunition concentrated on producing armour-piercing shells, hardening the nose of the round so that it achieved penetration before exploding within the enemy hull.

If *Warrior* rendered every other warship obsolete, technical developments were already in train that would quickly overtake her. Early in the American Civil War the Federals had been forced to abandon their naval base at Norfolk, Virginia, and with it the screw frigate *Merrimack*, which was burned to the waterline. The Confederates found that her lower hull and engines were repairable and they fitted her with an armoured superstructure containing ten guns. Simultaneously John Ericsson, a Swedish engineer, had been designing a revolutionary warship named *Monitor* for the Federal Navy. This consisted of a revolving armoured turret containing two 11-inch smoothbore guns, mounted on a wide armoured deck overhanging the hull, propeller and rudder. On 8 March 1862 *Merrimack* (now re-named *Virginia*) emerged to tackle the Federal squadron blockading the James River. She rammed and sank one ship and drove two more ashore, one of which was disabled and forced to surrender by her gunfire. *Monitor* arrived during the night and next morning the two ironclads fought an inconclusive duel in which each obtained about twenty hits on the other without penetrating the armour. *Merrimack* was subsequently burned when the Federals re-occupied the area, and *Monitor* foundered at sea because of her low freeboard; her name was to be perpetuated by a class of coastal bombardment vessels.

Nevertheless the two engagements, while small in themselves, were decisive. The first sounded the death-knell of unprotected wooden warships, and the second was to revolutionise warship design. *Gloire*, *Warrior* and *Merrimack* all mounted their guns in conventional broadsides, but *Monitor*'s revolving turret opened up new and exciting possibilities at a time when longer range was being sought. Longer range demanded longer guns, but there were obvious difficulties in mounting these in broadside vessels, notably the lack of space needed for loading, and the weapon's recoil. Turrets were suitable for breech-loading guns, but there were still plenty of muzzle-loaders about and for these a compromise system was produced. This was the barbette, an armoured breastwork over which the gun was fired, then traversed inboard and depressed for re-loading. Once turret and barbette mountings had been introduced, the need of broadside gun ports disappeared, thereby eliminating these vulnerable gaps in the armoured belt.

As warships came to rely more and more on steam, the need of sails declined and in 1871 the Royal Navy launched the first battleship without any provision for them, HMS *Devastation*. Automotive independence also led to the brief resurrection of an archaic weapon, the ram. As we have seen, this had claimed one victim for *Merrimack*, but its moment of glory came on 20 July 1866 when, during the Second Battle of Lissa, fought between Austrian and Italian fleets, *Ferdinand Max* rammed and sank *Re d'Italia* with heavy loss of life.

Moored mines – confusingly called torpedoes at the time – were first used by the Russians in the Baltic during the Crimean War. They were of the contact type and their use quickly became widespread, especially during the American Civil War. The device was refined by a remote detonation mechanism, activated electrically through a cable connected to a switchboard ashore. The Confederates also used 'spar torpedoes' (explosive charges fixed to the end of a spar) in their attacks on Federal shipping. These were fitted in the bows of the attacking vessel and simply rammed the side of the victim. In this way a steam-driven, trimmed-down, semi-submersible named *David* damaged the USS *New Ironsides* on 5 October

1863, and on 17 February 1864 the USS *Housatonic* became the first ship to be sunk by a submarine, the man-powered *H. L. Hunley*, which she took to the bottom with her.

GETTYSBURG, 1–3 JULY 1863

When the Confederate southern states seceded from the Union in 1861 the prospect of their obtaining a decisive military victory over their Federal northern adversaries was remote. The South had a population of only 5½ million, while that of the North was 22 million. As if these odds were not long enough, on the eve of what would inevitably evolve into an industrialised conflict, the South had only 8,500 miles of railway compared to the North's 22,000 miles. In the South agriculture played a more important role in the economy than industry and there were only 18,000 factories; in the North industry was just getting into its stride but already there were more than 110,000 factories. Furthermore industrial capital investment in the North was nearly ten times that in the South, which made the gap in productive capacity even wider.

The Confederacy was, however, able to field a higher proportion of its available manpower because much of its manual labour was performed by slaves, so that on the battlefield the odds between the two sides were much closer than might be suggested by the above. Well aware of the inequality of the struggle, it sought to preserve its independence either by attracting foreign support, especially that of Great Britain and France, or by inducing war weariness in the North. Psychologically, too, the Confederacy was the better prepared for war.

President Abraham Lincoln's Federal administration made the mistake of preparing for a short war. However, after the Confederate victory at Bull Run on 21 July 1861, it recognised that only the physical conquest of the South could bring the war to a successful conclusion, and that this would be a lengthy process. It therefore adopted the long-term strategy proposed by the US Army's General in Chief, Lieutenant General Winfield Scott, which became known as the Anaconda Plan. This envisaged an advance down the Mississippi to the Gulf of Mexico while the US Navy imposed a blockade on southern ports. The effect would be to cut the Confederacy in two, curtail its exports of cotton and tobacco, deprive it of foreign aid and, ultimately, strangle the greater part of it into submission.

When the war broke out the US Army numbered only 16,367 officers and men who were either employed on the western frontier or in coastal defence forts. Many Southern officers opted to fight for their own people and upon these respective rumps fell the burden of raising, equipping and training the huge armies that would be required. Once again the Federals made a serious mistake in that many regular officers remained with their own regiments while civilian political appointees received volunteer commissions and were promoted to absurdly high ranks for which they were quite unfitted. The Confederates, on the other hand, distributed their regular officers throughout the army where they would do most good. On both sides, states raised militia and volunteer regiments which required training from scratch.

The early encounters were fought by amateurs whose idealism and enthusiasm was ruthlessly blunted as pre-conceived ideas and defective training were exposed to reality. Hard experience sorted the wheat from the chaff and by the summer of 1862 the American genius for organisation had produced armies that were capable of doing their job. It was true that they lacked the spit-and-polish of their European contemporaries, but equally they were less inhibited by tradition, more flexible in their outlook and more innovative in their tactics.

Two years after the war had begun there were few signs that it could be ended quickly. It was being fought on two major fronts, with mixed results. In the west the Federals were winning slowly and had secured control of the Mississippi save for the fortress of Vicksburg, which was besieged by Major General Ulysses S. Grant's Army of the Tennessee. In the eastern theatre, where much of the fighting took place between the two respective capitals of Washington, DC, and Richmond, Virginia, the position came close to being reversed. Despite regular changes of command, the Federal Army of the Potomac was regularly defeated by the Confederate Army of Northern Virginia, commanded by General Robert E. Lee.

Lee was undeniably a charismatic leader, held in great affection by his men, who regarded him as the personification of the Southern gentleman. He had served with distinction during the United States' war with Mexico and was an excellent defensive strategist. When conducting offensive operations his touch was less sure and his judgement uncertain; in particular he seemed reluctant to impose his will on his immediate subordinates. In August 1862 Lee had carried the war into the North, hoping that a victory there would lead to offers of mediation, and thus tacit recognition of the Confederacy, by Great Britain and France. On 17 September he fought the Battle of Antietam (known in the South as Sharpsburg) against heavy odds and was only saved from defeat by the failure of a Federal corps commander to press his advantage and the timely arrival of Major General Ambrose Hill's division. In London Lord Palmerston's government was actively considering recognition of the Confederacy, but when the outcome of battle was known it deferred its decision to await developments. From then on the prospect of foreign intervention gradually receded. After Antietam Lee retired into Virginia and on 13 December he inflicted a serious defeat on the Army of the Potomac at Fredericksburg. In a battle lasting from 1 to 6 May 1863, he again defeated it at Chancellorsville.

In Richmond it was felt that the moment had come for Lee to lead the Army of Northern Virginia in another invasion of the North. One object of this would be to relieve the pressure on the defenders of Vicksburg, which could be achieved by destroying the bridge crossing the Susquehanna river at Harrisburg, as well as

large sections of the Pennsylvania Railroad, thereby seriously disrupting Federal communications with the western theatre of war. Once these tasks had been completed, Lee would be at liberty to menace Philadelphia, Baltimore or even Washington itself, which would cause such an uproar among the war-weary populace that President Lincoln's government would succumb to popular demand for a negotiated peace.

Chancellorsville had been an expensive victory for the Confederacy in that it cost the life of Lieutenant General Thomas (Stonewall) Jackson, mistakenly shot by his own pickets in the dark. Jackson and Lee had worked well together, but the Army Commander did not enjoy a similar mutual understanding with any of his remaining senior officers. It was equally unfortunate that Lee was himself no longer a well man. In March he had sustained an attack of pericarditis and although he had recovered sufficiently to command at Chancellorsville the after-effects of the disease, including pain and a general deceleration of the system, may have affected his conduct of the subsequent campaign.

After Chancellorsville Lee re-organised his army into three corps under Lieutenant General James Longstreet (I Corps), Lieutenant General Richard Ewell (II Corps) and Lieutenant General Ambrose Hill (III Corps). Supremely confident in their ability to perform their tasks, he ordered them to march on 3 June. After leaving the Fredericksburg area they crossed the Blue Ridge Mountains into the Shenandoah Valley then marched northwards, defeating a Federal force encountered at Winchester. The right flank of the move was covered by Major General J. E. B. Stuart's Cavalry Division until, on 9 June, it was surprised by Major General Alfred Pleasanton's Federal Cavalry Corps in its encampments near Brandy Station. In every previous encounter Stuart's troopers had chased their opponents off the field, but on this occasion they barely managed to hold their own. As the engagement provided proof of Lee's movements, Washington ordered Major General Joseph Hooker, commanding the Army of the Potomac, to conform, keeping his army between the Confederates and the capital.

The workings of both armies now became subject to the sort of internal friction noted by Clausewitz. A year earlier Stuart had ridden right round the Army of the Potomac, causing chaos among the Federals. Aware that Hooker's troops had also begun to march north, and still smarting from his reverse at Brandy Station, he proposed to Lee that he should harry their rear and then rejoin by a direct route when the Army of Northern Virginia was closer to its objectives. Lee agreed conditionally, permitting Stuart to leave with three of his six cavalry brigades. Hooker's command, however, was spread over so many miles that Stuart was forced to turn south before he was able to cross its rear. Furthermore the Federals were setting such a cracking pace that he was compelled to maintain a parallel route through Maryland. He did, however, cause damage to the enemy's railway system and captured a supply convoy of 125 wagons which he decided to take along, although they slowed him down. Temporarily unable to rejoin Lee, he decided to head for Carlisle, Pennsylvania, which lay on the latter's route to Harrisburg. The cumulative effect of Stuart's foray was, therefore, to deprive the Army of Northern Virginia of its eyes and ears at the very time they were most needed.

The Federals, too, had their problems. The arsenal at Harper's Ferry was indefensible and 'Fighting Joe' Hooker wanted to add its 10,000-strong garrison to his army. When his request was refused he resigned and since he had not been forgiven for the defeat at Chancellorsville his resignation was accepted. On 28 June Major General George C. Meade was appointed commander of the Army of the Potomac. Meade was neither a political animal nor was he a party to factional squabbles within the Army, and for this reason his appointment gave least offence to those who were. Having made it clear that he did not want the job, he had little alternative but to take it at a time when a major crisis was building up. While commanding a corps at Fredericksburg and Chancellorsville he had shown himself to be steady if unimaginative and cautious, all characteristics which he would display during the forthcoming battle.

The day upon which Meade received his appointment found the Army of Northern Virginia within striking distance of its first objective – Harrisburg. Ewell's II Corps had one division at Carlisle and another at York, while Longstreet's and Hill's corps had reached Chambersburg, where Lee established a temporary headquarters. The isolation of Stuart's cavalry far to the east had left Lee without any clear idea of his opponents' movements, but that evening a Confederate agent arrived. He told Lee that Hooker had been replaced by Meade, the Army of the Potomac's fifth change of command in ten months, that the enemy had passed through Frederick, Maryland, and was still marching north. The latter caused Lee considerable concern as Frederick was too close for comfort; also Lee had to assume that his new opponent was being kept well informed as to the Army of Northern Virginia's movements both by his own cavalry and the hostile civil population. He therefore decided to suspend operations against Harrisburg and, anticipating a major engagement, ordered his corps commanders to concentrate their troops at Cashtown.

Some eight miles east of Cashtown in the pleasant, rolling Pennsylvania countryside, was the sleepy little town of Gettysburg, remarkable only in that it was the meeting place of ten roads, was the terminus of an unfinished railway, and contained a Lutheran seminary. This unspoiled, rural scene was to provide the setting for the Civil War's bloodiest battle. The ground over which the decisive actions were fought lies to the south of the town and consists of two low parallel ridges running from north to south, the western feature being known as Seminary Ridge and the eastern as Cemetery Ridge. At the northern end of Cemetery Ridge is the appropriately named Cemetery Hill joined by its eastern shoulder to

**GETTYSBURG,
1–3 July 1863**

Union Corps
❶ Slocum XII
❷ Newton I
❸ Howard XI
❹ Hancock II
❺ Sickles III
❻ Sykes V
❼ Sedgwick VI
  (direction of
  approach)

A Culp's Hill
B Plum Run –
  stream
C Devil's Den
D McPherson's
  Ridge
E Peach
  Orchard
F Wheat field

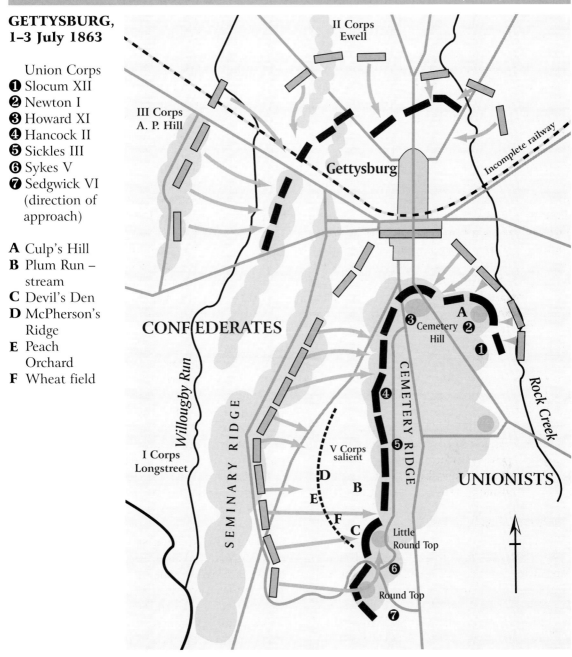

Culp's Hill. From Cemetery Hill the ridge extends southwards, losing height and terminating in a steep-sided valley through which flows a stream called Plum Run. Across the mouth of the valley is an area of gigantic, tumbled boulders deposited long ago by retreating glaciers, known locally as the Devil's Den. The southern slopes of the valley are formed by two hills suitably named Little Round Top and Round Top. The summit and western slopes of Little Round Top consist of granite boulders and scattered trees; the eastern slopes, the saddle connecting the feature to Round Top, and the whole of Round Top itself, are densely forested. Round Top was the higher of the two, but trees denied any view

157

from its summit. From Little Round Top, however, the whole of Cemetery Ridge is visible and within range, rendering it untenable if it should fall to an enemy, although this only becomes apparent to anyone who has actually climbed to the summit.

It was a shortage of boots within the Confederate ranks that resulted in Gettysburg becoming a battlefield. Many of Lee's men were marching barefooted and a report that there was a boot and shoe warehouse in the town led to a brigade being dispatched from Cashtown on 30 June to secure it. As it approached it became apparent that Gettysburg was occupied by Federal cavalry. No engagement took place, but the news that the two armies were once again in contact was quickly passed up their respective chains of command. Soon the Army of the Potomac, with eight corps numbering 97,000 men and 360 guns was approaching Gettysburg from the south and south-east, while the Army of Northern Virginia, with three corps, 75,000 men and 280 guns, converged from the west, north and north-east. Lee also dispatched messengers to find Stuart and order him to rejoin immediately.

Fighting began shortly after dawn on 1 July as the vanguards of the two armies clashed to the north and east of the town. Both sides pushed reinforcements into the fight as they came up. Advancing from the east, Hill's III Corps pushed the Federals off a feature known as McPherson's Ridge, then off Seminary Ridge. During the afternoon Ewell's II Corps came in from the north, threatening the Federal right until troops were deployed in its path. Like many encounter battles, it was confused and untidy from the command point of view. By evening, however, the Federal I and XI Corps had been ejected from Gettysburg town and had taken up positions on Cemetery Hill and the northern part of Cemetery Ridge.

During the night more and more troops arrived so that by the morning of 2 July the formal battle lines had been established. Because of Ewell's presence to the north, the Federal line offered a refused right flank and therefore resembled a fish-hook. The extreme right was held by XII Corps (Major General Henry W. Slocum), then came I Corps (Major General John Newton) on Culp's Hill with its left extending towards Cemetery Hill where it joined XI Corps (Major General Oliver O. Howard). From this point the line ran southwards along Cemetery Ridge with II Corps (Major General Winfield S. Hancock) and III Corps (Major General Daniel E. Sickles) holding the left flank. Some distance behind was V Corps (Major General George Sykes) in reserve. VI Corps (Major General John Sedgwick) was still marching towards the battlefield but would arrive during the late afternoon.

The Army of the Potomac was therefore in occupation of a sound defensive position and, for his part, Meade had no intention of throwing away this advantage by attacking his more experienced opponent. Nevertheless, one area did cause him serious concern. Sickles, commanding III Corps, was one of the Army's political appointees. Aggressive by nature, he had performed well as a brigade and divisional commander but was unsuited to the command of a corps. He was jealous of the newly promoted Meade and inclined to take matters into his own hands. On this occasion he had not liked the position allocated to his corps on the lower, southern end of Cemetery Ridge and advanced his divisions to somewhat higher ground 1,000 yards closer to the enemy. This had the effect of creating a salient, the left flank of which ran back to the Devil's Den, and it stretched his men very thinly along their front. Meade expressed his displeasure but it was already too late to do anything about a *fait accompli*. Curiously, at this stage neither Meade nor Sickles paid any attention to Little Round Top; the only troops that did so were a Signal Corps detachment which set up a semaphore station on the summit.

Lee's deployment paralleled Meade's. Ewell's II Corps was facing Culp's Hill and Cemetery Hill; Hill's III Corps was on Seminary Ridge; and Longstreet's I Corps was arriving. Stuart had been located at Carlisle the previous day and, breaking off an action with a Federal militia brigade, he had begun marching on Gettysburg immediately; he would rejoin the army at noon, but his men and horses were so tired that they would not be fit for action until 3 July.

When Longstreet joined Lee he expressed serious reservations about attacking the Federals in their strong position. A better course of action, he believed, would be to march south, inserting the Army of Northern Virginia between Meade and Washington; Meade would have to respond and Lee could defeat him decisively in a defensive battle fought on ground of his own choosing. This was excellent advice, but Lee was not in a receptive mood and he believed that he could inflict crippling damage on Meade's army

Below: Gettysburg. Massed Union artillery in action on Cemetery Ridge. A gun is being wheeled forward to replace one smashed by the Confederate bombardment. *Mollus Collection/US Army Military History Institute*

before it had been fully deployed. As that deployment was nearly complete, this was a faulty premise upon which to base a plan which required Longstreet's I Corps to overwhelm Meade's left and overrun the Round Tops while Hill and Ewell assaulted his right.

Longstreet, too, was to make a critical error. At about noon his divisions began marching across country towards their start-lines. Having covered some two miles, Longstreet realised that he was being observed by the signal station on Little Round Top. Not wishing to forfeit the element of surprise, he gave the order to counter-march then approach afresh using dead ground formed by the valley of a stream named Willoughby Run, which was further screened by trees on Seminary Ridge. It took two and a half hours to complete the manoeuvre against an objective which had been within 30 minutes' steady marching. It was 4 o'clock before I Corps was ready to attack and by then the chance of achieving surprise had all but slipped away.

Meade had held a command conference an hour earlier during which he had stressed that

Sykes' V Corps, forming the reserve, should also be responsible for the security of the Federal left. After the conference Meade asked his Chief Engineer, Major General Gouverneur K. Warren, to investigate the noise of firing on Little Round Top. This proved to be nothing more than a trick of sound reflecting the fire of skirmishers active between the two armies. On reaching the summit, Warren realised immediately that if the Confederates took the hill the whole of Cemetery Ridge would have to be abandoned, with disastrous consequences. Simultaneously the signallers drew his attention to suspicious movements beyond Seminary Ridge. Warren asked a battery in the Devil's Den to fire a round in that direction.

'As the shot went whistling through the air the sound of it reached the enemy's troops and caused everyone to look in the direction of it. This motion revealed to me the glistening of gun barrels and bayonets of the enemy's line of battle, already formed and far outflanking the position of any of our troops, so that the line of his advance from his right to Little Round Top was unopposed. This discovery was appalling.'

Warren's priority was now to get as many troops as possible onto the hill. He dispatched one of his staff officers to Meade requesting a division. At first Meade agreed, but then recalled that Sykes was already moving V Corps towards Little Round Top. A second officer found Sykes and the latter, mindful of Meade's instructions, sent up his 1st Division's 3rd Brigade, commanded by Colonel Strong Vincent.

By 4.30 the guns of both sides were in action. Longstreet's I Corps began its attack with two divisions forward, Major General John B. Hood's on the right and Major General Lafayette McLaws' on the left, their skirmishers driving the Federal sharpshooters before them. Hood's division was one of the best in the Confederate service, but during the advance its leading brigades became intermingled and at the critical moment a shell burst above Hood, wounding him so severely that Brigadier General Evander Law, the senior brigade commander, was summoned to take his

place. Law's own brigade, unaware of this development, remained effectively without a commander for the next two hours. Nevertheless the Confederates pressed home their attack, storming their way into the Devil's Den and capturing Round Top. Little Round Top immediately came under pressure from three directions as the attackers swarmed up its northern and western slopes from the Devil's Den and across the saddle from Round Top.

Vincent's Federal brigade was hard pressed, Vincent himself being killed while rallying his men. Seeing how matters stood, Warren, who had remained on the feature, rode down the reverse slope in a desperate search for reinforcements. By the greatest good fortune he encountered a brigade he had formerly commanded and returned with the 140th New York, which surged over the crest to beat off the attack on the northern and eastern sectors. Concurrently, the guns and limbers of Battery D, 5th US Artillery, were manhandled to the summit with much effort, each gun going into action as it arrived.

Around the southern shoulder of the hill, Colonel Joshua Chamberlain's 20th Maine was engaged in a furious close-quarter fight with the 15th Alabama on the saddle. When his regiment's ammunition began to fail, Chamberlain, a lecturer at a theological college in civilian life, ordered a bayonet charge which drove the Alabamians back to Round Top. The crisis on the extreme left of the Federal line was over.

To the north of the Devil's Den, however, the Federal line had almost given way. The Confederate gunners had made the salient formed by Sickles' III Corps their special target. Sickles lost a leg, being succeeded by Major General David Birney, but amid bitter fighting their troops were driven steadily back towards Cemetery Ridge by McLaws' division, assisted by Major General Richard Anderson's division from Hill's III Corps. Only the prompt action of Meade, Sykes and others in rushing reinforcements into the gap prevented a breakthrough. Counter-attacks drove the weary Confederates back and, with the arrival of

Sedgwick's Federal VI Corps, the moment of danger passed. The day was now too far gone for Longstreet to renew his attack.

Further north, the holding attack by Ewell's II Corps against Culp's Hill and Cemetery Hill had gone in too late to be of any use to Longstreet and had failed to prevent Meade moving troops from this sector to cover his threatened centre and left. Fighting continued long after dark, but while the Confederates were able to secure a small lodgement on Culp's Hill they were unable to make any real impression on the Federal lines.

During the night both commanders assessed the situation. Meade had sustained some 20,000 casualties in two days' fighting and his III Corps had been badly knocked about. On the other hand his entire army had now reached the battlefield, no ground of tactical value had been lost, and, with the Round Tops now securely held, the Federal position was actually stronger than it had been when the day began. He therefore told his corps commanders that, apart from eliminating the enemy lodgement on Culp's Hill, the army would remain on the defensive next day. He also predicted that Lee, having unsuccessfully attacked both flanks, would mount his next major attack against the right-centre of the line.

Across no-man's land, Lee was probably unaware of how close he had come to achieving a complete victory at Little Round Top. The Army of Northern Virginia had sustained about 16,000 casualties, but he still believed that it had the ability to deliver a concentrated knock-out blow and, as Meade predicted, decided that this would be delivered at the enemy's right-centre on the morrow, using 15,000 men. He was convinced that the attack would split Meade's army and to exploit the anticipated rout Stuart's cavalry was to be sent round to the Federal rear, east of Culp's Hill. Longstreet, who was in favour of unsettling Meade by manoeuvring against his sensitive left, south of the Round Tops, was horrified by the plan. As the troops involved in Lee's projected assault would have to cross a mile of open farmland, their losses would be heavy, even if the attack succeeded, and the South, with its limited manpower resources, simply could not afford to indulge in a battle of attrition. When the plan was proposed the previous evening he had objected strenuously, but Lee's stubborn response was that if the enemy were still present on Cemetery Ridge the following morning he must be attacked.

'If he is there,' replied Longstreet with implacable logic, 'It will be because he is anxious that we should attack him. A good reason, in my judgement, for not doing so.'

This was about as far as the conventions of discipline would permit him to go. When he met Lee shortly after dawn on 3 July, the latter had not changed his mind, although he did promise strong artillery preparation. Longstreet was to organise the attack, which would involve one division from his own corps, that of Major General George E. Pickett, which had been employed as wagon guards during the previous two days, and elements of Hill's corps who had not been in action since 1 July, including Major General Henry Heth's division, now commanded by Brigadier General James Pettigrew, two brigades from Major General William Pender's division, now commanded by Major General Isaac Trimble, and one brigade from Major General Richard Anderson's division under Brigadier General Cadmus Willcox. These formations would assemble in the lee of Seminary Ridge from which a grand battery of some 140 guns would fire the preparatory bombardment under the direction of Colonel E. P. Alexander.

Ewell's corps was also to play a part by renewing its attack on Culp's Hill, thereby concentrating Meade's attention on his right. In fact it was the Federals who initiated action on this sector shortly after dawn on 3 July. Heavy fighting continued throughout the morning, as a result of which the Confederates not only failed to make further progress but also lost their lodgement on the feature.

Meanwhile Meade observed the steady concentration of guns on Seminary Ridge and knew that he had divined Lee's intention correctly. His Chief of Artillery, Brigadier General Henry J. Hunt, concentrated some 80 of the 106 guns on Cemetery Ridge for the counter-battery role, a further 136 being held in reserve until the Confederate attack developed. Its weight would evidently fall on Major General Hancock's II Corps, the infantry of which had the protection of drystone walling for much of their front and entrenchments along the rest.

At 1 o'clock Alexander's guns opened fire and Hunt's responded, the artillery duel lasting for two hours. The Federal infantry sustained some casualties and one or two artillery limbers exploded when hit, but most of the Confederate fire was a little too high and passed over the crest of Cemetery Ridge to explode among the staff and supply troops beyond; several rounds struck Meade's headquarters, a small farmhouse below the reverse slope, and Hunt's artillery reserve wagons were forced to withdraw out of range. The less intense Federal reply was largely ineffective. During the bombardment Longstreet instructed Alexander to inform Pickett, whose division would form the right flank of the assault, when the guns had done their work. At 2.45 the Federal artillery fire slackened, suggesting that they had, although in reality Hunt was simply conserving ammunition to meet the attack. Alexander informed Pickett, who trotted over to Longstreet, saluted and said he was about to advance. Longstreet, only too aware of what was about to happen, simply nodded and shook his hand.

Although several formations were involved, what followed has become known universally as Pickett's Charge. It was, like that of the Light Brigade nine years earlier, an incredible demonstration of superhuman courage, deter-

Below: Gettysburg. The Confederate attack known as Pickett's Charge, the leading elements of which can be seen in the middle distance, approaches the Union position on Cemetery Ridge. The combination of the Springfield rifle and the Minié bullet meant that attacking troops began to come under fire at longer ranges than in previous wars. Even at this stage the Confederate ranks were too shredded to press home their attack effectively. *Mollus Collection/USAMHI*

mination and the utter futility of war. At 3 o'clock some 13,000 Confederates, their brigades arrayed in two or even three successive waves, emerged from the trees and began descending the forward slopes of Seminary Ridge. With their Colours to the fore, their dressing correct and mounted officers controlling the direction of their advance as though at a formal review, they marched steadily on. Signal flags began to wag on Little Round Top, but the blue-coated ranks on Cemetery Ridge were already aware what was happening. Hunt's gunners opened fire, initially causing more damage to the rear brigades than those in front. A steady trickle of wounded began limping its painful way back to the tree line.

Below: Gettysburg. The 'high-water mark' of Pickett's charge. Although some Union guns are pulling out of the line, this penetration by a comparative handful of courageous men was quickly contained and most became prisoners. From this moment the fortunes of the Confederacy were in decline. *Mollus Collection/USAMHI*

Along the bottom of the valley ran the road from Gettysburg to Emmitsburg. In the lee of its embankment the grey and butternut lines paused briefly to close up and attend to their dressing. Once across the road they became the focus of every gun from Cemetery Hill to the Round Tops, taking enfilade as well as frontal fire. As they came within killing range of II Corps' infantry, a hail of Minié balls began to slash through the ranks. Over the last 400 yards the pace quickened, but now the Federal gunners had switched to canister, double-shotted in many cases, and were blowing huge gaps in the lines. Hancock was everywhere, directing the defence, and Meade was rushing reinforcements into the threatened sector. A Vermont brigade wheeled out of the line to rake Pickett's division in flank. The head of the Confederate mass was obscured by dust and smoke through which men could be seen dropping in large numbers and fallen Colours repeatedly raised. Among the Federals admiration began to be tinged with pity. It was indeed more than mortal flesh and blood could stand, but even as survivors began to retire singly and

in small groups, an especially determined party of men led by Brigadier General Lewis Armistead fought their way through the Federal line and overran a wrecked battery. Armistead, waving his hat upon his sword, was mortally wounded at once. After a brief, savage fight, his men, numbering not fewer than 150 and not more than 350, were surrounded and forced to surrender by Federal regiments converging spontaneously on the penetration.

The great attack had failed. Its survivors made their weary way back across the valley, harried by artillery. Lee, horrified by the consequences of his mistake, rode out to meet them. To the men he spoke words of kindness and encouragement. To Pickett and other senior officers he frankly confessed: 'All this has been my fault. It is I that have lost this fight and upon my shoulders rests the blame.' Casualties were every bit as bad as Longstreet had feared. Only Pickett and one other officer of field rank remained of the 22 serving in the former's division. Overall, only three men in every ten answered the first roll call; later, as stragglers came in, the proportion rose to one in two. The rest were either dead, wounded or prisoners. Nor could Stuart's cavalry provide any comfort, for during their engagement to the east they had once again been fought to a standstill. On Cemetery Ridge soldiers of Hancock's II Corps emerged from their defences to pick up 28 Confederate Colours, 20 of which were found lying within an area of 100 square yards.

The Battle of Gettysburg was over. Throughout 4 July both armies remained in their positions. The weather, hot and humid the previous day, broke in a torrential downpour under cover of which Lee began to withdraw to Virginia. Meade, unwilling to hazard the results of a hard-won victory, followed at a respectful distance, for which he was subsequently criticised.

The battle cost the Army of the Potomac 3,155 killed, 14,529 wounded and 5,365 missing, a total of 23,049; the Army of Northern Virginia lost 3,903 killed, 18,735 wounded and 5,425 missing, a total of 28,063.

The South could not afford such losses and was never again strong enough to mount an invasion into the North. On 4 July its cause received another crushing blow when Vicksburg surrendered, and in Tennessee it suffered further reverses.

Nevertheless, it took two more years of hard fighting before the Confederacy surrendered. During this time Lee would recover his abilities and conduct a skilful defence, but once Grant had decided to impose the cruel strategy of attrition the end was inevitable. So great had become the firepower in the hands of troops holding defensive positions that during the final, decisive campaign, fought around Petersburg, Virginia, the troops of both armies entrenched themselves, and in so doing gave an ominous pointer to the nightmare battles of attrition that would characterise the fighting in the First World War.

VIONVILLE–MARS-LA-TOUR AND GRAVELOTTE–ST-PRIVAT, 16–18 AUGUST 1870

The lessons of the American Civil War were not fully digested by European general staffs until they were confirmed by the Franco–Prussian War of 1870–1. In the meantime, Prussia had achieved a surprisingly rapid defeat of Austria during the Seven Weeks War of 1866 and had become the dominant military power in the German-speaking world. This, the first demonstration of brilliant pre-planning by Moltke and the Prussian General Staff, reached its decisive conclusion at the battle of Königgratz (Sadowa) when the Prussian Elbe, First and Second Armies had converged on the battlefield to inflict a serious defeat on General Ludwig Benedek's Austrian Army. Because of a telegraphic failure, the result was not as neat as Moltke would have preferred, nor was it the reconstruction of Cannae that he sought, because Benedek was able to withdraw from the trap, covered by his cavalry and artillery.

Moltke learned some lessons from the war. The efficient Prussian mobilisation had been slightly marred by insufficient unloading facilities for railway trains arriving in the various army assembly areas, a problem subsequently solved by installing numerous extra sidings at the relevant stations. The Dreyse needle-gun had given the Prussian infantry a convincing advantage over their Austrian opponents, who were still armed with muzzle-loading muskets, but the Austrian artillery had proved superior and the Prussian Army was hurriedly re-equipped with Krupp's steel breech-loading guns.

However, when Chancellor Otto von Bismarck provoked the government of Emperor Napoleon III into declaring war on Prussia and her German allies on 15 July 1870, the respective balance of the two arms was reversed: the Dreyse was inferior to the Chassepot, but the Prussian artillery was superior to the French. The latter, however, did possess a secret weapon in the *mitrailleuse* – so secret, in fact, that no training had been done with the gun and no doctrine evolved for its use. Ultimately they decided to employ the *mitrailleuse* in batteries like the artillery, but experience quickly found them outranged and neutralised by the Prussian guns.

Nor were these the only differences between the two armies. King Wilhelm I was nominally in overall command, but the real power lay with Moltke, serving as his Chief of Staff. As before, Moltke planned to seize the initiative with a speedy mobilisation followed by the creation of circumstances that would result in a second Cannae. Three field armies were organised, the First under General von Steinmetz, the Second under Prince Friedrich Karl, and the Third under Crown Prince Friedrich Wilhelm. In cases where a member of a German royal house exercised command of an army or a corps, it was usual to attach an experienced professional as Chief of Staff to advise him. The Prussian rank-and-file were conscripts, some of whom had already seen active service during the war against Austria.

Initially the French deployed eight corps, known collectively as the Army of the Rhine, under the overall command of the Emperor and his inept Minister of War, Marshal Edmond Leboeuf. On 2 August, realising that this arrangement was too unwieldy to work well, Napoleon formed the three southern corps into the Army of Alsace under Marshal Marie MacMahon, designating the remaining five the Army of Lorraine under the command of Marshal Achille Bazaine. As neither army had a trained staff, their commanders had to improvise. Nor had any firm objectives been set beyond a vague idea of advancing on Berlin. France also had a conscript army, but as the men were drawn from a quota of each annual class and had to serve for a longer period they were more like regular troops. As a whole, the army was experienced and self-confident, having seen active service in the Crimea, in northern Italy, in Mexico and more or less continuously in North Africa. Unfortunately, while Leboeuf might boast that its readiness for war extended to the 'last gaiter button', its mobilisation arrangements were so chaotic that some reservists were still in transit to their units long after the issue had been decided. By the end of July, France had 224,000 men in the field; Prussia and her allies had 475,000, more than twice as many.

During the opening battles the French were thrown back from the frontier. All that could be said was that the Germans, who relied on speed, mass and weight to press home an attack, sustained the heavier casualties because of the effect of Chassepot fire on their dense formations. At this stage, having by far the greater number of men in hand, Moltke was not unduly worried.

MacMahon withdrew to regroup at Châlons-sur-Marne, closely followed by the Crown Prince's Third Army. Bazaine, accompanied by the Emperor, fell back on the fortress of Metz. On 12 August, recognising that he did not understand the new mechanics of warfare, Napoleon handed over command to Bazaine with instructions that he should withdraw to Verdun, where he could either co-operate with MacMahon or counter a Prussian move against Paris.

Bazaine, aged 59, had served with distinction in Spain, Algeria, the Crimea and Mexico.

He had shown himself a capable and courageous divisional commander, but had no experience of active command at corps or army level. All too conscious of his humble origins, he was afflicted by a sort of social paranoia yet was simultaneously driven by burning ambition. The result was depression, hesitancy and undue caution, all of which were reflected in the handling of his army.

Nevertheless, on 15 August he fought a successful delaying action against Steinmetz's First Army at Borny, east of Metz, but even this minor success worked against him because, to the south, Prince Friedrich Karl's Second Army was already across the Moselle and advancing north-westwards on an axis that would interdict the planned line of withdrawal from Metz to Verdun. By that very evening, in fact, the route was under direct surveillance by the Prince's cavalry.

Early next day Napoleon left for Verdun, escorted by two regiments of Chasseurs d'Afrique. Bazaine busied himself with the details of his army's continued withdrawal, for which two parallel routes were available, the northern through Doncourt, the southern through the villages of Rezonville, Vionville and Mars-la-Tour. These routes, however, all began at Gravelotte, to reach which the entire army and its 5,000 supply wagons had to travel along a single road from Metz, the centre of which had become a monumental traffic jam. The result was that while those corps encamped west of the fortress were ready to move off immediately, it would take several hours before the remainder of the army sorted itself out. Bazaine, aware that Steinmetz was closing in on the fortress from the east, and now conscious of the presence of German cavalry to the south, made the fatal decision to postpone the march until the afternoon.

The initiative now rested with Prince Friedrich Karl's leading formation commanders. Major-General von Rheinbaben, commanding the 5th Cavalry Division, was aware that he was confronted by the entire French army and, knowing that III Corps,

commanded by Lieutenant-General Constantin von Alvensleben, was coming up on his right, ordered his artillery to open fire on the French cavalry camp at Vionville. When Alvensleben arrived, his first impression was that Rheinbaben had become engaged with the French rearguard, but he quickly changed his mind. It was apparent that the French withdrawal could be stopped altogether if his corps mounted a holding attack until the rest of Second Army arrived.

The infantry of III Corps, consisting of the 5th and 6th Infantry Divisions, captured the villages of Flavigny and Vionville, but their further attacks were stalled with crippling casualties. Cavalry attacks by both sides were shot to pieces. By noon Alvensleben had cut the Metz–Verdun road between Rezonville and Vionville, and the French were holding an arc of downland with their left resting on Rezonville and their right being extended progressively westwards as more troops arrived. Had Bazaine wished, he could have destroyed Alvensleben's corps by reinforcing his right and mounting converging attacks. Instead, when he was not personally siting artillery batteries, which was hardly the business of an army commander, he reinforced his left, suggesting that he was more interested in preserving a line of retreat into Metz than re-opening the road to Verdun.

By 1.30 Alvensleben was in serious trouble. His casualties had been heavy, he had no further reserves to commit and his troops were running short of ammunition. Furthermore there were signs that the French formation opposite, Canrobert's VI Corps, was about to mount a counter-attack in strength. Against this, he had received a message to the effect that Lieutenant-General Constantin Voigts-Rhetz's German X Corps was approaching and that until it entered the line on his left he must hold on, whatever the cost. The situation was saved by the suicidal charge of Major-General Friedrich von Bredow's 12th Cavalry Brigade, some mention of which has been made earlier. The brigade, consisting of 7th Cuirassiers and 16th Lancers, was positioned in a hollow south

Above: Vionville–Mars-la-Tour. Major General von Bredow's 12th Cavalry Brigade overrunning a French battery. Although the brigade was all but destroyed when counter-charged by French cavalry, seen on the right, its action relieved pressure on the Prussians and was long cited as a justification for the retention of cavalry. *Otto Quenstedt, Historischer Bilderdienst*

of Vionville and was able to approach the French line up a shallow re-entrant leading to another hollow on Canrobert's right, features which provided a degree of cover both from view and the enemy's fire. On reaching the upper fold Bredow wheeled the brigade to the right and launched a headlong charge, overrunning a battery and putting the nearest infantry to flight. The brigade was then counter-charged in flank by French heavy cavalry and a furious mêlée ensued. Of the 500 men Bredow had led into action, only 194 regained their own lines, but Canrobert's corps had been so thoroughly disorganised that it was unable to mount its counter-attack.

During the afternoon the arrival of X Corps was matched opposite by that of Ladmirault's IV Corps and once again the German advance was stopped in its tracks by devastating Chassepot fire. On the western flank the battle ended in a major but indecisive cavalry combat, the last in western European history, involving no less than 49 French and German squadrons. Hardly had this ended when, at 7

o'clock, elements of Lieutenant-General von Goeben's VIII Corps, part of First Army, began entering the battle, pushing the French back on Rezonville before darkness put an end to the fighting.

Apparently, the battle of Vionville–Mars-la-Tour had ended in a draw, although both sides had some cause for satisfaction. The Germans, who had lost nearly 16,000 officers and men, had succeeded in halting the French withdrawal and successfully concentrated their First and Second Armies against Bazaine. The French, who sustained 14,000 casualties, could claim to have held all their ground and were ready to renew the contest on the morrow. In Bazaine's mind, however, the battle was lost.

167

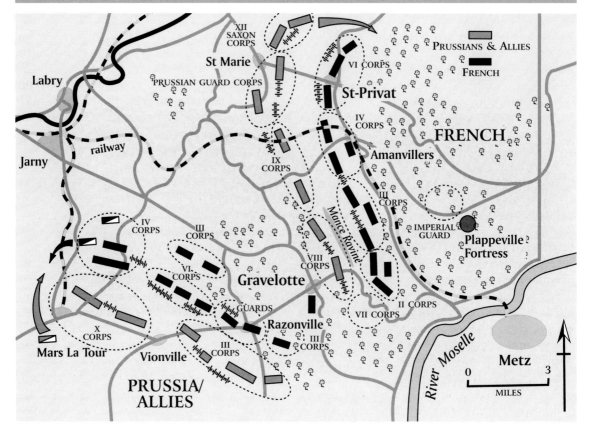

Gone were all thoughts of re-opening the road to Verdun. Instead, at midnight he ordered his corps commanders to fall back on a position closer to Metz, pivoting on Gravelotte, so that their new line faced west rather than south. Throughout 17 August the order was obeyed by bewildered and resentful troops who not only had to abandon some of their wounded but also burn badly needed supplies.

If Bazaine can be said to have played into Moltke's hands by allowing his army to be thus trapped, it can also be said that the new position offered defensive advantages that should have enabled him to inflict a costly reverse on an attacker. The new French line occupied a ridge running from north to south. The southern sector was fronted by a steep wooded ravine carrying a stream, the Mance, southwards towards the Moselle. This obstacle would itself disorder the Germans' close attack formations, and above the tree line the crest offered long fields of fire dominated by several

fortified farms linked by trenches and emplaced battery positions. The northern sector of the line, beyond the point where the Mance rose in the Bois de Genivaux, extended through Amanvillers to St-Privat-la-Montagne, but was different in that while the slopes were gentler they offered even longer fields of fire with no protection whatever for an attacker. Bazaine's headquarters was located in the incomplete fort of Plappeville, two miles behind his left wing and four from St-Privat, with the Imperial Guard in reserve nearby.

On the morning of 18 August Moltke had 188,000 Germans with 732 guns with which to attack 113,000 Frenchmen with 520 guns. His plan was that Steinmetz's First Army would mount heavy holding attacks against the French left while Prince Friedrich Karl marched north with the Second Army and turned Bazaine's right.

In the event, there were two battles, and in that at Gravelotte the Germans were heavily defeated. Experience had been a hard school and the local French commanders sited their *mitrailleuses* in concealed positions among the infantry, adding to the carnage inflicted by the rapid fire of the Chassepots. Steinmetz, a believer in brute force, flung one formation after another across the Mance ravine, only to have it founder in bloody ruin in front of the French defences. The survivors fell back to the ravine where infantry, cavalry and artillery units struggled to advance through the debris of earlier attacks until the whole area became a nightmare congestion, flayed mercilessly by the French guns. By 5 o'clock Steinmetz had exhausted his own reserves, yet still believed that one more assault would carry the day. By-passing Moltke, he appealed directly to the King for permission to use Lieutenant-General Eduard Fransecky's recently arrived II Corps, which belonged to Second Army. Wilhelm consented and the corps advanced towards the Mance. As it did so, the nerve of those in the ravine finally broke. In their thousands they fled in blind panic through Gravelotte, which had been set ablaze by enemy shellfire, halting only when they reached the comparative safety of Rezonville. Fransecky's troops, while shaken by the sight, maintained their discipline and in the fading light advanced across the ravine, now deserted save for its grisly carpet of dead and wounded. Climbing the slope beyond, they opened fire on troops dimly seen through the tree line. These were, in fact, those of Steinmetz's men who had not succumbed to the general panic and were now holding a weak line. For them, this onslaught from the rear was the last straw and they bolted, leaving an uneasy II Corps to take over their position.

The German First Army had effectively been routed. If Bazaine had counter-attacked he would probably have won a great victory, but he was personally unaware of the sudden enemy collapse and his corps commanders were under strict instructions to remain on the defensive. For Moltke, this was the worst moment of his professional life. First Army had been so badly mauled that at one stage serious consideration was given to escorting the King off the field, and the sound of battle from the north indicated only that Second Army was engaged in heavy and destructive fighting, the result of which was not yet known.

Friedrich Karl's problem was that he did not know where the French right rested. He believed that it lay in Amanvillers and time was wasted when Lieutenant-General von Manstein's IX Corps became involved in a fruitless frontal assault on that village. When it was discovered that Bazaine's right was situated in St-Privat, the battle had to be re-planned. The Guard Corps was ordered to mount a frontal assault while the Saxon XII Corps, commanded by the Crown Prince of Saxony, attacked from the north. It would take several hours before the Saxons would be in a position to launch their attack. In the meantime the French were cleared from a strong outpost in the village of Ste-Marie-les-Chênes at about 3.30. Friedrich Karl then concentrated the artillery of the Guard, III and XII Corps, a total of some 180 guns, around the village and began a bombardment of St-Privat, which was held by Canrobert's VI Corps. This was largely ineffective because the French had positioned themselves on the forward slopes below the village.

At about 5 o'clock the commander of the Guard Corps, Prince August of Württemberg, made the disastrous decision to attack alone instead of waiting either for the Saxons, who were still an hour's march from their start-line, or for direct support from the artillery. No reasonable explanation for this has ever been offered, although Friedrich Karl was nagging him to get on. Nor was his Chief of Staff able to restrain him; the latter's advice, in fact, resembled the legendary curate's egg, the better parts of which were largely ignored.

The Guard Corps formed up in assault columns behind a screen of skirmishers. It had a 3,000-yard advance to make across open ground. Most of this would be made in quick time with the last 100 yards covered at the double with levelled bayonets. The first mile was covered without incident and then the French line erupted in smoke and flame. It has been calculated that during every minute that followed the French fired 40,000 Chassepot rounds. First the skirmish line was shot away, and then the assault columns began to go down in heaps. The Prussians lowered their heads into the leaden sleet and kept moving, but some 800 yards from the objective they lay down and not even their renowned discipline

could get them moving again until the Saxons appeared. In 20 minutes they had sustained more than 8,000 casualties, including more than 2,000 killed, leaving hardly one of

Prussia's noble houses unaffected by the slaughter.

At about 6 o'clock the Saxons began to make their presence felt. Canrobert's men now began to regret their prodigal expenditure of ammunition for they had insufficient to meet an attack from two directions, the vengeful Guard Corps having now renewed its assault with the support of its own artillery. Canrobert sent a request that his withdrawal be covered by General Bourbaki with the Imperial Guard, and attempted to buy some time with a cavalry charge that was shot to pieces before it had covered 50 yards. Despite this, some of his infantry units fought so bitter a rearguard action that St-Privat was not securely in German hands until 8.30. By then the Guardsmen and Saxons were too exhausted to pursue.

Bourbaki had also received a request for help from Ladmirault, commanding the French IV Corps on Canrobert's left. Ladmirault believed that a counter-attack with fresh troops would inflict a decisive defeat on Manstein's corps, against which he had been engaged for much of the day. As in the first Napoleon's day, the role of the Imperial Guard was to administer the *coup-de-grâce* to a beaten enemy. Bourbaki therefore set off for Amanvillers with a division, full of high hopes. These were dashed when, at 7 o'clock, he reached the front to find Canrobert's corps retreating from St-Privat and large numbers of Ladmirault's wounded limping away from the firing line. He promptly gave way to hysterics. 'You promised me a victory!' he screamed at the aides who had brought him Ladmirault's request. 'Now you've got me involved in a rout! You had no right to do that!' Then he turned his Guardsmen round and marched them to the rear. The result was as predictable as it had been at Waterloo. For the French, if the Guard were retreating the

Left: Gravelotte–St-Privat. Having sustained over 8,000 casualties on the slopes below the village, the Prussian Guard Corps fights its way into St-Privat in vengeful mood. *Otto Quenstedt, Historischer Bilderdienst*

171

battle must be lost. All along the line they abandoned their positions and headed for the imagined safety of Metz. At about midnight the anxious Moltke learned that Second Army had won a victory, albeit at a terrible price. The Germans had sustained more than 20,000 casualties; French losses were in the region of 13,000.

Leaving sufficient troops to besiege Metz, Moltke turned westwards to co-operate with German Third Army. MacMahon's army, advancing to relieve the fortress, was trapped against the Belgian frontier at Sedan and was bombarded into surrender on 1 September. At last Moltke had his Second Cannae. The Second Empire collapsed days later and soon Paris itself was under siege. The leaders of the new Third Republic raised fresh armies of mixed quality but these were unable to influence events. Bazaine surrendered Metz on 27 October and when Paris capitulated the following January the war was virtually over. On 18 January 1871 King Wilhelm of Prussia was proclaimed Kaiser of the new German Empire in the Hall of Mirrors at Versailles.

Many Frenchmen, unable to understand the unbelievably rapid defeat of their armies and shamed by the severe peace terms imposed by Germany, harboured a desire for revenge that continued to simmer beneath the surface of national life and was one element in creating the even greater European tragedy of the First World War. The events of 16 and 18 August 1870 were therefore far-reaching in their political consequences; they were, too, indicative of the shape of things to come on the battlefield.

Commentary 9 – Armageddon Mark I

Although the major military powers of Europe remained at peace with one another for forty years after the Franco-Prussian War, there was almost continuous military activity elsewhere in the world. Simultaneously, armaments manufacturers refined the technical developments of the Industrial Revolution and inven-

tors produced new devices which could be adapted for war.

The introduction of the metallic cartridge case enabled Hiram Maxim to demonstrate the first true machine-gun in 1884. The weapon utilised its own recoil forces to operate the loading, firing and ejection mechanisms, the ammunition being fed into the chamber by a belt. Beyond the initial loading and cocking, no further manual assistance was necessary and the gun would continue to fire as long as the trigger was pressed. The metallic cartridge also led to the introduction of the magazine rifle, rapidly loaded from clips, which further increased the infantryman's rate of fire.

The same was true for the artillery once fixed shells were produced, but in this field the introduction of hydraulic recoil buffers also enhanced the gun's potential. The hydraulic system absorbed the shock of the recoil, so allowing the carriage to remain static, which obviated the need to re-lay the weapon after every discharge. Already used for naval and coastal artillery, the first field gun to employ it successfully was the French *Canon de 75mm Modèle 1897*, the legendary 'Seventy-Five', which could fire 20 rounds a minute without disturbing the carriage.

Added to all this, smokeless powder, the most efficient propellant yet produced, entered service in 1885, giving greater range and making it difficult to spot the source of hostile fire. Within a comparatively short period the battlefield had become even more dangerous than the slopes of Cemetery Ridge or St-Privat had proved to be. Concealment became all-important. Colours were no longer taken into action and, with the exception of the French, the smart uniforms of earlier years were discarded in favour of a less conspicuous drab service dress; the British Army, which had long opted for khaki drill in India and elsewhere, fought its last battle in scarlet coats at Ginnis in the Sudan on 30 December 1885.

The telephone first appeared in 1875. It was obviously a faster means of communication than the telegraph and therefore had wide-ranging military uses. These naturally included

Right: Attempts to apply industrial methods to fire-power were by no means new. Mr Puckle's machine gun of 1718 – really a rapid fire system – was a workable design but found little favour with the authorities.

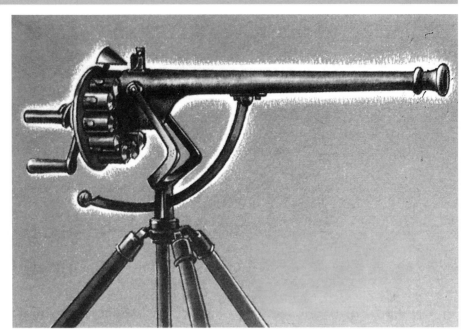

Right: British home service troops demonstrate the workings of the Gatling Gun in about 1880.

tactical command but were quickly extended to the control of long-range artillery fire. In 1885 the German army conducted a series of successful experiments in which forward observers were connected to their battery positions by telephone. Thereafter, the artillery became capable of firing concentrations and barrages of various types without the gunners ever seeing their targets. Communications took a further leap forward when, in 1901, Guglielmo Marconi transmitted a radio signal over a distance of 3,000 miles. Generals in the field and admirals at sea could now exercise immediate command over much wider areas, and as radios improved in the process of technical evolution their use spread downwards from the strategic to the tactical level. Naturally, hostile armies and navies set up intercept stations to monitor one another's transmissions, and so the use of codes proliferated, adding to the size of their intelligence staffs.

The internal combustion engine was to have even more profound social consequences than the railway. In the military sphere it would not only revolutionise transport but be used to power fighting vehicles. In 1902 a British engineer, Frederick Simms, demonstrated his armoured automotive War Car, armed with one heavy and two medium machine-guns. In common with many contemporary general staffs, the War Office could not decide whether the armoured car was a cavalry, infantry or artillery weapon and was unreceptive to the idea. It was conceded, however, that it had an application in colonial warfare and some countries with internal security problems, notably Imperial Russia, saw it as a useful addition to the police armoury. In 1913, however, the Italian Army deployed several to Libya during its war with Turkey and from this point it was apparent that, sooner or later, it would be have to be taken into service by major armies.

Cavalry now stood not the slightest chance against infantry armed with magazine rifles and machine-guns and could only expect to use the *arme blanche* against its own kind, though its advocates formed an influential lobby within every army. They claimed, with some justice, that they could still perform the reconnaissance and screening role, they heavily emphasised such rare successes as they achieved in shock action, and they pointed to its necessity in colonial and frontier warfare. This last context was only true up to a point, for experience showed that the best results were obtained when mounted infantry methods were employed, combining mobility with firepower rather than shock action.

The fortunes of the fortress engineer also continued to decline. No matter how ingenious he might be in providing armoured cupolas and other sophisticated forms of protection, the siege artillerymen always produced bigger guns firing yet more powerful armour- and concrete-defeating ammunition. The inescapable long-term conclusion was that the expensive fortress was little more efficient than entrenchments and earthworks, particularly if the latter were fronted with barbed wire, which had originally been produced as an economic means of containing livestock on large ranches where timber was scarce.

The powers of the defence therefore exceeded those of the attack by a wide margin. Battles now lasted weeks rather than days and the casualties incurred reached levels undreamed of in the worst nightmares. For example, in the Russo–Japanese War of 1904–5 the battle of Mukden lasted for seventeen days during which the Russians sustained some 100,000 casualties and the Japanese 94,000. At one time these numbers would have been regarded as intolerable, but population growth and conscription ensured that gaps in the ranks could be quickly filled. Yet during the first years of the 20th century the generals encouraged the offensive spirit as an article of faith. This was far from being the blimpish reaction of elderly men whose traditional military training had been outstripped by expanding technology. The truth was that in every major war from the 1860s onwards the side which retained the initiative, and therefore did most of the attacking, had emerged victorious, though often with much heavier casualties. This was true of the American Civil War, the

Franco–Prussian War, the Russo–Turkish War of 1877, the Spanish–American War, the Second Boer War, the Russo–Japanese War and several lesser conflicts. Because of this, all general staffs subscribed to the doctrine of *l'offensive à l'outrance*, that is, attack pushed to the point of ultimate success. This would have been all very well, had not the warning signals become clearly apparent. By 1864, so dangerous had life above ground become that Federals and Confederates alike resorted to trench warfare during the defence of Petersburg; and, as we have seen, by attacking *à l'outrance* at Gravelotte von Steinmetz all but destroyed his own army. These trends were emphasised in subsequent wars, their logical projection being that, sooner or later, no attack would stand the slightest chance of succeeding. Thoughtful writers such as Ivan Bloch predicted that the power of modern weapons would inhibit battlefield movement to the extent that war would become impossible; others suggested that, mainly for economic reasons, future wars would be of very short duration. Few army staffs planned for a protracted war; all planned for a rapid mobilisation followed by an immediate offensive which it was hoped would bring a quick victory.

In 1914 the diplomatic techniques of crisis management failed with the result that Europe was suddenly divided into two warring camps – the Triple Entente, consisting of Great Britain, France and Russia; and the two Central Powers, Germany and Austria–Hungary.

Germany, faced with a war on two fronts, opted for a defensive strategy in the east while she dealt with France in the west. As usual, German pre-planning envisaged a gigantic reconstruction of Cannae. The method, devised by Field Marshal Alfred Graf von Schlieffen, Chief of the German General Staff from 1891 to 1906, envisaged several armies making a huge wheel through neutral Belgium with the object of pinning the French against the German left wing and the Swiss frontier. However, Schlieffen's successor, General Helmuth von Moltke, nephew of the great Moltke and sometimes referred to with sarcasm as The Lesser, weakened the all-important right wing to reinforce his left. Then the physical demands made on the troops on the extreme right of the great wheel, notably General Alexander von Kluck's First Army, were too heavy given the exacting time scale. Next, at Mons and again at Le Cateau, those same troops were checked with serious casualties by the professional infantry of the British Expeditionary Force, whose riflemen fired up to 20 aimed rounds a minute into the packed ranks of the German attack formations. Finally, it was decided to wheel east to the north of Paris instead of to the south, as originally intended. The effect was to expose the German right wing to an Allied counter-attack and its exhausted troops were forced to withdraw after being defeated at the Marne. Meanwhile, to the east, the French opening offensive, code-named 'Plan XVII', had also failed at the horrific cost of 300,000 casualties. For the moment, neither side knew quite what to do next, beyond extending its open flank steadily northwards until it reached the Belgian coast. The armies then dug in until the trench lines extended from the North Sea to the Swiss frontier.

On the Eastern Front two Russian armies invaded East Prussia but were virtually destroyed during the battles of Tannenberg and the Masurian Lakes. Farther south, the Russians did a little better against the Austrians but were finally checked. Russia's losses in men and *matériel* had been extremely heavy, and when the Ottoman Empire joined the Central Powers the need to open another front in the Caucasus further drained her limited resources. By the end of 1914 the Austro–Hungarian Empire had also sustained crippling losses on the Eastern Front and in Serbia, similarly aggravated by the opening of a new front when Italy joined the Entente powers the following year. Indeed, without German support Austria could hardly have remained in the war, which caused senior German officers to comment that they were now 'shackled to a corpse'.

For all the war's global nature, the Western Front remained the primary theatre. At great cost and without success, both sides sought to achieve a breakthrough and restore mobile warfare. Attacks foundered in the teeth of artillery, machine-gun and rifle fire. Within every army artillery of all calibres proliferated, creating a huge expansion in the relative strength of the arm. The guns became the principal man killer, for even between offensives they were seldom silent, creating a daily toll of dead and wounded. Because of this a new factor began to emerge, known then as shell-shock and today as combat fatigue. In his book *The Anatomy of Courage*, Lord Moran makes the point that every soldier begins with a credit balance of courage, from which withdrawals are made during close, deadly contact with the enemy. This had barely been noted hitherto because even in protracted conflicts such as the Napoleonic and American Civil Wars such contacts were restricted to periodic battles, with long periods of reduced stress between in which the credit balance was restored. Now, foul living conditions, semi-permanent close proximity to the enemy and constant contact with death drew heavily on personal reserves until, in some cases, the mind refused to function properly. For all, the nightmare would continue, year in, year out, until the means of breaking the deadlock of trench warfare was found.

The face of naval warfare had also been changed beyond recognition by expanding technology. A Captain Luppis of the Austrian Navy, keen to develop the concept of the automotive torpedo, enlisted the help of Robert Whitehead, a British engineer working in Fiume. Whitehead used compressed air to launch the torpedo and drive its propeller. A hydrostatic valve and pendulum weight working in conjunction with horizontal rudders enabled the torpedo to run for 1,000 yards at a pre-set depth. The British Admiralty invited Whitehead to demonstrate his invention and was sufficiently impressed to purchase the manufacturing rights for £15,000 as well as offering him a job at Woolwich Arsenal. There he refined his torpedo by fitting a gyroscope which maintained direction through a vertical rudder. By 1875 the basic principles of the modern torpedo were firmly established and it remained only to increase its size and range. The torpedo was to have as revolutionary an impact on naval warfare as the gun-armed warships of Drake's day.

The torpedo was at first seen largely as a coast defence weapon to be used by small, fast, manoeuvrable craft emerging from harbour to deliver the death blow to much larger adversaries. In 1876 the Royal Navy began to commission a class of torpedo-boats that were capable of the then incredible speed of over 21 knots.

As other navies would obviously copy the idea, the Admiralty had to find a solution to the problem created by these very dangerous little ships. Its answer was to produce even faster craft armed with quick-firing and automatic weapons. These were originally known as 'torpedo-boat catchers', then as 'torpedo-boat destroyers', and then simply as 'destroyers'. The danger of fitting large powerful engines in small ships was that they could shake the hull apart. This was solved when a Mr Charles Parsons gave an unsolicited demonstration with his steam turbine boat *Turbinia* at Spithead during Queen Victoria's Diamond Jubilee Naval Review in 1897. Not one of the Royal Navy's fast craft came close to catching the intruder. Two destroyers were promptly built with Parsons' steam turbine engines as their power units. *Viper*, the first to be launched, reached the astonishing speed of 37 knots during trials, the Navy's representative being assured by the builders, Hawthorne, Leslie & Company of Hepburn-on-Tyne, that should the need ever arise she had a couple more in reserve! Thereafter, while conventional reciprocating engines remained in use for a time, the steam turbine formed an essential element of destroyer design.

A second class of warship for which the torpedo was particularly suited was the submarine. Ingenious minds had been tinkering with the idea for many years, the principal obstacle to progress being the means of propulsion when submerged. In 1886 a Spanish officer, Lieutenant Isaac Peral, showed that this could be done with battery-driven electric motors. In 1899 the French Navy launched *Narval*, propelled by steam when surfaced and by electric motors when submerged, the steam engine being connected to a dynamo which re-charged the batteries. The following year the US Navy accepted the design of an Irish schoolmaster, Mr John Holland, for a similar submarine in which steam was replaced by a petrol engine for surface running. Petrol engines, however, presented obvious dangers and as the concept evolved they were quickly replaced by less volatile diesels.

Understandably, the Royal Navy, which relied on its ironclad battleships to maintain control of the world's oceans, did not welcome the threat implicit in these developments. In the opinion of the Third Sea Lord, Rear-Admiral Wilson, submarines were 'underhand' weapons, their use was 'damned un-English', and their crews should all be treated as pirates and hanged. Despite such outbursts, submarines were now a fact of life and in 1914 the Royal Navy had eight flotillas operating in home waters and four more in the Mediterranean and the Far East.

Meanwhile, battleship evolution had also continued apace with such refinements as bigger guns mounted in powered turrets, mechanical handling of ammunition between magazines and turrets, thicker armour, electric searchlights for night fighting, and radio communication. Bigger guns meant that battles would be fought at ever longer ranges where experience revealed that a variable number of rounds were needed to obtain one direct hit. To achieve concentration and reduce ammunition expenditure, it became necessary to introduce centralised fire-control systems. In 1906 the Royal Navy launched HMS *Dreadnought*, which was the first battleship to concentrate all her main armament (ten 12-inch guns) in turrets, so arranged that eight of them could fire in broadside. Her secondary armament consisted of twenty-seven 12-pounder guns for repulsing torpedo-boat attacks, and five submerged 18-inch torpedo tubes. *Dreadnought* was also the first major warship to be powered by Parsons steam turbines and could achieve a speed of 21 knots. She made every other battleship in the world obsolete so that for many years people would refer to those built before her as pre-Dreadnoughts and to later designs simply as Dreadnoughts.

The tasks once performed by frigates, including scouting for the fleet, were now performed by cruisers, which were also ideal vessels for any navy with world-wide commitments. A new class of warship, the battle cruiser, intended to out-run and out-gun an enemy's cruisers, began entering service in 1906. The battle cruiser combined the hitting power of the battleship with the speed of the cruiser, achieved by limiting armoured protection. As opposing battle cruisers would inevitably encounter one another it can be seen that the risks involved were so great as to render the concept inherently flawed.

Since the Battle of Lissa there had been a number of naval actions from which conclusions could be drawn. In the Far East Japan had at last emerged from her self-imposed isolation and was fast expanding her military and naval potential. In 1894, Japan and China having gone to war over Korea, the two navies clashed off the mouth of the Yalu river. Each fleet had ten ships, but whereas the Chinese had two battleships and several other armoured vessels, the Japanese had only protected cruisers. Against this, the Chinese ships were slower, short of ammunition, and their gunnery was of a lower standard. Moreover the Japanese had 66 quick-firing guns and the Chinese only two, the result being that five of the latter's ships were sunk and the rest fled.

Four years later more numerous and technically superior warships of the US Navy inflicted predictable destruction on elderly Spanish squadrons off Santiago, Cuba, and in Manila Bay. During these actions the Spaniards' difficulties were compounded when wooden components in their ships' construction, notably the decks, caught fire under the impact of explosive shells.

In February 1904 Japan initiated her war with Russia with a pre-emptive strike against the latter's naval base at Port Arthur, during which two battleships and a cruiser were torpedoed. Both sides made successful use of minefields and there were a number of engagements between the Russian and Japanese fleets. By mid-August, however, the Russians had been confined to Port Arthur, now besieged by the Japanese Army, where their remaining battleships were sunk by artillery fire in December. On 2 January 1905 Port Arthur surrendered.

Meanwhile, in October 1904 the Russian Baltic Fleet, commanded by Admiral Zinovy Rozhestvensky, had been ordered to sail round the world and retrieve the situation. The fleet included a number of slow, obsolete vessels which reduced the common speed of the rest, a factor which, coupled with coaling and repair difficulties, meant that it did not enter the war zone until May 1905. The Russian crews were inexperienced and inadequately trained, particularly in gunnery, and they contained a high proportion of conscripted peasants with no knowledge of the sea. In some ships mismanagement and poor leadership had created a situation bordering on mutiny.

Knowing that Port Arthur had fallen, Rozhestvensky had little option but to make for Vladivostok with his entire fleet, which consisted of twelve battleships, eight cruisers, nine destroyers and a number of smaller craft. He decided to pass through the Straits of Tsu Shima where, on 27 May, he was intercepted by Admiral Heihachino Togo with ten battleships, eighteen cruisers, 21 destroyers and 60 torpedo-boats. Togo's fleet, fully trained, battle-hardened and its morale enhanced by recent victories, had the additional advantage of an average speed some two or three knots faster than that of the Russians, which enabled it to dictate the course of the engagement. As Japanese gunnery was excellent and the Russians' shooting went

from bad to worse, the battle was more of a massacre, ending the following morning when Togo ran down most of Rozhestvensky's fleeing survivors. Russian losses amounted to eight battleships sunk and four captured, four cruisers and five destroyers sunk, 4,830 men killed and 5,917 taken prisoner. Of the remnant of the Baltic Fleet, one cruiser and two destroyers reached Vladivostok and the rest fled to neutral ports where they were interned for the remainder of the war. The Japanese lost three torpedo-boats, 117 men killed and 583 wounded. The battle of Tsu Shima, sometimes referred to as the 'Trafalgar of the East', set Japan firmly on the road to becoming one of the world's great naval powers.

In the western hemisphere the unstable Kaiser Wilhelm II of Germany was insanely jealous of the global power and prestige enjoyed by his British uncle, King Edward VII. Germany, the strongest land power in Europe, had few overseas possessions and did not need a large navy. However, nothing would satisfy Wilhelm but that he should have a prestigious fleet comparable to the Royal Navy and, starting in 1900, he began building one. The new Imperial Navy was extremely efficient and in some respects, especially gunnery, night fighting and damage control, was superior to its British rival. All this had the predictable effect of forfeiting British goodwill and pushing the United Kingdom into a defensive *entente* with France. It also resulted in an extremely expensive naval construction race between Great Britain and Germany so that on the outbreak of war the relative strength of the two navies was as shown in the table.

	Britain		Germany	
	In Service	Building	In Service	Building
Dreadnoughts	22	8	16	5
Pre-Dreadnoughts	40	0	30	0
Battle cruisers	9	0	6	1
Armoured cruisers	48	0	15	0
Light cruisers	71	8	33	0
Destroyers	225	15	152	12
Submarines	75	0	30	0

The gun, of course, remained the primary weapon, but both navies were acutely aware of the threats posed by the mine and the torpedo and conscious of the need to deploy their lighter forces around the capital ships for protection.

On the outbreak of war the Royal Navy's first tasks were to impose a blockade on Germany and clear the seas of German surface units. The first was achieved without difficulty, but the latter was not completed without the loss of two cruisers off the coast of Chile during an engagement with the German East Asiatic Squadron, which was itself destroyed on 8 December 1914 during the Battle of the Falkland Islands. Even so, German commerce raiders disguised as merchant vessels continued to take a toll of British shipping.

The commanders of the German High Seas Fleet had no intention of risking a general engagement with the much larger British Grand Fleet, then based at Scapa Flow. Instead they sought to entrap and destroy part of the fleet, thereby writing down its strength, and to this end they mounted a series of provocative raids against the east coast of England. These were largely ineffective and resulted in the loss of the armoured cruiser *Blücher* when the raiders were intercepted by British battle cruisers on 24 January 1915. So far the High Seas Fleet was not earning its keep. The same was far from true of the German submarine arm, whose U-boats scored a steady stream of successes against surface warships and were beginning to make serious inroads into the British merchant fleet. However, the removal of some of the restrictions governing U-boat operations proved to be counter-productive. In particular, the sinking of the unarmed liner *Lusitania* on 7 May 1915, with the loss of 1,198 lives, including 128 Americans, hardened opinion against Germany within the United States. On the surface U-boats could be rammed or sunk by gunfire, but when submerged they were almost impossible to deal with. Mining their bases provided only a partial answer, although mines did account for approximately one-third of German submarines lost during the war. A more direct response, produced by the Royal Navy in 1915, was the depth-charge, a container filled with explosives, detonated by a hydrostatic pistol at a pre-determined depth when dropped above a U-boat's suspected position.

Ever since the Wright brothers demonstrated their flying machine at Kitty Hawk on 17 December 1903 it was apparent that a third dimension would be added to land and sea warfare. Development proceeded along two lines: aircraft that relied on the vacuum created above their wings for lift when in motion, and airships filled with hydrogen gas, which was lighter than air. In this second field Germany had a definite lead with the rigid airships named after their designer, Ferdinand von Zeppelin. The German Army and Navy both made extensive use of Zeppelins for strategic reconnaissance and for bombing raids on London and elsewhere, but the Italian Army had been the first to use aircraft in war. During its 1911–12 war against Turkey in Libya it employed a squadron of nine aeroplanes and two non-rigid airships from which small bombs were dropped. Elsewhere the concept of landing on and taking off from water was proved to be workable and with commendable speed the Royal Navy produced its first seaplane carrier.

In 1914 all the major combatants went to war with a rudimentary air arm at their disposal. Surprisingly, Russia, which was backward in so many ways, led with 300 aircraft and eleven airships; Germany came second with 264 aircraft and eleven Zeppelins; France had 160 aircraft and five airships, Great Britain 110 aircraft and six airships, and Austria–Hungary 35 aircraft and one airship. Beyond carrying out reconnaissance, none of these embryonic air forces had any clear perception of the various roles which lay ahead of them, but they learned very quickly from experience. For example, when scout pilots began potting at one another with rifles and pistols it was soon realised that better results could be obtained if their aircraft were fitted with a machine-gun, and so the fighter, capable of attacking other aircraft, came into being. Tracer ammunition, enabling pilots to see where their fire was going, was already in service in 1914 and was steadily improved. In 1916 incendiary ammunition became available and was used with deadly effect against the Zeppelin, penetrating its highly inflammable gas-bags to create a huge fireball. Thereafter the fortunes of the airship as a weapon of war declined rapidly. The bomber evolved from scouts dropping grenades on marching columns to larger and more powerful aircraft dropping purpose-built bombs on tactical or strategic targets. At sea, the viability of air-launched torpedoes was demonstrated with the sinking of a Turkish freighter by a Short seaplane on 19 August 1915. Other roles included directing artillery or naval gunfire by radio, and photo-reconnaissance which led to the production of accurate maps. In a remarkably short space of time air forces managed to develop their own infrastructure, involving everything from the design and manufacture of aircraft to pilot training and routine administration.

Although air power was not employed to any great extent during the opening stages of the war, its importance steadily increased to the point where resources had to be diverted into providing a defence against it. This involved the creation of a new branch of the artillery which began to develop aircraft tracking and target prediction techniques. Despite these, hundreds of rounds had to be fired for every certain kill, though the presence of anti-aircraft guns tended to keep hostile aircraft above a certain height. Against aircraft which deliberately carried out low-level missions such as trench strafing, massed rifle and machine-gun fire proved remarkably effective.

As the war progressed it became apparent that tactical operations mounted by the side which possessed control of the air above the battlefield stood a higher chance of success. This elevated air forces to the status of being a service within their own right. At the strategic level it was also appreciated that bombing attacks on the enemy's means of manufacture and distribution would seriously hinder his war effort.

JUTLAND, 31 MAY – 1 JUNE 1916

It was said that if there were one man who could lose the war in an afternoon it was Admiral Sir John Jellicoe, commander of the British Grand Fleet. If mistakes on Jellicoe's part resulted in serious loss the possibility of a German invasion of England would loom larger and to meet that threat British troops would have to be withdrawn from France and Flanders. This would leave the French Army, already weakened by nearly two years of war, to take over a much-extended sector of the Western Front at a time when it was already under intense pressure at Verdun. Russia, having already sustained one million casualties, was about to mount another offensive, but in the longer term was a spent force and was less than a year away from revolution. The consequences of a German naval victory in the North Sea would, therefore, be far-reaching; equally, the defeat of the German High Seas Fleet would have little immediate effect on the Central Powers.

The British, however, possessed not simply the advantage of numbers but also the German naval codes, recovered by the Imperial Russian Navy from the wrecked cruiser *Magdeburg* at Odensholm in the Baltic on 26 August 1914 and promptly passed to the Admiralty. Surprisingly, the Germans had not changed their codes and the British carefully concealed the fact that they were monitoring their radio frequencies.

On 30 May, alerted by careless radio chatter indicating that the Germans were mounting a major naval operation, Jellicoe correctly guessed that this would take place in the area of the Skaggerak and immediately led his battle fleet out of its anchorage at Scapa Flow and set a course to intercept, while the battle cruiser fleet, commanded by Vice-Admiral Sir David Beatty, left its base at Rosyth on the east coast of Scotland to scout ahead. Jellicoe's objective was the destruction of the High Seas Fleet in a general engagement which had been eagerly anticipated since the war began. The intention of Vice-Admiral Reinhard Scheer, commanding the High Seas Fleet, remained, as usual, to tempt part of the Grand Fleet into a local action and destroy it, avoiding a general engagement at all costs. The warships available to the two commanders were:

	British	**German**
Dreadnoughts	28	16
Pre-Dreadnoughts	–	6
Battle Cruisers	9	5
Armoured-Cruisers	8	–
Light Cruisers	26	11
Destroyers	78	61
Minelayers	1	–
Seaplane-carriers	1	–

Vital to Scheer's operational planning was the information to be provided by the navy's Zeppelins and a U-boat screen specially deployed for the purpose. However, poor flying weather prevented the Zeppelins from making any contribution, and details supplied by the U-boats were so fragmentary as to be useless. He therefore had no idea that the Grand Fleet was at sea and would probably have reversed course had he been aware of the fact. Incomplete decipherment of German signals meant that Jellicoe was equally unaware that the entire High Seas Fleet was in the offing. With their respective battle cruiser forces deployed well ahead, both fleets were now on a converging course, the British from the west the Germans from the south. It was an innocent Danish freighter, the *N. J. Fjord*, steaming equidistantly between the two fleets that precipitated the battle during the afternoon of 31 May. Cruisers from both battle cruiser forces were sent to investigate her smoke, sighted one another, and their heavier sisters closed in to engage.

Beatty had with him the six battle cruisers of the 1st and 2nd Battle Cruiser Squadrons (*Lion* (Flagship), *Princess Royal*, *Queen Mary*, *Tiger*, *New Zealand* and *Indefatigable*) supported by the four slightly slower dreadnoughts of the 5th Battle Squadron (*Barham*, *Valiant*, *Warspite* and *Malaya*) plus cruiser and destroyer units. Vice-Admiral Franz Hipper, commanding the German battle cruiser force, had five battle cruisers (*Lützow*, *Derfflinger*, *Seydlitz*, *Moltke* and *Von der Tann*) plus cruisers and destroyers. He turned south, intending to lead the British to destruction under the guns of the German battle fleet, and at 15.31 Beatty came on to a parallel course. At 15.48 both sides began exchanging salvos, closing the range from 18,000 to 12,000 yards. German gunnery was the better and obtained the greater number of hits. *Lion*, Beatty's flagship, had her midship turret knocked out and the ship was only saved from destruction when the mortally wounded Major F. W. Harvey of the Royal Marines flooded the magazine.

Below: A German shell explodes on Q (midships) turret of the battlecruiser HMS *Lion. Imperial War Museum Neg No SP1704*

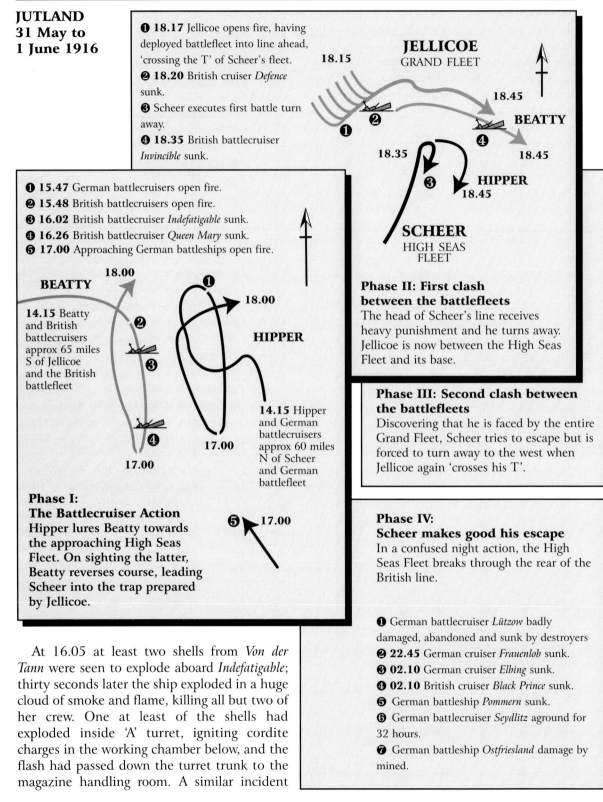

**JUTLAND
31 May to
1 June 1916**

❶ 18.17 Jellicoe opens fire, having deployed battlefleet into line ahead, 'crossing the T' of Scheer's fleet.
❷ 18.20 British cruiser *Defence* sunk.
❸ Scheer executes first battle turn away.
❹ 18.35 British battlecruiser *Invincible* sunk.

18.15

JELLICOE
GRAND FLEET

18.45

BEATTY

18.35   18.45

❸   **HIPPER**
18.45

SCHEER
HIGH SEAS
FLEET

**Phase II: First clash
between the battlefleets**
The head of Scheer's line receives heavy punishment and he turns away. Jellicoe is now between the High Seas Fleet and its base.

❶ 15.47 German battlecruisers open fire.
❷ 15.48 British battlecruisers open fire.
❸ 16.02 British battlecruiser *Indefatigable* sunk.
❹ 16.26 British battlecruiser *Queen Mary* sunk.
❺ 17.00 Approaching German battleships open fire.

18.00

BEATTY   18.00

14.15 Beatty and British battlecruisers approx 65 miles S of Jellicoe and the British battlefleet

HIPPER

14.15 Hipper and German battlecruisers approx 60 miles N of Scheer and German battlefleet

17.00   17.00

17.00

**Phase I:
The Battlecruiser Action**
Hipper lures Beatty towards the approaching High Seas Fleet. On sighting the latter, Beatty reverses course, leading Scheer into the trap prepared by Jellicoe.

❺   17.00

Phase III: Second clash between the battlefleets
Discovering that he is faced by the entire Grand Fleet, Scheer tries to escape but is forced to turn away to the west when Jellicoe again 'crosses his T'.

**Phase IV:
Scheer makes good his escape**
In a confused night action, the High Seas Fleet breaks through the rear of the British line.

❶ German battlecruiser *Lützow* badly damaged, abandoned and sunk by destroyers
❷ 22.45 German cruiser *Frauenlob* sunk.
❸ 02.10 German cruiser *Elbing* sunk.
❹ 02.10 British cruiser *Black Prince* sunk.
❺ German battleship *Pommern* sunk.
❻ German battlecruiser *Seydlitz* aground for 32 hours.
❼ German battleship *Ostfriesland* damage by mined.

At 16.05 at least two shells from *Von der Tann* were seen to explode aboard *Indefatigable*; thirty seconds later the ship exploded in a huge cloud of smoke and flame, killing all but two of her crew. One at least of the shells had exploded inside 'A' turret, igniting cordite charges in the working chamber below, and the flash had passed down the turret trunk to the magazine handling room. A similar incident had occurred aboard the cruiser *Kent* during the Battle of the Falkland Islands, but the damage had not been fatal and the Admiralty had paid little attention. However, at the Battle of Dogger Bank in 1915 two of *Seydlitz's* turrets had been similarly penetrated and only prompt flooding of the magazines had prevented a major explosion. Since then the German Navy had taken steps to remedy the

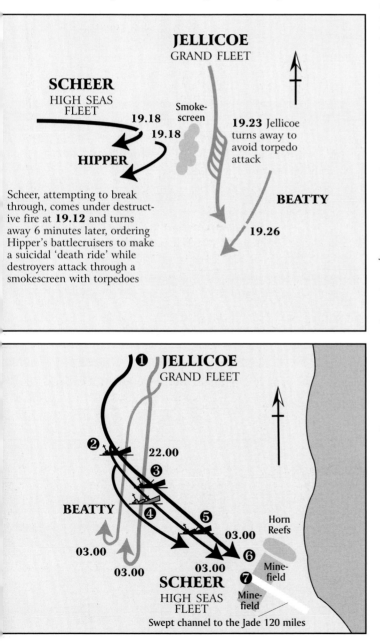

SCHEER
HIGH SEAS FLEET

JELLICOE
GRAND FLEET

HIPPER

BEATTY

Smoke-screen

19.18
19.18

19.23 Jellicoe turns away to avoid torpedo attack

19.26

Scheer, attempting to break through, comes under destructive fire at **19.12** and turns away 6 minutes later, ordering Hipper's battlecruisers to make a suicidal 'death ride' while destroyers attack through a smokescreen with torpedoes

❶ **JELLICOE**
GRAND FLEET

❷ **22.00**
❸
BEATTY
❹ ❺
03.00
03.00 **03.00**
SCHEER
HIGH SEAS FLEET

Horn Reefs

❻ **03.00**
Mine-field
❼ Mine-field

Swept channel to the Jade 120 miles

problem so that while some of its battle cruisers' turrets were penetrated with heavy loss of life the damage was contained.

Meanwhile, Beatty's four dreadnoughts, commanded by Rear-Admiral Hugh Evan-Thomas, had caught up with the battle and opened fire at 4.08 p.m.. Their shooting was better than that of the battle cruisers, resulting in *Von der Tann* being seriously holed below the water line. The German ships, however, were more compartmentalised than the British so that although 600 tons of water came aboard she not only stayed afloat but kept her place in the line. Again, a design flaw in the British 15-inch shells meant that if they struck at an oblique angle some broke up on impact instead of exploding inside the armour. 'It was nothing but the poor quality of the British bursting charges that saved us from disaster,' Hipper commented after the battle.

Two of the German ships, *Derff-linger* and *Seydlitz*, concentrated their fire on the battle cruiser *Queen Mary*, which blew up at 4.26 p.m. from precisely the same cause as *Indefatigable*. Only eight of her crew of 1,274 were saved. Beatty commented laconically, 'There seems to be something wrong with our bloody ships today,' then gave the order to engage the enemy more closely. Hipper, unable to stand the weight of shellfire, turned away and minutes later sighted the rest of the High Seas Fleet steaming north.

For the moment Scheer must have felt his ambition had been realised, for Hipper had led a sizeable portion of the Grand Fleet straight into his trap. It was not quite that simple, however. British and German destroyer flotillas forged ahead of their major units to launch torpedo attacks, becoming embroiled in a savage mêlée in which both sides

183

sustained loss, the only torpedo to find its mark being one fired by *Petard* which struck *Seydlitz* and caused flooding.

Beatty reversed course at 17.26, intending to turn the tables on Scheer by leading him northwards into a direct confrontation with the Grand Fleet. The move was covered by Evan-Thomas's battleships, which became the target of every German gun within range. They were saved by the quality of their armour and their own good shooting which obtained hits on *König*, *Grosser Kurfürst* and *Markgraf* at the head of Scheer's line as well as handing out further punishment to the enemy battle cruisers.

During the run north Hipper's ships continued to trade salvos with those of Beatty and Evan-Thomas. Scheer was somewhat handicapped in that the speed of his battle fleet was restricted to the 15 knots attainable by his pre-dreadnoughts. Jellicoe, having been advised of Scheer's presence, was heading south-east at maximum speed with the Grand Fleet's dreadnoughts in six columns, spearheaded by the 3rd Battle Cruiser Squadron (*Invincible*, *Inflexible* and *Indomitable*) under Rear-Admiral H. L. A. Hood. Shortly after 18.00 Beatty sighted Jellicoe and began turning eastward so that he would remain at the head of the line into which the Grand Fleet had begun deploying on the port column. Visibility on this grey, misty evening was further reduced by the drifting funnel smoke of so many warships steaming at full speed. At about 18.15 Scheer emerged from the murk to find, to his horror, that Jellicoe had crossed his T with the entire Grand Fleet, so that while the latter could engage with all its heavy guns only those of the leading German ships could reply. At 18.17 gun flashes flickered along the length of Jellicoe's line. A furious general engagement ensued in which Hipper's battle cruisers and the foremost of Scheer's ships became the focus of the concentrated British fire. *Lützow*, Hipper's flagship, was so badly damaged that the Admiral transferred his flag to a destroyer. For the next two hours the battle cruisers were commanded by Captain Hartog in *Derfflinger*, which had already sustained 20 hits, was holed in the

bows and had lost wireless communications. *Seydlitz* had also taken fearful punishment and was awash from the bows as far as her middle deck. All *Von der Tann*'s turrets had been put out of action, leaving only *Moltke*, which Hipper was eventually able to board, in any way fit to continue the fight. In Scheer's line *König* was hit repeatedly and took on a severe list, and *Markgraf*, hit in the engine room, was forced to reduce speed. Between the two fleets lay the German cruiser *Wiesbaden*, crippled and sinking. Of her two assailants, the armoured cruisers *Defence* and *Warrior*, the former was blown apart by the heavy guns of *Derfflinger* and four German battleships, while the latter, badly damaged, managed to escape only because of the timely intervention of *Warspite*.

Scheer had anticipated the predicament in which he now found himself and had exercised his ships in a manoeuvre the Germans called *Gefechtskehrwendung* (battle turn-about) in

which they all reversed course simultaneously at a given signal. At 6.35 p.m. he gave that signal and, to the surprise of the British, the High Seas Fleet simply faded into the mist. Jellicoe's satisfaction at having caused severe damage to the enemy was marred when, just as Scheer had reached his decision, the last salvo from *Derfflinger* struck Admiral Hood's flagship, the battle cruiser *Invincible*, which was blown apart by yet another magazine explosion. Just six survivors were left clinging to floating wreckage. 'I have never seen anything more splendid than these few cheering as we raced by them,' wrote one of *Indomitable*'s officers. Shortly after this they were picked up by a destroyer.

Jellicoe now had two options. He could embark on a direct pursuit of Scheer to the west in which he would probably be able to sink a few damaged stragglers but not achieve the decisive result he sought; or he could maintain a southerly course which would interpose the Grand Fleet between the Germans and their base, so bringing on another general engagement. Without hesitation he chose the latter.

Scheer had been badly rattled. At 18.55 he decided to reverse course again and head directly for his base. It was a decision of which he later commented, 'If I had fought such an action in a peacetime exercise, I should have lost my command – but it was necessary to escape.' The manoeuvre was observed by Commodore W. E. Goodenough in the cruiser *Southampton*, who reported it to Jellicoe at 19.04. Shortly afterwards three German destroyer flotillas emerged from the mist to

Below: A painting by Robert Henry Smith showing the Grand Fleet deploying from columns into line of battle as it crosses the T of the German High Seas Fleet. *Imperial War Museum PIC 1728*

Right: The destruction of the battlecruiser HMS *Invincible.* The explosion of the midships magazine broke the ship in half so that she sank in 10–15 seconds with the loss of 1,025 officers and men out of 1,031. The photograph also shows the start of a secondary explosion in the forward magazine and the mainmast falling. *Imperial War Museum Neg SP2468*

launch an unsuccessful torpedo attack on the British line. At 19.10 the German fleet appeared out of the murk to the west. Two minutes later, at ranges between 10,750 and 14,000 yards, Jellicoe's battle squadrons erupted in smoke and flame, sending one accurate salvo after another into Scheer's ships. The crippled *Lützow* was reduced to a sinking wreck and, clearly unable to make port, was later torpedoed by her own escorting destroyers. *Von der Tann*'s control turret was smashed, killing everyone within and leaving only one gun in action, but she remained in line in the gallant hope of drawing fire away from her consorts. Fires began to rage aboard *Seydlitz* and *Derfflinger*. *Markgraf*, *Grosser Kurfürst* and *König* were all badly hit, the last two shipping 800 and 1,600 tons of water respectively. Once again, to his horror, Scheer discovered that Jellicoe had crossed his T. At 19.15, now thoroughly shaken, he ordered his

fleet to make a second about-turn. To achieve this, he was prepared to sacrifice Hartog's four remaining battle cruisers, which were instructed to 'Close the enemy and ram! Ships will fight to the death!' It was an order that would go down in German naval history, but it was pointless because even if it could have been carried out, which seems very unlikely, it would at best have removed only four of his opponents. Evidently, on reflection, Scheer thought so too, for two minutes later he told Hartog simply to 'Operate against the enemy's van,' and, having done so the latter conformed to the about-turn.

More to the point was a fresh torpedo attack mounted by two German destroyer flotillas which also laid a smoke-screen to cover the withdrawal of Scheer's battle squadrons. They were counter-attacked by British light cruisers and destroyers and engaged by the battleships' secondary armament, six being severely

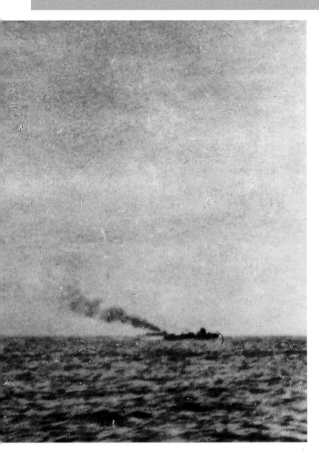

to stop engines or even go astern to avoid collisions, suggesting that the High Seas Fleet had begun to lose some of its former cohesion. He appreciated, correctly, that Scheer's sole priority had become escape to his base in the Jade estuary and, with a further interception in mind, he turned south, as Scheer had already done.

Gathering darkness compounded the mist, but at 19.45 Jellicoe received a signal from Beatty, now some miles ahead of the Grand Fleet, confirming that he was once more in contact with the enemy. At 20.20 Beatty opened fire on the German battle cruisers, inflicting further damage on *Derfflinger* and *Seydlitz*. The German gunnery officers could see little more than the British gun flashes against the darker eastern horizon and, unable to make effective reply, Hartog's battle cruisers turned away. Scheer had meanwhile sent his pre-dreadnought squadron, now leading the German battle line, to their assistance, but after hits were scored on *Schleswig-Holstein*, *Pommern* and the cruiser *Stettin*, they too turned away westwards until they were out of range.

The two fleets continued on their parallel southerly course, the British, being several knots faster, pulling ahead. Jellicoe, knowing that Scheer would have to make for the swept passage through the minefields south of the Horns Reef, dispatched the fast minelayer *Abdiel* to seal the entrance. Scheer dared not risk a renewal of the battle at first light, which would appear at about 03.00, but he was prepared to risk a night action with the Grand Fleet if it meant that most of his ships could escape. At 21.30 he gave the order to steer south-east and, as luck would have it, broke through the light units covering the tail of Jellicoe's battle line. The Germans were the better prepared for night fighting and, while few in the British battle squadrons were aware of the reason for the uproar far astern, those closest to the enemy inexplicably declined to engage without specific instructions from their commodores. The result was a chaotic series of midnight clashes involving close-range gunfire,

damaged and a seventh sunk, but they pressed their attack to within 8,000 yards and launched 31 torpedoes. In the face of such an attack, commanders could either turn towards or away from it, thereby reducing the target area presented by their ships. Jellicoe chose to turn away, the accepted wisdom being that by so doing he would out-distance the torpedoes' maximum range. In the event only ten of them reached and passed through the British line, the battleship *Marlborough* having a lucky escape when one went by ahead, another just astern and a third, running too deep, slid under her.

With hindsight, Jellicoe has been criticised for turning away from instead of towards the attack since his course was now easterly and he was moving steadily away from his opponent. He had, however, observed that on this occasion the German turn-about had been executed with a degree of confusion, some ships having

torpedo attacks, collisions and sinkings. The British lost several destroyers, the armoured cruiser *Black Prince*, which blew up under a rain of heavy shells, and the light cruiser *Tipperary*, while the cruisers *Southampton* and *Dublin* were severely damaged. The German cruisers *Frauenlob* and *Rostock* were torpedoed and sunk, and *Elbing*, having been crippled by torpedoes, was subsequently rammed by one of her own dreadnoughts, *Posen*, and abandoned; the pre-dreadnought *Pommern*, torpedoed by the destroyer *Obedient*, blew up and sank in two halves; the battle cruiser *Seydlitz* with thousands of tons of water aboard and drawing 42 feet forward, ran aground off the Horns Reef and had to be towed into harbour stern first next day; and finally, at 05.20, the dreadnought *Ostfriesland* struck one of *Abdiel*'s mines laid in May, the previous night's minefield being a little too far to the south.

Jellicoe remained off the Horns Reef until 11.00 when, in rising seas which claimed the severely damaged *Warrior*, now under tow, he steamed back to Scapa Flow and Rosyth, where his ships dropped anchor the following morning. In the United Kingdom there was an acute sense of disappointment that the battle had not been a second Trafalgar, best expressed in a signal sent by King George V to Jellicoe on 3 June:

'I mourn the loss of brave men, many of them personal friends of my own, who have fallen in their country's cause; yet even more do I regret that the German High Seas Fleet was enabled by misty weather to evade the full consequences of an encounter they have always professed to desire, but for which, when the opportunity arrived, they showed no inclination.'

Below: With fires raging aboard and thousands of tons of water in her hull, the German battlecruiser SMS *Seydlitz* was towed into harbour. She was out of commission for many months after the battle. *Imperial War Museum Neg No SP2158*

Ever since that grey, mist-shrouded day the outcome of the battle has been debated. The Grand Fleet lost three battle cruisers, three armoured cruisers and eight destroyers, a total of fourteen ships. The High Seas Fleet lost one pre-dreadnought battleship, one battle cruiser, four light cruisers and five destroyers, a total of eleven ships. British casualties totalled 6,097 killed and 510 wounded; the Germans lost 2,551 killed and 507 wounded. On the basis of these figures, plus the fact that the High Seas Fleet had escaped destruction, Scheer could claim a tactical victory, as did a large section of the Central Powers' press. The more thoughtful *Berliner Tageblatt*, whose naval correspondent seems to have examined the fearful damage inflicted on the majority of Scheer's returned ships, expressed a less palatable truth: 'Germany narrowly escaped a crushing defeat; it is clear that this battle must and should be the last one.'

To examine the bald statistics another way, on the day following the Grand Fleet's return to harbour, Jellicoe could report it as being at four hours' readiness with 24 undamaged dreadnoughts and battle cruisers. In sharp contrast, Scheer had only ten undamaged capital ships and could only promise the Kaiser that the High Seas Fleet would be ready for sea in six or seven weeks. Again, while Beatty had eight capital ships undergoing heavy repair, the last being completed on 2 August, Scheer had ten, including all four surviving battle cruisers, of which *Seydlitz* and *Derfflinger* were not completed until 16 September and 15 October respectively.

Small wonder, then, that the neutral press should remain unconvinced by German claims of victory. As one New York newspaper put it: 'The German fleet has assaulted its jailer, and is still in jail.' In that sense Jellicoe had won a decisive strategic victory, for after Jutland the High Seas Fleet as a whole rarely put to sea again. It remained at its anchorages in Kiel and Wilhelmshaven, its best officers and men being drained away for service in the U-boat arm, which was producing results the surface fleet could never hope to equal. So successful were the U-boats that in 1917 the United Kingdom had only a few weeks' food supply in hand. Belatedly the Admiralty introduced an effective convoy system which brought the menace under control. The British blockade of Germany, however, continued to produce shortages, rising prices, inflation and industrial unrest. Against this background, the enforced idleness, poor rations and inadequate accommodation which was the lot of those crewing German surface warships resulted in a gradual decline in morale. This was accelerated by leftist agitation following the Russian Revolution and by the realisation in 1918 that the defeat of the Central Powers was inevitable. In the words of the French naval historian Jacques Mordal: 'The spirit had gone out of the High Seas Fleet, which was as dead as if it had been destroyed at Jutland.' Unwisely ordered to sea during the final stages of the war, it mutinied, initiating the collapse of Imperial Germany. Its last voyage was to internment in Scapa Flow, where it was scuttled by its skeleton crews the following year in protest against the terms of the Treaty of Versailles. Such was the ultimate result of Jutland, the last action to be fought between battle fleets in which the gun was the primary weapon.

THE SOMME, 1 JULY – 18 NOVEMBER 1916

Ever since the deadlock of trench warfare had set in on the Western Front during the last months of 1914, both sides had tried by various means to restore mobility to their operations. The Germans had used gas but this had proved a two-edged weapon, especially as the prevailing west wind generally favoured the Allies. The British and French had tried heavier and heavier artillery bombardments in the vain hope that these would eliminate resistance in the enemy's ever deeper and more complex trench systems, but their subsequent infantry assaults had usually foundered in the teeth of concentrated machine-gun fire and defensive barrages. For a while the vague idea persisted that if a sufficiently wide breach be created the cavalry could pass through and restore movement to the battlefield. This never amounted to more than a pious hope, for even a couple of well-sited machine-guns could stop a cavalry regiment in its tracks. Even if the cavalry could get through, the chances of exploiting a breach were virtually nil because the attackers would have to bring forward their artillery and supplies across two trench systems and a shell-torn, wire-tangled no-man's land, a laborious process costing priceless time during which the defenders would be able to seal off the breach with reinforcements rushed into the area over unspoiled ground. The generals were therefore faced with an insoluble problem in which the odds were always heavily weighted in favour of the defence. As has been said elsewhere, their dilemma was akin to that of the savage who, being unfamiliar with the screw, tries to pull one from a piece of wood; when it refuses to move, his answer is to apply more and more force. Like the savage, the generals lacked both an appropriate screwdriver and the knowledge to use it. Behind the scenes, however, inventive minds were already working to produce a suitable mechanical solution.

Germany had planned for a short, victorious war and when her opening campaign in the west failed to produce the desired result she adopted a broadly defensive stance while her strategy was re-thought. In September 1914 von Moltke the Younger had been replaced by General Erich von Falkenhayn as the German Army's Chief of General Staff. Falkenhayn was fully aware of the problems posed by trench warfare and recognised that, for the moment, no conventional solution existed. On the other hand, he appreciated that a falling birth-rate in the past years had seriously reduced French manpower resources and believed that this situation could be exploited by imposing attrition at a point he knew the French would defend at all costs. The object was, quite simply, to bleed the French Army white to the point where it would request an armistice; the British, left isolated, would be forced to withdraw to their island or seek terms. On 21 February 1916, having received the Kaiser's

approval, Falkenhayn implemented his strategy by opening a major offensive against the fortress of Verdun, which lay in a salient covered by the German artillery. The French reacted as he had hoped they would, fighting tenaciously for every yard of ground and rotating their divisions regularly through what became a slaughterhouse. It mattered little to him that Frenchmen and Germans were killing one another in approximately equal numbers, for Germany had the greater reserves.

General Joseph Joffre, the French Commander-in-Chief, saw the crisis looming and asked his allies for help. The Russians responded in March with an offensive in the Lake Naroch area, but this failed at a cost of more than 70,000 casualties. In June they tried again, this time with greater success, their South West Front under General Alexei Brusilov driving the Austrians back to the Carpathians. The Russian and Austrian armies each sustained about one million casualties, leaving their respective empires fatally weakened. Russia's situation was further aggravated when, in August, Romania declared war on the Central Powers and collapsed almost immediately, so creating an extended Eastern Front which the Russian Army could not afford to man.

In the west, Joffre and General Sir Douglas Haig, commander of the British Expeditionary Force, discussed various proposals for an offensive on the Somme sector. It was finally decided that this would commence on 29 June and involve a general assault along 21 miles of front, the objects being to relieve the pressure on Verdun, to inflict loss on the enemy, to eject the Germans from the higher ground of the Thiepval–Pozières ridge, and to create a breach or exploit the advance to the limit of its capability.

The attack would be made by General Fayolle's French Sixth Army astride the Somme on the right, the main blow being delivered by General Sir Henry Rawlinson's Fourth Army, the left flank of which was to be protected by two divisions of General Sir Edmund Allenby's Third Army. On 3 July a breakout force, known as the Reserve Army, consisting of the cavalry corps and two of Rawlinson's infantry divisions, was to be formed under Lieutenant-General Hubert Gough.

The preparations required for this, the greatest offensive as yet undertaken by the British Army, were intense. Some 2,000 artillery pieces were to fire a preparatory bombardment lasting five days and for this huge quantities of ammunition had to be delivered and stockpiled; 7,000 miles of additional telephone cable were laid and buried, together with 120 miles of water piping; new supply dumps, field hospitals and tented camps suddenly appeared; roads leading to the front were improved and new railway track, both standard and narrow gauge, was laid.

By now, the BEF had become a citizen army. The Regular and Territorial divisions had been seriously thinned both by the battles of 1914 and 1915 and by the need to provide a backbone of experienced personnel for Kitchener's New Army divisions, and their ranks had been filled out with volunteers. The New Army divisions consisted in the main of enthusiastic volunteers many of whom had enlisted in the 'Pals' battalions recruited from friends and neighbours or men with similar backgrounds who wished to fight together. Some regular commanders and their staffs, lacking confidence in the training of these formations and their ability to execute such elementary tactical movements as controlled rushes over fire-swept ground, were to insist that they attack in straight lines at walking pace. Ten Commonwealth divisions – five from Australia, four from Canada and one from New Zealand – would also take part in the battle, as would a brigade of South Africans. These men, too, were mostly volunteers, but they differed from their New Army counterparts, many of whom were city dwellers, in that they were of better physique and healthier; they also tended to be more flexible and placed greater store on personal initiative.

Rawlinson's planned scenario for the attack envisaged a situation in which the long preparatory bombardment would cut the enemy's wire, demolish his strongpoints, sever his communications, neutralise his artillery and lower his morale. At selected points the Royal Engineers were excavating tunnels in which mines would be exploded beneath the defences just before the attack went in. The infantry would advance according to a timed programme, storming the German front line as soon as the bombardment lifted to targets beyond. It was unlikely, some were told, that they would find anyone alive. The same method would be used to secure the German second line and the various objectives beyond.

Across no-man's land the German positions were sited advantageously on ground which had been occupied in 1914. South of the Ancre, those on the Thiepval–Pozières ridge overlooked the British trenches. In places, the Germans had dug in on the reverse slopes and were concealed, but air reconnaissance showed that their front and second lines of defence extended to a depth of 5,000 yards. Falkenhayn's reserves were earmarked for the Eastern Front or Verdun and, having no reinforcements available, he had insisted on a major programme of defence works elsewhere along the Western Front. On the Somme these consisted of barbed wire aprons 50 yards deep, sometimes shaped so as to channel attacks into a killing-ground swept by concealed machine-guns; hundreds of fortified machine-gun posts, some within reinforced concrete blockhouses; and huge dugouts some 30 feet or more beneath the surface, equipped with running water, ventilation, electric lighting and emergency rations.

The Somme sector was held by General Fritz von Below's Second Army. Although the Royal Flying Corps had achieved air superiority over the area, the extensive British preparations could hardly be concealed altogether from the German artillery spotters in their observation balloons. Below asked Falkenhayn for reinforcements, but all he received was a battery of captured Russian howitzers.

On 24 June the preparatory bombardment began, continuing day and night with little rest for the sweating gunners; the sustained rumble was audible in southern England. It turned many of the German trenches into a series of craters, cut gaps in the wire, albeit unevenly, exploded ammunition dumps, smashed gun positions and caused casualties as far back as the enemy's rest areas. Unfortunately, low cloud and poor visibility made it difficult for the Royal Flying Corps to adjust the fire on the deeper targets, notably the German artillery, which escaped much of the punishment intended for it. Patrols also confirmed that long stretches of wire remained uncut and for these reasons the infantry assault was put back until 1 July. Nor did the bombardment, in which no less than 1,732,873 shells were expended, have much effect on the enemy's deep dugouts. It did, however, stretch the nerves of those within to the point where they longed for the assault to begin, granting some respite from the pounding and, temporarily at least, releasing them from their claustrophobic subterranean prisons into fresh air and daylight.

At 7.30 a.m. on Sunday 1 July the bombardment suddenly lifted to the German rear trenches. Whistles shrilled all along the line as the British and French went over the top to form the first assault wave. On the right, all went well. The French, not being subject to British tactical restrictions, broke through the German first line with a series of disciplined rushes. Their neighbours, the British XIII Corps, also captured their objective, ironically with two New Army divisions, the 18th and the 30th. The former had only 200 yards of no-man's land to cross and arrived in strength before the enemy could put up a coherent defence, and although the latter had more than twice as far to go it found the German wire aprons had been adequately cut and was able to press home its attack. By 4 p.m. Montauban ridge was firmly in Allied hands, but Rawlinson forbade any further advance.

These were the only successes of the day, and even they cost XIII Corps some 6,000 casualties. Everywhere else, the story was one of supreme courage and terrible failure. Machine-guns sliced swathes through the stolidly advancing ranks; the German artillery's defen-

sive barrages presented walls of blast and flying steel that were impenetrable by flesh and blood; and where mines were exploded too rigid adherence to timetables meant that the craters were in German hands before the British could take advantage of them. Here and there, brave but inexperienced groups penetrated beyond the front line, but they failed to clear the deep dugouts and many were shot down from behind; others found themselves cut off and were either killed or forced to surrender. The few local lodgements secured were mostly lost to counter-attacks.

Holding the line opposite Authieule and to the south of Thiepval was the Swabian 180th Regiment (26th Reserve Division). On this sector the attack was delivered by 8th Division (III Corps) and 32nd Division (X Corps) which, together, contained battalions from all over the United Kingdom. In 1920 its tragic course was recorded, not unsympathetically, by a German officer named Gerster in his book *Der Schwaben an der Ancre*. It must surely be one of the most harrowing passages in military history.

'The first line appeared to continue without end to right and left. It was quickly followed by a second line, then a third and a fourth. They came on at an easy pace, as if expecting to find nothing alive in our front trenches.

'"Get ready!" was passed along our front from crater to crater, and heads appeared above the crater edges as final positions were taken up for the best view.

'A few minutes later, when the leading British line was within a hundred yards, the rattle of machine-gun and rifle fire broke out along the whole line of shell-holes. Some fired kneeling so as to get a better target over the broken ground, while others, in the excitement of the moment, stood up regardless of their own safety, to fire into the crowd of men in front of them. Red rockets sped up into the blue sky as a signal to the artillery, and immediately a mass of shells from the German batteries in rear tore through the air and burst among the advancing lines. Whole sections seemed to fall, and the rear formations, moving

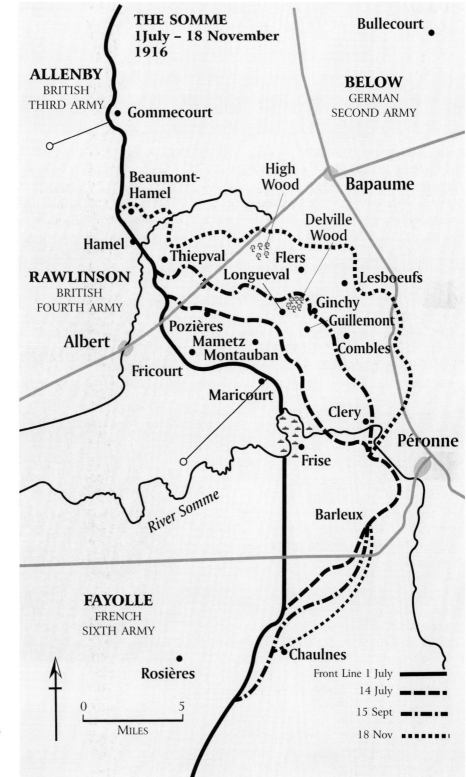

THE SOMME
1 July – 18 November
1916

ALLENBY
BRITISH
THIRD ARMY

● Gommecourt

BELOW
GERMAN
SECOND ARMY

Bullecourt ●

Beaumont-
Hamel

High
Wood

Bapaume

Delville
Wood

Hamel ●

● Thiepval

● Flers

Longueval

Lesboeufs

RAWLINSON
BRITISH
FOURTH ARMY

Ginchy
Guillemont

Albert ●

Pozières
Mametz ●

Combles

Fricourt

Montauban

Maricourt

Clery

Péronne

Frise

River Somme

Barleux

FAYOLLE
FRENCH
SIXTH ARMY

Rosières ●

● Chaulnes

Front Line 1 July
14 July
15 Sept
18 Nov

0   5
MILES

THE SOMME,
1 July to
18 November
1916

Right: Trench fighting was savage and personal, with both sides incurring heavy casualties.
Illustrated London News

in close order, quickly scattered. The advance rapidly crumpled under this hail of shells and bullets. All along the line men could be seen throwing up their arms and collapsing, never to move again. Badly wounded rolled about in their agony, and others, less severely injured, crawled to the nearest shell hole for shelter.

'The British soldier, however, has no lack of courage and is not easily turned from his purpose. The extended lines, though badly shaken and with many gaps, now came on all the faster. Instead of a leisurely walk they covered the ground in short rushes at the double. Within a few minutes the leading troops had advanced to with a stone's throw of our front trench, and while some of us continued to fire at point-blank range, others threw hand-grenades among them. The British bombers answered back, while their infantry rushed forward with fixed bayonets. The noise of battle became indescribable. The shouting of orders and the shrill cheers as the British charged forward could be heard above the violent and intense fusillade of machine-guns and rifles and bursting bombs, and above the thundering of the artillery and shell explosions. With all this were mingled the moans and groans of the wounded, the cries for help and the last screams of death. Again and again the extended lines of British infantry broke against the German defence like waves against a cliff, only to be beaten back.'

By 10 a.m. it was all over. All along the front the khaki bodies lay thick in the skeletal woodland where undergrowth grew obstinately between the shattered trees, among the millions of wild poppies carpeting fields untilled for two years, and in the villages long since pounded to fragmentary walls and brick-dust that stained the chalkland. In no-man's land the survivors limped or crawled back to their own lines or waited patiently in shell-holes for the cover that darkness would provide. Sated with slaughter, and with admiration for their opponents' contempt of death now tinged with fellow-feeling, Germans left their trenches to give what help they could. As another of their officers put it, the day's

fighting had provided 'an amazing spectacle of un-exampled gallantry, courage and bulldog determination on both sides'.

That evening, as the British reserve brigades came forward to hold the line, everyone knew that there had been a disaster. The unanswered roll calls, the numberless stretcher cases encountered in the communication trenches and the long lines of walking wounded filing past the battery positions all confirmed the fact. When figures finally became available they showed that on 1 July the British Army had sustained the highest casualty rate for a single day's fighting in its entire history, with 19,240 killed, 35,493 wounded, 2,152 missing and 585 known captured, a total of 57,470.

It is frequently asked why, in the light of the above, did Haig decide to continue with the offensive when he had previously promised Rawlinson that it would be closed down if strong resistance prevented capture of the first objectives? The reasons were partly military and partly political. First, he was initially unaware of the scale of Rawlinson's casualties, which he thought to be in the region of 40,000 – unwelcome but acceptable in view of the scale of the operation. Secondly, the gains made on the right confirmed that the German front was not impregnable. Finally, he had committed his support to Joffre and could not withdraw it without creating serious strains within the Entente at the highest levels.

During the ensuing weeks Rawlinson therefore persisted in his attacks, although these were much smaller in scale and designed to secure local objectives and erode the German defences. There were signs, too, that the Germans were being hurt, for Falkenhayn insisted that the essence of positional warfare involved the recapture of lost ground by prompt counter-attacks. This had the effect of exposing the German infantry to the same sort of ordeal by fire as had been endured by the British on 1 July, and in this connection the newly issued Lewis light machine-gun was used to telling effect. On 11 July the Allies had their reward, for as a result of the demands on the Eastern Front, and now the Somme, Falkenhayn suspended offensive operations against Verdun. The initiative on that sector passed to the French who in due course recovered most of the ground they had lost. Nor did Allied pressure on the Somme slacken, so that now it was the German Army that was being put through the meat-grinder.

On 14 July Rawlinson introduced a new tactical concept to the battle, namely a night attack delivered behind a creeping barrage.

This was intended to break through the German second line between Longueval and Bazentin-le-Petit with four infantry divisions, then exploit the breach with four cavalry divisions as far as High Wood, Leuze Wood and Martinpuich. Artillery preparation began on 11 July, but the final bombardment was to be restricted to five minutes followed by the creeping barrage. At 03.20 on 14 July an immense flash of gunfire tore the night sky apart and five minutes later the infantry rose from their start-lines in the middle of no-man's land to follow the moving curtain of high-explosive and shrapnel. Taken by surprise, the Germans were unable to co-ordinate their resistance. By 08.00 their second line had been breached along a front of 6,000 yards. Bazentin-le-Petit, Bazentin-le-Grand and Trônes Wood had all been taken although resistance continued in parts of Longueval. The British cavalry was ordered forward, but it was located ten miles to the rear and as it would have to traverse the cratered, wire-strewn battlefield at a walk it would be some time before it would make its presence felt. In the meantime the infantry had pressed on as far as the edges of Delville Wood and High Wood. The latter was there for the taking by 7th Division but the commander of XV Corps forbade it to advance further on the grounds that the wood was a cavalry objective. It should, perhaps, be pointed out that because the British Army had expanded so rapidly, most corps commanders had been brigadiers less than two years previously and were inexperienced at the higher level, as indeed were their staffs. When the cavalry had still not arrived at noon, XV Corps obtained Rawlinson's permission for 7th Division to advance into the wood, but confused reports regarding the situation in Longueval delayed the move until 19.00. By then German reinforcements had arrived and the chance of taking the wood, which would become the scene of bitter fighting in the weeks ahead, had gone. During the evening two cavalry squadrons finally reached the high ground between Delville and High Woods. At 21.30 they charged some infantry and machine-guns hidden among the crops but they were too few in numbers to achieve much and finally took over a section of the line near Longueval.

Next day the 1st South African Brigade, part of 9th Division, was ordered to take Delville Wood at all costs. The South Africans, recruited from both the British and Dutch populations, were experienced soldiers, having already served in German South West Africa and against the Senussi in North Africa before moving to the Western Front. Their advance through the tangle of smashed oaks, birches and undergrowth all but cleared the 156-acre wood, but the cost was high. The Springboks' ordeal, however, was only just beginning, for the enemy reacted to this latest penetration with extreme violence. Counter-attacks from the north and east began almost immediately, only to be broken up by British artillery, machine-gun and rifle fire; so fiercely were they pressed that in many cases the last of the attackers fell on the edge of the South African trenches. When the wood was not under direct attack it was bombarded with high-explosive, shrapnel and gas shells. Such importance did the Germans attach to the wood that at one time the fire of 116 field and more than 70 medium and heavy guns and howitzers was focused upon it, blasting the confined area with 400 rounds per minute. Days and nights merged as the South Africans' casualties mounted steadily, forcing them to give ground. Many of them were crack shots and, as their numbers dropped they collected five or six rifles each from the dead and wounded, keeping them ready to meet each new attack with a heavy volume of fire. Relief of the brigade began on 18 July but was not completed for two days. When the roll was called on 21 July it was answered by only 29 officers and 751 other ranks. So far the Somme had cost the Springboks 1,080 killed or missing and 1,735 wounded; only eight of their officers remained unwounded.

By the end of July the wood and Longueval were finally cleared. At about the same time Haig received a letter from General Sir William Robertson, Chief of the Imperial General Staff, expressing the concern of those at home regarding the mounting casualties that were being incurred for such comparatively minor gains. He replied to the effect that he intended to continue the process of wearing down the enemy, who had already suffered heavy losses and would, in his view, be faced with a manpower crisis in about six weeks. Minor but costly attacks therefore continued throughout August on an horrific battlefield where the living shared their trenches with the dead, over-gorged rats and swarms of flies. Even journeys to and from the line were fraught with hazard as the artillery of both sides had every route zeroed to the nearest yard. The British continued to make slow progress, matched by the French astride the Somme. The Germans, having lost the protection of their deep dugouts, took to holding their front with linked outposts and a strong counter-attack force to the rear. This policy resulted in their incurring even higher casualty levels, and at the end of August loss of confidence in Falken-hayn's methods led to his replacement by Field Marshal Paul von Hindenburg and General Erich Ludendorff, the latter with the appoint-ment of Quartermaster-General.

Haig used this period to prepare for another major attack, this time using a new and secret weapon. Once trench warfare had set in the British and French had appreciated the need of a fully tracked armoured vehicle that could negotiate no-man's land, crush barbed wire, cross trenches and eliminate machine-gun posts. The British had taken the remarkably short time of a year to create a viable design which they had put into production under the thinly veiled cover story that it was a mobile water tank, a name which stuck. The genius of the British design lay in its rhomboidal shape, which has never been bettered for cross-country performance. The Tank Mark I could travel at about one mile per hour over going such as that presented by the Somme battle-field. Its crew were protected against small-arms fire and shell splinters, although they could receive minor injuries from bullet splash

penetrating visors or joints between the armour plates and also from shards of red hot metal flaking off interior surfaces as a result of external strikes. On the other hand, a direct hit by an artillery round could smash through the boilerplate armour and turn the vehicle into an inferno. Main armament consisted of either two sponson-mounted 6-pounder guns plus four Hotchkiss machine-guns for the 'male' version, or one Hotchkiss and four Vickers machine-guns for the 'female'. The eight-man crew worked in intense heat generated by the Daimler 105hp engine, compounded by petrol and cordite fumes, and received a jolting, unpredictable ride from the unsprung rollers. They belonged to the recently formed Heavy Section Machine Gun Corps and were volunteers who believed that in the tank they possessed a weapon capable not only of breaking the deadlock of trench warfare, but of winning the war itself.

Early in September 'C' and 'D' Companies HSMGC, with a total of 49 tanks between them, detrained at Bray, just behind the Somme front. Haig planned that they should lead a major attack on the Flers–Courcelette sector on 15 September and allocated seven-

Above: The Somme. Men of the Wiltshire Regiment commence an attack on the Thiepval sector, 7 August 1916. *Imperial War Museum Negative No. QII42*

teen each to XIV and XV Corps, dividing the rest between III Corps and the Canadian Corps. In the event only 32 reached the start-line. Of these, nine broke down, five became ditched, another nine were unable to keep up with the infantry but were able to assist in the subsequent mopping-up, leaving just nine with which to lead the assault. The results they achieved, however, while the subject of mixed views at the time, were to prove revolutionary.

Zero hour had been set for 6.20 a.m., but the main assault was to be preceded by a preliminary attack, timed for 5.15 a.m., against a German position known as Hop Alley, to the east of Delville Wood. This was carried out by Captain H. W. Mortimore's section of three tanks and two companies of the 6th King's Own Yorkshire Light Infantry. One of Mortimore's tanks broke down immediately and another became ditched shortly after, but he continued across no-man's land with the third, 'D1', while the KOYLI followed, using an old communication trench for cover. His gunners engaged machine-gun flashes ahead, evidently to some effect, because the infantry charged past with fixed bayonets and secured the objective. Mortimore then positioned 'D1' astride another trench which he raked with his machine-guns, observing that the enemy's reaction was either dumb bewilderment, fear, blind panic or passive surrender. When the main attack started he joined in the general advance but was halted only 300 yards further on by a direct hit from a shell which broke the starboard track, smashed in the sponson and killed two of his crew. The vehicle nevertheless continued to engage targets within the enemy trenches until the infantry passed through.

Elsewhere the tanks enjoyed mixed fortunes, the most spectacular success of the day being obtained at Flers by 'D6' (Lieutenant Legge), 'D16' *Dracula* (Lieutenant Arthur Arnold) and 'D17' *Dinnaken* (Lieutenant Stuart Hastie), which suppressed the opposition so effectively that the infantry were able to take possession of the village by 08.00. Later in the day Legge, accompanied by Lieutenant Blowers in 'D5', advanced from Flers to Gueudecourt, which would almost certainly have fallen as well if the infantry had kept up. As it was, the two tanks had advanced farther than anyone else and now found themselves being engaged by two German artillery batteries over open sights. Both were knocked out, but not before they had inflicted casualties and destroyed a gun. The hamlet fell on 26 September, largely because of the action of a single 'female' tank, 'D4'. commanded by Second Lieutenant C. E. Storey, which turned parallel to the formidable Gird Trench, crushing its wire for a considerable distance while the gunners fired belt after belt into the trench itself.

When it came to assessing the part played by the tanks, Haig was able to report that despite their mechanical shortcomings the fact was that when they were present the attack had succeeded, and when they were not it had failed. That he considered the weapon to be of value is beyond doubt, as he asked for a thousand more. He has been criticised for not waiting until large numbers were available before committing them, thereby forfeiting surprise and the possibility of a major success. While there is a degree of truth in this, it was necessary for the tank crews to gain some operational experience, and the other side of the coin must be examined as well. The appearance of the tanks had indeed caused panic among the enemy, but on a very local scale. When the Germans subsequently examined several knocked-out tanks they concluded that they were nothing more than an experimental novelty, mechanically unreliable and vulnerable not only to artillery but also to the German 'K' ammunition, which was already in use against armoured bunker slits. They therefore decided that for the moment they would not embark on a tank production programme of their own, a short-sighted view which failed to allow for the British putting these faults to rights in future production models.

After Flers–Courcelette Haig shifted the emphasis north to the Ancre sector of the Somme battlefield. During October a series of local attacks finally cleared the Thiepval–Pozières ridge. Haig's critics are probably justified in their view that he should have closed down the offensive at this point, for the autumn weather had finally broken and as the chalk absorbed heavy rain it dissolved into dirty, foot-deep slime in which movement on the battlefield and the approaches to it became difficult and exhausting. Nevertheless, he persisted. During the third week of November Gough's Fifth Army, as the Reserve Army had recently become, took Beaumont Hamel, which had been an objective on the first day, and then Beaucourt. On the night of 17/18 November it snowed and little progress was made next day. The snow thawed, turning the whole shattered area into a swamp. As further offensive operations were impossible, the battle ran down of its own accord.

As to what it accomplished, the relief of Verdun was achieved quite early in its course. No accurate figures exist for German casualties because the records were destroyed during the Second World War, but most estimates put them in the region of 650,000. The Allies had gained a strip of territory some 20 miles long and up to seven miles deep. More importantly, as Haig intended, the magnificent German Army of 1914 was finally destroyed on the Somme, most of its professional junior officers and senior NCOs having been killed. There were, too, signs that the German soldier's morale had begun to crack; latterly his letters home contained the common theme of crippling losses, the terrible nature of the ordeal and the hope of peace. Hindenburg and Ludendorff reached the conclusion that their troops could not withstand the combination of intense artillery bombardments and sustained infantry attacks for much longer. The following February they voluntarily surrendered several more miles of territory and pulled back to a shorter, even stronger defensive position. There was a recognition, too, in Imperial Germany's higher command echelons, that Great Britain had become the principal enemy. It was decided to embark upon a campaign of unrestricted submarine warfare to bring her to her knees, even at the risk of bringing the United States into the war.

British casualties amounted to 418,000 and French to 194,000. Of the former it is true to say that many of the best of their generation, the volunteers who in the normal way would have risen to become leaders in many facets of national life, perished on the Somme, and their loss could not be easily or quickly replaced. The flow of volunteers shrank to a trickle and the following year conscription was introduced to maintain manpower levels. Idealism was replaced with bitter cynicism, reinforced by the trench battles of the following year, notably Third Ypres, otherwise known as Passchendaele. Thus innocence, too, died on the Somme, for with a very few exceptions the British have never again trusted their leaders, political or military, in the way they did prior to the battle. In the complete tapestry of the First World War, the Somme can be seen to have its place as the offensive in which the groundwork for the defeat of the German Army was laid. To its participants it was simply endless carnage and misery without apparent meaning.

Below: Until the tank could be employed in any numbers, artillery was the dominant arm. Here, beside an old communication trench, a battery of 6-inch howitzers drawn by caterpillar tractors moves forward to new positions along the Albert–Fricourt road. *Imperial War Museum Neg Q4146*

AMIENS, 8 AUGUST 1918

If there were one group of British soldiers which retained its optimism throughout the equally dismal trench battles of 1917 it was the Tank Corps, as the HSMGC had become. After seeing their vehicles squandered in the atrocious going at Arras and the Ypres salient, they had been given the opportunity to show what they could do over hard downland in an attack on the Cambrai sector of the Western Front. On 20 November 1917, operating under the overall command of General Sir Julian Byng's Third Army, nine battalions with a total of 476 tanks had smashed through the thoroughly prepared defences of the Hindenburg Line on a 13,000-yard frontage and by 16.00 had penetrated to a depth of 10,000 yards. The infantry of III and IV Corps, who had followed up the tank attack, sustained only 6,000 casualties, considered trifling by the standards of the Somme and Passchendaele, where losses in the region of 250,000 had been incurred to achieve a similar advance. The breach was to have been exploited by the Cavalry Corps, but, as at High Wood the previous year, the horsemen were positioned too far to the rear and those that did get into action were too late and too few to affect the issue. For the Germans the shock was the greater in that by digging their trenches wider and deeper they had considered them tank-proof, a problem the Tank Corps had solved by dropping huge fascines into the gaps to provide causeways. For the first time in the war the church bells were rung in celebration of a clear-cut British victory.

By degrees the tanks were withdrawn for essential repairs and maintenance. Then, on 30 November, the Germans counter-attacked with astonishing speed and drive, recovering much of the ground they had lost, and a little more besides. There seemed to be no logical reason for this dramatic reversal of fortune and indeed the only men capable of supplying one were now on their way to prison camps. Some survivors noted a marked increase in ground strafing by the Imperial German Air Service, but that was only part of the story.

Three months earlier, at Riga on the Baltic, the Germans had developed their own means of breaking the deadlock of trench warfare. Their Eighth Army, commanded by General Oskar von Hutier, was ordered to eliminate a Russian bridgehead on the west bank of the Dvina, but instead of launching a direct assault on the bridgehead, as most of his contemporaries would have done, Hutier chose to attack upstream then wheel northwards to the coast, severing the Russians' line of communication. His infantry were instructed to rely on speed and infiltration to work their way through the Russian defences while waves of ground-attack aircraft raked the enemy trenches. Furthermore, Hutier's artillery commander, Colonel Bruchmuller, had a supply of the new phosgene gas shells which enabled him to deliver gas with pinpoint accuracy, and he incorporated these into his five-hour preparatory bombardment, together with high-explosive, shrapnel and smoke. Choking and blinded, the Russians were unable offer coherent resistance to Hutier's indirect assault and took to their heels before the trap closed round them.

The following month the Austro–German offensive against the Italians on the Isonzo Front, now more generally known as the Battle of Caporetto, employed similar tactics. In less than three weeks the Italians were thrown back more than 70 miles, sustaining a staggering 300,000 casualties and losing 2,500 guns. This blow came near to knocking Italy out of the war and resulted in the dispatch of sorely needed British and French divisions from the Western Front to stiffen their defence.

Hindenburg and Ludendorff were now satisfied that they had a war-winning formula. The demands on Germany's manpower resources had eased with the collapse of the Russian war effort, and for 1918 they planned a series of offensives on the Western Front with the intention of defeating Great Britain and France before American troops could arrive in Europe in any numbers. Fit men of proven initiative were creamed off the rest of the Army to form the storm troop battalions which would lead the attack. Their preferred weapons were the grenade, the light machine-gun and the manpack flame-thower, and they were trained to move in groups, by-passing opposition and pressing on towards the enemy's formation headquarters, receiving direct support from ground-strafing battle flights the while. Behind them came specially trained battle groups whose function was to reduce the strong-points left unsubdued by the storm troopers, followed by the mass of the infantry divisions. The artillery preparation was to be orchestrated by Bruchmuller, who was given a 'travelling circus' of medium and heavy guns which would move up and down the front as required. The successful employment of British armour at Cambrai had changed the Germans' attitude to the tank, so for good measure they formed their own tank arm, using captured British vehicles and a tank of their own design, the A7V. At the higher levels, commanders who had previously committed their reserves against the toughest centres of resistance were now required to employ them only in support of successful penetrations, thereby increasing the whole tempo of the battle.

Ludendorff's first offensive, lasting from 21 March to 5 April, effected a breakthough along a 60-mile front and penetrated to a depth of 40 miles, overrunning the old Somme battlefields. It virtually destroyed Gough's Fifth Army, caused 255,000 Allied casualties, including more than 90,000 men taken prisoner, and captured 1,100 guns. Somehow, the line held, often because of self-sacrificial stands and small *ad hoc* groups of stragglers, cooks, drivers, clerks and batmen thrust into the gaps. The offensive therefore failed in its primary purpose of separating the British from the French by a drive to the Somme estuary. Moreover, the 250,000 German casualties were heavier than had been anticipated, notably among the storm troop battalions. On 26 March Marshal Ferdinand Foch was appointed co-ordinator of the Allied response and on 3 April he became Supreme Commander.

It was Ludendorff's belief that if the British were defeated the French would seek an armistice, and his next offensive, lasting from 9 to 30 April, was aimed at the British left. It recovered all the ground lost during Passchendaele, plus Messines Ridge, and inflicted 82,000 casualties, but it did not achieve a breakthrough to the Channel ports and itself sustained the loss of 98,000 men.

Next, from 27 May to 6 June, he attacked the French on the Chemin des Dames in the hope that they would withdraw their reserves from Flanders, enabling him to strike a decisive blow against the British. Once again losses were heavy on both sides and although the Germans won a tactical victory which took them across the Aisne and on to the Marne, this proved to be counter-productive in that too few troops were now available to man the extended line formed by the new salient.

This meant that Ludendorff had to abandon whatever plans he might have had for the British. Instead, he mounted a fourth offensive along the 25-mile stretch of front between Noyon and Montdidier, intending to shorten the line between the salients formed by his first and third offensives. By now, however, the Allies had become familiar with the new German method of attack and were prepared for it. In itself, the offensive was a tacit admission that Germany was nearing the end of her resources and it achieved nothing.

The cumulative effect on German morale was disastrous. The troops had been promised that their efforts would result in victory but they had not. Most of the storm troopers were now dead and the remaining troops were of lesser quality. The manpower reserve provided by the all but defunct Eastern Front had been used up. In contrast, the Allies seemed to have all the tanks, guns, men, rations and supplies they needed. The first American troops, equipped by the British with tanks and steel helmets and by the French with tanks and artillery, were now entering the line. Significantly, during their first actions they displayed a youthful vigour and aggression that had not been seen among the British and French armies for many months.

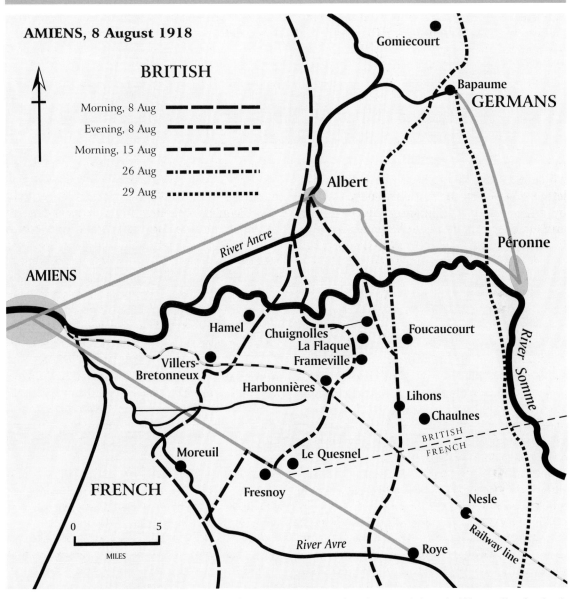

AMIENS, 8 August 1918

BRITISH

Morning, 8 Aug	——— — — —
Evening, 8 Aug	—·—·—·—·
Morning, 15 Aug	– – – – –
26 Aug	▪—·—▪—·—▪
29 Aug	············

GERMANS

Gomiecourt

Bapaume

Albert

Péronne

River Ancre

AMIENS

River Somme

Hamel

Chuignolles

La Flaque

Frameville

Foucaucourt

Villers-Bretonneux

Harbonnières

Lihons

Chaulnes

BRITISH
FRENCH

Moreuil

Le Quesnel

FRENCH

Fresnoy

Nesle

0   5

MILES

River Avre

Roye

Railway line

Having ridden out the storm, the Allies went on the offensive with a series of counter-attacks. On 4 July sixty of the new Mark V tanks supported an attack by ten Australian battalions and four American companies on a frontage of 3½ miles. The objective was the village of le Hamel, which lay on a shallow ridge to the north of Villers-Bretonneux, 1½ miles behind the German lines. It was taken within an hour at the cost of 775 Australian and 134 American casualties; Tank Corps losses amounted to only thirteen wounded and

five tanks damaged by shellfire, all of which were recovered; 1,500 prisoners were taken, together with two field guns and 171 machine-guns. A fortnight later French and American divisions, spearheaded by 346 tanks, punched a four-mile dent into the flank of a salient south of Soissons. During the next few days the offensive ran down, enabling the Germans to retreat in good order to a shorter line, although they left 25,000 prisoners in Allied hands. On 23 July the Tank Corps' 9th Battalion, on loan to the 3rd Division of the

203

Above: German view of a tank attack. Much of the wire has already been cut by artillery fire and the tanks will have no difficulty in crushing their way through the rest. *Imperial War Museum Neg Q45352*

French First Army, led a successful attack which enabled the infantry to take their objectives at a cost of only 1,891 casualties, capturing 1,858 prisoners, five field guns and 275 machine-guns. The 9th Battalion lost 54 men killed or wounded, plus eleven of its 34 tanks knocked out, but it was awarded a corporate *Croix de Guerre* and the right to wear the emblem of the 3rd Division.

The success of these local operations prompted General Sir Henry Rawlinson, commanding Fourth Army, to suggest that a major offensive, spearheaded by the Tank Corps, be mounted east of Amiens, using British III Corps, the Australian Corps and the Canadian Corps. His choice of Dominion troops was deliberate because their divisions were still largely up to strength and had retained their aggressive spirit, while most British formations were still recovering from the ordeal of Ludendorff's spring offensives and were seriously short of men; infantry brigades, for example, had already been reduced from four to three battalions in which the fatigued rifle companies were operating at about half their established strength. Rawl-

inson's suggestion was adopted and preparations for what was to be the greatest armoured assault of the war went ahead in great secrecy, covered by an elaborate deception plan.

Fourth Tank Brigade (1st, 4th, 5th and 14th Battalions) was allocated to the Canadian Corps on the right of the attack; 5th Tank Brigade (2nd, 8th, 13th and 15th Battalions), plus the Austin armoured cars of 17th Battalion, to the Australian Corps in the centre; and 2nd Tank Brigade (reduced to a single battalion, the 10th) to British III Corps, covering the left flank of the attack to the north of the Somme. Once again the Cavalry Corps was given the task of exploiting the breakthrough in conjunction with 3rd Tank Brigade (3rd and 6th Battalions), which was equipped with the Whippet, a new, much faster, three-man tank armed with three Hotchkiss machine-guns, that had been designed to support cavalry operations and had already given a good account of itself during the Ludendorff offensives. In total, the attack would involve 324 Mark V or V* heavy tanks, with a further 42 in immediate reserve, 96 Whippets, 120 supply tanks, more than half of which were allocated to the infantry, and 22 gun carriers, which were cut-down Mark I chassis designed to carry 60-pounder guns or 6-inch howitzers across no-man's land. Artillery, air support and reserves were available on a larger scale than at Cambrai.

The deception plan involved concealing the movement of the Canadian Corps into the area by maintaining an appropriate flow of dummy radio traffic from its former positions. Elsewhere, intense tank activity was simulated with dust and noise. All movement into the concentration area took place at night. Roads were strewn with straw, and wheels were muffled with rope. Artillery fire was maintained at routine levels, newly arrived batteries simply registering their designated targets then lapsing into silence under their camouflage. Ultimately, Fourth Army had 684 heavy guns and 1,386 field guns and howitzers available, and the French First Army, which would extend the right flank of the attack southwards, had 826 heavy and 780 field guns. During the night of 6/7 August the tanks arrived by train, the rumbling of their move into operational assembly areas being drowned by the steady drone of low-flying aircraft.

Across the lines was General von der Marwitz's Second Army. Of his eleven divisions, each with an average strength of 3,000 men, he considered only two to be in fully battleworthy condition. The remainder were demoralised by recent failure and the growing unrest at home. Their positions were nothing like as strong as those they had occupied during the previous two years. Although they had been issued with a new anti-tank rifle capable of punching a 13mm round through the thickest British armour at 200 yards, it was in short supply. Understandably, the thought of a tank attack made them jumpy – so much so in fact, that Second Army HQ was angered by

the number of false tank alerts it was receiving daily and issued a sharp rebuke. In the final analysis, the German infantryman would have to rely on his field artillery for anti-tank defence, as he always had done.

At 04.20 on 8 August the Allied artillery thundered out, firing a rolling barrage while the long lines of tanks and infantry moved forward through a morning mist thickened to fog by smoke shells. Above the incessant explosions, the Germans could hear the rumbling of hundreds of approaching engines, accompanied by the distinctive sound of clattering tracks. Then, quite suddenly, the monstrous shapes emerged from the grey curtain at point-blank range, spitting machine-gun fire, high-explosive shells and scything case shot, crushing wire, straddling trenches and rearing over them. The German machine-gunners, scattered in depth among shell-holes and behind every available cover, remained dedicated to the last, continuing to feed belts into their weapons until they were shot down or crushed. In contrast, riflemen by the hundred threw up their hands and surrendered to the fast-moving British, Australian and Canadian infantry, which had now adopted the storm troopers' infiltration tactics. Between 06.30 and 07:00 the German front line was overrun with such ease that it might never have existed.

For the Tank Corps, the real fighting now began. At 06.45 the mist began to lift and the tanks were suddenly exposed to the German field gunners, who went into action over open sights. No quarter was sought or given in these duels and as the infantry came up they too brought the gun crews under fire. By the end of this phase of the battle, no fewer than 109 tanks had been reduced to flaming wrecks or were inoperable, but the German divisional artillery regiments had ceased to exist. The attack rolled on, securing the second objective by 11.00 and the third by 13.00.

A huge gap, eleven miles wide and up to seven miles deep, had been torn in the German line and the moment had come to unleash the Cavalry Corps. Not wishing to see a repetition of the mistakes made at High Wood and

Cambrai, Haig had told the corps commander, Lieutenant-General Kavanagh, that he must keep in close touch with events as they developed. Kavanagh had done so and soon, as recalled by one tank commander on the Canadian Corps sector, the battlefield presented a spectacle few had ever expected to see:

'Streaming up the long southern track they came, headed by a regiment of lancers. As far as the eye could reach there were trotting columns of horses while in the middle track batteries of horse and field artillery were arriving at a gallop. A cloud of dust on the northern track heralded the Whippets, 40 of them, moving almost as fast as the artillery and going hell-for-leather for the next objective.'

The cavalry were desperate to do well and in places did so, capturing a large rail gun, field batteries and machine-guns, as well as rounding up prisoners by the score. But cavalry and tanks were not compatible. When there was no opposition the horsemen cantered ahead, leaving the Whippets far behind; but when serious opposition was encountered, the cavalry was pinned down and unable to keep up with the Whippets.

One Whippet, *Musical Box*, commanded by Lieutenant C. B. Arnold, broke away and created mayhem in the German rear areas for several hours before being knocked out eight miles behind the original front line. What a whole brigade let loose might have achieved can well be imagined. Some idea can be formed from the activities of 17th Battalion's armoured cars on the Australian sector. Heavy tanks pulled the cars across fascines which had been dropped in the trenches, and also towed away trees which the Germans had felled to block the Amiens–St-Quentin road. Once past the tangle, the cars passed through their own infantry and out into enemy-held country beyond. There they fanned out along side roads to the north and south, raiding into the villages of Framerville, Harbonnières, La Flaque, Chuignolles and Foucaucourt. They

Above: Canadian troops and wounded prisoners beside Lieutenant Clement Arnold's Whippet, photographed a day or two after her protracted rampage behind enemy lines. Signs of the fire which gutted the vehicle are clearly visible. *IWM Neg (E(1914)2880)*

Above: Some of the German prisoners taken during the battle. *IWM Neg Q9271*

chased lorries, destroyed convoys, killed mounted staff officers, shot up troops in their billets, exploded the boilers of several steam wagons, disabled a train and ambushed fugitives streaming back from the broken front. Best of all was the capture of a hurriedly evacuated corps headquarters at Framerville; within was found a complete set of plans of a twenty-mile stretch of the Hindenburg Line which was put to good use the following month.

On the morning of 9 August only 145 tanks were fit for action. Next day the figure was even lower and as fresh German divisions were being rushed in from everywhere to seal off the penetration it was clear that the battle was over. Haig, however, had finally broken the enemy's will, as the German official report made perfectly clear:

'As the sun set on 8 August the greatest defeat which the German Army had suffered since the beginning of the war was an accomplished fact. The positional divisions between the Ancre and the Somme which had been struck by the enemy attack were nearly annihilated. The troops in the front line north of the Somme had also suffered seriously, as had the reserve divisions thrown into the battle during the course of the day. The total losses of the units deployed in Second Army's sector can be put down as from 650 to 700 officers and 26,000 to 27,000 men. More than 400 guns and an enormous quantity of machine-guns, mortars and other *materiél* were lost. More than two-thirds of the total German losses were due to prisoners. Almost everywhere it was evident that German soldiers had surrendered to the nearest enemy or thrown away rifles and equipment, abandoned trench mortars, machine-guns and guns, and sought safety in flight.'

207

Left: From small beginnings in 1914 air warfare expanded quickly until it became an essential element within operational planning. Here a Royal Flying Corps FE2b 'pusher' is bounced by a Fokker triplane of the German Imperial Air Service.

The report understated the position. Total German losses during the battle were in excess of 75,000, including nearly 30,000 prisoners. British casualties totalled 22,000 killed, wounded and missing, those of the French First Army during the same period being about half that figure.

In his memoirs Ludendorff was to refer to 8 August as 'the Black Day of the German Army', not because of the physical damage sustained but because it 'put the decline of our fighting powers beyond doubt'. Shortly after the disaster he summoned Second Army's divisional commanders and other senior officers to a conference at which the reasons for the collapse were examined:

'I was told of behaviour which, I openly confess, I should not have thought possible in the German Army; whole bodies of our men had surrendered to single troopers or isolated squadrons. Retiring troops, meeting a fresh division going into action, had shouted things like "Blackleg" and "You're prolonging the war," expressions that were to be heard again later. The officers in many places had lost their

influence and allowed themselves to be swept along with the rest. Our war machine was no longer efficient.'

In the circumstances he could only advise the Kaiser that a German victory was no longer possible. It was decided to initiate peace negotiations through the offices of the neutral Queen of The Netherlands while the Army continued to fight defensively in the hope that the gains made during the early months of the war would place Germany in a strong negotiating position. It was not to be, for all along the front the Allies went over to the offensive, slowly eroding those gains week by week. By November the Army had little option but to continue its fighting withdrawal, there was revolution at home, the Kaiser had abdicated and an armistice had become an urgent necessity.

In considering the effects of Amiens, however, the battle had not simply accelerated the end of the war on the Western Front. To a greater degree than Cambrai it had ended the era in which the powers of defence dominated the battlefield and it had demonstrated that exploitation could be carried out effectively by mechanical means. If the war had continued, the Allies would have adopted a plan devised by Colonel (later Major-General) J. F. C. Fuller, the Tank Corps' Chief of Staff. Subsequently known as 'Plan 1919', this envisaged disorganisation of the enemy's command structure before the main attack on his front began. During the first phase, Fuller conceived a Disorganising Force, consisting of fast medium tanks with air cover, effecting a penetration and driving deep into the enemy's rear to neutralise corps and army headquarters; simultaneously, bombers and ground-attack aircraft would add to the confusion by strafing road and rail centres and supply dumps. As soon as the command system had been paralysed, a Breaking Force of heavy tanks, infantry and artillery would smash through the enemy's front. Because of the confusion and panic caused by the Disorganising Force in Phase I, protracted resistance was not anticipated. Once the front had been broken, a Pursuing Force of fast tanks, lorried infantry and cavalry would harry the routed army until its will to fight was broken. Curiously, within weeks of Amiens, many aspects of Fuller's plan were to be demonstrated on a distant battlefield; the irony was that, for the last time in history, it would be the horse which supplied the bulk of the motive power.

MEGIDDO, 18 SEPTEMBER – 31 OCTOBER 1918

As far as grand strategy was concerned, the British War Cabinet was divided into Westerners who believed that Germany could only be brought to her knees by the defeat of the main mass of her armies on the Western Front, and Easterners, who prefered the more indirect approach of knocking out her weaker eastern allies, the Ottoman Empire, Bulgaria and Austria-Hungary, in turn, thus leaving her isolated.

For much of the time the Westerners' views prevailed, although the Easterners could point to tangible successes in the Middle East. In March 1917 General Sir Frederick Maude's troops had captured Baghdad and occupied the greater part of Mesopotamia, now Iraq. In October of that year General Sir Edmund Allenby's Egyptian Expeditionary Force inflicted a sharp defeat on the Turks at the battle of Gaza/Beersheba and advanced north to capture Jerusalem on 9 December. It is possible that Allenby could have finished off the Turkish armies in Palestine during the spring of 1918, but he was obliged to send large numbers of troops to France because of the crisis generated by Ludendorff's offensives. By the following September, however, he had received reinforcements and was again ready to take the offensive.

The opposing lines stretched from a point north of Jaffa on the coast over the Judean hills and across the Jordan valley into the desert beyond. Allenby's opponent, General Liman von Sanders, had three Turkish armies under command: General Jevad Pasha's Eighth, nearest the sea; General Mustapha Kemal Pasha's Seventh, in the centre, and General Mohammed Jemal Kuçuk Pasha's Fourth, in the Jordan valley. All were controlled through a main telephone switchboard at Afula, south of Sanders' GHQ at Nazareth. Altogether, including the German Asia Korps serving with Eighth Army and tactical reinforcements, his army group numbered 3,000 cavalry, 32,000 infantry, 370 guns and, west of the Jordan alone, more than 600 heavy machine-guns. Elsewhere some 6,000 men were deployed along the Hejaz Railway, leading south into the rebellious province of Arabia, but of these only the garrison of Amman was likely to become involved in large-scale operations. Far to the north and spread across a wide area between Damascus and the Taurus was the 5,000-strong Turkish Second Army, too weak and too distant to be of much assistance if trouble flared on the Palestine Front. Sanders, an advocate of positional warfare, had made his dispositions solely with static defence in mind, giving no consideration to the possibility of having to conduct a withdrawal. Believing that Allenby intended attacking north up the Jordan valley, he concentrated the bulk of his strength on that sector. Although aware that the British outnumbered him by two to one, this did not concern him unduly because the conventional ratio for a successful attack was considered to be three to one. With the exception of the Asia Korps, however, the condition of his army group was less than satisfactory. The fact that the holy cities of Mecca, Jerusalem and Baghdad were now in rebel or enemy hands was demoralising proof enough that the fortunes of the Ottoman Empire were in terminal decline. Widespread sickness, neglect of the troops' welfare and general maladministration further undermined morale, compounded by the mutual antipathy of the Anatolian and Arab elements of the army.

Allenby's army numbered 11,000 cavalry, 56,000 infantry and 552 guns. It consisted of the Desert Mounted Corps (Lieutenant-General Sir Harry Chauvel) with four cavalry divisions; XX Corps (Lieutenant-General Sir Philip Chetwode) with two infantry divisions; XXI Corps (Lieutenant-General Sir E. S. Bulfin) with five infantry divisions and a French brigade; and a number of independent units. The Royal Air Force Middle East (Major-General W. G. H. Salmond) had seven squadrons and a balloon company and was operating directly under Allenby's control. Across the Jordan was an Arab irregular army led by the Emir Feisal and Colonel T. E. Lawrence.

The character of the army was Imperial. Within the infantry, only 54th (East Anglian) Division retained its British composition. The rest were now essentially Indian divisions with one British battalion in each brigade. Also present were two battalions of the British West Indies Regiment and two battalions raised from Palestinian volunteers.

Chauvel's Desert Mounted Corps consisted of 4th and 5th Cavalry Divisions, the Australian and New Zealand (ANZAC) Mounted Division and the Australian Mounted Division. Again, both cavalry divisions were Indian in character, each brigade consisting of one British regiment, Yeomanry being substituted for the usual Regular units, and two Indian cavalry regiments that were accustomed to professional soldiering in hard climates. The ANZAC and Australian Mounted Divisions consisted of Australian Light Horse or New Zealand Mounted Rifle regiments, trained and temperamentally suited to fight a fast-moving mounted infantry battle. They were, moreover, very flexible in their approach and, after experiences the previous year the Australian Mounted Division had also received training with the sword, at its own request. Also serving with this division was a regiment of French *Chasseurs d'Afrique*, who were at a slight disadvantage in that their Arab horses lacked the stamina of the big Walers on which the Australians were mounted. Chauvel's corps troops included two Light Armoured Motor Batteries (LAMBs) with twelve Rolls-Royce armoured cars apiece, and two Light Car Patrols, equipped with Model T Fords mounting Lewis light machine-guns. Chauvel is considered to have been the best cavalry leader of the modern era and under his command the Desert Mounted Corps had achieved great things during the previous two years, assisted by the fact that neither the number of the enemy's guns and machine guns per mile of front, nor, save at Gaza, the overall depth of the defences, nor barbed wire, of which the Turks never had enough for their needs, was sufficient to inhibit mobile operations. These were notable not only for the speed with which they were executed, but also for the aggression and determination with which attacks were pressed home with bayonet or sword, regardless of loss. Consequently the Turks were somewhat in awe of this corps and their own less numerous cavalry was disinclined to try conclusions with it.

Allenby planned nothing less than the complete destruction of Sanders' army group. In essence, the plan was very simple, involving a breakthough by Bulfin's XXI Corps on the coastal sector, exploited with a huge wheel to the right by the Desert Mounted Corps, severing Turkish communications as it carved its way north-eastwards to the Jordan valley. At the crucial point the 8,000 Turks with 130 guns in the coastal sector would find themselves under attack by 35,000 infantry and 9,000 cavalry with 383 guns, plus two

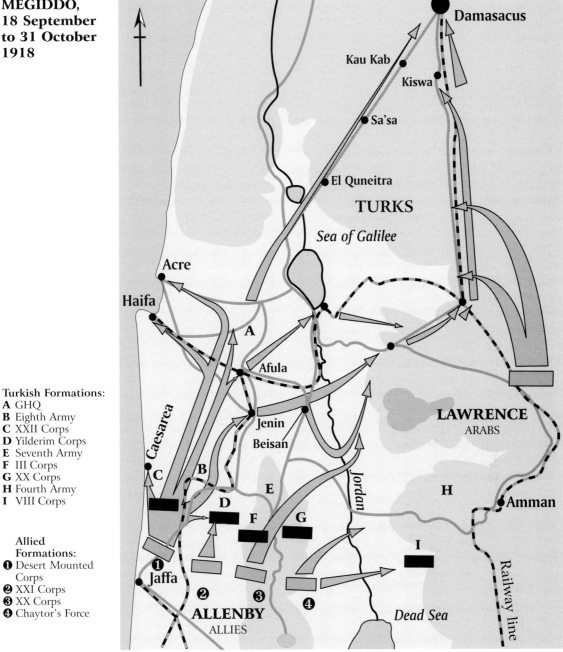

**MEGIDDO,
18 September
to 31 October
1918**

Turks formations labels on map:

TURKS

Sea of Galilee

LAWRENCE
ARABS

Turkish Formations:
A GHQ
B Eighth Army
C XXII Corps
D Yilderim Corps
E Seventh Army
F III Corps
G XX Corps
H Fourth Army
I VIII Corps

**Allied
Formations:**
❶ Desert Mounted
   Corps
❷ XXI Corps
❸ XX Corps
❹ Chaytor's Force

ALLENBY
ALLIES

Map location labels: Damasacus, Kau Kab, Kiswa, Sa'sa, El Quneitra, Acre, Haifa, Afula, Caesarea, Jenin, Beisan, Jaffa, Jordan, Amman, Dead Sea, Railway line

destroyers offshore providing direct gunfire support. Simultaneously the RAF would destroy Sanders' telephone links, paralysing command of his army group, then concentrate on strafing Turkish columns retreating from the front, thereby eroding the enemy's will to continue the fight.

Every aspect of the coming offensive, including the artillery plan, engineering, logistics and signals, received the most minute scrutiny, especially the deception plan. Sanders, as we have seen, suspected that Allenby would strike in the Jordan valley and had deployed 15,000 men and 185 guns to meet the threat. Allenby

211

therefore decided to reinforce his opinion, not simply because this would continue to leave the coastal sector comparatively weak, but also because when his trap closed that many more Turkish troops would be enmeshed within it. The ANZAC Mounted Division was detached from the Desert Mounted Corps and, with other troops, allocated to a force under Major-General Sir E. W. C. Chaytor in the Jordan valley. Chaytor's Force was to simulate the presence of the entire Desert Mounted Corps, which it did by constructing dummy horse lines, battery positions and camps, creating much apparent bustle, raising dust clouds with mule-drawn sledges, and lighting many campfires. Across the Jordan, Lawrence's Arabs intensified their attacks on the Hejaz Railway. At the opposite end of the line, where the real attack would go in, troops arrived by night and moved into concealed bivouacs or camps constructed two months earlier. They remained under cover during daylight hours, were permitted no fires and cooked with smokeless solidified alcohol. The RAF concentrated successfully on keeping Turkish and German airmen on their own side of the lines. Finally, two rumours were leaked to the civil populace in the certain knowledge that Turkish sympathisers would carry them straight to Sanders. The first was that Allenby was moving his GHQ into the most comfortable hotel in Jerusalem for the winter, and the second was that there would be a race meeting near Jaffa on 19 September, attended by the Egyptian Expeditionary Force's senior officers. Despite elaborate security, the details of Allenby's true intentions were communicated to the Turks on 17 September by a captured *havildar*. Sanders, believing them far-fetched and that the man was a plant, did nothing.

His suspicions regarding an offensive in the Jordan were temporarily reinforced when, during the night of 18/19 September, Chetwode's XX Corps launched a heavy attack on the east-central sector of the front. This, however, was merely a diversion. Shortly after midnight the RAF bombed the headquarters of the Turkish Seventh and Eighth Armies, destroying the latter's wireless station and wrecking the main telephone exchange at Afula. Sanders, therefore, had lost the greater part of his communications net at the critical moment.

The next few hours were passed quietly in routine patrol activity. Then, at 04.30, the British bombardment opened, rising to a crescendo of more than 1,000 rounds per minute, the heaviest ever mounted in this theatre. The Turkish artillery replied briefly but ineffectually as its shells exploded in empty trenches, Bulfin's infantry having already quit them and moved to their start-lines in no-man's land, and was then silenced by counter-battery fire. Most of the Turkish were too stunned or confused to offer much resistance when their trenches were rushed. Many surrendered on the spot, others streamed away from the broken front in crowds. Soon the British infantry had penetrated as far as the artillery zone and captured several batteries.

The 3rd (Lahore), 7th (Meerut) and 60th Divisions now began to swing eastwards like an opening gate to create a protective hard shoulder for the gap through which the Desert Mounted Corps was about to pass. The objective of 60th Division, with 5th Light Horse Brigade (temporarily detached from the Australian Mounted Division) under command, was the town of Tul Karm which until a few hours earlier had contained the headquarters of the Turkish Eighth Army. It was quickly isolated by the Light Horsemen who then pursued the crowds of Turkish fugitives eastwards along the road to Nablus. The Turks, under simultaneous air attack, willingly surrendered, and that day the brigade took over 2,000 prisoners, fifteen guns and a large haul of supplies. At 17.00, 60th Division, having advanced more than sixteen miles through enemy territory in thirteen hours, captured Tul Karm, taking a further 500 prisoners and twelve guns. The Desert Mounted Corps, led by 4th Cavalry Division on the right and 5th Cavalry Division on the left, followed by the Australian Mounted Division, was already pouring through the gap and across the Plain of Sharon. When encountered, the enemy usually surrendered or fled.

As Allenby had intended, Liman von Sanders spent the day groping in the densest fog of war imaginable. All communication with HQ Eighth Army at Tul Karm had ceased at 07.00, but at about 09.00 he received a message via HQ Seventh Army from Colonel von Oppen, commander of the Asia Korps, to the effect that the British had broken through on the coastal sector and cavalry was advancing northwards; Seventh Army was apparently holding but was withdrawing to its second line under pressure. At this point the line went dead when the RAF again put the repaired switchboard at Afula out of action. Nor could Sanders gain any more information from his air force, which was effectively grounded by the RAF sitting above its airfields. Unable to form a coherent picture, he believed that Turkish XXII Corps, closest to the coast, was retiring before the British

advance; in fact it had ceased to exist when its trenches were stormed and its commander was now a fugitive behind enemy lines. Sanders did, however, give some consideration to the possibility of deep penetration by British cavalry and dispatched a Major Frey with six reinforced companies from the depot regiment at Nazareth to occupy the northern end of the important Musmus Pass at El Lajjun, near the site of ancient Megiddo.

The pass, which provided a good route through the Samarian Hills, was the objective of Major-General Barrow's 4th Cavalry Division. When an officer prisoner disclosed that a Turkish force was on its way to block the defile, Barrow cut short the division's evening rest period and dispatched the 2nd Lancers, commanded by 30-year-old Captain D. S. Davison, plus two armoured cars of the 11th LAMB, into the pass. The remainder of 10th Cavalry Brigade was ordered to follow as quickly as possible, but dawdled and lost its way twice in the dark. Barrow dismissed the brigade commander on the spot and sent 12th Cavalry Brigade after the lancers.

Below: Megiddo. Indian infantry storming the Turkish front line. Most Turks were so stunned by the initial bombardment that they simply bolted. *Illustrated London News*

At 03.00 on 20 September Davison's command reached the northern end of the pass to find Frey's advance guard, about 100 strong, sitting round a fire with their arms piled, singing. They were too surprised to offer resistance. When 12th Cavalry Brigade emerged from the pass at 04.30, its commander, Brigadier-General T. J. Wigan, ordered Davison to capture Afula and cut the railway there. An hour later Davison came across Frey's main body at the village of Birket el Fuleh. In a neat little action involving fire, movement and a charge pressed home with the lance, this was dispersed in little more than five minutes at the cost of one man wounded and five horses killed; forty-six of the Turks were speared and 470 captured.

Approaching Afula at 07.45, the lancers came under fire from its garrison. Shortly after this the Deccan Horse from 5th Cavalry Division also mounted an attack and at 08.00 the enemy, 75 German and 200 Turkish troops, surrendered. The booty included ten locomotives, 50 lorries, three aircraft on the airfield and a fourth shot down as it came in to land, a petrol dump, a stock of champagne and, of course, Sanders' battered main switchboard. Twelve German lorries attempting to escape along the road to Beisan were run down by the armoured cars.

The 4th Cavalry Division concentrated at Afula throughout the morning. At 13.00 it resumed its advance along the Jezreel valley to Beisan which by 18.00 had been taken without difficulty. Guns and prisoners by the hundred were captured, more coming in to surrender during the night. With one exception, the division's men and horses could now rest, having covered 70 miles in 34 hours. The exception was the 19th Lancers, reinforced with additional machine-guns and an engineer squadron, which had spent the afternoon resting at Afula. The regiment's task was to secure the railway bridges at Jisr el Majami, where the river Yarmuk flowed into the Jordan. At 19.30 it set out on a 20-mile march across country and reached its objective before first light on the 21st. The Turks holding the railway fled, the

bridges were prepared for demolition and Allenby's trap was sprung.

Elsewhere Major-General Macandrew's 5th Cavalry Division had crossed the Samarian Hills over rough tracks during the night of 19/20 September. In the lead was 13th Cavalry Brigade under Brigadier P. J. V. Kelly, which had as its mission nothing less than the capture of Sanders and his GHQ at Nazareth. While the brigade was trotting across the Plain of Esdraelon and up into the foothills towards Nazareth, Kelly fragmented its strength in diversions which in other circumstances might have been tactically justified, but given the nature of his mission wasted much valuable time. It was first light on the 21st before it reached a point south of the town, where Kelly detached a squadron of the 18th Lancers to cover the road from Afula. Almost immediately this intercepted a convoy of lorries escorted by 400 Turks. The escort surrendered after a brief fight, but neither the interception nor a chest containing £20,000 in gold coin and notes discovered in one lorry, were worth the alarm raised in the town by the shooting. Sanders, according to his housekeeper, made a hasty escape in his car, dressed in pyjamas, but later returned to direct the fighting. Kelly meanwhile strove to capture the town and its barracks with the 1st Gloucestershire Yeomanry and the remnant of the Lancers. Some German and Turkish troops, half asleep and taken unawares, surrendered at once, but others, notably the German GHQ Staff and their clerks, put up a terrific fight. At 06.50 Kelly, burdened with 1,200 prisoners, asked Macandrew for assistance. This was refused but he was given permission to withdraw. Although his casualties had been remarkably light given the circumstances, he lacked the resources to capture the town and pulled out some three hours later. Sanders left Nazareth at 13.15 and drove first to Tiberias and then to Samakh at the southern end of the Sea of Galilee where he established a temporary GHQ during the evening. The raid on Nazareth had deprived the Turkish army group of its commander for a further day, but Kelly was subsequently dismissed his command; although he cannot escape criticism, this was generally considered to be harsh. To the south, another of Macandrew's formations, 14th Cavalry Brigade, operated against the Nazareth–Afula road, capturing two more convoys and, as we have seen, assisted in the capture of Afula itself.

Major-General H. W. Hodgson's Australian Mounted Division, it will be recalled, had already detached 5th Light Horse Brigade to work with 60th Division. Its 4th Light Horse Brigade was now temporarily broken up to provide escorts for Chauvel's Corps HQ and various transport convoys, so that by the time he reached El Lajjun the only troops remaining to Hodgson were Brigadier-General L. C. Wilson's 3rd Light Horse Brigade and divisional units. At 14.15 Chauvel received an air reconnaissance report that large numbers of the enemy were retreating northwards from Jenin, to the south of Afula. At his direction Hodgson sent Wilson to intercept the fugitives with two of his regiments, plus the 11th LAMB, which had reverted to Corps control. This he did to good effect, penetrating as far as Jenin where huge supply dumps were already burning. By evening the Australians were heavily outnumbered by the 3,000 prisoners they had taken. During the night a continual stream of weary, demoralised Turks converged on Jenin, some being bluffed into surrender while others gave up willingly. Dawn revealed that Wilson's men were guarding no less than 8,000 prisoners and the situation was becoming dangerous. In response to urgent messages Hodgson sent up two regiments of 4th Light Horse Brigade, which had re-assembled at El Lajjun. On their arrival the prisoners were marshalled into columns and marched to their compounds.

Elsewhere the infantry of XX and XXI Corps had maintained their pressure throughout the day, especially against the crumbling western flank. By noon the headquarters of Seventh and Eighth Armies had sanctioned limited withdrawals, but their instructions became meaningless as, hour by hour, reports came in confirming that the British cavalry had blocked all escape routes to the north. Soon it became apparent that the only way out of the trap lay to the east across the Jordan fords. During the evening Sanders cobbled together a plan for an emergency defence line stretching southwards from Lake Hula down the Jordan valley to the Sea of Galilee and then eastwards from Samakh to Der'a. Beyond the Jordan, Jemal Kuçuk's Fourth Army had not as yet been seriously affected, although it had been subjected to air attack, and Arab raids against the Hejaz Railway had intensified. Jemal, however, was aware that a disaster had taken place and, although he had not heard from Sanders for two days, reached the correct conclusion that the remnant of the army group would be retiring on Damascus, covered by his own army. He gave orders for his II Corps to abandon Ma'an and move north.

At dawn on 21 September the RAF spotted the bulk of Mustapha Kemal's Seventh Army withdrawing along the Wadi Far'a. From that moment on it was bombed and strafed without mercy. Although comparatively few casualties were caused, the Turks gave way to blind hysteria and fled into the hills, leaving the road choked with a tangle of carts, lorries, guns and dead animals. It took several days to extract 100 guns from the wreckage, which in some areas could only be cleared by burning. This was the first occasion in history when an army was virtually annihilated by air power alone. To the north, Nazareth was promptly occupied when its garrison was found to have left during the night.

Sanders' rearguard consisted of Colonel von Oppen's badly mauled Asia Korps and elements of the Turkish 16th and 19th Divisions. Oppen had intended following the Seventh Army along the Wadi Far'a, but on learning that this was blocked he decided to try for the Jordan ford at Jisr el Damiya. By now, however, Chaytor's Force, having been released from its diversionary role, was playing an active part in operations. At 13.00 on 22 September it captured the ford, causing Oppen to think again. Abandoning his baggage and guns he made his way over a difficult cross-country

Above: The Turkish Seventh Army, struggling to retreat through the Wadi Far'a, ceased to exist after continuous strafing by the RAF. This was the first occasion in history when a major ground formation was wiped out by air power alone. *IWM Neg Q12311*

route with the intention of attacking Beisan and breaking through to Samakh. This was forestalled by Jevad Pasha, who ordered him to cross the Jordan by the ford at Mekhadet Abu Naj. By the time the ford came under attack, most of his men were across.

So far the Desert Mounted Corps had taken some 15,000 prisoners and the infantry about 20,000. Allenby had every cause for satisfaction although there remained some tidying up to do. On 23 September 5th Cavalry Division was ordered to capture the ports of Acre and Haifa and 4th Cavalry Division was detailed to block the remaining Jordan fords. Acre fell quickly but the garrison of Haifa, occupying naturally strong positions, chose to make a fight of it. Two regiments of Brigadier-General C. R. Harbord's 15th Cavalry Brigade, the Mysore Lancers and the Jodhpur Lancers, charged with such aggression across the rocky summit of the dominant Mount Carmel and along the narrow neck of land into the town that resistance collapsed. The cost amounted

to only three killed and 34 wounded although the horses suffered severely, 64 being killed, 83 wounded and many more lamed and exhausted.

The task of blocking the Jordan fords was given to Brigadier-General C. L. Gregory's 11th Cavalry Brigade which advanced down both banks of the river. In places, particularly at Makhadet Abu Naj, the Turks fought very hard in the belief that they were within sight of safety, but they were very sensitive to movement against their flanks or rear and would nowhere stand against a mounted charge. By the time the fords had been sealed off, their dead littered the surrounding area and 9,000 more prisoners had been taken. During the

Above: Megiddo. Australian Light Horsemen escorting a column of prisoners. Such was the speed with which Allenby's offensive developed that the Turks, their command structure completely dislocated, willingly surrendered in their thousands. The prisoner in the foreground has a leg wound and seems to be riding his officer's horse. *IWM Neg Q12382*

night a 29th Lancer patrol made contact with the Worcestershire Yeomanry, the cavalry regiment of XX Corps. To the south, Chaytor's Force had advanced into trans-Jordan and by 18.30 had taken Es Salt. Next morning, having been ordered by Allenby to stop the Turkish withdrawal from Amman, Chaytor sent 100 men of the Auckland Mounted Rifles to destroy a section of the Hejaz Railway north of the town.

On 25 September the Australian Mounted Division renewed pressure against the enemy's rapidly disintegrating army group. At Samakh, the hinge of Sanders' projected defence line,

the reinforced garrison had had several days in which to strengthen their defences and had been ordered to hold to the last man. The town was the objective of Brigadier-General W. Grant's 4th Light Horse Brigade, from which 4th ALH had been detached to guard Chauvel's headquarters and five troops of 12th ALH were away escorting prisoners, leaving only 11th ALH at full strength. Grant had been promised reinforcements, but instead of waiting for them he took advantage of the darkness and attacked at first light. At 04.25 11th ALH charged across open ground from the south-east, supported by machine-guns. In the teeth of the defenders' fire the Australians broke through the eastern defences and closed with the rifle and bayonet. After an hour's ferocious hand-to-hand fighting, to which Grant committed a squadron of the 12th ALH, held in reserve, the town and its station had been cleared. About 100 German troops were killed, but, significantly, among the 364 prisoners taken were about 200 Turks who had shown no

217

interest in the fighting. Australian casualties were comparatively heavy, amounting to 78 killed and wounded and 100 horses, most of which were killed. Grant ordered a squadron of 12th ALH to patrol up the western shore of the lake towards Tiberias. On the way it encountered a squadron of 8th ALH and 12th LAMB; the combined force occupied the town, taking 100 prisoners and thirteen machine-guns.

Across the Jordan, Chaytor continued his advance from Es Salt to Amman, the defences of which were stormed by 2nd Australian Light Horse Brigade (Brigadier-General G. de L. Ryrie) and the New Zealand Mounted Rifles Brigade (Brigadier-General W. Meldrum), resulting in the capture of 2,563 prisoners, ten guns, numerous machine-guns, 300 horses and a large quantity of forage. In waiting so long for his II Corps, which had still not arrived from Ma'an, Jemal Kuçuk had compromised the withdrawal of the remainder of Fourth Army because, thanks to the activities of Chaytor's Force and the Arabs, the Hejaz Railway was now inoperable as far north as Der'a. His men were now faced with a long, hot, thirsty march, knowing that if they straggled they would receive no mercy from the hovering Arabs.

Having destroyed Sanders' Seventh and Eighth Armies and mauled his Fourth, Allenby set about planning the final ejection of the Turks from Palestine and Syria, his next objectives being Beirut and Damascus. From XXI Corps 3rd Division would take over the Nazareth–Samakh sector, 7th Division would relieve 5th Cavalry Division at Haifa, and 54th Division would begin marching north along the coast. In the Desert Mounted Corps, Australian Mounted Division followed by 5th Cavalry Division were to cross the Jordan at Jisr Banat Yukub and advance over the Golan Heights through Kuneitra to Damascus; 4th Cavalry Division was to march on Der'a and then, together with the Arab army, advance northward through Kiswe to Damascus.

Sanders, meanwhile, was doing his best to stop the rot. Recognising that Damascus was not defensible, he finally re-established his GHQ at Ba'albek and ordered Mustapha

Kemal to establish a new front at Riyaq using the remnant of the Asia Korps, which had been hurriedly transported by train from Der'a for the purpose, and such reinforcements as Second Army could send down from the north. The so-called Tiberias Group, holding the line of the Jordan between Lake Hula and the Sea of Galilee, was placed under Jemal Kuçuk's command with the idea that it and the Fourth Army should carry out a fighting withdrawal through Damascus to the new defence line.

Barrow's 4th Cavalry Division clashed with the Turkish rearguard at Irbid on 26 September and again at El Remte next day. On the 28th the division reached Der'a to find that it had been captured by the Arabs the previous afternoon. Barrow rode into the town with 10th Cavalry Brigade and was sickened to find the Arabs massacring the patients of a recently arrived hospital train in reprisal for atrocities committed in their villages by the retreating Turks. The incident soured the relationship between Barrow and Lawrence but did not affect the course of the campaign.

Farther south, the troops of Turkish II Corps, some 4,000 strong, indicated their willingness to surrender but declined to lay down their arms until enough troops had arrived to defend them against the vengeful Arabs. Chaytor dispatched 2nd Light Horse Brigade, followed by the New Zealand Mounted Rifles Brigade, who escorted the captives into Amman. This brought the operations of Chaytor's Force to an end. During its short career it had, at the cost of some 140 casualties, taken all its objectives and captured 10,322 prisoners, 57 guns, eleven locomotives, a large quantity of rolling stock and much else besides.

When the Australian Mounted Division reached Jisr Banat Yakub on the morning of 27 September it found the bridge partially demolished and the far bank of the Jordan held in strength. A fierce fire fight ensued until alternative fords were located; crossings were made overnight, but by now the enemy had vanished. Passing through Kuneitra, the Australians caught up with the Turkish rearguard at Sa'sa on the morning of the 29th. The Turks were holding a strong position but again decamped during the night when it was apparent they were being outflanked. They were also unsettled by the advance of Barrow and the Arabs to the east. When, on the morning of 30 September, Hodgson came up with them once more at Kau Kab, eleven miles from Damascus, they broke and ran rather than face a full divisional attack. At about the same time, Macandrew's 5th Cavalry Division came into line between Hodgson and Barrow, intercepting and capturing a 2,000-strong column at Kiswe.

The remnant of Jemal Kuçuk's Fourth Army and the Tiberias Group were now streaming through Damascus. Some were heading north on the road to Homs, but most were escaping westwards through the Barada Gorge towards Riyaq and Beirut. At about 16.30 elements of Australian Mounted Division reached the cliffs on the southern edge of the gorge and opened fire on packed troops, transport vehicles and railway trains below. When the firing ceased the Fourth Army no longer existed; 4,000 prisoners were taken and 400 Turkish and German bodies were found amid a tangle of wrecked vehicles and dead transport animals which took several days to clear. Next morning the Desert Mounted Corps and the Arabs entered Damascus.

Little or nothing in the way of serious opposition now lay in Allenby's path, but two problems were causing him grave concern. The first was that the Desert Mounted Corps' horses were utterly exhausted. Many, indeed, had foundered and been destroyed, and of those that remained the artillery was entitled to claim the fittest. Equally serious was an epidemic of malaria and influenza contracted from Turkish prisoners, which, during its worst

Below: The remnant of the Turkish Fourth Army was destroyed as it attempted to escape through the Barada Gorge, near Damascus. *IWM Neg Q12360*

week put more than 3,000 men in hospital. Even Macandrew's division, the healthiest in the corps, could muster only 1,500 sabres. Against this, an additional LAMB and Light Car Patrol had reached the front. Allenby therefore allocated 2nd, 11th and 12th LAMBs and 1st, 2nd and 7th LCPs to Macandrew as 5th Cavalry Division's mechanised advance guard, and placed an RAF squadron at his disposal.

Sanders no longer had the manpower to hold his projected defence line and on 6 October Riyaq was abandoned. Next day probing armoured cars discovered that the enemy had evacuated Beirut as well. XXI Corps' cavalry regiment and 7th Indian Division reached the city on 8 October and were ordered to push on to Tripoli, which was occupied five days later. Allenby's troops were now being supplied regularly through the captured ports of Palestine and Syria, which removed some of the burden of their extended overland lines of communication.

Macandrew meanwhile was pushing north towards Homs, having divided his division into two: Column A, the mechanised units plus 15th Cavalry Brigade, a combination of mobility and firepower; and Column B, the remainder of the division, which would follow on and be committed as required. Homs was taken on 16 October and the advance continued down the valley of the Orontes, with an Arab force operating on its eastern flank. By the 24th Column A was two days' march ahead of Column B. Next day Mustapha Kemal rejected a call to surrender Aleppo, but abandoned the city that night in response to an Arab threat against his line of retreat. Although Column A engaged his rearguard at Haritan on 26 October his withdrawal continued. On the 29th Muslimiye Junction, through which ran the enemy's rail lifeline to the Mesopotamian Front, was also captured.

The probability is that the defeat would on its own have led Turkey to seek terms, but the sudden collapse of her ally Bulgaria had already impelled the Grand Vizier to request an armistice, which was granted on 31 October.

In the 38 days since the start of the Battle of Megiddo, Allenby's troops had destroyed three Turkish armies, advanced 350 miles, and captured 76,000 prisoners, 360 guns and 89 locomotives; no accurate figures exist for the numbers of enemy killed and wounded. The cost, negligible by the standards of the Western Front, had been 782 killed, 4,179 wounded and 382 missing.

Won before the first shot had been fired, Megiddo was fought in accordance with the principles Fuller was propounding in his 'Plan 1919' and it contained all the elements of what subsequently became known as the *Blitzkrieg* technique. It mattered not that the primary instrument of Allenby's victory was horsed cavalry rather than armoured formations, although armoured vehicles did play a significant part from time to time. What counted was mobility and in this respect the Desert Mounted Corps' daily rate of advance between 19 and 21 September was actually *twice* as fast as that of armoured formations during the German invasion of the USSR in 1941 or the Allied breakout from the Normandy beachhead in 1944. At Cambrai and Amiens the tank had finally broken the power of the defence; now, Allenby's methods at Megiddo had demonstrated how the restored power of the offensive could be used to devastating effect.

Commentary 10 – Armageddon Mark II

During the twenty years following the end of the First World War the pace of technical development accelerated even more rapidly than it had in the pre-war years. By the end of the war the French Army had produced its Renault FT 17 tank in which the main armament was housed in a turret with all-round traverse, a feature which was adopted as standard the world over. Improved power units, transmissions, track design and methods of joining armour plate meant that numerous tank designs proliferated. These included heavy tanks intended to perform the breakthrough role, medium tanks designed to support infantry operations, fast, or cruiser, tanks for deep penetration operations, and light tanks and tankettes which could perform the reconnaissance role as well as operate in a colonial environment.

How tanks were to be employed was the subject of much controversial debate. Some armies took the view that they were best used in support of infantry operations, in the manner of Cambrai and Amiens. Others believed that they should be employed in large formations with their own organic mechanised artillery, infantry and engineer units, and operate in the manner of Fuller's 'Plan 1919' or Allenby's use of the Desert Mounted Corps at Megiddo. Others strove, not very successfully, to allow for every potential scenario.

As a consequence of the cut-backs in her armed services that would leave her unprepared for the Second World War, Great Britain's contribution was largely intellectual, but exercises did demonstrate that it was possible to control such formations by radio. The writings of Fuller and Captain Basil Liddell Hart were widely read abroad, especially in Germany, and when Adolf Hitler repudiated the restrictive clauses of the Treaty of Versailles, the German Army had no hesitation in forming panzer divisions along the lines suggested and, later, grouping these into panzer corps. Senior officers, schooled in the tradition of the Annihilation Battle, found no difficulty in absorbing the concepts of strategic paralysis and deep penetration expressed by the British authors. The German armoured corps was, therefore, implacably opposed to providing tanks for infantry support, but the subject could not be ignored altogether and to meet the infantry's requirements a new arm of service, the Assault Artillery, was brought into being, equipped with assault guns. These were initially armed with a short 75mm howitzer in a fixed superstructure mounted on the chassis of a Pz Kpfw III tank.

Naturally the response to the tank was the anti-tank gun, but here the designers generally seem to have under-estimated the requirements. In 1939 most armies went to war with a 37mm or similar calibre anti-tank gun; that issued to German troops was known derisively by its crews as 'the door-knocker'. As heavier anti-tank guns came into service, tank designers increased the thickness of their armour which led to the demand for even more powerful guns, and so it went on. In theory there was no restriction on the size of an anti-tank gun, but the difficulties in crew handling, emplacing and digging-in imposed their own limit on weight and bulk. For the Americans this was reached with the 3-inch M5, for the British with the 17-pounder, for the Germans with the 75mm PaK 40 and for the Russians the 57mm M1943, none of which weighed less than a ton while some weighed over two tons. Curiously, two of the best tank killers, the German 88mm anti-aircraft gun and the British 25-pounder (87mm) gun-howitzer, were not purpose-built anti-tank guns at all.

For the tank, once it had broken through a screen of static anti-tank guns, mobility provided its own protection. Therefore, just as the powers of defence had dominated much of World War I, those of the attack dominated the first half of World War II. The balance was restored by a phenomenon known as the Monroe Effect, in which a conical, copper-lined hole in the end of a cylindrical charge focused the explosion of the latter into a narrow jet of immense power which could blast its way through the thickest armour and kill the tank crew. Rounds of this type did not require a powerful delivery system and were therefore suitable for issue to the infantry. They could be fired from a spring-loaded spigot mortar or, more efficiently, fitted with a small rocket motor and fired through a tube aimed from the shoulder, the best-known examples being the American Bazooka and the German *Panzerfaust*. Once the infantry had acquired their own close-quarter protection against the tank, the latter ceased to be Queen of the Battlefield and became one among equals, dependent for its success upon close co-operation with other arms.

Elsewhere on the battlefield, the artillery weapons and ammunition of the Second World

War were considerably more efficient than those of 1914–18. Radio not only permitted their fire to be controlled more effectively than in the days of vulnerable telephone lines and observation balloons, but also introduced a flexibility that enabled the fire of hundreds of guns to be switched quickly between targets as the situation demanded. For the infantry, the heavy tripod-mounted machine-gun still had a role to play, but the light machine-gun with its own bipod, had evolved to much the same form it has today and was issued on the scale of one per infantry section or squad. The machine-pistol and machine-carbine, some clumsy versions of which had appeared in 1914–18, had also been developed into deadly close-quarter weapons, carried by platoon and section leaders. The infantry platoon of 1939–45 therefore possessed far greater fire-power than that of 1914–18, especially in the German Army.

In the air, technical development had been equally rapid. By the end of the 1930s the biplane was giving way to the monoplane and more manoeuvrable aircraft were flying faster and higher than ever before. The fighter and the bomber had been joined by the dual-role fighter-bomber, the dive-bomber, capable of delivering its payload with great accuracy, the torpedo-bomber, which had actually claimed its first victim in 1915, and the large transport from which airborne troops could be dropped by parachute behind enemy lines or air landed on previously secured airfields.

As with armoured warfare, there were conflicting theories as to the correct employment of air forces. Of these the most influential were expounded by General Giulio Douhet, a former chief of the Italian Army's air arm, in his book *The Command of the Air*, published in 1921. Douhet's basic tenet was that air power could be used to win wars by destroying an enemy's cities and inducing terror among his civilian population, a theory put to the test during the Spanish Civil War and the Italian conquest of Ethiopia. To this end he advocated air forces completely independent of military or naval control. At that time, only Great

Britain had formed the Royal Air Force as an autonomous arm of service, although Italy followed in 1925 and France in 1934. The USA and Japan maintained separate army and naval air forces, and the Soviet air force was a branch of the army. Within air forces there was debate as to whether air power was best applied at the tactical level in direct support of military and naval operations, or against more distant strategic objectives, the only area of common agreement being that without air superiority neither armies nor navies could operate efficiently. When the Luftwaffe was formed in 1934 it was an apparently well-balanced air force capable of performing at both the strategic and tactical levels, willing to apply Douhet's terror theory to weaken an enemy's will to fight. However, as the German view was that wars would be won by the army, the Luftwaffe's primary employment would be to provide direct support on the battlefield, once air superiority had been attained.

Improved radio communications meant that air commanders at all levels could exercise control of their units. Likewise, the permanent attachment of radio-equipped forward air controllers to ground formations ensured that air power could be summoned quickly to eliminate stubborn centres of resistance or break up counter-attacks. Another use for radio, introduced during the 1930s, was the directional beam, originally developed as a foul-weather landing aid, which could be used to direct bombers to their target along a given path. To ensure accuracy a second beam was directed at an angle to intercept the first above the target area, so that when receivers aboard the aircraft indicated that the beams had met the raid could be delivered regardless of navigational difficulties caused by poor visibility or darkness.

The most important electronics breakthrough of the period, however, was radar. It had been known for many years that metallic objects reflected electromagnetic radiations. In 1934 the idea was developed in Britain as an aircraft detection device in which the reflections were displayed on a screen. By 1938 its feasibility had been proven and a chain of radar stations was built as part of the country's air defence system. As transmitters and receivers became smaller and more efficient the application of radar technology to naval as well as air warfare became a natural progression.

In the naval sphere the Washington Treaty of 1922 laid down that the ratio of capital ships possessed by the British, USA and Japanese Navies should stand respectively at 5:5:3. In theory the purpose of the conference was to prevent another expensive naval construction race. In practice its result was a tacit admission by Great Britain that the economic consequences of 1914–18 meant that she could no longer afford to be the predominant power at sea.

Navies still consisted of battleships, battle cruisers, cruisers, destroyers and submarines, and the gun and torpedo were still considered to be the weapons of decision. Guns would indeed decide the issue during a number of surface actions during the Second World War and naval gunfire support was an essential element of every amphibious operation. The torpedo, too, retained its importance, and in this connection the Japanese Long Lance 24-inch torpedo deserves special mention. A fearsome weapon fitted with a warhead twice the size of its Allied counterparts, it was powered by oxygen-enriched fuel to a distance of 44,000 yards at 36 knots or half that distance at 50 knots, giving the Japanese a marked advantage in that it was capable of inflicting fatal damage at ranges that could not be equalled.

Nevertheless things had been changing very quickly and the aviation aspects of naval warfare were becoming steadily more important. In 1917 the battle cruiser HMS *Furious* was converted as an aircraft carrier and in 1918 the Grand Fleet was joined by *Argus*, purpose-built for the role. During the next few years the USA and the Imperial Japanese Navies added aircraft carriers to their fleets. In 1921 General William Mitchell of the US Army Air Corps began a series of tests in which the surrendered German dreadnought *Ostfriesland* and several older American battleships were sunk by bombing. Mitchell's traditionalist opponents

scoffed at the results, commenting that the targets were at anchor and unable to fight back, but the unpalatable truth was that aircraft could sink battleships. Once the aircraft carrier had become an established element within the fleet its strike force consisted of dive- and torpedo-bomber squadrons plus fighters for their protection. Again, once it had been accepted that attack by land- or carrier-based aircraft would become an inevitable part of naval operations, warship armament was supplemented by a growing proportion of anti-aircraft guns.

It was the Japanese Navy which paid the greatest attention to its naval air arm between the wars, becoming remarkable for its efficiency and the high standards demanded from its aircrew entrants. Its first instructors were a team of former Royal Naval Air Service personnel led by Lord Sempill, who was to comment on his return home: 'The general ability in pilots is distinctly high, possibly higher than we are accustomed to find in this country, though it would seem likely that there is a smaller percentage of abnormally good pilots.' For their part, the Japanese maintained an interested watch on Royal Naval carrier operations during the early years of the Second World War, drawing the appropriate conclusions from the emasculation of the Italian battlefleet at Taranto in November 1940 and the crippling of the German super-battleship *Bismarck* the following May. It was, therefore, her own carrier strike force which led the attack on the US Pacific Fleet at Pearl Harbor in December 1941 and every major naval operation for the next six months. When, as we shall see, that strike force was destroyed at the Battle of Midway, what remained was of lesser quality and unable to withstand the powerful carrier task forces which the expanded US Navy was able to deploy. In the Atlantic, too, the aircraft carrier made a decisive contribution in the struggle against the U-boat and the Luftwaffe. By 1945 aircraft carriers had become the most important units of any fleet, rendering the battleship and the battle cruiser obsolete.

223

FRANCE, BELGIUM AND HOLLAND, MAY – JUNE 1940

It is not surprising that the outbreak of the Second World War was greeted with none of the enthusiasm that had marked that of its predecessor. The German Supreme Command (OKW = *Oberkommando des Wehrmacht*) did not believe that its forces would be strong enough to fight a major war for another four or five years, and indeed the German Army could not have gone to war at all if it had not absorbed Czechoslovakia's entire tank fleet when it invaded that country. Once again the mistake had been made in planning for a short war, compounded on this occasion by failure to plan for the second generation of tanks and aircraft that would be needed. Again, the army had been equipped in breadth but not depth, having evolved into a two-tier organisation in which the panzer and mechanised divisions formed the mobile cutting edge while the great mass of infantry divisions still plodded along with horse-drawn artillery and transport. The one area in which the German armed forces excelled was the application of modern technology to their traditional concept of the Annihilation Battle, suitably adapted to absorb the lessons of Cambrai, Amiens and Megiddo.

The Germans' strategic plan was to maintain a defensive stance along the West Wall (Siegfried Line) and deal with Poland quickly before the French and British armies could be fully mobilised, then attack in the west. Unfortunately for Poland, she was bounded on the north by East Prussia and on the south by German-held Slovakia, so that any penetration in these areas would prejudice the position of her armies holding the western frontier. Predictably, the Germans mounted a double envelopment, the inner jaws closing on Warsaw and the outer on Brest-Litovsk. The Luftwaffe quickly won air superiority then switched to interdiction missions and tactical support, the psychological effect of sustained dive-bombing doing much to break the defenders' will. Once they had broken through the defence zone, the armoured formations accelerated their advance into the Polish hinterland, disrupting the enemy's command and logistic infrastructure. The Poles, having a strong cavalry arm but few tanks, were unable to offer an effective counter. Their country ceased to exist for several years when the Soviet Army, keen to grab a share of the spoils, crossed its eastern frontier.

In effect, the Wehrmacht had destroyed the 1.5 million-strong Polish Army during the first ten days of fighting. German losses totalled 8,000 killed and 32,000 wounded, plus about 400 tanks of which half were destroyed by enemy action and the rest considered to be beyond economic repair either because of battle damage or mechanical failure. During the campaign's early stages the panzer divisions, forgetting that most of the danger lay behind them, were reluctant to drive deep into enemy territory, but with experience came confidence and their daily rates of advance grew longer. For its part, the Luftwaffe generated such terror among the civilian population that Polish reinforcements were prevented from reaching the front because the roads were jammed with refugees.

Overjoyed by his easy victory, Hitler was keen to mount a similar offensive in the west as soon as re-deployment was complete, and he treated his generals to an hysterical outburst of anger when they pointed out the impossibility of this. One reason was that time would be required for the panzer divisions to rebuild their tank strength, but even more important was the fact that continuous bad weather over the winter months seriously affected the Luftwaffe's ability to provide close ground support. Nevertheless, in October the generals put together a plan, codenamed Yellow. It involved three army groups – Army Group B under Colonel General Fedor von Bock deployed along the border with Holland and Belgium, Army Group A under Field Marshal Gerd von Rundstedt facing Luxembourg, and Army Group C under Colonel General Wilhelm Ritter von Leeb opposite the Maginot Line – in what amounted to nothing more imaginative than a mechanised resurrection of the old

Schlieffen Plan. The consensus was that the fighting would take the form of the later Western Front battles of 1918. At best the offensive might be expected to secure most of Belgium, including the coastline, and possibly reach the positions from which the German Army had withdrawn in 1918. This was exactly what the Allies expected and was the one situation for which they were prepared.

In the west the Allies remained sufficiently passive for this period to be known as the Phoney War. The operational pause thus granted enabled OKW to re-plan its offensive. The new plan was the brainchild of Rundstedt's Chief of Staff, the then Lieutenant-General Erich von Manstein, who was to emerge from the war with the reputation of possessing the finest strategic mind in the German Army. He had seen a way in which the Allied obsession with the Schlieffen Plan could be turned to decisive advantage. First an invasion of Holland and Belgium could be used to draw the British and French north into the Low Countries, like a matador's cloak. Next, a major armoured thrust through the Ardennes, across the Meuse and on to Amiens and the Channel, would have the effect of trapping and ultimately *annihilating* those Allied forces north of the Somme instead of merely defeating them, as envisaged in the original Plan Yellow. Such a thrust was possible because the French, for political reasons, had not extended the formidable Maginot defences along their frontier with Belgium. Once the breakthrough had been achieved, the French High Command would have to allow for three possibilities: that the Germans would turn south behind the Maginot Line; or would drive on Paris; or would continue westwards to the sea. However, the French lacked sufficient reserves to cover every contingency.

Rundstedt approved Manstein's plan, but neither the army's Commander-in-Chief, Field Marshal Walther von Brauchitsch, nor his staff at OKH (*Oberkommando des Heeres*), cared for the idea. By devious means, however, the plan was placed before Hitler who, to his credit, immediately saw its potential and ordered Brauchitsch to implement it. Rather less cred-

itably, Hitler was to claim the plan as his own while Manstein, who had irritated Brauchitsch by his persistence, was packed off to command an infantry corps at Stettin, far from the scene of action.

In April 1940, while detailed planning was under way for the coming offensive, code-named *Sichelschnitt* (sickle-slash), Hitler launched an invasion of Norway and Denmark with the object of securing Germany's iron ore supplies, which travelled by rail from Swedish Lapland to Narvik in northern Norway and thence south by sea, where it was at risk from the Royal Navy. Paratroops were dropped to seize important airfields to which air-landing formations were flown in, and amphibious landings were made at strategic points on the coast. The German surface fleet sustained crippling losses, but British and French troops who were landed to support the Norwegians, lacking adequate air cover and armour, were immediately thrown on to the defensive and forced to retreat to their embarkation ports. Throughout, the Germans enjoyed the twin advantages of air superiority and the support of small numbers of tanks. By 3 May the Allies had completed their withdrawal.

The campaign deepened the sense of inferiority which had afflicted the Allies since the rapid conquest of Poland. The morale of the French Army had declined to the point where in some formations whatever fighting spirit might have existed in September 1939 had evaporated by May 1940. Of the two million men mobilised, only 600,000 were between the ages of 20 and 25, the prime years for soldiering. The remainder had families or were middle-aged reservists with businesses to run and other responsibilities. Months of pointless inactivity, political disillusionment, poor living conditions, low pay, lack of leave, sheer boredom and an unsatisfactory relationship between officers and men, all contributed to the general apathy and disinterest. There were some efficient divisions of good quality, but for the most part lax discipline, desertion and slovenliness raised serious doubts in the minds of British liaison officers.

The French Army remained formidable nevertheless. It had a tank fleet of some 3,000 vehicles, outnumbering that of Germany by a wide margin, even if the MG-armed light Pz Kpfw Is and IIs, of no use at all in a tank v. tank battle, were included in the latter's total. In some respects, too, French tank designs were superior to German. For example, the 47mm gun mounted by the Char B and the Somua was a better armour-defeating weapon than the 37mm of the Pz Kpfw III, Pz Kpfw 35(t) and Pz Kpfw 38(t); again, while the Char B had 60mm armour and the Somua 55mm, the best protection available to German tanks was 30mm. On the debit side, French tanks had a smaller operational radius and the preference for one-man turrets meant that the tank commander, who also acted as his own gunner and loader, was overworked.

The two most important types of armoured formation in the French order of battle were the *Divisions Légères Mécaniques* (DLM) and the *Divisions Cuirassées* (DCR). The former was intended to execute a mechanised version of the cavalry's traditional roles, namely providing a screen for the main body of the army, carrying out reconnaissance *en masse* and exploiting a victory. The DCR, three of which had been hastily raised after the Polish campaign, while a fourth was forming, was intended to perform the breakthrough role. Neither possessed the inherent flexibility of the German panzer divisions but even more serious was the failure to provide specially trained corps headquarters capable of handling a possible concentration of DCRs. Altogether, the French had 500 tanks serving with the DCRs and 800 with the DLMs and mounted cavalry divisions, the remainder of their tank strength being dispersed in infantry support battalions.

During the inter-war years, as today, the British armed services had been subjected to a criminal degree of political neglect. A re-armament programme started in the late 1930s had barely begun to take effect. The British Expeditionary Force serving in France, commanded by Field Marshal Lord Gort, consisted of ten good-quality infantry divisions but only one armoured formation, the incomplete 1st Army Tank Brigade with 100 heavily armoured (80mm) Infantry Tanks, of which the majority were the little two-man MG-armed Mark I, joined by a handful of 2-pounder Mark IIs (the legendary Matilda II). Also available were 210 MG-armed light tanks serving with two light armoured reconnaissance brigades and the divisional cavalry regiments. In theory 1st Armoured Division, still in England with its 174 light and 156 2-pounder Cruiser tanks, could be shipped across the Channel at short notice; in reality the division had so many equipment deficiencies that it was barely operable.

If, however, the German armoured corps would fight at a disadvantage save in matters of organisation, technique and experience, the Luftwaffe had a distinct and decisive advantage. It could put up 1,268 fighters (Bf 109 and 110), 1,120 medium bombers (Heinkel He 111H and Dornier Do 17Z), 350 Junkers Ju 87B-1 dive-bombers, and a large fleet of Junkers Ju 52 transports, against which the French *Armée de l'Air* could oppose only 700 fighters of inferior performance (Morane-Saulnier, Potez, Bloch and Dewoitine) and up to 175 Breguet and Leo bombers; nor could the gap be bridged by the BEF's Air Component of 500 fighters and light bombers, many of its types such as the Gloster Gladiator biplane and the Boulton-Paul Defiant fighters and the Fairey Battle light bomber being obsolete and only the few Hurricane squadrons present being able to compete on even terms.

Commander-in-Chief of the Allied forces in France was General Maurice Gamelin. Aged 68, he might have been considered too old for his task, but he had served on Joffre's staff and actually drafted the orders which resulted in the defeat of the original Schlieffen Plan on the Marne in 1914. As France's eastern frontier was guarded by the formidable defences of the Maginot Line, he believed that the only option open to the Germans was a mechanised version of the same plan, and his opinion was reinforced in January 1940 when a German military aircraft crash-landed in Belgium; its occupants were in possession of the details of

Plan Yellow and the Belgians promptly passed these to the Dutch, French and British. Gamelin's intention was to counter the attack with his own Dyle–Breda Plan, which would involve the BEF and the best of the French armies racing north to join the 23 Belgian and eleven Dutch divisions, having first halted the German advance along the line of the river Dyle. He believed that, confronted by a combined French, British, Belgian and Dutch front, the over-extended German Army would be beaten in the long term. That his plan dovetailed so neatly with the requirements of Manstein's *Sichelschnitt* provides grounds for further reflection on the ability of the best strategists to achieve victory long before battle is actually joined.

The stage was now set for the German offensive. The matador's cloak which would draw the Allies into the Low Countries would be provided by Bock's Army Group B (Sixth and Eighteenth Armies) led by two panzer corps, XXXIXth with one division, which would operate in Holland, and XVIth with two, destined for central Belgium. Bock's task would be eased by paratroops dropped near Rotterdam, The Hague, Moerdijk and Dordrecht, and the arrival of air-landing divisions once suitable bases had been secured. In the Maastricht Appendix, separating Belgium from Germany north of their common frontier, parties of German soldiers dressed in Dutch uniforms or as civilians, known as Brandenburgers, were to take and hold the bridges over

THE GERMAN INVASION OF THE LOW COUNTRIES AND THE ALLIED REACTION, May 1940

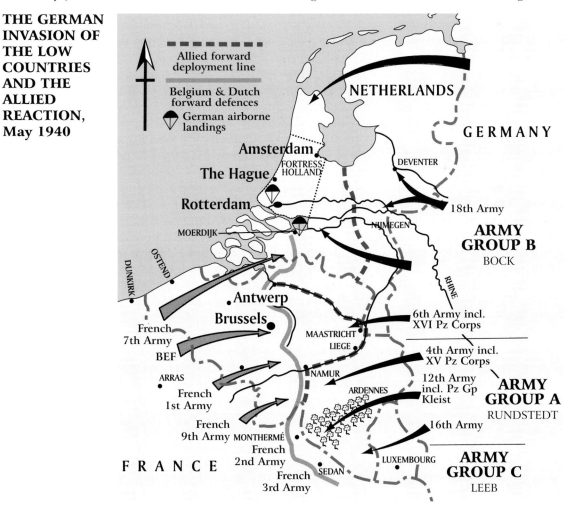

the Maas, so opening the door into Belgium itself. At the junction of the Albert Canal with the Maas the allegedly impregnable Fort Eben Emael was to be captured by a specially trained and equipped force of paratroops landing on top of the defences in gliders. Simultaneously, Rundstedt's Army Group A (Fourth, Twelfth and Sixteenth Armies), led by three panzer corps with a total of seven panzer divisions, would thread its way through the Ardennes and secure bridgeheads across the Meuse while the infantry of Leeb's Army Group C made diversionary attacks between the Siegfried and Maginot Lines and along the upper Rhine.

The offensive began in the early hours of 10 May with Luftwaffe attacks on Dutch, Belgian and French airfields. These caused damage and destroyed aircraft on the ground but did not neutralise the Allied air forces. Nor was the follow-up an unqualified success. In Holland, the northern end of the airborne corridor suffered a complete disaster. The paratroops were unable to capture some airfields and others were too muddy for operational use, the result being that when the air-landing transports arrived they were badly shot up. The attack on The Hague was cancelled, 600 casualties were incurred and numerous Ju 52s were destroyed. In Rotterdam, however, the city centre bridges were taken by a company which landed on the New Maas in Heinkel He 59C-2 floatplanes, reinforced by paratroops who dropped into a football stadium and commandeered trams to take them into town. South of Rotterdam the bridges over the Hollandch Diep at Moerdijk, the bridge over the Old Maas at Dordrecht and Waalhaven airfield all fell to successful drops. Further up the Maas, the fortunes of the Brandenburgers were equally mixed. At Maastricht, Nijmegen, Neerbosch and Grave the Dutch blew the bridges at the first sign of trouble, but enough bridges were captured to allow the invasion to proceed without serious check. The 9th Panzer Division (XXXIX Panzer Corps) immediately began its drive across Holland with the dual object of breaking through to the units forming the

airborne carpet and preventing a junction between the Allied and Dutch armies.

At Fort Eben Emael the arrival of the German gliders at 04.25 took the Belgian garrison by complete surprise. Employing shaped charges, which as yet had only been adopted for assault engineering use, the attackers blew in the fort's reinforced steel gun cupolas and kept the Belgians confined deep within the defences by means of more demolition charges and flame-throwers. Shortly after noon next day the fort surrendered. The Belgian Army had hoped to fight a delaying action along the line of the Albert Canal and the Meuse until Allied assistance arrived, but with the fall of Eben Emael the hinge of its first line of defence was lost even before serious fighting had begun.

Army Group B was now flooding across the frontiers of Holland and Belgium. Gamelin was delighted: 'On les aura!' (We have them!) he exclaimed. His Dyle–Breda Plan was implemented immediately, the Seventh Army racing northwards towards Antwerp while the BEF and French First Army wheeled to the right to come in alongside the Belgians along the river Dyle. Simultaneously, Ninth and Second Armies pivoted on Sedan and closed up to the Meuse, thereby forming a continuous front facing east.

At the head of Seventh Army's advance, 1e Division Légère Mécanique reached Breda only to find that the Dutch troops it was to join had been withdrawn northwards. The divisional commander, suddenly wary, split his advance guard into a reconnaissance screen, part of which had an unexpected brush with 9th Panzer Division between Breda and Tilburg. When other elements reached Moerdijk, the German paratroops called up their dive-bomber support and soon the whole of 1st DLM was under air attack. Its commander, having stuck his head into a hornets' nest, ordered his troops to fall back on Antwerp. This enabled 9th Panzer Division to break through to Moerdijk at dawn on 12 May and pass along the airborne corridor to Rotterdam.

The Dutch were now completely isolated, but their air force fought itself to destruction and the army continued to fight stubbornly against odds, with little hope. On 14 June the Luftwaffe carried out its threat to reduce the commercial quarter of Rotterdam into an inferno. One thousand civilians were killed in the raid, which caused widespread revulsion abroad, not least in the USA. As the royal family, with great reluctance, had already sailed for England, followed by the government, the Dutch General Staff decided that since there was no hope of repelling the invaders it was not justified in exposing the population to further air attacks. It therefore agreed to a general surrender with effect from 20.30 that evening. In eliminating Holland the Luftwaffe had lost 170 aircraft plus a similar number damaged, while casualties among the parachute and air-landing troops had been extremely heavy in proportion to the numbers involved. Notwithstanding this new mode of warfare had clearly demonstrated its ability to produce results quickly and the Germans decided to expand their airborne arm.

The 3rd and 4th Panzer Divisions (XVI Panzer Corps) had crossed the Maastricht Appendix and advanced across Belgium until they reached the Gembloux Gap. There, throughout 12 and 13 May, they fought a fierce tank battle against 2nd and 3rd DLMs of

General Prioux's 1st Cavalry Corps, which was screening the deployment of the French First Army along the Dyle. The French had the greater number of gun tanks but this was counter-balanced by the intervention of the Luftwaffe. Both sides claimed victory, the French because they had successfully fulfilled their mission, the Germans because Prioux had finally withdrawn; each claimed to have knocked out about 100 of the other's tanks, although the Germans retained the battlefield and were able to recover many of their vehicle casualties. The encounter may have imposed a temporary check on Army Group B, but it also served to concentrate Gamelin's attention on central Belgium and he dispatched 1st and 2nd DCRs, the most powerful formations of his central reserve, northwards into the trap.

Meanwhile the three panzer corps of Army Group A, two of which werer operating as a panzer group under the overall command of General Ewald von Kleist, were winding their way through the wooded valleys of the Ardennes, considered by the French to be tank-proof. The Luftwaffe had prevented the Allied air forces from getting a clear picture of what was taking place, but sufficient information reached Gamelin to cause him some concern. Such doubts as he had, however, were brushed

Right: Deliberate German air attacks on refugees were used to create terror. Refugee columns also hindered Allied movements. *IWM Neg F4505*

away by General Joseph Georges, Commander-in-Chief of the North East Front, who assured him that the situation was under control.

During the evening of 12 May the leading units of all three panzer corps had closed up to the Meuse along a forty-mile stretch running from Dinant in the north to Sedan in the south. Once again the French deployment could not have suited the requirements of *Sichelschnitt* better, for opposite them and straddling the boundary between French Second and Ninth Armies were four divisions of middle-aged reservists, manning what Gamelin considered would remain a quiet sector of the line.

At 09.00 on 13 May the bombers of General Hugo Sperrle's Third Air Fleet began subjecting the crossing sites to an intense attack lasting six hours, paying particular attention to the French artillery positions. The constant howling of the dive-bombers, incessant explosions, blinding smoke and the screams of the wounded would have provided a severe test for veteran regulars, let alone family men dragged unwillingly into uniform. For the infantry, cowering in trenches and bunkers, the ordeal induced widespread shock, but for the less protected artillerymen it was far worse.

Yet, incredibly, when the bombers finally droned away and the German motorised rifle troops began their assault crossing, these same men fought back, sending the first wave of rubber boats drifting downstream in tatters. The German divisional commanders rapidly formed fire bases with tanks, anti-aircraft and anti-tank guns, and indeed any heavy weapon available. By direct gunfire these systematically reduced the French bunkers, eating away at the defences until by dusk all three panzer corps had obtained a footing on the far bank. At about 18.00 a badly shaken artillery officer of the French 55th Division, covering Sedan, spotted tanks in the village of Bulson. They were French, moving up to a position from which they could give support, but he reported them as being German. The divisional artillery limbered up and headed for the rear and the infantry, thus abandoned, followed suit. Soon

the withdrawal became a panic which infected the neighbouring 71st Division, which also streamed away from the line.

There was now a yawning gap between the French Second and Ninth Armies, growing wider by the hour. While the German engineers worked at speed to put in the bridges that would allow their own tanks to cross, the Allied air forces launched repeated attacks on the bridge sites. This had been anticipated, and though the pilots with suicidal bravery pressed home the attack through intense anti-aircraft fire and swarms of Messerschmitt fighters, their efforts were foiled. The already weakened Air Component of the BEF and the *Armée de l'Air* lost, respectively, 70 and 40 aircraft to no purpose.

While German tanks continued to pour across the river, a shaken Gamelin prepared his response. This was to have been a converging attack on the expanding bridgehead by 1st DCR from the north, 2nd DCR from the west and 3rd DCR from the south, and the critical question was whether the French could deliver their counter-stroke before the Germans broke out? As already mentioned, there existed no formation headquarters capable of co-ordinating the operations of the three DCRs which, thanks to unbelievably bad staff work, were subjected to orders, counter-orders and needless delay. The Germans won the race by a wide margin and commenced their breakout on 14 May.

At 09.00 next day 7th Panzer Division (XV Panzer Corps), commanded by the then Major-General Erwin Rommel, ran into 1st DCR near Flavion. During the previous day the French division had run its fuel tanks dry as it strove to reach the battlefield along roads congested with refugees and the remnant of broken units. When Rommel arrived it was replenishing in close laager so that many of its powerful Char Bs were unable to get into action. Rommel, however, was more interested in making ground to the west and swung round the flank, calling up his dive-bombers to occupy the French until 5th Panzer Division (also XV Panzer Corps) arrived to engage them. The ensuing battle lasted most of the day. The

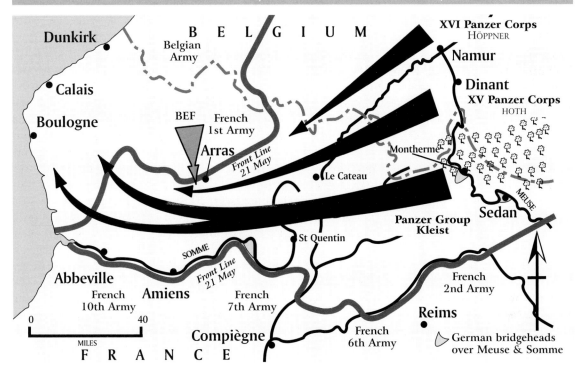

French claimed to have knocked out up to 100 tanks but also lost a considerable number of their own when the Germans discovered that their tracks and prominent radiator louvres were vulnerable. Many more were lost when 1st DCR disengaged at dusk, leaving a trail of vehicles abandoned and destroyed by their own crews because of fuel shortage or mechanical failure. By dawn next day the division could muster a mere seventeen tanks.

The 2nd DCR never fought as a division. During the afternoon of 15 May part of its artillery was overrun by XLI Panzer Corps and the rest of its wheeled vehicles sought safety south of the Aisne, leaving the armoured units north of the river. The division never re-assembled although its tanks attached themselves to infantry formations and fought on for as long as they could without the support of their supply echelons.

The fate of 3rd DCR was equally unfortunate. The division reached Sedan in good order on 14 May and was in a position to inflict serious damage on General Heinz Guderian's XIX Panzer Corps as it prepared to break out. It almost beggars belief that the local corps commander, General Flavigny, should have immediately deprived the division of its mobility by cancelling the counter-attack and deploying its tanks as static pillboxes in an 8-mile line along the southern edge of the German penetration. By morning the chance had gone, and during the next few days the division's strength was whittled away in local counter-attacks against strongly held German positions at Stonne.

There were now seven panzer divisions carving a 40-mile-wide corridor across northern France, followed by motorised and marching infantry divisions whose task was to protect the flanks of the penetration. There was little serious opposition, a few bursts of machine-gun fire often being all that was required to induce the mass surrender of French troops retreating from the disasters on the Meuse, or of bewildered reinforcements trying to establish new positions only to find German tanks already bearing down on them. To maintain continuous progress, the panzer divisions topped up their fuel at civilian garages or from supplies dropped by the Luftwaffe onto recently captured airfields.

On 17 May the southern flank of Guderian's XIX Panzer Corps was counter-attacked at Laon by the newly raised 4th DCR under Major-General Charles de Gaulle. The French, inexperienced and unused to working as a team, were easily fended off by 1st Panzer Division. Of greater annoyance to Guderian were the restrictions placed on his corps' movements by Kleist, the Panzer Group commander. Inevitably these led to a serious row in which Rundstedt intervened, endorsing Kleist's authority but permitting Guderian to perform 'reconnaissance in force', a term which the latter defined in the broadest possible terms. On 20 May he reached the sea, closing the trap on the Allied armies north of the corridor.

On the same day the French Prime Minister, Paul Reynaud, replaced the unfortunate Gamelin with General Maxime Weygand who proposed that the panzer corridor be cut by converging thrusts from north and south the following day. This would be no easy matter, for on 21 May there were nine panzer divisions in the corridor, XVI Panzer Corps having now joined Army Group A. Furthermore they were echeloned back to the right and beginning to swing northwards into the rear of the Allied Northern Army Group, which was already under unremitting pressure from Bock's Army Group B.

The attempt had to be made, but Weygand's southern thrust never really developed although near Arras the British 50th (Northumbrian) Division and 1st Army Tank Brigade broke into the 7th Panzer Division's line of march behind its armoured spearhead, inflicting serious loss on its two motor rifle regiments and putting to flight the neighbouring SS Motorised Infantry Division *Totenkopf*. By massing his entire divisional artillery, including his 88mm anti-aircraft guns, Rommel personally managed to check the advance, but his Panzer Regiment 25, returning to counter-attack, ran into an anti-tank gun screen and was further mauled by the remnant of the French 3rd DLM. Nevertheless by evening the threat had been contained and the panzer corridor remained intact.

Rommel's report that his division had been attacked by 'hundreds' of tanks was a wild exaggeration prompted by a degree of self-justification, but it set alarm bells ringing up the entire German chain of command. In particular, Hitler, who had personally sanctioned *Sichelschnitt*, had become a prey to worries that his prized armoured force would be cut off far to the west, and now his worst fears seemed about to be realised. The great drive was abruptly halted and XLI Panzer Corps was actually ordered to retrace its steps towards the apparently dangerous situation developing around Arras. By the time the advance was resumed 24 hours later, it ran into tougher and more resolute resistance.

For the Allies' Northern Army Group, now penned inside a shrinking pocket with its supply lines cut, the failure of Weygand's plan left only one option – withdrawal to the coast and, if possible, evacuation. The fall of Calais on 25 May gave the situation an added urgency. Next day Vice-Admiral Bertram Ramsay, Flag Officer Dover, began the evacuation under the code-name Operation Dynamo, assembling more than 1,000 vessels, including destroyers and smaller warships, cross-Channel ferries, pleasure steamers, coasters, trawlers and craft as small as cabin cruisers, manned by their civilian owners.

On 24 May the advance of the panzer divisions was again halted by Hitler, this time at Rundstedt's urging. The Allied Army Group North had effectively been destroyed, as Manstein had intended, and what happened within the Dunkirk pocket became less important with every hour that passed. Equally, large French forces still existed south of the corridor and the panzer divisions urgently needed time to untangle their long lines of communication, allow their breakdowns and repaired battle casualties to catch up, carry out essential maintenance and deploy for the final battle against them. At the request of its Commander-in-Chief, Reichsmarschall Hermann Göring, the Luftwaffe was to be allowed to deliver the *coup de grâce* against the pocket. This it proved incapable of doing, despite the surrender of the Belgian Army on 27 May, for the RAF threw in its modern Spitfire squadrons, flying from airfields in England. In air battles which took place far beyond the evacuation beaches, the RAF shot down 189 German aircraft for the loss of 99 of its own, inflicting on the Luftwaffe the first defeat in its history. This

Below: The French Char B heavy tank was the most formidable opponent encountered by the German panzer divisions. This example was disabled by a shot near the radiator louvre and attempts to recover it have clearly been abandoned. *IWM Neg F4635*

was not apparent to those awaiting evacuation on the beaches, who had to endure the bombing and strafing of those German aircraft which did break through, and until the situation was clarified there existed a feeling of bitterness between the British Army and the RAF.

Operation Dynamo continued until 4 June. More than 336,000 Allied troops, one-third of whom were French or Belgian, had been taken off, although they left behind all their heavy weapons and most of their small arms. The cost had been six British and three French destroyers sunk and nineteen damaged, plus 56

Left: The evacuation of the BEF. Virtually all of the Army's heavy weapons had to be left behind. *IWM Neg F4824*

other ships and 161 small craft sunk. Together, the saga of the little ships of Dunkirk and the leadership of Prime Minister Winston Churchill inspired a fighting spirit throughout the British nation that hitherto had been latent, but, as Churchill himself was quick to point out: 'Wars are not won by evacuations.'

While most of the BEF was being evacuated from Dunkirk, other British troops were landing at Cherbourg. They included 1st Armoured Division which, lacking half its tank strength, its motorised infantry, artillery and much else besides, was described by its own commander as 'a travesty of an armoured division'. Nor were the French in much better case, having lost three DLMs, two DCRs and all the infantry support tank battalions sent north. All that remained were part of 3rd DCR, the newly raised 4th DCR and some scattered tank battalions. Nevertheless, Weygand set about building a new line

stretching along the Somme and Aisne to the Maginot Line. This consisted of a zone several miles deep, based on towns, villages and woods. Where possible these strongpoints were mutually supporting, with the areas between registered as artillery killing grounds. When, on 5 June, the Germans opened the second phase of their offensive they were at first checked by determined resistance, but once again the Luftwaffe made the enemy artillery its special target. When the guns had been silenced and the few French tanks knocked out, gaps began to appear in Weygand's line and through these the panzer formations flooded into empty space. The British 1st Armoured Division, having fought on the Somme sector, hastily re-embarked at Brest and Cherbourg, but most of the crack 51st (Highland) Division was trapped at St-Valéry and forced to surrender to Rommel's 7th Panzer Division. Paris, having been declared an open city, was entered on 14 June. Panzer Group Kleist drove south through Dijon to capture Lyons. To the east, Guderian's armour finally created the conditions envisaged by the Schlieffen Plan, trapping several French armies with their backs to the Swiss frontier and the Maginot Line, which was also under attack by Leeb's Army Group C, the pocket thus formed yielding half a million prisoners. Italy entered the war as Germany's ally on 10 June. Two days later Weygand recommended that Reynaud seek an armistice. This was granted and hostilities formally ended on 25 June.

It had taken just six weeks to destroy the French, British, Belgian and Dutch armies. The *Service Historique de l'Armée de Terre*'s recently published *Sedan 1940* gives French losses as 85,000 killed, 120,000 wounded and 1,552,000 missing or taken prisoner, these figures being somewhat lower than previously published estimates but indicative of the scale of the tragedy. British, Belgian and Dutch casualties (killed, wounded and missing) totalled respectively 68,000, 23,000 and 10,000. German losses totalled 27,000 killed, 111,000 wounded and 18,000 missing. The Luftwaffe lost 1,284 aircraft as against the RAF's 931 and the *Armée de l'Air*'s 560. On the mainland of Europe the Allied armour had been eliminated altogether. At the end of the campaign the German armoured corps' tank strength showed a reduction by half, partly as a result of battle and partly because of breakdowns caused by hard usage and several hundred miles' running.

The rapid German conquest of Poland, Norway, Holland, Belgium and France gave rise to a new word, *Blitzkrieg* (lightning war, coined by a popular British newspaper, but never used by the Germans), to describe the manner in which these campaigns had been fought by rapidly moving armour closely supported from the air. Hitler was now at the pinnacle of his power, the fruits of success soured only by the illogical defiance of the United Kingdom, lying apparently defenceless within sight of his victorious troops at Calais.

THE BATTLE OF BRITAIN, JULY – OCTOBER 1940

In the wake of his stunning victories in western Europe, Adolf Hitler intimated that he was ready to conclude a peace treaty with Great Britain on what he considered to be generous terms. To his bewilderment and annoyance his approaches were not acknowledged and on 16 July he issued his War Directive No 16:

'Since England, in spite of her militarily hopeless situation, shows no sign of coming to terms, I have decided to prepare a landing operation against her and, if necessary, to carry it out. The objective of this operation is to eliminate the English home country as a base for the continuance of the war against Germany, and if this should prove unavoidable, to occupy it to the full extent .... The preparation for the operation must be completed by mid-August .... The operation will carry the code-name "Sealion"'.

Göring, as head of the Luftwaffe, was enthusiastic. Brauchitsch, Commander-in-Chief of the Army, was confident that his troops could overrun the United Kingdom provided that they could be got ashore and their supply lines maintained. Rather less sanguine, however, was Grand Admiral Erich Raeder, the Navy's Commander-in-Chief, who pointed out that as a result of the heavy losses sustained during the invasion of Norway, he lacked the necessary units with which to escort the invasion fleet. Furthermore, mounting a cross-Channel invasion was a very different matter from a river crossing, whatever the Army might think. It involved tides which rose and fell, flowing first one way and then the other, as well as wind, weather and light conditions. These considerations in themselves restricted the landing periods to a number of tactical 'time windows' in which the operation could be carried out successfully. With the onset of autumn and the winter gales, the frequency of useable 'windows' would decline rapidly. Raeder accepted that while the number of suitable invasion beaches was fewer than had been anticipated, these would suffice, although an absolute pre-requisite to the operation would be complete air superiority over the Channel and the invasion zone. This Göring assured him would be the case, adding that such coast defences as the British possessed would be

neutralised by airborne troops landing immediately behind them. Raeder, by no means convinced, set about the immense task of collecting barges from Europe's inland waterways, causing considerable economic dislocation in the process, and concentrating them in western harbours where they were suitably adapted.

At this time the Luftwaffe possessed about 1,460 medium bombers (Junkers Ju 88, Heinkel He 111, Dornier Do 17 and the long-range Do 215), 280 dive-bombers (Junkers Ju 87), 760 single-engined fighters (Messerschmitt Bf 109E), 250 twin-engined fighters (Messerschmitt Bf 110) and some 170 reconnaissance types, a total in excess of 2,700 aircraft of which more than 2,000 would be serviceable at any one time. These were deployed in three *Luftflotten* (air fleets): Field Marshal Hugo Sperrle's *Luftflotte 3* in France south of the Seine; Field Marshal Albert Kesselring's *Luftflotte 2* in northern France, Belgium and Holland; and General Hans-Jürgen Stumpff's smaller *Luftflotte 5* in Denmark and Norway. During the recent campaign the Luftwaffe had lost 3,000 aircrew killed and 1,400 wounded plus 28 per cent of its aircraft strength. It needed time in which to regroup and re-deploy from operations against the French to fresh axes converging on England, which occupied much of July. Although its crews may have needed rest, its morale was uniformly high for it had enjoyed a career of uninterrupted victory stretching back to the Spanish Civil War, save for the failure at Dunkirk, which was unwisely forgotten in the general euphoria.

If one looked a little deeper, however, there was cause for concern. The Luftwaffe, primarily a tactical air force, was being asked to perform a strategic role. Its bombers would be required to destroy the RAF's airfields, radar stations, aircraft factories, industrial targets and communications centres, many of which lay well within the English hinterland. They would have fighter protection for much of the way, but the Bf 109E's limited fuel endurance meant that it could only provide cover as far as London before turning for home. Indeed, even against much closer objectives its restricted range ensured that it could only remain for minutes above the target area. Once the fighter squadrons had gone the bomber crews could only rely on their own inadequate defensive armament to protect them from British fighters. This situation was to provide a continuous thread throughout the coming battle.

In the immediate aftermath of Dunkirk the British Army was so lacking in equipment of every kind that it could only have offered minimal resistance. The Home Fleet could not be exposed to the risk of air attack by bringing it south from Scapa Flow to southern bases. In practical terms, the defence of the United Kingdom rested with Royal Air Force, and in particular with Fighter Command, led by Air Chief Marshal Sir Hugh Dowding. At this period Fighter Command could muster only 446 modern single-engined fighters, with a further 36 in reserve. Churchill, however, had appointed Lord Beaverbrook to the post of Minister of Aircraft Production. Ruthlessly, Beaverbrook sheared through bureaucracy and rationalised industrial methods so that just ten weeks later there were 704 fighters in front-line service and 289 in reserve.

Heavily outnumbered, Fighter Command excelled only in organisation and the quality of its aircraft. Dowding sub-divided the Command into Groups, 10 Group being responsible for south-west England and south Wales, Air Vice-Marshal Keith Park's 11 Group, upon whom the weight of the battle would fall, for south-east England, Air Vice-Marshal Trafford Leigh-Mallory's 12 Group for the Midlands and much of East Anglia, and 13 Group for the north. The high-level radar early warning stations had been extended to cover the entire south and east coasts, and low-level stations had been established in the areas where the threat was greatest. Once the raiders had passed inland they were tracked by an efficient Observer Corps. Together, radar and Observer Corps reports were passed simultaneously to Fighter Command and the relevant Group headquarters. Fighter Command would

Left: A Messerschmitt Bf 110 fighter goes down as Spitfires attack the formation of Heinkel He 111 bombers it is escorting. In the middle distance, a Messerschmitt Bf 109 fighter. If the artist's portrayal seems exaggerated to modern eyes, there really were moments when the skies over south eastern England were this crowded.

speed its controls would become heavy. The Hurricane had a maximum speed of 335mph and was armed with eight wing-mounted machine-guns. Its all-round performance was not as good as that of the Bf 109E, but its turning radius was smaller, giving it a slight advantage in a dogfight. The Spitfire had a maximum speed of 355mph and was more agile than the Bf 109 in every way save climbing and diving. It was armed with eight wing-mounted machine-guns positioned, like those of the Hurricane, to converge in a shattering cone of fire; the Mk IIB version which entered service during the later phases of the battle was armed with four machine-guns and two 20mm cannon. The Spitfire was a more complex aircraft to build than the Hurricane and was never as numerous at this period, yet such was its performance that it became a legend, partially eclipsing the Hurricane which actually formed the mainstay of the defence. In general terms, they could be used to complement one another; the Spitfires tackling the enemy's fighter escort while the Hurricanes broke through to wreak havoc among the bomber formations below.

German plans to achieve the air superiority required for *Sealion* were divided into two phases. During the first, for which four days had been allowed, the RAF fighter defences were to be neutralised south of the line London–Gloucester. The second, designed to destroy the British aircraft industry and whatever remained of the RAF, would consist of a major offensive code-named *Adlerangriff* (Eagle

assess the threat and decide whether assistance would be required from other Groups, while Group would pass the information to sector control stations which would scramble squadrons and vector them by radio to meet the raiders. The system not only provided an indication of enemy intentions, but also dispensed with the need for standing patrols and thus saved fuel and wear on aircraft.

In the battle between the fighters, only the single-engined Hawker Hurricanes and Supermarine Spitfires could engage the enemy's Bf 109Es on equal terms. The Bf 109E had a maximum speed of 354mph and was armed with one 20mm cannon firing through the propeller boss and four machine-guns. When climbing or diving its performance was regarded as being second to none, although at

Attack), lasting an estimated four weeks. This was scheduled to begin on 10 August so that the invasion phase of *Sealion* could be activated during the first two weeks of September, before weather in the Channel began to deteriorate.

Preliminary sparring took place throughout July and into August. It took the form of attacks on shipping in the Channel, coastal towns and the nearest RAF bases in the hope of provoking Fighter Command into a large-scale air battle. Dowding refused to be drawn and as far as possible his fighters concentrated on the enemy bombers. By 11 August the Luftwaffe's losses amounted to 109 bombers destroyed and 27 seriously damaged, plus 82 fighters destroyed and 25 seriously damaged, these being considered somewhat heavier than had been anticipated but nonetheless sustainable. During the same period Fighter Command had 120 aircraft destroyed and 41 seriously damaged.

Fighting intensified during the days immediately prior to *Adlertag*, which had been put back from 10 to 13 August. On 12 August a series of heavy raids was mounted against six radar stations and several of 11 Group's airfields in Kent. Five of the stations were operational again very quickly, but that at Ventnor, Isle of Wight, was knocked out and was not replaced until 23 August. All the damaged airfields were back in action within 24 hours.

Adlertag itself was something of an anticlimax because the attacks did not begin until afternoon. *Luftflotte 2* again raided airfields in Kent and shipping in the Thames estuary without much in the way of tangible results, while *Luftflotte 3* pounded three airfields in Hampshire, none of which were occupied by aircraft of Fighter Command. Against this, the Spitfire factory at Castle Bromwich, near Birmingham, was damaged in a successful night attack.

At this stage, the Luftwaffe was satisfied that the battle was going according to plan, a belief encouraged by Colonel Josef Schmidt, its principal intelligence analyst. Schmidt had a tendency to ignore entire areas of relevant information and present his superiors with only the most favourable reports. According to him successful attacks had been carried out against 30 airfields between 8 and 14 August removing the squadrons based thereon from Fighter Command's order of battle. During the same period he claimed the destruction of 300 British fighters when the actual figure was less than a third of that figure. The moment had come, he suggested, for 'decisive daylight operations because of the inadequate air defences of the island'. In the days to come senior officers responsible for mounting operations would grow more than a little tired of Schmidt and his claims that Fighter Command was tottering on the brink of extinction. If that were the case, they asked, who was doing all the fighting?

Air activity was at a lower level on 14 August, but next day the Luftwaffe put in the sort of effort that had been expected on *Adlertag*, flying no fewer than 1,786 sorties of which 520 were by bombers. Once again southern England was heavily attacked, but in the mistaken belief that Dowding had brought 12 and 13 Groups south to reinforce 11 Group, *Luftflotte 5* was brought into the picture. Flying from Stavanger in Norway, sixty-five Heinkel He 111 bombers, escorted by thirty-five twin-engined Messerschmitt Bf 110 long range fighters, set course for targets on Tyneside, while further south 50 unescorted Junkers Ju 88 bombers, operating from Aalborg in Denmark, headed for the Yorkshire coast. The raiders were intercepted over the sea by 12 and 13 Groups and sustained such a drubbing that apart from night attacks and the provision of replacement aircraft and crews, *Luftflotte 5* was unable to play any further part in the offensive. The fighting on 15 August was the most widespread of the entire battle, resulting in the destruction of 75 German aircraft and 34 British fighters.

On 16 August the Luftwaffe flew a further 1,700 sorties against southern England, losing 45 aircraft to Fighter Command's 21. For the next week fierce air battles continued to rage over Kent and Sussex, covering the sky with intricate contrails. In terms of aggression, the British pilots, fighting for national survival in full view of their own people, developed something of an edge, honed by an instinctive personal animus best expressed by veterans of the battle: 'Who did these people think they were, coming over here with their big formations and their black crosses?' During this period the slow Junkers Ju 87 dive-bomber squadrons, once the terror of Europe, were so cut to pieces that they were withdrawn from the battle. Likewise, the twin-engined Messerschmitt Bf 110 fighter, though heavily armed, had proved no match for Hurricane and Spitfire and was subsequently employed only for specific tasks. During the period 12–25 August the Luftwaffe's losses amounted to 178 bombers shot down and eleven seriously damaged, plus 191 fighters destroyed and twelve seriously damaged. During the same period Fighter Command lost 171 aircraft with five seriously damaged.

Problems were beginning to mount for Göring. Admiral Raeder required a full ten days' notice in which to activate the Navy's part in *Sealion* and time was running out. The date for the invasion had been set for 15 September, but as Fighter Command's powers of resistance seemed undiminished Hitler postponed it until 21 September. Göring, therefore, must achieve air superiority by 11 September at the latest, and it was decided that the entire strength of the Luftwaffe should be employed to destroy Fighter Command's sector control airfields, which were sited in a ring around London. The Luftwaffe, however, was beginning to show signs of strain. It was already suffering an unacceptable rate of attrition relative to the total force available and the loss of experienced aircrew was mounting. Furthermore there was growing friction between the bomber and fighter elements, the former claiming that they were receiving inadequate protection. The size of escorts was increased and the fighters were instructed to remain with the bombers. For their part the fighter pilots bitterly resented Göring's comments on their lack of aggression, pointing out that tying the Bf 109Es to the bombers would forfeit the very qualities inherent in their design. Given the

aircraft available at the time the problem was not easily solved. In a famous exchange during which Göring attempted to smooth ruffled feathers by offering his fighter pilots anything they needed, the response of the then Major Adolf Galland, already a notable ace, was to request a squadron of Spitfires!

From 24 August until 6 September 11 Group's sector control airfields at Kenley, Biggin Hill, Hornchurch, North Weald and Debden were all raided regularly. Each day, about 1,000 German aircraft, of which between 250 and 400 were bombers and the rest fighter escorts, crossed the British coast, and on the last two days of August the overall figure reached 1,500. Thanks to Herculean efforts none of the sector stations was put out of action, despite the heavy damage sustained, although Biggin Hill was reduced to controlling a single squadron instead of the usual three. To Luftwaffe crews it seemed inexplicable that, given the scale of their attacks, the number of British interceptions remained undiminished. During this phase of the battle 86 German bombers were destroyed and 37 badly damaged, and 226 fighters were shot down and fourteen badly damaged; Fighter Command's losses amounted to 267 aircraft destroyed and twelve badly damaged.

For Dowding, rotating his tired squadrons, the crisis of the battle had been reached. It was not so much that deliveries of aircraft from the factories were barely keeping pace with the numbers lost, although this was serious enough; rather it was because soon there would be too few trained pilots to fly those that remained. True, Fighter Command had been strengthened by volunteers from all over the Commonwealth, the USA and Ireland, and by vengeful French, Belgian, Polish and Czech airmen; also the shooting down of British fighters did not necessarily mean the loss of their pilots, many of whom managed to parachute uninjured to safety and return to operations immediately, an advantage which the Luftwaffe did not possess. What mattered was that wastage in killed and wounded was exceeding the output of the flying schools;

equally, as the new arrivals lacked the experience of the men they replaced, their average life expectancy was tragically short. Dowding, however, did not know that Göring's all-out assault on the sector control airfields was intended to be of comparatively short duration, and it seemed to him that while Fighter Command was just coping, it would find itself in difficulties as September wore on.

Battles, and wars, tend to be won by the side which makes fewest mistakes, and Dowding made very few. Hitler, anxious to avoid the unfavourable publicity created by the bombing of Warsaw and Rotterdam, had specifically forbidden attacks on London, but during the night of 24/25 August a German bomber crew, unsure of their whereabouts, jettisoned their bombs over the capital. Churchill responded the following night with an attack on Berlin by 81 aircraft of Bomber Command, thereby deflating Göring's boast that he would never allow such a thing to happen. In a paroxysm of hysterical rage Hitler directed the Luftwaffe to bomb London and other British cities by day and by night. A less emotional view, expressed

Below: The gun camera of a British fighter dramatically shows machine-gun fire focusing on a doomed Heinkel He 111. *IWM Neg CH1823*

by Field Marshal Kesselring, was that such a course would involve Fighter Command in even heavier fighting, paralyse the apparatus of government and possibly terrorise the population into surrender even before the invasion began. In the event the decision cost the Luftwaffe the battle. The sector control airfields were allowed the breathing-space they needed to recover, aircraft production overtook wastage, government continued to function and civilian morale actually hardened.

What became known as the Blitz began during the afternoon of 7 September when 372 bombers escorted by 600 fighters converged on London in waves. Huge fires were started in the docks, serving as beacons for the 250 bombers which continued the attack after dark. Whenever weather permitted, this pattern was repeated for the rest of the month, although it never reached the same level of intensity. Large areas of the docks, the City and the East End were laid waste. The balloon barrage kept the raiders above a certain height and the concentrated fire of anti-aircraft guns unsettled bomb-aimers although it brought down comparatively few aircraft.

During the day, Fighter Command became expert at meeting and breaking up raids before they reached the capital, the weight of the counter-attack being reinforced by 12 Group's newly introduced big wings in which several squadrons attacked together, bouncing enemy formations which had already been harried to distraction by 11 Group's squadrons. The resultant heavy casualties further demoralised the bomber crews, some of whom simply jettisoned their bombs and turned for home.

At night it was a different matter. Before the introduction of airborne radar the British night-fighters were compelled to grope blindly in a three-dimensional search. At this stage of the war the odds against interception were compared to the improbable collision of two table tennis balls bouncing around in a space the size of Waterloo station. Consequently the bombers flew unescorted, ranging at will over London, Bristol, Cardiff, Liverpool, Manchester and other cities. They did sustain losses, but they were trivial in comparison with those incurred during daylight raids, amounting to only nineteen aircraft from all causes during the period from 9 September to 6 October.

In the meantime, on his own initiative Admiral Raeder had begun concentrating his invasion barges in the Channel ports and estuaries. By 6 September air photo-reconnaissance revealed that there were 205 of them packed into Ostend harbour alone. The British government issued a warning that invasion could be

expected within three days; when the Luftwaffe began its attacks on London the following day the warning period was reduced to twelve hours. Bomber Command immediately began an air offensive of its own against the French and Belgian ports, flying 88 day and 1,862 night sorties in September alone. Its Blenheims, Hudsons and Battles could hardly avoid inflicting severe punishment in the congested target areas. Approximately 10 per cent of the barges were sunk and more sustained serious damage, all for the loss of only seventeen aircraft. It was a sobering thought for the commander of an invasion armada which had yet to sail.

On 15 September the Luftwaffe mounted another mass attack. This was intercepted by 11 Group before it reached Canterbury and scattered when a five-squadron wing from 12 Group waded into the fight, many of the

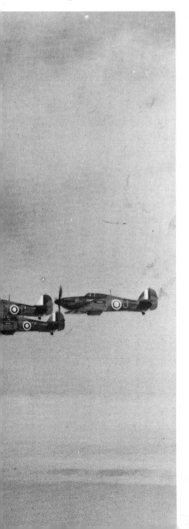

Left: Although the Spitfire is most commonly associated with the Battle of Britain, Hurricanes such as these formed the greater part of the RAF's fighter strength. *IWM Neg CH1508*

bombers jettisoning their loads over the south London suburbs. Later in the day a second raid was similarly dealt with. Of the 230 bombers and 700 fighters dispatched by Göring, 60 were destroyed. Fighter Command lost 26 aircraft but recovered thirteen of their pilots.

Hitler had become hesitant about giving the invasion order, despite encouraging reports from Göring, but the events of 15 September made up his mind. Fighter Command was clearly as active as ever and the Luftwaffe was unable to achieve the necessary air superiority. On 17 September he postponed *Sealion* until further notice, and on 12 October announced that it would take place in 1941. That meant never, for he soon reached the decision to attack the Soviet Union instead

Raeder thankfully dispersed his barges, but Göring, unwilling to accept defeat, continued the battle into October with fighter-bomber intrusions carried out by modified Messerschmitt Bf 109s, Bf 110s and Junkers Ju 88s. These achieved very little. Comparative figures for the period 9 September–6 October show that the Luftwaffe lost 134 bombers plus 59 seriously damaged, and 176 fighters plus 27 seriously damaged; Fighter Command lost 228 aircraft plus 24 seriously damaged.

While *Sealion* had become a dead duck, the Luftwaffe continued night raids on British cities and industrial targets until the following May, when most of its strength was transferred to the east for the invasion of the Soviet Union. These raids killed some 40,000 civilians, injured another 46,000, and destroyed or damaged one million homes as well as much industrial and commercial property, for the cost of about 600 aircraft. It is only in fairly recent years that German historians have come to regard the Battle of Britain as an issue complete in itself rather than as part of the continuous German air activity directed against the United Kingdom from July 1940 to May 1941. During the battle itself the Luftwaffe lost 1,733 aircraft and Fighter Command 915.

Could the Luftwaffe have won the battle? Air Vice-Marshal J. E. Johnson, a participant, provides a chilling answer in his book *Full Circle*

– *The Story of Air Fighting*: 'Göring went about it the wrong way. He should have put out the eyes of Fighter Command by destroying the 19 radar stations between the Wash and the Isle of Wight, destroyed RAF fighters by strafing and their communications by bombing. Simultaneously with the radar attacks the six fighter airfields near the coast between Tangmere and the Thames, the five sector stations near London, and the Headquarters of Fighter Command and 11 Group, at Bentley Priory and Uxbridge respectively, should have been struck. Small, compact formations should have attacked each of these 32 targets two or three times a day until reconnaissance showed that further blows were unnecessary. The enemy's night bombers should have been dovetailed into the same plan and directed against the sector stations and aeroplane factories.' Fortunately, Göring possessed neither the insight nor the professionalism to reach such conclusions.

The Battle of Britain was a decisive event in history not only because it provided the first check to Hitler's career of conquest, but also because if the Luftwaffe had triumphed the world today would be a different place. More immediately, Great Britain's lonely stand as the bastion of freedom and democracy earned world-wide admiration. In its immediate aftermath she recovered her self-confidence and, with generous American assistance, grew stronger by the month. Before the year ended she would, with slender resources, cripple the Italian battle fleet in Taranto harbour and inflict a crushing defeat on the large Italian army in North Africa.

Of the 3,080 pilots who flew with Fighter Command at some period of the Battle of Britain, 481 were killed and 422 were wounded or seriously injured. Of the remainder, more than 800 would be killed before the war ended. While the battle was at its height, Winston Churchill, reflecting upon the nature of the fighting and the young men who daily took off to face apparently impossible odds, passed his immortal judgement on Dowding's pilots: 'Never in the field of human conflict was so much owed by so many to so few.'

MIDWAY, 4–6 JUNE 1942

To bring her war with China to a victorious conclusion, Japan needed the vital supplies of tin, rubber and oil that could only be obtained from territories under British, French, Dutch or American control. When those supplies were denied her, she embarked on a series of pre-emptive strikes to secure them, believing that this would place her in a strong position when the time for negotiations came. Her success, both on land and at sea, was won by her ability to deploy concentrated air power in overwhelming strength against disjointed Allied forces scattered across a vast area. In particular, her naval air arm was the largest and best-equipped in the world, demanding the highest standards from its aircrews.

The Japanese may have seen nothing dishonourable in beginning their attacks before a state of war formally existed and, it will be recalled, had begun the Russo–Japanese War of 1904–5 in a similar manner. Nothing, however, could have been more calculated to enrage American public opinion than the treacherous attack on the US Pacific Fleet at Pearl Harbor on 7 December 1941, a date described by President Roosevelt as 'a day which will live in infamy'. Furthermore, although the USA had withdrawn into isolation between the wars and maintained only small regular armed forces, her industry had recovered from the world economic recession of the early 1930s and was geared to the concept of mass production, which could easily be applied to the manufacture of aircraft, tanks and warships. For all her apparent success, all Japan had succeeded in doing was waking a sleeping giant who, in the long term, was absolutely determined to crush her.

Meanwhile the Imperial Japanese Navy went where it liked and did what it wanted. In March 1942 its aircraft carriers penetrated the Indian Ocean, sinking one British carrier, HMS *Hermes*, two cruisers and a destroyer for trifling loss, while a raiding force entered the Bay of Bengal and sank 150,000 tons of merchant shipping. The following month sixteen USAAF Mitchell bombers, flying off the carrier USS *Hornet*, raided Japan itself, causing consternation but little damage. On 7 and 8 May the Japanese received an unexpected check at sea when, as a result of the Battle of the Coral Sea, they were forced to abandon a landing at Port Moresby, New Guinea. This was the first occasion in naval history when the opposing fleets never sighted each other, relying exclusively on carrier strikes delivered from a range of about 120 miles. Of the two US carriers present, *Lexington* sustained bomb and torpedo damage that proved fatal and *Yorktown* was sufficiently damaged to require repair at Pearl Harbor; the Americans also lost a destroyer sunk and a tanker damaged. Of the three Japanese carriers, *Shoho* was sunk and *Shokaku* was badly hit and took several months to repair, while during the air fighting so many of *Zuikaku*'s aircrews were lost that she was withdrawn for a month while their replacements were trained. In material terms the Japanese had come off slightly the better, but strategically the Americans were the victors and in the weeks to come the absence of *Shokaku* and *Zuikaku* was to have a bearing on subsequent Japanese operations.

Easy conquests had made the Japanese a prey to what they now call the Victory Disease. Admiral Isoroku Yamamoto, Commander-in-Chief of the Imperial Navy's Combined Fleet, was one of those who believed that Japan could not afford a protracted war with the USA and he warned against what he called 'mindless rejoicing'. Concerned by the US air attack on Japan and the result of the Coral Sea battle, he was anxious to extend the area of Japanese power eastwards to include islands in the Aleutian chain and Midway Atoll, halfway across the Pacific. This, he reasoned, would make life very difficult for his opponent, Admiral Chester Nimitz, Commander-in-Chief of what remained of the US Pacific Fleet, in that Midway lay within striking distance of Pearl Harbor. Furthermore, on Midway, a mere three square miles of which lay above sea level, the Americans had already built an air base, and as Nimitz could hardly ignore a threat to

this the opportunity presented itself for a major battle in which the Pacific Fleet could be destroyed altogether.

There were numerous elements in Yamamoto's complex scheme. Northern Force under Vice-Admiral Hoshiro Hosagaya, led by Rear-Admiral Kakuta's 2nd Carrier Striking Force, consisting of the small carriers *Ryujo* and *Junyo*, two cruisers and three destroyers, was to leave for the Aleutians on 25 May, followed two days later by escorted transports carrying the troops detailed for the invasion of Attu and Kiska Islands. Should Nimitz attempt to interfere he would find that a Guard Force under Vice-Admiral Shiro Takasu, consisting of four battleships, two cruisers and twelve destroyers, had been positioned on the direct route between Pearl Harbor and the Aleutians. Meanwhile, Vice-Admiral Chuichi Nagumo's 1st Carrier Striking Force, consisting of the fleet carriers *Akagi*, *Kaga*, *Hiryu* and *Soryu*, escorted by two battleships, four cruisers, a light cruiser and eight destroyers commanded by Vice-Admiral Nobutake Kondo, was to neutralise Midway's defences with an air attack on 4 June, after which the invasion force would take possession of the atoll with direct gunfire support provided by four heavy cruisers and two destroyers under Vice-Admiral Takeo Kurita. The Japanese Main Body, commanded personally by Yamamoto in his new flagship *Yamato*, armed with eight 18-inch guns and the biggest battleship afloat, also contained two 16-inch gun battleships, the light carrier *Zuiho*, a light cruiser, nine destroyers and two seaplane tenders. This force was to be positioned centrally so that it could intervene decisively in whichever threat Nimitz chose to counter. As a precaution, two flying-boats delivered by submarine to French Frigate Shoal, 500 miles north-west of Hawaii, were to keep Pearl Harbor under observation from 31 May to 3 June and report on US activity. Additionally, submarine patrol lines were to be established north, north-west and west of Hawaii by 2 June.

Yamamoto's plan was ingenious if over-complicated, and contained typically Japanese elements of bluff and double-bluff. Unfortu-

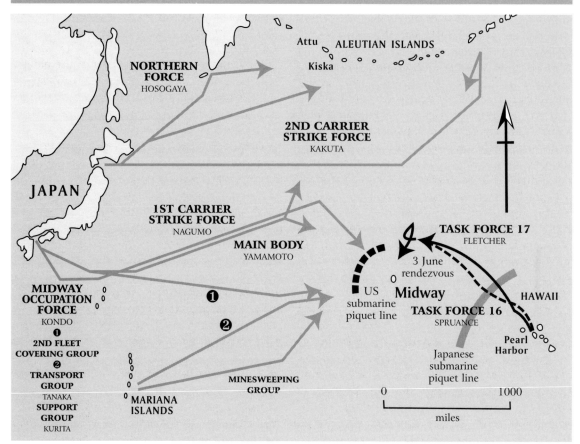

nately for him US cryptanalysts had cracked the Japanese naval code and its broad outline was already in Nimitz's possession. From the outset, therefore, the diversionary nature of the Aleutian operations was apparent, although Nimitz, anxious for the future security of Alaska, did detach a task force of five cruisers and ten destroyers northwards.

On 26 May the US carriers *Enterprise* and *Hornet* of Task Force 16 (TF 16) entered Pearl Harbor. The task force commander, Vice-Admiral William F. Halsey, was ill and required immediate hospitalisation, his place being taken by Rear-Admiral Raymond A. Spruance. Having replenished, Spruance's carriers left again on 28 May and, escorted by six cruisers and nine destroyers, disappeared over the western horizon. Meanwhile *Yorktown*, the surviving carrier of TF 17, had entered Pearl Harbor the previous day, still bearing plentiful signs of the battle damage sustained in the

Coral Sea. Dockyard crews immediately swarmed over her and, working round the clock, returned her to a battle-worthy state within 48 hours. On 30 May TF 17, consisting of *Yorktown*, two cruisers and five destroyers, sailed again under the command of Rear-Admiral Frank Fletcher, who was to assume overall operational command when his ships joined TF 16 in an area designated 'Point Luck', some 350 miles north-east of Midway.

Fletcher had a definite advantage in that he was aware of the enemy's general intentions. Yamamoto, moreover, was not even aware of his presence in the area, for both task forces had sailed over the Japanese patrol lines before the scouting submarines reached them and the flying-boat mission had been aborted when French Frigate Shoal was discovered to be in American hands. In other respects, however, the odds were stacked against Fletcher. He had three carriers to pit against five, no battleships at all, eight cruisers against sixteen, and fourteen destroyers against 46. In the air, the balance was more even, for although his carriers could put up 230 aircraft against the Japanese 262, some 50 aircraft already based on Midway could be added to the equation.

It was a Midway-based Catalina flying-boat which first sighted the Japanese, some 700 miles west of the atoll, early on 3 June. During the day nine USAAF B17 bombers delivered three high-altitude attacks on the enemy ships without loss to either side. Taking advantage of bright moonlight, four Catalinas launched a torpedo strike in the small hours of 4 June, hitting a tanker but not inflicting fatal damage. This activity was duly noted by Fletcher, who ordered TFs 16 and 17 to steam to a position 200 miles north of Midway.

Shortly before dawn on 4 June scouting aircraft left Nagumo's 1st Carrier Striking Force to search areas extending 300 miles to the east and south. Simultaneously, the decks of his four large carriers were busy preparing the force that was to carry out the preliminary air strike on Midway. This consisted of 36 Nakajima B5N2 Kate torpedo-bombers each armed with a 1,770-pound bomb-load, 36 Aichi D4A2 Val dive-bombers each with one 551-pound bomb, and an escort of 36 Mitsubishi A6M2 Zero fighters. By 04.45 the raiders were well on their way.

At 05.20, however, a Catalina was observed shadowing the Japanese carriers, and although some of their fighter screen set off in pursuit it vanished into the clouds. At 05.34 its radio operator began transmitting details of Nagumo's force, including its position and composition, direct to Fletcher, together with a report that numerous enemy aircraft were heading towards Midway. By 06.03 Fletcher knew that Nagumo was just 200 miles away to the south-west. He ordered Spruance to proceed with TF 16 in that direction and attack as soon as the enemy carriers had been located; he would follow with TF 17 as soon as *Yorktown* had recovered her scout aircraft.

On Midway radar picked up the incoming raiders at 05.53. During the next seven minutes every aircraft on the island was scrambled, the bombers and flying-boats to remain out of harm's way to the south, the Marine Corps fighters, mainly consisting of the elderly Brewster Buffalo, climbing to their combat altitude, while a counter-strike force of ten Avenger and Devastator torpedo-bombers set off for the enemy carriers.

As the raiders closed in, the Marine fighters swooped down on them, shooting down four of the bombers and damaging more. The Zero escort then intervened, shooting down sixteen of the American fighters and damaging a further seven beyond repair, at a cost of two of their number. Three more Japanese aircraft were destroyed by anti-aircraft fire, but the remaining bombers broke through to release their bombs on hangars, fuel tanks and other installations; significantly, the Japanese did not bomb the runways, which they required for their own use. By the time the raiders droned away, Midway's fighter cover had been reduced to five aircraft. Nor did the counter-strike force fare any better. Although it lacked fighter protection, several of its aircraft broke through the swarm of defending Zeros at about 07.10 and launched their torpedoes. At this stage of the war the American torpedo was comparatively slow-running and the Japanese were able to take evasive action. Only three of the torpedo-bombers returned to the island. The Midway garrison, however, refused to be intimidated and immediately began preparing a second and larger counter-strike with its bombers.

It was to be a strange and recurring theme throughout the battle that even apparent Japanese successes contained the seeds of destruction. At 07.00 the officer responsible for the raid on Midway, a Lieutenant Tomonaga, had signalled Nagumo to the effect that a second strike would be required to suppress the island's defences. At that moment *Akagi* and *Kaga*'s Kate torpedo-bombers were ranged on deck, armed with torpedoes against what seemed the remote possibility of intervention by American surface units. Tomonaga's report was reinforced by the first Midway counter-strike which confirmed that the garrison was still evidently full of fight. Five minutes after it had been beaten off, Nagumo gave orders that the Kates were to be struck down and re-armed with fragmentation, incendiary and high-explosive bombs, a process that would take about an hour.

At 07.28, however, Nagumo received an alarming transmission from the cruiser *Tone*'s scout aircraft, which had been late leaving because of technical problems with her catapult. It reported the presence of ten apparently enemy warships an estimated 240 miles from Midway, but did not specify their type. Nagumo was now on the horns of a dilemma, for if the enemy force included carriers he must launch a strike as soon as he was within range. At 07.45 he gave orders for the Kates to re-arm with torpedoes and armour-piercing bombs. Even among a people as polite and a service as disciplined as the Japanese, the comments of the sweating hangar crews cannot have been less than sulphurous. When, at 08.10, *Tone*'s scout reported that the enemy force consisted of five cruisers and five destroyers, Nagumo visibly relaxed.

The respite was to be of short duration, for within minutes Midway's second counter-strike came in. It was delivered by fifteen USAAF B17s which attacked from 20,000 feet, and 26 Marine dive-bombers and light bombers which came in much lower. This time the interception was less severe and only two Vindicators were lost. On the other hand, while some of the Japanese carriers temporarily vanished behind curtains of water thrown up by exploding bombs, no hits were obtained. At this point the American submarine *Nautilus*, one of twelve forming a screen west of Midway, entered the fight. Commanded by Lieutenant Commander William H. Brockman, *Nautilus* had penetrated Nagumo's screen of escorts and her periscope revealed a scene of bursting bombs, barking anti-aircraft guns, snarling aircraft and ships taking evasive action. Her plume of spray caused further confusion, attracting wild gunfire while escorts closed in with their depth-charges. Brockman fired two

torpedoes at a battleship then took *Nautilus* down to 150 feet, where she was forced to endure protracted depth-charging. His courage deserved better immediate reward, for one torpedo stuck in its tube and the battleship evaded the other, but the submarine's presence would ultimately produce what proved to be decisive results.

In the midst of this uproar *Tone*'s scout transmitted a further report containing the news that Nagumo least wanted to hear: a carrier had been identified as part of the American force. Simultaneously he became a prey to the demands of the moment and conflicting advice. His deputy, Rear-Admiral Tamon Yamaguchi, urged an immediate strike against the US task force. However, at that moment the aircraft which had raided Midway began to return, some shot up and all running short of fuel. If the strike was mounted they would be compelled to ditch because the carriers were unable to launch and recover aircraft concurrently. Nagumo turned to his operations officer, Commander Minoru Genda, for advice. Genda, against wasting either aircraft or trained pilots, pointed out that it would take just half an hour to recover Tomonaga's force, after which the strike against the American task force could proceed. Nagumo accepted this and, once more, every aircraft on deck was struck down while the raiders came in. Refuelling and re-arming began immediately, the aircraft being re-ranged on the flight decks as soon as they were ready. At 09.18 Nagumo ordered 1st Carrier Striking Force to alter course towards the reported American task force; for the moment Midway would have to wait.

Admiral Spruance's aircraft had begun getting airborne at 07.02, but all had not gone well for them. In four groups, they had headed for Nagumo's estimated position, but found nothing because the Japanese had altered course. *Hornet*'s dive-bombers and their fighter escort had flown on until fuel exhaustion forced the former either to land on Midway or return to their ship, while all of the latter ditched in the sea. At about 09.30, however,

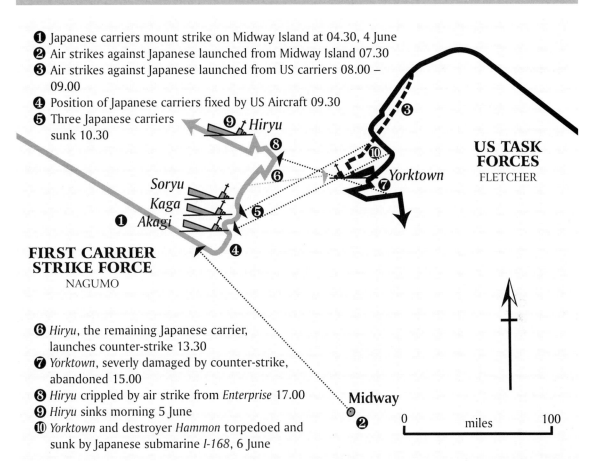

❶ Japanese carriers mount strike on Midway Island at 04.30, 4 June
❷ Air strikes against Japanese launched from Midway Island 07.30
❸ Air strikes against Japanese launched from US carriers 08.00 – 09.00
❹ Position of Japanese carriers fixed by US Aircraft 09.30
❺ Three Japanese carriers sunk 10.30

US TASK FORCES
FLETCHER

Hiryu

Yorktown

Soryu
Kaga
❶ *Akagi*

FIRST CARRIER STRIKE FORCE
NAGUMO

❻ *Hiryu*, the remaining Japanese carrier, launches counter-strike 13.30
❼ *Yorktown*, severely damaged by counter-strike, abandoned 15.00
❽ *Hiryu* crippled by air strike from *Enterprise* 17.00
❾ *Hiryu* sinks morning 5 June
❿ *Yorktown* and destroyer *Hammon* torpedoed and sunk by Japanese submarine *I-168*, 6 June

Midway

0   miles   100

the torpedo squadrons from *Enterprise* and *Hornet*, commanded respectively by Lieutenant Commanders Eugene Lindsey and John Waldron, had turned north and were rewarded almost immediately with the sight of the enemy's funnel smoke. They were out of contact with their fighters but decided to launch an immediate attack, knowing this to be suicidal. Waldron went in first, his lumbering Devastators ploughing low through the wall of anti-aircraft fire from the escorting cruisers and destroyers, only to be bounced by the Zeros of the carriers' combat air patrols. Although a torpedo was launched here and there, and easily evaded, the result was a massacre. Five minutes later it was the turn of Lindsey's squadron, which near-missed *Hiryu* and *Soryu* but lost ten of its fourteen aircraft. Hardly had the Zeros chased off the survivors than *Yorktown*'s air group arrived, having set out

later than those of TF 16 but flown straight to the target area. Whereas the two previous attacks had been delivered against the enemy's starboard side, Lieutenant Commander Lance Massey, commanding *Yorktown*'s torpedo-bombers, decided to approach from the opposite side, escorted by six Wildcat fighters. Although two torpedoes passed within 50 yards of *Kaga*, the result of the attack was the same; only two of the Devastators survived, one Wildcat was shot down and two more were driven off, severely damaged. Wild jubilation took hold of the Japanese carrier crews, now more convinced than ever that I Carrier Striking Force was invincible. Within minutes, however, events would take place that would alter the entire complexion of the battle.

Enterprise's dive-bomber squadron, under Lieutenant Commander C. Wade McClusky, had reached the anticipated point of interception only to find the sea deserted. It had continued on a south-westerly course for a while before beginning a sweep to the north-west. During this, McClusky spotted a Japanese destroyer steering north-east at high speed. She was the *Arashi*, left behind to depth-charge the *Nautilus*. McClusky, correctly deducing that she was hurrying to rejoin the carrier force, decided to follow. He arrived above Nagumo's carriers just as *Yorktown*'s dive-bombers, under Lieutenant Commander Maxwell Leslie, were approaching from the opposite direction.

Aboard the carriers, most eyes were watching the destruction of the Wildcats and Devastators, whose self-sacrifice had not been in vain. Nagumo had given the order to launch the strike against the American task force and the attention of senior officers was concentrated on their flight decks, where the massed aircraft were ranked tightly together. Suddenly, at about 10.25, the rising note of engines caused them to look up. To their horror, they saw the first of McClusky's and Leslie's 35 Dauntless dive-bombers, growing larger by the second as they bored down on their targets. Frantic helm orders set the carriers turning to port or starboard. Desperately, Zeros of the combat air patrol, their ammunition all but expended after the sea-level battle with the Devastators and Wildcats, strove to gain height. It was all too late.

In *Akagi*, Nagumo's flagship, one bomb landed among the packed aircraft. Exploding petrol tanks, bombs and torpedoes created a gigantic fireball which killed everyone in the vicinity and threw wrecked aircraft about like toys. A second bomb penetrated the flight deck to burst in the hangar below, where the discarded bombs from successive re-armings still lay about. Explosion followed explosion, the raging fires quickly becoming an inferno as they were fed by ruptured fuel lines. Captain Taijiro Aoki, the carrier's commander, knew at once that his ship was doomed and persuaded Nagumo to transfer to the light cruiser *Nagara*.

One bomb exploded just forward of *Kaga*'s superstructure, hitting a parked fuel truck, the fireball from which swept back over the bridge, incinerating everyone there. Three more came down among the ranked aircraft, triggering such huge fires and explosions that it was quickly apparent that the ship was beyond saving. On *Soryu* the story was the same. One bomb penetrated the hangar deck, its explosion flinging the aircraft lift back against the bridge; two more landed among the parked aircraft. Twenty minutes later the order was given to abandon ship.

The three blazing hulks remained afloat throughout the day, *Kaga* and *Soryu* to sink during the evening while *Akagi* was dispatched by torpedoes from one of her own destroyers. In the interim, the submarine *Nautilus* had reappeared and fired a torpedo into *Kaga*, but like so many American torpedoes at this time it failed to explode. Most Zero pilots of the combat air patrol, having no home to return to, flew until their fuel was exhausted and splashed down beside the escorts to await rescue.

In less then ten minutes the balance of naval power in the Pacific had altered dramatically, although the battle of Midway had far from run its course. The carrier *Hiryu* had escaped the disaster because her manoeuvres to avoid the Devastators' torpedoes had taken her some distance from her sisters and when McClusky and Leslie had delivered their attack she was obscured by cloud cover. Aboard her, Rear Admiral Yamaguchi promptly ordered a retaliatory strike which began taking off at about 11.00, following the direction taken by the retiring US aircraft. Shortly after noon the incoming raiders were picked up on *Yorktown*'s radar. They were cut to pieces by the combat air patrol and anti-aircraft fire, but, displaying the same self-sacrificial courage as their American counterparts, several broke through to land three bombs on the carrier. The first of these started a hangar fire but this did not have the same catastrophic results as those in the Japanese carriers because the fuel system had been drained down and flooded with inert carbon dioxide gas. The second penetrated deep within the ship, starting fires which threatened the forward fuel tanks and magazine until brought under control. The third exploded inside the funnel, extinguishing half-a-dozen furnaces and destroying three boiler uptakes. The carrier lost way and within twenty minutes was lying dead in the water. Fletcher transferred his flag to the cruiser *Astoria*, returning full tactical control of TF 16, some 60 miles distant, to Spruance.

At first it was thought that the carrier would have to be taken in tow but her own engineers quickly effected repairs and she was soon working up to 20 knots. At this moment the second wave of the Japanese strike appeared. Led by Lieutenant Tomonaga, it consisted of escorted torpedo-bombers, many of which fell victim to the US fighters and anti-aircraft fire. Once again, however, the survivors bored in to drop their torpedoes at point-blank range. Two struck *Yorktown* on her port side, blowing holes in her fuel tanks and causing flooding which quickly resulted in a list of 26 degrees. At about 15.00, with all power lost and the possibility of capsize apparently imminent, Captain Elliott Buckmaster gave the order to abandon ship.

On *Enterprise*, Spruance, aware that the fourth enemy carrier was still at large, received a report of her whereabouts from one of *Yorktown*'s search aircraft. At 15.30 twenty-four dive-bombers, including ten which had flown across from *Yorktown*, took off from *Enterprise*, followed at 16.00 by sixteen more from *Hornet*. Yamaguchi's combat air patrol, reduced to thirteen Zeros, did not spot them until they began their dive at about 17.00. Twist and turn as she might, *Hiryu* could not evade the rain of bombs. One peeled back the forward lift like the lid of a sardine tin and four more caused the same fatal series of explosions and fires that had destroyed her sisters. The strike was followed by a medium-level attack delivered by *Midway*'s B17 bombers. No hits were obtained but it was already apparent that the carrier was finished. Her crew continued to fight the fires until 02.30 then abandoned her to be torpedoed by the escorting destroyers.

At midnight Yamamoto, some 350 miles away with his Main Body, was thunderstruck to learn not only that Nagumo had lost all his carriers, but also that Midway's defences were

Right: Midway. The Japanese carrier *Hiryu*, ablaze and with her flight deck peeled back like a sardine tin. The loss of all four Japanese carriers radically altered the naval balance in the Pacific. *IWM Neg MH6492*

still intact. Detaching the light carrier *Zuiho* to render what assistance she could, he concentrated his battleships and steered east in the hope of pounding the US task force to destruction in a night action. Spruance had anticipated this reaction and, as his pilots were not trained for night flying, at sunset he too turned eastwards, maintaining the distance between the opposing fleets. At midnight he reversed course to bring his carriers within supporting distance of Midway by daylight. Yamamoto, having digested the full implications of the previous day's losses, not least of which was that the American carriers had a striking range 30 times greater than that of his battleships, became less emotional. Recognising that the enemy did not lie within his grasp, he ordered a general withdrawal at 02.55, together with a dawn bombardment of Midway by Vice-Admiral Kurita's squadron of four heavy cruisers.

Even in this, luck was running against the Japanese. As they approached the atoll from the west, the cruisers spotted the American submarine *Tambor*, commanded by Lieutenant Commander John W. Murphy, observing them in the moonlight. The submarine dived almost immediately, but Kurita, taking no chances, ordered his ships to make an emergency turn to port. The flashed signal did not reach the rearmost cruiser, *Mogami*, which collided heavily with her next ahead, *Mikuma*, sustaining very serious damage. Aborting his mission, Kurita left *Mikuma* and two destroyers to escort the crippled *Mogami* and set off to rejoin the fleet.

Tambor had got off a contact report at 03.00. Three hours later Midway's B17s took off but were unable to find the ships because of early morning haze. At 06.30, however, a Catalina reported 'two battleships streaming oil' 125 miles west of the atoll. Marine dive-bombers took off and, following the oil slick, launched an attack shortly after 08.00. No direct hits were scored, but Captain Richard E. Fleming's burning aircraft crashed on *Mikuma*'s after turret. Petrol spewed down the starboard engine room air intakes and exploded below, killing the crew and causing extensive damage. Both cruisers were now reduced to a maximum speed of 12 knots.

Below: The American carrier USS *Yorktown*, damaged by air attack and subsequently torpedoed by a Japanese submarine. *IWM Neg OEM22400*

During the afternoon of 5 June Spruance, thinking that Yamamoto could be found somewhere in the vicinity of the previous day's action, launched a strike of 58 dive-bombers. They found a solitary destroyer, Commander Motomi Katsumi's *Tanikaze*, sent by Nagumo to confirm that *Hiryu* had finally sunk, which they promptly attacked. Katsumi, however, knew his business. Twisting, turning, circling and doubling back at high speed, he evaded every bomb aimed at his ship, including those from a later B17 strike, and even shot down one of his attackers. The destroyer's only damage came from a near miss when a bomb fragment penetrated her No 3 turret, causing an explosion which killed the six men within.

The abandoned *Yorktown* had remained afloat during the night, and at noon on 5 June she was boarded by a salvage party and taken in tow. Unfortunately her continued presence had already been reported to Yamamoto by the cruiser *Chikuma*'s scout plane at 06.52, and he

had immediately ordered her to be sunk by Lieutenant Commander Yahachi Tanabe's submarine *I-168*.

During the night *I-168* had been bombarding Midway. On receipt of this new order Tanabe set course for his target 150 miles to the north. At first light on 6 June he approached from the west, the sky still dark behind him, slipped under the escorting destroyers to launch four torpedoes, then made good his escape. One torpedo struck the destroyer *Hammann*, moored alongside *Yorktown* to provide electric power for the salvage party, sending her to the bottom; two more exploded against the carrier's starboard side, blasting great holes through which the sea flooded into the hull. Even then, she refused to give up easily and did not slip under until 06.00 next day.

Elsewhere on 6 June Yamamoto sent Admiral Kondo south to assist the stricken *Mikuma* and *Mogami* with the light carrier *Zuiho*, six cruisers and eight destroyers. In the event, Admiral Spruance's dive-bombers found them first, sinking *Mikuma* and inflicting further damage on *Mogami*. Thanks to the seamanship of her skipper, Captain Akira Soji,

Below: In the later stages of the battle the Japanese cruiser *Mikuma* was reduced to a sinking wreck by American air attack. *IWM Neg NYF17584*

and the work of her damage control officer, Lieutenant Suruwatari, *Mogami*, more floating scrapyard than warship, succeeded in reaching her base at Truk with 40 feet of her bows missing.

That evening Spruance abandoned his pursuit and reversed course to rendezvous with his supply tankers. The Battle of Midway was over. In the immediate reckoning the Americans lost one carrier, one destroyer sunk, 147 land- and carrier-based aircraft and 307 men killed. Japanese losses amounted to four carriers and one heavy cruiser sunk, one heavy cruiser and two destroyers severely damaged, 332 aircraft, including those being transported to Midway for operational use after its capture, and about 3,500 men killed. The consequences of the battle went far deeper than mere statistics, as Masanori Ito comments in his book, *The End of the Imperial Japanese Navy*:

'Newspapers in Japan reported merely what Imperial General Headquarters authorised, which was that one American carrier had been sunk and one seriously damaged in a great naval battle, that Japan had won a great victory in invading the Aleutian Islands, and that there had been a naval action in the vicinity of Midway. News of the loss of four fleet carriers was dribbled out to the homeland public over a period of a year following the battle. In addition to Japan's loss of ships and planes there was a serious loss of men, especially of skilled pilots, who were thereafter in short supply for the remainder of the war. Survivors of sunken ships were held incommunicado until re-assigned, and they were under strict injunction to keep silent about the terrible defeat Japan had suffered. The facts of the Midway battle were not divulged to the people of Japan until after the end of World War II.'

In contrast, the US press reported the victory won by Fletcher and Spruance with banner headlines, taking much pleasure in the fact that the four enemy carriers sunk had all participated in the treacherous attack on Pearl Harbor. Yet, if Midway signalled the beginning of the end for the Imperial Japanese Navy, there was also sober recognition that a hard road still lay ahead. From August 1942 until January 1943 both sides sustained heavy losses in a series of fierce naval battles around the Solomon Islands. However, while the Japanese were unable to absorb such a severe rate of attrition, US shipyards were producing carriers by the dozen, cruisers by the score and destroyers, destroyer escorts and assault craft by the hundred. Inexorably, during the next three years, the Americans advanced island by island across the south and central Pacific and finally destroyed the remnant of the Imperial Japanese Navy off Okinawa.

SECOND ALAMEIN, 23 OCTOBER – 4 NOVEMBER 1942

So complete had been the defeat inflicted by General Sir Archibald Wavell's small army on Marshal Rodolfo Graziani's much larger Italian forces during the winter of 1940/41 that Hitler was compelled to dispatch German troops to shore up Mussolini's tottering North African empire.

In command of what became the Deutsches Afrika Korps was the then Lieutenant-General Erwin Rommel, who we last met commanding 7th Panzer Division during the 1940 campaign in France. Rommel had served as a company commander during the First World War and been awarded Imperial Germany's highest decoration, the *Pour le Mérite*, for his part in the Battle of Caporetto. He had enjoyed Hitler's favour since the latter had read his book *Infanterie Greift An* (*Infantry Attack!*) and at one stage had even commanded the Führer's bodyguard. Now aged 49, he possessed immense drive, energy and ambition. He had a genius for putting together *ad hoc* battle groups and leading them against what he correctly perceived to be an opponent's weakest point, but his impatience with higher authority and inclination to take unjustifiable risks were only vindicated by the remarkable results he produced. Luck, as Napoleon said, was the quality which separated the outstanding commander from the merely competent, forgetting perhaps that it was the lady's nature to be fickle.

Rommel's instructions were to recover the Libyan province of Cyrenaica. He was lucky in that most of Wavell's army had been sent to Greece and the remaining troops in the Western Desert were inexperienced and scattered. In a whirlwind offensive he swept across the province, failing only to take the port of Tobruk, which was to remain a thorn in his side. The rest of 1941 was taken up with British attempts to relieve the fortress. In hard fighting from 18 November to 20 December this was finally achieved and heavy losses forced Rommel to withdraw into Tripolitania. In January 1942, however, he received reinforcements and again mounted an offensive, catching his opponents off balance. On this occasion, while recovering the Benghazi Bulge, he only managed to advance as far as Gazala, where the two armies took up positions behind minefields stretching southwards to Bir Hacheim.

At this stage of the war, Axis strategy in the Mediterranean was sub-divided into two distinct phases. In the first, *Venezia*, the British Eighth Army was to be decisively defeated and Tobruk captured. There would then be an operational pause in the desert war during which *Herakles*, an airborne and amphibious invasion of Malta, would take place. In the opinion of Field Marshal Albert Kesselring, the capture of Tobruk would mean little unless the island of Malta, presenting as it did an incessant threat to Axis communications with North Africa, could be secured as well. Only when Malta was captured could sound plans be made for further operations against the weakened British presence in the Middle East. Hitler accepted this view, as did Göring and, for the moment, Rommel himself.

Rommel launched his offensive on 28 May, sweeping round Bir Hacheim with the intention of striking towards the coast and isolating Eighth Army. He was roundly beaten on the first day and forced back against the British minefields. Inexplicably his opponents delayed in delivering the *coup de grâce*. By the time they did mount piecemeal attacks he had been reinforced through minefield gaps and easily

Right: A Stuart light tank crew carrying out daily maintainance. The rail along the vehicle's side supported the dummy lorry canopy and cab known as 'the sunshade' and was subsequently used to stow packs and other items of personal kit. *IWM Neg E16097*

255

fended them off. He then broke out and, striking with concentrated force, defeated the British armour in detail. By 14 June the Gazala Line was no longer tenable and Eighth Army had begun a disorderly retreat into Egypt. On 21 June he stormed Tobruk and his triumph was complete.

Together, the Battle of Gazala/Knightsbridge and the capture of Tobruk won Rommel his field marshal's baton. Now, however, he became a prey to hubris. Ignoring the fact that the successful completion of *Venezia* was to have been followed immediately by *Herakles*, he used the huge quantities of fuel and vehicles captured in Tobruk to mount a pursuit which was intended to eliminate the British presence in Egypt altogether. Hitler, delighted, did not attempt to restrain him.

General Sir Claude Auchinleck, Commander-in-Chief Middle East, selected a defensive position running 40 miles south from El Alamein on the coast to the cliffs bordering the impassable Qattara Depression. When the badly battered Eighth Army retired into this, with the Axis Panzerarmee Afrika hot on its heels, he assumed personal command and in a hard-fought series of actions, known collectively as the First Battle of Alamein (1–27 July), halted Rommel's advance. Both armies dug in and began laying deep mine belts along their front.

Rommel was now faced with the unpalatable truth that he and his men were captives of his decision to penetrate so far into Egypt. The captured fuel and stores had been used up and with them went any chance of resuming his advance, yet retreat would promptly initiate the sort of mobile battle that the Axis armour lacked the resources to sustain. Because the RAF were mounting continuous raids on the ports of Benghazi, Derna, Tobruk and Bardia, most of his supplies were still coming through Tripoli, 1,000 miles to the west, so the amount of fuel reaching the front was barely enough to meet daily requirements. This was allocated to armoured formations in preference to the Luftwaffe and Regia Aeronautica, so the level of air support he had enjoyed at Tobruk was no longer available. To add to these difficulties submarines operating from Malta sank four supply ships in August, while aircraft accounted for a further three, a total of 40,043 tons.

Meanwhile, across the lines, there had been changes. Auchinleck was replaced by General Sir Harold Alexander and the largely unknown Lieutenant-General Bernard Montgomery assumed command of Eighth Army. To those who did know him, Montgomery had a reputation for orthodoxy, meticulous preparation and iron will. He was also noted for his abrupt manner, his ruthlessness and for being a bad enemy, yet to the few who became close to him he was also a good friend. Significantly, he came of that generation of infantry officers who had witnessed at first hand the slaughter on the Western Front in 1914–18 and were determined that never again would their troops be exposed to such pointless carnage.

Montgomery arrived in Egypt with two clear objectives in his mind. First, he was determined to root out the heresies that had bedevilled Eighth Army's operations for more than a year. Dispersion, in particular, would be replaced by concentration; instead of armour, infantry and artillery fighting their own individual battles, there would be sustained co-operation between all arms at every level; and it was quickly evident that the terms box, battle group and Jock column, so beloved in the old free-wheeling days, had no place whatever in current thinking. Senior officers unable or unwilling to accept this philosophy were quickly sent packing.

His second objective was to eliminate from his men's minds the deeply rooted and pernicious idea that Rommel was a super-general. He had taken over an army in which tired, demoralised men had become cynical about their generals' abilities, about the role of other arms and even whether British and Commonwealth divisions were pulling their respective weight. He therefore toured every unit possible, making himself personally known to the troops. As he wrote in his *History of Warfare*: 'My determination to deal firmly with Rommel

Above: A B-25 Mitchell bomber overflying a Sherman squadron in the Western Desert, 1942. *National Army Museum*

and his army once and for all was clearly expressed – to hit the Axis forces right out of Africa. But I was equally determined not to begin the attempt until we were fully prepared, and I said as much to officers and men.' Any new commander might have said much the same, but there was something about his incisive manner, his promise that there would be no more withdrawals, that the army would fight where it stood, and win, that created an instinctive trust in a leader who clearly knew what he was about. The soldiers also thought he was rather different from the usual run of generals: 'Doesn't wear his brass hat – borrowed a black beret from some bloke in the Royal Tank Regiment and hung on to it ever since!'

Before Montgomery could begin preparations for his decisive battle he had one other matter to deal with. Rommel, acutely conscious not only of the dilemma in which he had placed himself, but also that Eighth Army was being reinforced at a rate which he could not hope to equal, had accumulated sufficient fuel for one last desperate gamble. This would consist of a breakthrough on the southern sector of the front, followed by the same right hook with which he had begun the Gazala

battle. This had been predicted by intelligence sources as early as 27 July and was subsequently confirmed by Ultra decrypts of transmissions on the German high-level command frequencies.

When Rommel began his attack during the night of 30/31 August nothing seemed to go right for him. The British minefields were deeper than had been anticipated and well covered with defensive fire. Casualties among the mine-lifting parties and their covering infantry were heavy, so progress was maddeningly slow. Several senior officers were killed or wounded while urging their troops forward. When, at first light, the RAF added to his torment, Rommel had been on the point of cancelling the operation, but at that moment his leading elements broke out of the minefields. Even then, further progress was delayed by a sandstorm and an area of soft going, so that it was not until late afternoon that the Axis spearheads swung north towards Alam Halfa ridge, lying directly across their path. Here they ran into a carefully prepared defence incorporating tanks, anti-tank guns and concentrated artillery fire. Unable to make progress, and lacking the fuel with which to manoeuvre, Rommel decided to abort the operation. During the next few days he retired slowly behind his own minefields, harried from every direction and bombed regularly by the RAF. The battle cost him 49 tanks, 60 guns,

400 transport vehicles, some 2,800 casualties and his precious reserve of fuel, all squandered without tangible result. Eighth Army lost 67 tanks, many of which were reparable; it had, moreover, recovered its confidence in itself.

Montgomery was now free to concentrate on his opponent's destruction. He planned to fight a 'crumbling' battle in which he would attack first in one place and then another, forcing Rommel to react and in so doing burn up his limited fuel supplies. Without fuel his tanks could not operate, nor could water be distributed to his troops, and without water the Axis army would disintegrate. Yet, because both sides had resorted to positional warfare, Montgomery appreciated that the battle would be akin to those of 1918, albeit fought with modern weapons, and therefore, as he put it, 'a killing match'. Much thought was therefore given as to how best to contain casualties.

It was immediately apparent that the infantry would play a more important role in the coming battle than ever before in the desert war. It would be they who protected the mine-clearing sappers while they worked, they who would fight to secure breaches in the enemy defences through which the armoured formations were to pass, and they who would write down their opponents in attritional combat. The infantry, therefore, would fight mainly at night and be given their own specialist armoured support. This consisted of Brigadier G. W. Richards' 23rd Armoured Brigade (8th, 40th, 46th and 50th Royal Tank Regiments) equipped with the Valentine Infantry Tank Mk III, under-gunned but reliable and well armoured. Richards evolved suitable tactics, the essence of which was that if the infantry were held up by machine-gun posts the tanks would deal with them, and if the tanks were held up by anti-tank guns, these would be eliminated by the infantry. Furthermore, once the infantry had taken an objective the tanks would remain with them to beat off counter-attacks until the former's anti-tank guns had been brought up and emplaced. Richards' brigade group, which included a regiment of Bishop self-propelled guns (25-pounders mounted on Valentine chassis) for good measure, rehearsed endlessly with the infantry divisions with which it was to fight, and in so doing broke down many of the prejudices which had grown up between the two arms.

As part of the return to orthodoxy, divisional and corps artillery was concentrated so that the fire of large numbers of guns could be switched from area to area by an efficient control system established by Brigadier Sidney Kirkman, Eighth Army's senior artillery officer, who had flown from the United Kingdom at Montgomery's request. Kirkman required every one of his batteries to contribute to the overall fire plan, even the Bofors light anti-aircraft batteries firing short bursts of tracer at timed intervals during night attacks to mark the axes of advance and the boundaries between brigades.

When Tobruk had fallen President Roosevelt had generously suggested to Churchill that the US 2nd Armored Division be sent to the Middle East. This would have been a lengthy process and instead it was decided to send 300 Sherman tanks and 100 M7 (Priest) 105mm howitzer motor carriages. These reached Egypt shortly after Alam Halfa. Like the Grant, which had served Eighth Army well at Gazala and Alam Halfa, the Sherman was armed with a 75mm gun, but whereas the Grant's was housed in a limited-traverse sponson, the Sherman's was mounted in a fully rotating turret and thus conferred numerous advantages, including the ability to fight fully hull-down. On the eve of the battle the Eighth Army had 1,035 gun tanks (Shermans, Grants, Valentines, Crusaders and Stuarts) in first-line service, plus 200 more in immediate reserve and approximately 1,000 more undergoing repair or modification in workshops, and coming on stream. In armoured brigades forming part of armoured divisions, regiments consisted of two 'heavy' squadrons with Shermans or Grants and one 'light' squadron with 2- or 6-pounder Crusaders, except in 4th Light Armoured Brigade which was equipped with fourteen Grants and 67 Stuarts. In addition, Eighth Army had 435 armoured cars of various types.

Apostle of orthodoxy though he was, Montgomery also accepted the valuable contribution that could be made by special forces, in which a few highly trained and motivated men could achieve results denied to larger formations. Of those available to him, the Long Range Desert Group and the 1st Special Air Service Regiment were particularly important. The LRDG, originally formed by a notable desert traveller, Major Ralph Bagnold, operated from oases far to the south of the main battle area, its patrols penetrating the vast empty spaces far to the enemy's rear, there to carry out reconnaissance of specific objectives, intelligence-gathering missions which included surveillance of traffic on the coast road, insertion and extraction of agents and SAS teams, and occasionally direct action such as harassing attacks, ambushes and minelaying.

The SAS, originally known as 'L' Detachment Special Air Service Brigade, had been formed the previous year as a specialist long-range raiding unit under Captain David Stirling, a Scots Guards officer serving with a Commando unit. Such was its success that by October 1942 'L' Detachment's strength had risen to 30 officers and 300 men and, under Stirling's command, it became the 1st Special Air Service Regiment. In the period immediately prior to Second Alamein it attacked German and Italian airfields, raided Benghazi and Tobruk and shot up traffic on the coast road. Such was its success that GHQ in Cairo signalled it to leave the Mersa Matruh–Tobruk railway alone because it would be needed after the battle. The SAS said they were sorry, but they had just blown it up! Altogether, they raided it seven times, depriving the Axis of its use for thirteen of the crucial 20 days before the battle began.

The deception plan for Second Alamein was similar to Allenby's at Megiddo, but on a much larger scale, the intention being to convince Rommel that the major blow would be struck on the southern sector of the front. It was under the overall control of Lieutenant-Colonel Charles Richardson, a prominent member of whose team was a Royal Engineer officer named Jasper Maskelyne, a stage magician in civilian life and now a camouflage expert. Maskelyne's most notable invention was the 'sunshade', a wood and canvas lorry canopy and cab which could be mounted on a tank and quickly removed. In this way the appearance of apparently harmless lorry parks in the north concealed the concentration areas of armoured formations, the tank tracks being obliterated by real lorries. In the south, the number of tank laagers began to increase steadily, but many of the tanks were expertly painted dummies mounted on truck chassis, their tell-tale tyre marks eliminated by weighted trailers with track links fastened to the wheels. Guns were similarly hidden or duplicated from scrap, and on the critical northern sector no increase in daily ammunition expenditure was permitted. In the north, too, more sunshields and bivouac tents hid stockpiled stores, while in the south just sufficient clues were left for the enemy's air reconnaissance to identify fuel and ammunition dumps that were really stage props. On the southern sector clearly defined tracks appeared, leading from base areas to the front, as did a 'water pipeline' made from fuel drums, complete with 'pumping stations' and 'storage towers' that were serviced daily by real vehicles and labour gangs. Likewise, make-believe armoured formations consisting of imaginary regiments began to simulate normal radio traffic on the southern sector, making just sufficient procedural slip-ups as to suggest that they were in the line and preparing for action. Finally, lest curious and unsympathetic Egyptians discover the truth and find ways of communicating with the Axis, Richardson had Eighth Army sealed off from the local populace during the final stages of preparation.

As deployed for battle, Montgomery's army now consisted of three corps. On the northern sector was Lieutenant-General Sir Oliver Leese's XXX Corps, consisting of 9th Australian Division, 51st (Highland) Division, 2nd New Zealand Division (containing two infantry brigades and 9th Armoured Brigade), 1st South African Division, 4th Indian Division and 23rd Armoured Brigade Group. On the southern sector was Lieutenant-General B. G. Horrocks' XIII Corps, consisting of 7th Armoured Division (including 1st Fighting French Brigade Group), 44th Division and 50th (Northumbrian) Division, which had sustained serious losses at Gazala and now incorporated 2nd FF and 1st Greek Infantry Brigade Groups. Behind XXX Corps and over-laying its rear areas was Lieutenant-General H. Lumsden's X Corps containing 1st and 10th Armoured Divisions. Montgomery's plan for Operation 'Lightfoot', the opening phase of the battle, required XIII Corps to mount holding attacks on the southern sector while XXX Corps delivered the main blow in the north, capturing the minefields and clearing two corridors through which the armoured divisions of X Corps were to pass.

Following his repulse at Alam Halfa, Rommel could only prepare to meet the coming onslaught as best he could. His advance into Egypt had resulted in the cancellation of *Herakles* (the invasion of Malta) but his Panzerarmee Afrika had been reinforced with two formations that had been earmarked for that operation, the German Ramcke Parachute Brigade and the Italian *Folgore* Parachute Division. Neither possessed adequate transport, but without their presence the line could not have been held adequately. As it was, German units were dispersed along its length to stiffen poorly equipped Italian formations which were luke-warm in the common cause. To meet the coming assault, the minefields were extended to a depth of between two and five miles. The infantry was ordered to hold its forward line with a minimum of troops and to occupy a main position well to the rear, where it would escape the worst effects of the British bombardment. Unsettled by Richardson's deception plan, Rommel divided his four armoured divisions into two groups, 15th Panzer and *Littorio* in the north and 21st Panzer and *Ariete* in the south. Should the British armour succeed in emerging from the minefields it was to be halted by dug-in anti-tank gun screens and counter-attacked before it could deploy its superior numbers.

Panzerarmee Afrika would be at a serious disadvantage in terms of *matériel*. Against the substantial numbers fielded by Eighth Army it could deploy only 520 tanks. Of these, thirty were the long-barrelled 75mm Pz Kpfw IVF2, the most powerful tank on either side; eighty-eight were up-gunned 50mm Pz Kpfw III Model Js, eighty-five were short 50mm Pz Kpfw IIIs and the rest obsolete and unreliable Italian M13s. In workshops were a further thirty-two tanks, mostly Pz Kpfw IIIs. Given the obvious format of the coming battle, there would be little use for the 192 armoured cars. In artillery the contrast was equally marked, 908 British field and medium guns being opposed by 500 field and eighteen heavy guns. Anti-tank guns, however, were a special case, for while the British possessed 1,451 of them and the Axis only 800, of which the 300 Italian 47mm guns were obsolete, the Germans had a marked qualitative edge. Their dual-purpose 88, of which they had eighty-six, was a fearsome long-range tank killer, the 76.2mm PaK 36(r), a captured Russian weapon, had proved extremely efficient, and the excellent 75mm PaK 40 was reaching the front in small numbers. Even the older 50mm PaK 38, while not effective against the Sherman, Grant and Valentine, except at short range, could give a good account of itself against the Crusader and Stuart. It was therefore apparent that for all the British *matériel* superiority on the ground and an air superiority of five aircraft to three, breaking through the Axis position would not be a pushover. Having done everything he could, Rommel, worn down with stress, departed for home and sick leave on 23 September, handing over temporary command of Panzerarmee Afrika to General Georg Stumme.

The battle began at 21.40 on 23 October with a heavy bombardment by 592 British guns, 456 of which had been crammed into XXX Corps' sector, firing concentrations which exploded in the Axis artillery positions until 21.55. From 22.00 to 22.07 further concentrations were fired against selected targets at the forward edge of the defended area and then the guns reverted to divisional control. While diversionary attacks went in on the southern sector, XXX Corps' mine-clearing parties, the infantry and their supporting Valentines began moving forward through the thundering dark-

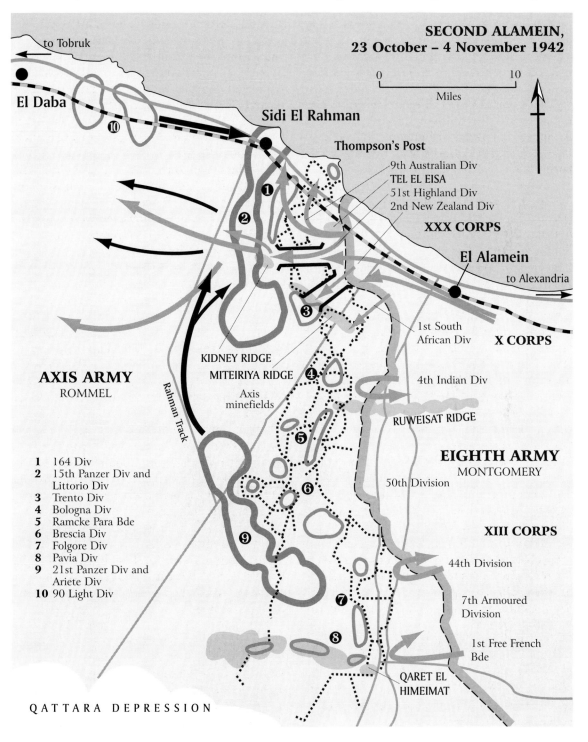

SECOND ALAMEIN,
23 October – 4 November 1942

0 10
Miles

to Tobruk

El Daba

Sidi El Rahman

Thompson's Post

9th Australian Div
TEL EL EISA
51st Highland Div
2nd New Zealand Div

XXX CORPS

El Alamein

to Alexandria

1st South
African Div

X CORPS

KIDNEY RIDGE
MITEIRIYA RIDGE

4th Indian Div

Axis
minefields

RUWEISAT RIDGE

AXIS ARMY
ROMMEL

Rahman Track

EIGHTH ARMY
MONTGOMERY

50th Division

1 164 Div
2 15th Panzer Div and
   Littorio Div
3 Trento Div
4 Bologna Div
5 Ramcke Para Bde
6 Brescia Div
7 Folgore Div
8 Pavia Div
9 21st Panzer Div and
   Ariete Div
10 90 Light Div

XIII CORPS

44th Division

7th Armoured
Division

1st Free French
Bde

QARET EL
HIMEIMAT

QATTARA DEPRESSION

261

ness, illuminated periodically by flickering gun flashes as they pushed lanes through in the Meteiriya and Kidney Ridge areas. Unexpectedly tough resistance delayed headway and although progress was made towards the enemy's main line, neither 10th Armoured Division in the north, nor 7th Armoured Division on the southern sector, had been able to break out of the congested lanes by morning.

Next day Stumme succumbed to a fatal heart attack and command of the Axis army devolved on Lieutenant-General Wilhelm Ritter von Thoma, commander of DAK. That night further attempts to get 7th and 10th Armoured Divisions through the minefields again proved abortive. On the 25th Montgomery decided to abandon the attempt and begin the process of 'crumbling' the enemy's front, ordering Lieutenant-General Sir Leslie Morshead's 9th Australian Division to attack on the coastal sector while Major-General

Raymond Briggs' 1st Armoured Division generated pressure on the enemy to the west of Kidney Ridge.

Rommel returned to the front that evening and immediately reached the conclusion that he was involved in 'a battle without hope'. He was shaken by the volume and flexibility of the enemy's 'tremendous' artillery fire and depressed by the way in which the British infantry and their Valentines kept gnawing into his defences in night attacks in which 'everything went methodically and according to a drill'. Despite the best efforts of his logisticians, his fuel stocks barely rose beyond the level required for two days' fighting. In the long term his prospects were even more bleak for between 26 October and 1 November the RAF

Below: A 5.5-inch medium howitzer opens fire. *IWM Neg E16776*

sank four ships carrying thousands of tons of fuel and ammunition, one of them on the point of entering Tobruk harbour.

As in most battles, some episodes during Second Alamein were really battles in themselves. About two miles to the west of Kidney Ridge lay the Rahman Track, which was the Axis army's principal means of lateral communication. In accordance with Montgomery's instructions to maintain pressure in the area, Briggs decided to cut it, but as the terrain between Kidney Ridge and the track was dangerously open he sent out two of his motor battalions during the night of 26/27 October to secure two intervening localities code-named Woodcock and Snipe for use as a firm base for a further westward thrust by 1st Armoured Division.

Woodcock was found to be untenable and was only occupied briefly, but the 2nd Battalion The Rifle Brigade, under Lieutenant-Colonel Victor Turner, reached and consolidated a large hollow which it believed to be Snipe, the true location of which lay some 900 yards to the north. At this point it should be mentioned that the motor battalion was much smaller than the conventional infantry battalion but had higher firepower and greater mobility. Turner had thirteen 6-pounder anti-tank guns of his own, plus six manned by 239 Battery, 76th Anti-Tank Regiment, Royal Artillery, and while these were being dug-in and camouflaged with scrub around the perimeter he sent out his tracked carriers to reconnoitre. They soon discovered that the outpost had been established close to two tank laagers formed by 15th Panzer and *Littorio* Armoured Division. One of these they cheekily shot up, leaving enemy transport burning as they retired into the darkness. At about 03.45 the disturbed laager broke up, the nearest column heading straight for Snipe, unaware that the hollow was now in British possession. The leading vehicle, one of the priceless Pz Kpfw IV F2s, was knocked out at 30 yards' range and a tracked tank destroyer was also destroyed. The rest of the column sheered off to form a new laager to the west. The performance of the newly issued 6-pounders was clearly so superior to that of the old 2-pounders that the jubilant little garrison was in a mood to take on all comers. At 04.00, however, it sustained its first serious loss when the artillery's forward observation officer left the perimeter to examine the surrounding terrain and was captured by a German patrol. His absence was keenly felt, for now Turner lacked adequate means of controlling his supporting artillery.

With first light, at about 06.15, both enemy laagers broke up, still apparently oblivious of the menace concealed in the hollow. Turner's guns immediately went into action at ranges of up to 800 yards, destroying eight tanks from each group. The rest hastily made off to the west but by now the secret was out. Artillery fire, which was to last with varying intensity throughout the day, began to land in and around Snipe. At about 07.45 24th Armoured Brigade reached the crest of Kidney Ridge. One of its regiments, 47 RTR, began firing into Snipe from the rear and continued to do so until 08.00 when the outpost's guns began engaging 25 German tanks hull-down 1,000 yards to the west, setting three of them ablaze, whereupon 47 RTR moved forward to enter Snipe and 41 RTR came up on their left. Unfortunately instead of easing the situation this made it far worse. Intense tank, anti-tank, field and medium artillery fire flayed the area until 47 RTR, reduced to eleven tanks, pulled back behind Kidney Ridge at 09.00, leaving six of their Shermans burning inside the perimeter; 41 RTR, having lost twelve tanks, conformed to the move. Snipe's riflemen and gunners, albeit left to fend for themselves once more, were glad to see them go.

Almost immediately, Italian infantry were observed forming up for an attack to the south of the post. Turner sent out Lieutenant Dick Flower's carriers and, Brens hammering, they quickly put them to flight, inflicting heavy casualties and destroying two vehicles towing captured British 6-pounders. Next, thirteen Italian M13s came in from the south-west, backing off after four of them were knocked out. At 10.00 the Germans mounted a major

Above: Grant squadron advancing across good hard going. The Grant mounted a 75mm gun in the sponson and a 37mm gun in the turret. *The Tank Museum*

counter-attack against 24th Armoured Brigade, passing to the south of Snipe, detaching part of their force to overrun the post. This meant that the thin side armour of the tanks attacking Kidney Ridge was exposed to Snipe's guns, and that of those attacking Snipe was exposed to the British tanks on the ridge. Cross-trumped, the Germans withdrew at 11.00 after eight of their tanks had been set ablaze.

Apart from shelling, Snipe was now left alone for a while. The interior of the outpost had become a shambles of smoking tank hulks, shattered vehicles, wrecked guns and sprawled casualties. Only thirteen guns remained in action; 6-pounder ammunition was running low and no replenishment was possible across the bullet-swept open space separating Snipe from Kidney Ridge. Turner sent out the most seriously wounded in his three remaining carriers, one of which was hit in the process.

Meanwhile, British radio intercept operators were monitoring the enemy's command frequencies. If Turner's embattled riflemen and gunners had but known, Briggs' attempt to sever the Rahman Track was causing uproar. Rommel was determined to restore the situation with a major counter-attack, for which 21st Panzer Division was already driving north

along the track; in the meantime, the stumbling-block presented by Snipe must be removed from the path of the operation.

At 13.00 the brief lull ended when eight Italian tanks and a *Semovente* assault gun launched an attack against the south-western perimeter. Only one gun, that of Sergeant Charles Calistan, would bear, and Turner acted as his loader while Lieutenant J. E. B. Toms brought up ammunition in a burning jeep. Opening fire at 600 yards, Calistan set six of the enemy ablaze. When the survivors, disregarding their loss, still came on with machine-guns rattling, Calistan took them out with one round apiece, then calmly placed a can of water on the burning jeep to brew tea for three. The attack had been halted less than 200 yards from the defences.

The shelling continued. Turner's helmet was penetrated by a steel splinter, but, having had the wound dressed, he continued to make the rounds of his gun teams until he began hallucinating. By now most of the battalion's officers had been killed or wounded and senior NCOs were commanding some sectors of the perimeter. As the afternoon wore on, 2nd Armoured Brigade's tanks began appearing on Kidney Ridge to the north-east. Their supporting artillery regiment subjected Snipe to further bombardment for several minutes until advised of their error.

The enemy's counter-attack could be seen forming up some 1,200 yards west of Snipe. Two groups could be discerned: one of approximately 40 German and Italian tanks and the other of 30 German tanks. At 17.00 they began moving forward, but were evidently unfamiliar with the area for their route took them past the northern perimeter of Snipe, the presence of which they clearly did not suspect. The guns of 239 Battery opened fire at 200 yards' range and tanks lurched to a standstill, belching smoke and flames. Those that turned angrily towards Snipe were promptly engaged in flank by 2nd Armoured Brigade.

Below: A 6-pdr anti-tank gun crew undergoing live ammunition training. It was guns like this that inflicted a sharp defeat on the Axis armour at Outpost Snipe. *IWM*

Subjected to the same sort of cross-trumping that had taken place during the morning, the enraged German battle group commander had no alternative but to reverse off the killing-ground. As he did so, he ordered fifteen tanks from his second wave to attack the outpost's western perimeter. They came on steadily, machine-gunning continuously, covering one another's movements with their fire and taking advantage of every fold in the ground. Only three guns, those of Sergeant Hine, Sergeant Miles and Lieutenant Holt-Wilson, would bear, and their remaining ammunition averaged ten rounds apiece. When Miles was hit, Colour-Sergeant J. E. Swann crawled 30 yards from his own wrecked gun to take his place. At 200 yards the 6-pounders let fly, punching their rounds into four of the tanks. The rest came on, but when two more met a similar fate, the last within 100 yards of Swann's gun, they backed off to a distant hollow from which they continued to fire until last light, when they were seen moving away towards their laager.

This was the last attack directed against Snipe, and it had been the most dangerous. When it ended, the guns were down to three

rounds apiece and Turner had ordered his adjutant, Captain F. W. Marten, the senior unwounded officer, to burn the maps and codes.

At 23.00 Marten received permission to withdraw. Nearby the enemy were out picking up their own wounded and, by tacit agreement, neither side interfered with the other. Snipe's dead would have to be left where they lay, but the worst of the wounded were placed aboard what little transport remained to the battalion. The walking wounded were supported by their comrades in a small column, 200 strong, which trudged back towards the ridge. Only one of 239 Battery's guns could be brought out; the rest, their breech-blocks and sights having been removed, had to be left behind. In and around the now silent hollow lay the hulks of nearly 70 tanks and self-propelled weapon systems, only seven of which were British.

Word of the tremendous fight at Outpost Snipe spread through the Eighth Army like wildfire. The following month a Committee of Inquiry visited the site, reaching the intentionally conservative conclusion that the outpost had been responsible for the complete destruction of 21 German and eleven Italian tanks, plus five assault guns or tank destroyers, and that a further fifteen, possibly twenty, tanks had been knocked out and recovered, although it was doubtful whether these had been repaired by the time Second Alamein ended. This produced a grand total of 57, of which nineteen were awarded to 239 Battery and 38 to the 2nd Battalion The Rifle Brigade. The enemy's personnel losses could not be assessed, but were obviously much higher than the 72 casualties incurred by the garrison of Snipe. Turner received the Victoria Cross, Calistan the DCM and subsequently a commission; a high proportion of the officers and men present were also decorated. For his part, Rommel could claim to have prevented interdiction of the Rahman Track, but he could neither afford to lose tanks at this rate nor burn such quantities of fuel and commented personally on the outpost's 'tremendous anti-tank defence'.

Elsewhere, Morshead's Australians, regarded by Rommel as the finest assault infantry on either side, had maintained the crumbling process on the coastal sector. During the night of 28/29 October they had, with the support of 46 RTR, almost succeeded in isolating a heavily defended locality known as Thompson's Post, held by the German 164th Light Afrika Division and Bersaglieri. Rommel recorded that in a bitter battle lasting six hours a gap was blown in his line and that by morning III/Panzergrenadier Regiment 125 had been all but wiped out, while II/125th and a *Bersaglieri* battalion were cut off but still resisting fiercely in Thompson's Post.

The Australian attack was renewed during the night of 30/31 October with a northwards thrust towards the coast, designed to complete the isolation of the pocket. The railway was crossed, then the coast road, but casualties were severe and at first light the Australians dug in. Throughout the hours of darkness their supporting armour, Lieutenant-Colonel J. L. Finigan's 40 RTR, had made an agonisingly slow approach through minefields while the sappers cleared a path for them. Having personally had two tanks immobilised under him by mine damage, Finigan dismounted and led his regiment forward the rest of the way on foot, off-setting the dangers of mines and shellfire against the need to support the Australians. Near the railway he met Lieutenant-Colonel H. H. Hammar, commanding the Australian 2nd/48th Infantry Battalion. Hammar, suffering from a face wound, said that he doubted whether more than 60 of his men were still on their feet and asked Finigan to keep the enemy's heads down. Finigan therefore led the 40th across the railway, deploying it along the western edge of the Australian salient to engage targets of opportunity. At this stage the regiment was down to 32 Valentines although reserve crews were drawing repaired tanks and would be bringing them up during the day.

Rommel was immediately notified that 30 heavy (*sic*) tanks were attacking Panzer Grenadier Regiment 361, part of 90th Light Division, which formed his last line of defence.

Above: The Eighth Army's four Valentine regiments were brigaded together for infantry support on the northern sector of the front. The Valentine was well-armoured and reliable, but despite the impressive muzzle flash of its 2-pdr it was out-gunned by most German tanks. *IWM Neg E17437*

Determined that a breakthrough on the sensitive sector of the coast road must be prevented at all costs, he moved his headquarters to the ruined mosque of Sidi Abd el Rahman. At 10.00 he was joined by Thoma and they planned a counter-attack by 21st Panzer and 90th Light Divisions. This began at about 11.30 but made little progress against the incredibly stubborn defence put up by 40 RTR, supported by the 6-pounders of 289 Anti-Tank Battery, field artillery concentrations and periodic air attacks. The burden of the defence, however, was borne by the under-gunned Valentines, which became the target not only of the enemy's tanks and tank destroyers, but also of his anti-tank guns and artillery; for a while, too, they were engaged from the rear by unsubdued anti-tank gunners within Thompson's Post, until their own artillery dropped in smoke-shells that provided an eerie backdrop to this and further counter-attacks put in throughout the afternoon. Obstinately, 40 RTR refused to yield an inch although they were losing four tanks to the Germans' one and their personnel casualties amounted to nine officers and 35 men, a high proportion of the 3-man crews. From time to time the Australians peered over the edge of their slit trenches at the single line of Valentines which

267

was all that stood between them and being overrun. Some of the tanks were burning, some were smoking sullenly with their crews sprawled beside them, but always there were others banging away with their 2-pounders or spitting machine-gun fire. Once the sharpest critics of British armour, the Australians watched the unequal battle in something like awe. Their official history contains the following passage:

'No other comment need be made on the performance of the commanders and crews of the Valentines than that of the historian of the 2/48th Battalion, who had earned the right to judge how others fought. "The courage of these men", he wrote, "Made their action one of the most magnificent of the war."'

When dusk put an end to the fighting, the 40th rallied to re-arm and replenish just south of the railway. Even those of their Valentines which had not been penetrated had sustained varying degrees of internal damage from the continuous impact of projectiles of every kind. This included ruptured radiators, fuel tanks and leads as well as cracked batteries from which the electrolyte had drained away, so that once engines had been switched off the regiment was left with very few runners.

If Rommel was close to the end of his tether, Montgomery also had troubles, although they were of a different kind, stemming from the impatience of the War Cabinet in London, keen to announce a clear-cut victory yet presented daily with news of an apparently endless stalemate. Alexander shielded his army commander from the worst effects, but Montgomery could not fail to be aware of the criticism that was building up behind his back. He had calculated that it would take thirteen days to achieve the destruction of Panzerarmee Afrika and saw no reason why his basic plan should be altered to please the politicians. Nor was he unduly worried by renewed pressure on the Australians, forcing them to give up just

Below: British infantry advance past an abandoned German tank. *IWM Meg E16837*

sufficient ground for the Axis garrison in Thompson's Post to escape, as this clearly demonstrated that Rommel's attention was now firmly fixed on the coastal sector. That being the case, he again shifted the emphasis of the battle, planning a three-phase breakthough just north of Kidney Ridge under the code-name Supercharge.

The first phase was mounted by Major-General Freyberg's 2nd New Zealand Division which was now so short of men that the assaulting brigades were drawn from 50th and 51st Divisions, deployed with 151 Brigade, supported by the Valentines of 8 RTR, on the right, and 152 Brigade, supported by those of 50 RTR, on the left. At 01.05 on 2 November both brigades crossed their start-lines and advanced behind a creeping barrage towards their objectives while sappers toiled to complete minefield gaps. Casualties were sustained but large numbers of prisoners were taken and by 05.30 the break-in was complete. Significantly, a number of dug-in tanks were discovered in the enemy's forward defences, confirming that he was beginning to run short of fuel. Some were knocked out by the Valentines, some were stalked by infantry who lobbed grenades into the turrets, and some were simply abandoned by their crews. Others of the enemy, however, simply went to ground as the attack rolled over them and were to make a great nuisance of themselves during the day.

The second phase of Supercharge required Brigadier John Currie's 9th Armoured Brigade (3rd Hussars, Royal Wiltshire Yeomanry and Warwickshire Yeomanry) to advance through the newly established front line at 05.45 and overrun the anti-tank gun screen covering the enemy's main position beyond the Rahman Track; most of this was sited in depth on the shallow slopes of Aqqaqir Ridge, at the southern end of which was the mound of Tel el Aqqaqir which would give its name to the battle. Currie had been told that, if necessary, Montgomery was prepared to accept the complete destruction of the brigade, provided it could complete its task, and this was communicated to his regiments, though kept from those below the rank of squadron commander.

Two of the regiments reached the Phase II start-line on time, but the third, delayed in the minefields, was late. Currie, though aware of the risks, was determined to strike a concentrated blow and postponed the attack for 30 minutes. When, at 06.15, all three regiments, deployed in line and led by Currie in person, began what amounted to a mechanised cavalry charge, they were silhouetted against the lightening sky to the east. Nevertheless, the leading squadrons got in among the guns, crushing some or shooting down the crews of others, before being shot to pieces themselves. The remainder of Currie's tanks then became engaged in a murderous duel not only with the anti-tank guns but also with tanks from 15th and 21st Panzer Divisions.

The third phase of Supercharge required two armoured brigades from Briggs' 1st Armoured Division to pass through Currie's brigade, destroy the enemy's armour and break out into the desert beyond. Brigadier A. F. Fisher's 2nd Armoured Brigade (The Queen's Bays, 9th Lancers and 10th Hussars) was first to arrive, debouching from the minefield lanes at about 07.00. To their front lay a scene of fiery desolation. Most of 9th Armoured Brigade seemed to be burning, but here and there small groups of tanks were still firing defiantly. In the distance enemy tanks were also burning and wrecked anti-tank guns were strewn about the slopes of Aqqaqir Ridge. Closer to hand, British infantry and dismounted tank crews were fighting smaller but equally vicious battles against the German infantry who had been by-passed during the night.

2nd Armoured Brigade moved in among the wreckage of Currie's brigade and took up the fight, the intensity of which reached new levels as Rommel fed all his remaining armour into the battle. At 07.40 the situation changed dramatically. The sun emerged from the desert to the east, its piercing horizontal rays shining straight into the eyes of the German and Italian gunners. Now it was the British who began to score heavily, the fire of their tanks supplemented by that of 360 field and medium

Above: Axis tanks, self-propelled artillery and tank destroyers captured during the battle. *IWM Neg No E26958*

guns battering the defenders of Aqqaqir Ridge, which was also visited at regular intervals by Mitchell bombers. Overhead, approaching Stuka dive-bomber formations were bounced by Allied fighters, jettisoning their bombs on their own troops as they broke up and fled for home. A vivid description of this, the climactic tank battle of the desert war, is provided by the historian of the 9th Lancers:

'All day we were fired at continually from three sides by 88s and 105s [*sic*]. For hours the whack of armour-piercing shot on armour plate was unceasing. Then the enemy tank attacks started. Out of the haze in serried lines they came, the low, black shapes. B and C Squadrons repulsed no fewer than six determined attacks and the regiment finished the day with a score of 31, of which 21 were set on fire. In addition, five guns were knocked out by putting air-bursts just over their pits. Passing the gunpits later we saw whole crews lying across their guns.

'The terrific cross-fire was taking its toll. Two of C Squadron's Shermans were burnt out, one cruiser destroyed and five other Shermans knocked about. Our own infantry, dug in on the battlefield, suffered terribly, being killed by shells meant for us. In that torrent of shot and shell any man who moved was killed. We did what we could for them, but our attention was taken up in fighting for dear life.

'Time and again our tanks ran out of ammunition and as we could not afford to have one single tank out of the line the [supply] lorries had to rush forward across the shell-swept ground, taking what cover they could behind each tank.'

Not surprisingly, the common theme in the histories of those regiments present is that this was one of the hardest day's fighting they experienced in the entire war.

Thus far, Supercharge had succeeded in creating a deep, blunt salient in the enemy line. Shortly after 09.30 a strong counter-attack began to develop against the northern flank of this. It was met by the Valentines of 8 RTR, which had remained with their infantry, and the tiny but still belligerent remnant of Currie's brigade, amounting to little more than a squadron. At about 10.00 the leading regiment of Brigadier E. C. N. Custance's 8th Armoured Brigade, the Staffordshire Yeomanry under Lieutenant-Colonel James Eadie, began to emerge from the minefield. Observing the threat developing to the north, Eadie sent his Crusader squadron to assist in the defence, followed by the two 'heavy' squadrons as they arrived. After a protracted exchange of gunfire the enemy turned away, leaving several tanks and wrecked anti-tank guns behind. The rest of 8th Armoured Brigade, 3 RTR and the Nottinghamshire Yeomanry (Sherwood Rangers), were directed to the south-western sector of the salient, coming in on the left of 2nd Armoured Brigade, which took ground to its right.

Fighting continued until dusk descended on the battlefield. For those British units most closely involved it was difficult to say what, if anything, Supercharge had achieved. Currie's 9th Armoured Brigade had begun the operation with 94 tanks of which 75 had been knocked out, and 230 of its 400 crewmen had been killed or wounded. Yet its sacrifice had not been in vain, for 1st Armoured Division's losses for the day amounted to only 44 tanks knocked out and a further 40 damaged. Moreover, during the panic caused by Currie's attack, two squadrons of the Royal Dragoons, an armoured car regiment, had bluffed their way through the lines south of Tel el Aqqaqir and were now deep inside the enemy's rear areas, shooting up his transport and reporting his movements.

In fact, Supercharge had inflicted a fatal blow on Panzerarmee Afrika. Two-thirds of the anti-tank gun screen had been destroyed, as had 77 German and 40 Italian tanks. Thoma informed Rommel that, at best, he could field 35 German tanks on the morrow; that the Italians were unsettled and unwilling to hazard their thin-skinned M13 tanks in another such slugging match; and that there were no more German reserves to commit to the battle. Despite Hitler's demands that he stand fast,

Rommel decided that he must salvage what he could of his army. Those units that still had motorised transport should start withdrawing, covered by the defenders of Aqqaqir Ridge; the remainder would have to take their chance.

On 3 November Briggs and Thoma continued their battle of attrition, the former gaining some ground without being able to achieve a breakthrough. During the night, however, probes by 51st (Highland) and 4th Indian Divisions to the south of Tel el Aqqaqir revealed that the enemy had gone, and 4th South African Armoured Car Regiment slipped out to the west. The 7th Armoured Division, brought north in preparation for the break-though, fell on and destroyed the remnant of the Italian XX Corps, thus outflanking 15th and 21st Panzer Divisions on Aqqaqir Ridge, which were compelled to withdraw on 4 November. While he was co-ordinating the movements of his rearguard, Thoma's tank was knocked out and he became a prisoner of 2nd Armoured Brigade. On 5 November Custance's 8th Armoured Brigade, swinging north towards the coast, ambushed and destroyed a column of fourteen German and 29 Italian tanks, four guns and 100 trucks at Galal.

The Second Battle of Alamein was over. Montgomery had accurately predicted its length and also his own personnel casualties, which amounted to 13,500 of whom approximately 4,500 were killed. Five hundred of his tanks had been knocked out, of which all but 150 were repairable, and 110 guns had been destroyed by shellfire. In the air, 77 British and 20 American aircraft had been lost. Total Axis casualties amounted to 55,000 including 30,000 prisoners of whom 11,000 were German; matériel losses included 450 tanks, 1,000 guns and 84 aircraft.

Montgomery's pursuit was inhibited by torrential rain which reduced the desert to a quagmire and prevented the lumbering fuel trucks from keeping up with the tanks. Rommel, however, had no intention of fighting, for within days of starting his retreat he received the numbing news that the Anglo–American First Army had landed in

Morocco and Algeria on 8 November. He could do no more than head for the Tunisian redoubt which Hitler and Mussolini had chosen to hold, reflecting bitterly on their sudden ability to find the resources which would have made all the difference to his own campaign had they been made available to him in July or August.

The Second Battle of Alamein, as Winston Churchill was to comment, marked the end of the beginning of the Second World War. Strategically and psychologically, it ranks as one of the war's most decisive battles in that it initiated the Axis decline. When the German and Italian forces in Tunisia surrendered in May 1943, more than a quarter of a million troops marched into captivity. Two months later Mussolini was overthrown and on 3 September Italy concluded an armistice.

STALINGRAD,
19 AUGUST 1942 – 2 FEBRUARY 1943

During Operation Barbarossa, Hitler's invasion of the Soviet Union in 1941, the German armoured formations carved out nine major and thirteen smaller pockets yielding more than three million prisoners, 14,000 tanks and 26,000 guns. Yet despite these remarkable gains, the invasion failed in its primary purpose, that of capturing Moscow, the hub of the Soviet political and railway systems. Various causes contributed to the failure. Barbarossa had started late with the result that it had stalled in the mud generated by the autumn rains and finally ground to a standstill in the unimaginable cold of one of the severest winters on record; Hitler had meddled with the conduct of operations, creating further delay; the vast distances covered had strained the mechanical endurance of the panzer divisions to its limit; the German Army as a whole, in which most divisions still relied on horse-drawn artillery and transport, was quite unprepared for a winter war; and finally, the Red Army had counter-attacked with tough, well-equipped Siberian divisions, inured to the bitter cold, and thrown back the German spearheads. At this point, with terrible conse-

quences for Germany, Hitler dismissed the ailing von Brauchitsch and taken over as Commander-in-Chief of the Army. He immediately issued strict orders that there would be no further withdrawals and was later to claim that these had saved the army during its terrible winter ordeal. In fact, the sheer instinct for survival, coupled with the comparative weakness of the Soviets at this period, had a far greater effect on preserving the integrity of the front. The Germans simply stayed under cover in the more important towns and villages along the major road and rail links and quickly devised numerous ingenious ways of keeping themselves alive and healthy.

There was no doubt that the Red Army had been savagely mauled. On the other hand, Stalin had limitless manpower resources, vast spaces in which to reconstitute his shattered formations, and he had already moved his tank and other armament factories far to the east, beyond the reach of the Luftwaffe. He also enjoyed a priceless asset in the Lucy spy ring, which had reliable sources of information within OKW and kept him informed of Hitler's intentions. The question now was could the unwieldy, demoralised Red Army ever be forged into a weapon capable of defeating the Wehrmacht. During the 1930s he had developed a paranoid fear of Praetorianism and ruthlessly purged the officer corps from top to bottom, leaving the survivors so cowed that most were frightened to use their initiative; even those still inclined to do so were required to have their decisions approved by the political commissars attached to every major formation. Consequently much reliance was placed on centralised planning and rehearsal, with no variation permitted once an operation was under way. This had proved disastrous and a new system was introduced in which officers at various command levels were allowed to sanction minor variations to the master plan. Even this fell hopelessly short of the flexibility available to German commanders, especially when, in Soviet tank regiments, battalion commanders considered themselves lucky if they possessed a radio. Nevertheless, a start had to be made somewhere, and for the moment commanders concentrated on gaining experience with much smaller formations than the huge unmanageable mechanised corps that had been cut to pieces during Barbarossa.

The one area in which the Red Army had a distinct edge over the Germans was in tank design. In 1941 much of its tank fleet, the largest in the world, was either obsolete or unsuited to the prevailing tactical conditions, but two recently introduced designs had provided the panzer divisions with a severe headache. The first and more obvious of the two was the KV (*Klimenti Voroshilov*) heavy tank, armed with a 76.2mm gun capable of knocking out any German tank in service, and protected by 90mm armour which was almost impenetrable by the tank guns of that time. The assets of the second, the T34, were less apparent. Although smaller, it too was armed with a 76.2mm gun. Its 500hp diesel engine could give a maximum speed of 31mph, and its wide tracks and a Christie suspension ensured a superlative cross-country performance over all types of going, including mud and snow. The angled hull overhung the tracks and the glacis plate, though only 45mm thick, was angled back at 45° to provide the equivalent protection of 90mm. Field Marshal von Kleist unhesitatingly described it as the best tank in the world, and indeed its balanced combination of firepower, mobility and protection is widely regarded as being the starting-point of modern tank design. In addition, its very simplicity rendered it suitable for training recruits whose technical education did not match that of their western counterparts.

At a stroke the German armoured corps discovered to its horror that even the best of its tanks were now bordering on obsolescence. It thus became necessary to produce a new generation of tanks at short notice. Plans for an experimental breakthrough tank were hastily activated and put into production as the Tiger E, and work started on a new medium tank, the Pz Kpfw V Panther. As neither would be available for many months, stopgaps had to be found immediately. Only the 75mm Pz Kpfw

IV and the StuG assault gun could be up-gunned to the new Eastern Front standard, but obsolete tank chassis were converted to tank destroyers by fitting them with 75mm or 76.2mm anti-tank guns and with these, plus the Pz Kpfw III up-gunned to 50mm, the army would have to make do.

Both armies therefore began the 1942 campaigning season in something of a state of flux. It was the Russians who struck first. On 12 May, at Stalin's direction, Marshal Semyen Timoshenko's South-West Front struck west out of the salient at Izyum with the object of swinging north to recapture Kharkov. The Germans immediately counter-attacked through both flanks of the salient. Suddenly Timoshenko's men found themselves struggling for survival within a contracting pocket. When the fighting ended, 1,200 Soviet tanks had been destroyed and more than 250,000 men began their march into prison camps. The Red Army still had much to learn.

Hitler had already decided on the form his own offensive would take. His intention was to secure the oilfields of the Caucasus, representing this as a master-stroke of economic warfare which would cripple the Soviet Union's ability to make war. General Franz Halder, Chief of Staff at OKH, pointed out that such a deep penetration would expose a vulnerable left flank that should be protected by a defensive front stretching south from Voronezh on the Don to Stalingrad on the Volga. Hitler accepted this, but during the planning stage became so absorbed by the possibility of simultaneously eliminating the industrial capacity of Stalingrad that this began to assume equal weight with the drive into the Caucasus. The plan, code-named Case Blue, was not only wildly ambitious but also, as Fuller was to comment, radically unsound. Fuller's point was that the capture of the vital rail junction and river transport centre of Saratov, 200 miles upstream from Stalingrad, would if properly exploited, have produced better results for less effort, because it would put a stranglehold on the Caucasus oil supply, greatly restrict the flow of Allied aid reaching Russia via Persia and the

Caspian, and unhinge the whole southern sector of the Soviet line. Hitler, however, was not given to such refined considerations as the Indirect Approach, and he had neither the patience, nor training, nor ability to pursue the traditional German objective of securing a crushing victory in the planning stage. Instead, considering himself to be the natural heir of Frederick the Great and the elder von Moltke, he preferred to employ what he described as his 'intuition' in flashy but impracticable game-board solutions to his problems.

Activity on the northern and central sectors of the Eastern Front was to remain at a low level while Case Blue was implemented. Army Group South was divided into two new Army Groups designated A and B of which the former, under Field Marshal Sigmund List, would make the deep penetration into the Caucasus while the latter, under Field Marshal Fedor von Bock, acted as flank guard and established the defensive front along the axis Voronezh–Stalingrad.

Despite the information supplied by the Lucy ring and the capture of revealing documents, a clever deception plan convinced Stalin and his *Stavka* (General Staff) that, once again, the German offensive would be directed at Moscow, so when Case Blue began on 28 June, both were caught wrong-footed and their response was muddled. Altogether, some 1,200 tanks, including the 600 belonging to the newly formed Fifth Tank Army, were directed to converge on Army Group B's spearhead. Stalin ordered his Chief of Armoured Troops, General Fedorenko, to assume personal control of armoured operations without clarifying the position of the local Front Commander, General Golikov. In a climate of black farce the two generals issued, and ignored, an increasingly angry series of orders to each other while *Stavka* further muddied the waters by bombarding Golikov with instructions about *armoured* operations. At lower levels, the disrupted chain of command left commanders without the slightest idea where their troops were, and the troops without orders. Not surprisingly, the Germans defeated their oppo-

nents in detail with almost contemptuous ease, tearing open a 40-mile gap in the front. The Russians, however, had learned the previous year's lessons and retreated out of harm's way before the panzer spearheads could close behind them. Chagrined by this failure to repeat the spectacular captures of Barbarossa, Hitler was also annoyed that Bock was taking longer than expected to secure Voronezh, and when Bock had the temerity to criticise an OKH directive he was summarily dismissed, his place as commander of Army Group B being taken by Colonel-General Baron Maximilian von Weichs.

Hitler next meddled with the internal workings of Army Group B. As originally drafted, Case Blue required General Hermann Hoth's Fourth Panzer Army to lead the advance on Stalingrad, followed by General Friedrich Paulus' much slower Sixth Army. On 17 July Hitler decided to transfer Fourth Panzer Army to Army Group A, where it would assist Kleist's First Panzer Army to secure crossings of the Don as a prelude to a great battle of encirclement in which the Soviet South Front would be pinned against the coast. *Stavka*, however, had already ordered South Front to withdraw across the Don and it had done so, leaving long stretches of the river undefended. Hoth's journey was therefore not only pointless but deprived Sixth Army of fuel, causing it to halt its advance on Stalingrad at Kalach. In the short term Hitler's intervention was unfortunate in that the city could probably have been taken without undue difficulty at this time; in the long term it was to prove catastrophic.

On 1 August Fourth Panzer Army reverted to Army Group B. Having crossed the Don at Tsimlyanskya, it advanced north-east along the Novorossisk–Stalingrad railway while Paulus' Sixth Army resumed its offensive from Kalach. At first they made reasonable progress but the closer they got to Stalingrad the tougher resistance became until, by the third week of August, they had been fought to a standstill. It now became obvious that the defenders of the city, the Soviet 62nd Army under General Vasili Chuikov, had been ordered to fight to the

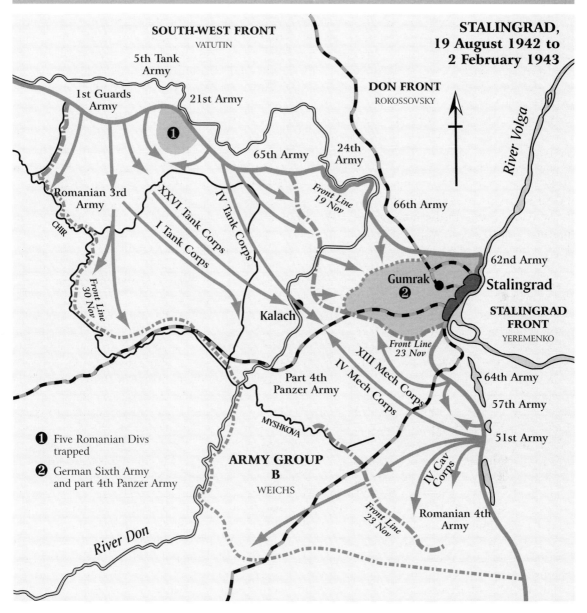

STALINGRAD,
19 August 1942 to
2 February 1943

SOUTH-WEST FRONT
VATUTIN

5th Tank
Army

1st Guards
Army

21st Army

DON FRONT
ROKOSSOVSKY

River Volga

❶

65th Army

24th
Army

Front Line
19 Nov

66th Army

Romanian 3rd
Army

XXVI Tank Corps

IV Tank Corps

CHIR

I Tank Corps

Front Line
30 Nov

Gumrak
❷

62nd Army

Stalingrad

STALINGRAD
FRONT
YEREMENKO

Kalach

Front Line
23 Nov

64th Army

Part 4th
Panzer Army

XIII Mech Corps

IV Mech Corps

57th Army

MYSHKOVA

51st Army

❶ Five Romanian Divs
trapped

❷ German Sixth Army
and part 4th Panzer Army

ARMY GROUP
B
WEICHS

IV Cav
Corps

Front Line
23 Nov

Romanian 4th
Army

River Don

last man among the ruins, regardless of the fact that they had a wide river at their back. Until the Russian Civil War the city had been known as Tsaritsyn, being subsequently re-named in honour of Stalin, who had played a wildly exaggerated part in its unsuccessful defence against the Whites.

In reaching Stalingrad Army Group B had actually fulfilled its mission of providing flank protection for the drive into the Caucasus. In these circumstances the physical possession of

the city was not really important, given the fact that the huge suburban industrial plants sprawling along the Volga for some 20 miles were within range of the German artillery and Luftwaffe. However, since the Red Army clearly intended denying it to Hitler, the more determined he was to have it. The whole of Paulus' Sixth Army and a large part of Fourth Panzer Army was committed to a struggle whose mounting ferocity sucked in reserves and supplies originally destined for Army

275

Above: An artist's impression of savage street fighting during the battle for Stalingrad. The Russians in the foreground are wearing a pre-war pattern of steel helmet. *Illustrated London News*

Group A. The story of this terrible battle, a modern re-enactment of Verdun set amid mountains of rubble and burning ruins beneath a pall of smoke and dust, was to become an epic of endurance for both sides.

The effects of Hitler's obsession quickly became apparent. When, on 6 September, List complained that Army Group A was being weakened by the demands of Stalingrad, he was dismissed. Next to go, on 24 September, was Halder, the Army's Chief of Staff, whose offence lay in warning Hitler that Sixth Army was in a potentially dangerous situation and should be withdrawn. Manstein, who had returned to the Leningrad sector after completing the conquest of the Crimea, kept his own counsel but agreed with Halder, believing that, sooner or later, the Russians

would turn the Führer's fixation with Stalingrad to their own advantage.

In fact, on 12 September Marshal Georgi Zhukov, together with Colonel Generals Alexandr Vasilevsky and Nikolai Voronov, had begun planning a counter-offensive that would turn the whole battle on its head. Like Halder and Manstein they had perceived that Sixth Army's fatal weakness lay in its immediate neighbours, which were armies contributed by Germany's allies to the Eastern Front. They were usually under-equipped and Manstein had little regard for the soldierly qualities of some of them, but they could be usefully employed on quieter sectors of the front while German troops were committed to the more serious fighting. So, from north to south, Army Group B's protective shoulder actually consisted of the weak German Second Army at Voronezh, Hungarian Second Army, Italian Eighth Army, Romanian Fourth Army, German Sixth Army and part of Fourth Panzer Army at Stalingrad, and Romanian Fourth Army. The Soviet plan, code-named Uranus, involved three Fronts, the Russian term for Army Group. In the north General Nikolai Vatutin's South-West Front would break out of the bridgeheads it had retained on the right bank of the Don with Fifth Tank and Twenty-First Armies, smashing through Romanian Third Army; to the south General Andrei Yeremenko's Stalingrad Front would attack with Sixty-Fourth, Fifty-Seventh and Fifty-First Armies, breaking through Romanian Fourth Army so that its spearheads would meet those of Vatutin in the area of Kalach, thereby trapping the entire German Sixth Army within a pocket; simultaneously, General Konstantin Rokossovsky's Don Front would mount holding attacks between these major thrusts. On the eve of Uranus the Red Army had one million men, 13,541 guns and other artillery weapons, 894 tanks and 1,115 aircraft poised to take the offensive.

Meanwhile the savage battle for the city continued. Areas such as the dominant hill of Mamayev Kurgan, Railway Station No 1, the Krasny Oktyabbr, Barrikady and Tractor Factories were fought over time and again with little quarter sought or granted. For the infantrymen of both sides, the street fighting was bitter and personal, survival depending upon holding their own few yards of rubble or the gutted house in which they had established a strong-point. Individual buildings began to assume immense importance. A Sergeant Pavlov and 60 men of 13th Guards Division, for example, turned a four-storey house into a fortress and held it against all comers for 58 days, their epic defence of 'Pavlov's House' becoming one of the legends of the siege. Despite this, Paulus'

Sixth Army was still attacking and had reached the Volga in several places when the storm broke.

At 07.30 on 19 November the forward positions of Romanian Third Army were struck by innumerable missiles fired from Katyusha rocket-launchers, known to the Germans as 'Stalin organs' because of the howling sound which accompanied their discharge. This area saturation bombardment was immediately followed by heavy conventional concentrations, then more saturation fire and barrages from which emerged wave after wave of Soviet infantry and T34 tanks. The under-equipped Romanians, unable to offer a coherent defence, simply fell apart. Five of their divisions were penned in a pocket which surrendered four days later. Others retreated across the Chir, a tributary of the Don, or fled north to join the Italian Eighth Army, or fell back on Stalingrad. On 20 November it was the turn of Romanian Fourth Army, which shared a similar fate, part seeking refuge in Stalingrad while the rest retreated to the south-west. On 23 November the spearheads of South-West and Stalingrad Fronts met at Kalach, isolating German Sixth and part of Fourth Panzer Armies.

Paulus immediately requested permission to abandon Stalingrad and break out of the trap to the west. In this he was supported by Weichs, his Army Group commander, and by General Zeitzler, the Army's new Chief of Staff. Hitler seemed inclined to give his approval, but at this critical moment Göring intervened. During the previous winter the Luftwaffe had kept a modestly sized German pocket supplied with food, fuel and ammunition, and he now announced that everything Paulus needed could also be sent in by air. This was an absurd boast, as basic requirements were set at 600 tons per day whereas the Luftwaffe's total lift capacity amounted to only half that figure. Furthermore, while the Luftwaffe had enjoyed air superiority during the former operation, its pilots would now be confronted by no less than 1,000 anti-aircraft guns and a strong Red Air Force presence above the battlefield. Without taking any of these factors into

Above: Though crudely finished and lacking refinements, the Soviet T34 is regarded as being the starting point of modern tank design. The speed with which their Sixth Army was encircled at Stalingrad took the Germans completely by surprise. *IWM Meg RR853*

account, Hitler accepted Göring's word and ordered Paulus to hold what he described as Fortress Stalingrad while operations to relieve it were organised. In the event, the average daily total flown into the Stalingrad perimeter amounted to less than 100 tons, despite the suicidal courage of the aircrews. The long-term future of Sixth Army was bleak, although to its credit the Luftwaffe did manage to bring out more than 25,000 of its more seriously wounded.

Hitler chose Manstein to take charge of the relief operation, forming Army Group Don for the purpose. This consisted of Sixth Army, Fourth Panzer Army and Romanian Fourth Army, but as these formations were either besieged or had been badly mauled by the Soviet offensive, Manstein was forced to await reinforcements. These included a panzer corps borrowed from Army Group A and a panzer division released from OKW reserve. At length thirteen divisions were assembled under General Hermann Hoth for the relief attempt. Code-named Wintergewitter (Winter Storm), this began on 12 December. By the 18th it had advanced some 40 miles from the restored German line and was within 35 miles of the Stalingrad perimeter. Further progress was barred at the river Myshkova by Second Guards Army, rushed into the area by Stavka for the purpose. Manstein transmitted the agreed code-word Donnerschlag (Thunderclap) to Paulus, indicating that he should begin break-out operations at once. Paulus declined to do this, choosing instead to place a literal interpretation on a recent Führer directive that he should remain in his existing positions. This

Right: A group of German infantrymen takes cover during heavy street fighting. *IWM Neg HU5131*

one slim hope of retrieving a disastrous situation was already passing, for on 16 December South-West and Voronezh Fronts had opened Operation Saturn, a major offensive aimed at the Italian Eighth Army. Within three days the Italians had been routed and Soviet armour was streaming west and south-west through the gap so created. Simultaneously Hoth came under intense pressure and by 29 December had been pushed back to the point from which his relief attempt had started.

There was nothing more that Manstein could do for Paulus and his freezing, hungry troops, who would now have to fight on within their shrinking defences. Instead, he was forced to give his entire attention to an even more serious situation which had developed, for if Zhukov chose to strike hard for Rostov and the Sea of Azov it would not only be Sixth Army which found itself trapped within an iron ring, but the whole of Army Group A as well. Once the danger had been explained to Hitler he reluctantly sanctioned the abandonment of the Caucasus. Manstein's primary task now was to hold open a corridor through which most of Army Group A, now commanded by Kleist, could withdraw, while the remainder were evacuated by sea to the Crimea. This involved a series of actions in which the Russians were held at bay by the tactical expertise of the German armoured formations.

The re-vitalised Red Army still had one hammer blow to deliver. On 15 January 1943 the Voronezh Front launched a new offensive which quickly routed the Hungarian Second Army. Now outflanked to the south, the German Second Army was forced to abandon Voronezh itself shortly after. Almost all the German gains made the previous year had now been lost.

Within Stalingrad, the condition of Sixth Army worsened progressively as, one after another, its airfields were overrun. Ragged. emaciated, frost-bitten, the troops now lived underground, burdened by numerous wounded for whom there was little available treatment.

279

The dead went unburied, organised distribution of rations and supplies ceased, and discipline began to break down. Yet still Hitler insisted that Stalingrad be defended 'to the last man and bullet'. On 31 January Paulus, elevated to the rank of field marshal the previous evening, surrendered; two days later the last of his troops laid down their arms. The meeting of victors and vanquished is vividly described by a surviving officer, Joachim Wieder, in his book *Stalingrad – Memories and Reassessments*:

'What first attracted my attention was the fresh, healthy appearance of the victors, their simple, enviable winter clothing and good weapons. Submachine-guns everywhere and the uniform picture of sheepskins, padded jackets, felt boots and fur caps with broad ear muffs swinging up and down. The warmly bundled-up, well-nourished and splendidly equipped men of the Red Army, with their chunky, mostly red-cheeked faces, formed a stark contrast to our deathly pale, filthy, bearded and freezing figures of misery who hung exhausted and sick in their makeshift winter clothing, consisting of all kinds of furs, blankets, scarves, field-grey headgear, woollens and inadequate footwear. This sudden meeting and comparison at once showed me how low we had sunk and how little we had been prepared for this murderous battle.'

Wieder was one of 91,000 prisoners taken at Stalingrad, only 5,000 of whom would see their homes again after many years of cruel captivity in the Soviet Union; about 120,000 of Paulus' men had died in the fighting or from disease. German equipment losses during the battle amounted to 3,500 tanks and self-propelled mountings of various types, 3,000 aircraft, 12,000 guns and mortars and 75,000 vehicles. Three panzer divisions were lost in the general surrender but were re-formed in France later that year. A chastened Hitler, admitting personal responsibility for the disaster, ordered a period of national mourning during which solemn music was played on the German radio, simultaneously expressing regret that the newly promoted Paulus had not committed suicide.

In the immediate aftermath of Stalingrad two Soviet Fronts, Golikov's Voronezh and Vatutin's South-West, advanced rapidly westward across the now open steppe, the former to secure Kharkov and the latter to swing south as

Below: German infantry attack, supported by the fire of an assault gun. *IWM Neg HU5151*

soon as it reached the Dnieper, trapping Manstein's re-constituted Army Group South in a huge pocket with the sea at its back. Manstein was able to plan his counter-stroke in the security of his own headquarters, which, unlike OKW, had not been penetrated by the Lucy ring, and, for once, Hitler was not inclined to meddle. Although Manstein had only 350 tanks at his immediate disposal, these would give him a local superiority of seven to one at the point of contact, while in the immediate vicinity the Luftwaffe had three times as many aircraft as the Red Air Force. Calculating the precise moment when his opponents would have out-run their ramshackle supply organisation, he struck into Vatutin's southern flank on 20 February. Stalled for want of fuel, the Russians quickly exhausted their ammunition and fled across the Donets. By the end of the month South-West Front's losses amounted to 615 tanks, 400 guns, 23,000 dead and 9,000 prisoners. Golikov, in danger of being isolated and under attack from the west as well, was forced to abandon Kharkov and beat a hasty retreat, leaving behind 600 tanks, 500 guns and 40,000 of his men. Only the spring *rasputitsa*, turning hard, frozen going into deep, clinging mud, put an end to the German counter-offensive.

Despite the success of Manstein's brilliant riposte, the German Army never really recovered from the catastrophe of Stalingrad. In July 1943 its offensive capacity was finally destroyed in futile attempts to eliminate the huge Kursk salient. Week by week the Red Army grew stronger, better equipped and more practised in large-scale mechanised operations. It proved impossible to hold back the Soviet war machine and in June 1944, while the western Allies were consolidating their Normandy beachhead, it destroyed the German Army Group Centre, thanks largely to another of Hitler's no withdrawal orders, simultaneously isolating Army Group North. Coupled with the failure of the July bomb plot against Hitler, this meant that Nazi Germany would inevitably be crushed by converging pressure from east and west.

D-DAY, 6 JUNE 1944

'You will enter the continent of Europe and, in conjunction with other United Nations, undertake operations aimed at the heart of Germany and the destruction of her armed forces.'

Such was the simple order given to General Dwight D. Eisenhower, US Army, Supreme Commander Allied Expeditionary Force, early in 1944. Behind it lay years of hard fighting to obtain mastery over the German submarine arm in the North Atlantic, thereby permitting the transport of those US forces to Great Britain without whom an invasion of Europe would have been impossible, as well as the essential air superiority above the projected invasion zone. These factors, together with immensely detailed planning and preparation initially co-ordinated by Lieutenant General F. E. Morgan, Chief of Staff to the Supreme Allied Commander (COSSAC), and his American deputy, Brigadier General R. W. Barker, would finally result in the greatest amphibious operation in history under the code-name Overlord.

During those same years Hitler, conscious that the British and Americans would one day attempt a cross-Channel invasion of western Europe, had spared no effort to perfect the defences of what he chose to call his Atlantic Wall, which stretched from Norway to the Spanish frontier. Priority was given to the main port areas, which by 1944 had become virtually impregnable to seaborne assault. Next came those areas which offered good landing beaches along the coasts of the English Channel, Belgium and Holland. Elsewhere, as in the Bay of Biscay, where an invasion seemed improbable, or where coastal conditions were unsuitable, fixed defences were fewer on the ground.

The defences were many and various. They ranged from immense, ugly coastal artillery batteries, observation towers, command posts and communication centres through more numerous smaller bunkers containing anti-tank and machine-guns covering the beaches with direct fire, to well-designed anti-tank walls which denied exit from the beaches into the interior, all constructed by slaves of the notorious Todt Organisation, using millions of tons of concrete. The beaches themselves were, of course, mined and covered by wire entanglements, while below the high-water line bristled steel tetrahedra or lines of stakes to rip the bottoms out of landing-craft or blow them up with contact explosive charges. If an attack succeeded in penetrating beyond the beach, it faced opposition from fortified houses, machine-gun and anti-tank posts, mines and anti-tank ditches. Farther inland waited the artillery's field and medium batteries, ready to engage the invasion fleet.

The officer commanding the German armies in France during much of 1944 was Field Marshal Gerd von Rundstedt. In the north was Army Group B, consisting of Seventh Army with sixteen divisions in Normandy and Brittany, and Fifteenth Army with 25 divisions covering an area from the Seine to Holland, under the command of Field Marshal Erwin Rommel. In the south, General Johannes Blaskowitz's Army Group G, consisting of First and Nineteenth Armies with a total of 17 divisions, was responsible for defence of the Biscay and Côte d'Azure coastlines.

During this period there were a number of fundamental disagreements within the higher echelons of the German command as to how the invasion was to be countered. Hitler insisted that Rundstedt should prepare for an invasion anywhere along the Atlantic Wall from Holland southwards, thereby forcing his Commander-in-Chief West to spread his troops more thinly than he cared. Furthermore, while Rommel, who had done much to strengthen his own sector since he took it over in February 1944, wished to defeat the invaders at the water's edge, Rundstedt was prepared to allow them to advance inland beyond the range of their naval gunfire support and then defeat them with a concentrated counter-attack. In either respect the role of the panzer divisions would be critical, but here an absurdly over-

complicated situation arose. On the eve of the Allied invasion there were nine panzer divisions in France and the Low Countries, known collectively as Panzer Group West, under the overall command of General Geyr von Schweppenburg, who was responsible for their training and would command them in action. Rommel wanted them deployed forward so that they could deliver an immediate counter-stroke, but Rundstedt and Schweppenburg were for holding them to the rear until it became apparent how the situation was going to develop. The compromise imposed by Hitler produced the worst of all possible solutions since of the six panzer divisions in Army Group B's area three were designated as a strategic reserve under OKW control, and three were allocated to Rundstedt, *provided OKW sanctioned their movement or commitment*. Thus, neither Rundstedt nor Rommel would be able to mount the type of counter-offensive measures they considered necessary without, in effect, obtaining Hitler's personal approval.

The remainder of the German Army in France included first-line infantry divisions and second-line static divisions manning the coastal defences. Both would put up an extremely stubborn fight, although the latter contained a high percentage of conscripted central and eastern Europeans, including Poles who had fought against Germany in 1939 and would do so again when given the chance to change sides once more, Russians and Yugoslavs.

For the Allies the story can be said to have begun in 1942 when Stalin warned Churchill that he would consider making a separate peace with Hitler unless a Second Front were opened quickly in the west. On 19 August of that year a large raid on Dieppe failed with heavy Canadian casualties, although it did prove that for the moment a Second Front was not a practical proposition.

The Dieppe raid also provided invaluable lessons that would be put to good use two years later. Clearly it would be impossible for the Allies to secure a heavily defended French port in working order, so it was decided to invade over the open beaches of Normandy, bringing their own pre-fabricated harbours with them. The German defences were studied in detail and it was decided that after the invasion fleet had approached the coast through swept channels, the assault landing would be made at half-tide, when the water was beginning to rise but the lines of obstacles were still exposed. These would be tackled by demolition teams of naval frogmen, who would first disarm the explosive devices then clear 50-yard gaps for the passage of landing craft. Beyond this, the reduction of the enemy defences became the responsibility of the ground troops, and on this occasion it was considered appropriate that they should be neutralised by specialist armoured engineer vehicles that would land in the first wave, rather than by infantry.

That task was given to Major-General P. C. S. Hobart, an irascible genius who had begun his career with the Bengal Sappers and Miners. Hobart was informed that the Army's specialist tank and assault engineering units would be concentrated within his own 79th Armoured Division to develop techniques and equipment for breaching the Atlantic Wall. Hobart recognised that not even specialist armour could be expected to produce the required results without direct gunfire support from other tanks. To solve the problem he turned to the DD (Duplex Drive) 'swimming tank'. The concept of this amphibian, kept afloat by a collapsible canvas screen attached to the hull and driven by a screw drawing power from the main engine, had been pioneered by a Mr Nicholas Straussler during the inter-war years. The theory was that once the vehicle had reached the shoreline the buoyancy screen would be lowered and the normal drive engaged so that it could perform as a normal gun tank. Successful trials had been carried out with the Valentine and the Stuart, but for the Normandy landings the choice fell on the Sherman because of its superior firepower. Hobart envisaged that during the early stages

Below: A Sherman flails its way through a mine-field. The gun had to be traversed to the rear while flailing was in progress. *The Tank Museum*

Above: The versatile Churchill AVRE (Assault Vehicle Royal Engineers) posed obvious problems for its commander when loaded with a fascine but in this and other forms solved numerous problems on D-Day. *IWM Neg B11135*

of the fighting the DDs would provide fire support from the shallows until the specialist armour had created sufficient elbow room, then fight as the situation demanded. A total of five British, two Canadian and three American tank battalions were trained in the use of the DD.

Various mechanical methods of mine clearing existed, but experience at Alamein had shown that the best results were obtained by flailing, that is by beating the ground ahead of a tank with chains attached to a rotating drum powered by the vehicle's main or auxiliary engine, so exploding any mines in its path. The most successful design was the Sherman Crab, which was capable of clearing a lane ten feet wide at 1.25 miles per hour, as well as fighting as a gun tank when it was not flailing. From November 1943 one complete brigade within 79th Armoured Division was equipped with the Crab.

Without doubt, the most versatile vehicle in the division's armoury was the AVRE (Assault Vehicle Royal Engineers), which had been developed as a direct result of experiences at Dieppe. The hull of the Churchill infantry tank was selected as the basis because of its heavy armour, roomy interior and obvious adaptability. The AVRE was fitted with a specially designed turret mounting a 290mm muzzle-loading demolition gun, known as a petard, which could throw a 40-pound bomb, designed to crack open concrete fortifications, to a maximum range of 230 yards, reloading being effected through a sliding hatch above the co-driver's seat. Standardised external fittings enabled the AVRE to be used in a variety of ways. For example, it could carry a fascine, 8 feet in diameter and 14 feet wide, which could be dropped across an anti-tank ditch to form a causeway; or lay a small box girder bridge with a 40-ton capacity across gaps of up to 30 feet or to the top of an anti-tank wall; or be fitted with a bobbin which unrolled a carpet of hessian and metal tubing ahead of the vehicle, so creating a firm track across soft going and shingle; or place demolition charges against an obstacle or fortification and fire them by remote control after it had reversed away; or push mobile Bailey bridges into position; and, on going too soft for the Crabs, it could be fitted with a plough to bring mines to the surface. The 1st Assault Brigade RE, consisting of three assault regiments each with 60 AVREs and a number of D8 armoured tractors, joined Hobart's division during the summer of 1943.

As no two sectors of the German coastal defences were alike, Hobart's division would function as a gigantic plant hire corporation. Liaison officers were attached to each of the British and Canadian divisions forming the first wave of Lieutenant-General Sir Miles Dempsey's British Second Army, on the left of the Allied invasion force. After detailed study of maps, models, air-reconnaissance photos and intelligence reports, the appropriate assault engineering equipment was allocated and formed into teams which received a similarly detailed briefing on their own specific tasks. These facilities were also offered to Lieutenant General Omar Bradley, Commander of the US First Army, which formed the right wing of the assault, but apart from the DD battalions mentioned above they were declined for reasons which have never been satisfactorily explained.

Simultaneously work was going ahead on the two prefabricated harbours, code-named Mulberry, through which the troops would be supplied once they had secured their beachheads. These were formed from more than 200 huge concrete caissons, some the height of a five-storey building, that would be towed across the Channel and sunk as breakwaters, supplemented by sunken blockships. Within the harbours were piers for supply craft,

connected to the shore by floating roadways. Every tug in Great Britain would be required to tow the Mulberries, plus more from the USA and Canada. Yet another imaginative device was the Pipeline Under The Ocean, code-named PLUTO. Fabricated from flexible aluminium alloy and wound on huge drums fixed in the sterns of cable-laying ships, it would be laid on the sea bed and fuel for the invasion force would be pumped through it from stations on the south coast of England.

The choice of Normandy as the invasion area was heavily influenced by air and naval considerations. Air cover had to be provided for the sea passage from England and as half the available fighter aircraft were Spitfires, which carried just sufficient fuel to attack a cross-Channel target and return to base, the possible invasion frontage was restricted to the area between Flushing and Cherbourg. This narrowed even further when the distinct possibility of Atlantic gales was taken into account, as the only shelter lay in the lee of the Cherbourg peninsula. Furthermore, except for one sector between Arromanches-les-Bains and the river Vire, which featured cliffs and submerged rock ledges, the Normandy coast was generally suitable for assault landings.

Operation Neptune, the naval aspect of the invasion, was under the command of Admiral Sir Bertram Ramsay, who had masterminded the Dunkirk evacuation. It embraced the conveyance of the Allied armies from England through swept channels in the enemy's minefields, and protection of the seaward flanks of the invasion fleet. The statistics are a source of wonder, as no fewer than 6,939 vessels were employed, including 864 merchant ships. Of the 1,213 naval combatant vessels, 79 per cent were drawn from the Royal and Royal Canadian Navies, 16 per cent from the US Navy and 4 per cent from Allied European navies generally operating under British control, including French, Norwegian, Dutch, Polish and Greek ships. No fewer than 137 vessels, including seven battleships, two 15-inch gun monitors, 23 cruisers, two gunboats and 103 destroyers, would form the main bombardment force. There were 221 escorts of various types, 287 minesweepers, four minelayers, one seaplane carrier, eight headquarters landing-ships, anti-submarine escort groups including three escort carriers, 495 motor torpedo- and motor gun-boats and rescue launches from the coastal forces, and even two midget submarines which would act as boundary markers. By far the greater part of Ramsay's armada, however, consisted of landing-ships and landing-craft of various types to the number of 4,126. Of these 340 were armed with guns, rockets and automatic weapons to give additional close fire support to the assault landing; some British LCTs carried tanks, field artillery and anti-tank guns intended to engage targets while still afloat.

Among the 736 ancillary vessels were repair, salvage, wreck dispersal, survey, anti-aircraft and fighter direction ships and smoke-making trawlers. Among the merchant vessels were ten hospital ships, cargo carriers of every type and 59 blockships to be sunk as part of the Mulberry breakwaters, four of them being obsolete warships.

The task of marshalling and administering this huge assembly of shipping was Herculean, even though the invasion fleet was divided into two main groups. Of these, the Western Naval Task Force, under Rear-Admiral A. G. Kirk, US Navy, and the Eastern Naval Task Force under Rear-Admiral Sir Philip Vian, were responsible respectively for the landings on the American and British sectors.

From mid March 1944 the RAF and USAAF carried out widespread attacks on targets within the invasion area and against the enemy's air installations and lines of communication. These were carefully structured to give the impression that the Allied intention was to land in the Pas-de-Calais rather than in Normandy. Thus, for every target designated in Normandy, two were attacked in the Calais region. Interdiction raids across Belgium and northern France destroyed rail junctions, bridges, viaducts, embankments and cuttings so thoroughly that by 3 June the German railway authorities frankly doubted the point

of trying to repair them. Likewise road bridges across the same area were systematically destroyed. Overall the effect would be to isolate the German armies in what would become the battle zone, leaving them without reinforcements and supplies during the critical period. No fewer than 200,000 sorties were flown during these preliminary operations, at the cost of some 2,000 aircraft. When the moment came, the French Resistance would also be mobilised to destroy what remained of the enemy's communications infrastructure and carry out extensive acts of sabotage. On D-Day itself, in addition to further interdiction missions flown by bombers, no fewer than 3,700 Allied fighters would be in the air, with fifteen squadrons providing cover for shipping, 54 providing beach cover, 36 flying in direct support of ground operations, 33 engaged in offensive operations or escorting bomber formations and a further 33 available for immediate deployment as required.

Operation Bodyguard, the deception plan intended to convince the Germans that the landings would be made in the Pas-de-Calais area, was also designed to give the impression that they would take place some six weeks later than would be the case. Dummy camps, roads and airfields were constructed all over Kent and southern East Anglia, apparently peopled by an army group under General George S. Patton, which maintained extensive radio traffic. Dummy tanks, guns, transport and gliders provided the impression of a steady build-up, as did scores of dummy landing-craft which appeared in the south-eastern ports and the creeks of the Thames estuary. Information leaked to known double agents and in unreliable diplomatic circles all suggested that the Pas-de-Calais was the target area, while lesser deceptions in Scotland and Northern Ireland gave the impression that diversionary landings would take place in Norway or Denmark. As late as 4 June Admiral Krancke, the German naval commander of the Channel ports area, submitted a report expressing doubts that the Allied invasion fleet was ready. *Bodyguard* continued even after the Normandy landings were a fact, leaving Hitler convinced that they were a diversion, with the result that substantial German forces in northern France were tied down at his orders.

One aspect of the Overlord planning which perhaps deserves more attention than it usually receives is the sustained psychological warfare effort made to demoralise the German defenders. One important element of this was the radio station known as *Soldatensender Calais*, which broadcast from England using the most powerful medium-wave transmitter in Europe. *Soldatensender* put out a first-rate German forces' radio programme which retransmitted the Führer's speeches live, plus accurate, verifiable news, the latest dance music from America and even requests for known – and somewhat surprised – members of German units. It provided compulsive listening for everone manning the Atlantic Wall. From the beginning of 1944 it began asking unsettling questions. Why was the best equipment always sent to the Eastern Front? Could the Polish, Ukrainian and Croat elements within the army be relied upon? Where was the Luftwaffe? Could the fortifications withstand the latest British and American weapons, the power and effect of which were described? And what right had the high-living Party bosses to meddle in military matters of which they knew nothing? Such questions were already passing through the minds of men who knew that they

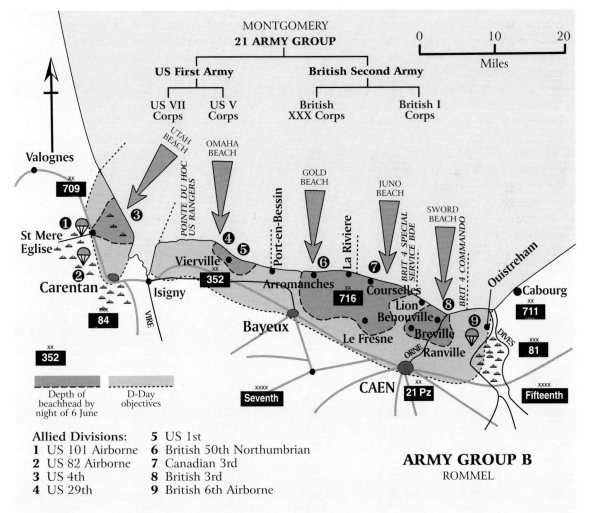

Allied Divisions:

1 US 101 Airborne	**5** US 1st
2 US 82 Airborne	**6** British 50th Northumbrian
3 US 4th	**7** Canadian 3rd
4 US 29th	**8** British 3rd
	9 British 6th Airborne

ARMY GROUP B
ROMMEL

were about to undergo a severe ordeal, and there were no satisfactory answers to them.

Early in 1944 General Morgan and most of the COSSAC staff were absorbed into the Supreme Headquarters Allied Expeditionary Force (SHAEF). Here, Eisenhower, the Supreme Commander, had as his Deputy Air Chief Marshal Sir Arthur Tedder, Lieutenant General Walter B. Smith as his Chief of Staff, Admiral Ramsay as Naval Commander-in-Chief and Air Chief Marshal Sir Trafford Leigh-Mallory as Air Commander-in-Chief. General Sir Bernard Montgomery was made responsible for planning the assault landings and would command ashore until such time as the number of American troops committed to the battle exceeded those of Great Britain and Canada; at that point Eisenhower would assume overall command of the armies and Montgomery would revert to command of British 21st Army Group.

The actual assault would be delivered by US First Army astride the Vire on two beaches designated Utah and Omaha, and by British Second Army on three beaches designated 'Gold', 'Juno' and 'Sword', lying between Port-en-Bessin and Ouistreham. The right flank of the operation would be secured by night-dropping the US 82nd and 101st Airborne Divisions on the hinterland behind Utah, and the left flank by a simultaneous air assault by British 6th Airborne Division north-east of Caen, where bridges across the Caen Canal and the river Orne would be captured, a coastal battery neutralised and bridges over the Dives demolished. A further preliminary operation would be a Commando-style attack by American Rangers on another coast defence battery at Pointe du Hoc, east of the Vire.

During the final week of May those troops forming the assault wave were moved into camps near their embarkation ports and virtually held incommunicado until the moment arrived for them to board their transports. D-

Below: Troops and vehicles, including DD Shermans, AVREs and an armoured bulldozer, stream ashore on the British sector. *IWM Neg MH2021*

Day had been provisionally set for 5 June, but heavy weather in the Channel forced a postponement. The meteorologists predicted that this would abate for a day or two on 6 June, although there would be a swell, variable cloud and some mist. It was decided to proceed on this basis, the alternative being another uncertain wait of two weeks, which would be unfair to troops already keyed to fighting pitch. At midnight on 5 June, therefore, engines thundered into life on the airborne divisions' airfields while from ports along the south coast of England the huge armada began converging on its assembly area to the south-east of the Isle of Wight, there to form up and head south towards the invasion beaches.

On the western flank the two American airborne divisions soon ran into problems. Their difficult approach to the drop zones

Below: D-Day. Infantry and DD Sherman tanks reach the shore on the American sector. *IWM Neg AP25726*

involved careful navigation which was not assisted by heavy cloud and anti-aircraft fire against which inexperienced pilots took over-evasive action. The result was that the paratroops and glider infantry of both divisions were widely dispersed, although by dawn they had begun to rally and tackle their objectives. There was, nevertheless, an unforeseen bonus in that the presence of so many armed and determined men, spread across such a wide area, generated confusing reports among the Germans and seriously unsettled the defenders of Utah Beach. To the east, British 6th Airborne Division, led by the gliders of its *coup de main* party, made an accurate landing. By dawn it had taken all its objectives, consolidated a bridgehead east of the Orne, and was preparing to stand off a series of very determined counter-attacks until relieved by seaborne troops. At Pointe du Hoc the American Rangers found their objective unarmed and deserted. Later in the day they discovered the battery's 150mm guns, still unmanned, some way inland and wrecked them.

From 03.15 to 05.00 RAF Bomber Command attacked targets along the invasion frontage, dropping 6,000 tons of bombs. Such a rain of explosives was beyond the experience of those within the fortifications, but far worse was to follow. At 05.30. a little before first light, the naval bombardment began, its intensity reducing some men to mind-numbing incoherence. The effect of the heavy shells fired by battleships and monitors was literally shattering as seemingly impenetrable concrete splintered and cracked wide, while in the smaller bunkers even near misses moved entire structures within the earth. The crescendo of sound and fury continued to rise. At 05.50 the daylight bombers of US Eighth and Ninth Air Forces arrived. The Utah defences alone were pounded by 269 medium bombers while elsewhere along the invasion front 1,300 Flying Fortress and Liberator heavy bombers arrived in 36-wide waves, to drop a further 3,000 tons of bombs, breaking off just ten minutes before the first assault craft were due to beach.

German reaction to the events of the night had been hesitant. Rommel, taking advantage of the bad weather, was on leave in Germany. He did not learn of the invasion until 10.15 and left for France immediately. His Chief of Staff, Lieutenant-General Spiedel, had already contacted Rundstedt's headquarters at 05.15, but on the basis of the evidence available at that time the Commander-in-Chief West was not prepared to take decisions. Closer to the front, Colonel-General Friedrich Dollmann, Commander of German Seventh Army, had ordered his LXXXIV Corps (91st Air Landing, 352nd and 716th Divisions) to take appropriate action against the British and American paratroops and at 07.00 he allocated 21st Panzer Division, his only armoured formation, to assist in the task. Dollmann was quite clear that an invasion was being mounted but was uncertain whether it was a diversion or the main Allied effort. His northern neighbour across the Dives, Colonel-General Hans von Salmuth, commanding German Fifteenth Army, had actually issued an invasion alert the previous evening, based on intercepted trans-

missions to the French Resistance, but his attention was concentrated on the Pas-de-Calais. Admiral Krancke saw no cause for undue alarm until, shortly after 03.00, his torpedo-boats from Le Havre ran into the eastern flank of the invasion fleet. After sinking a Norwegian destroyer they beat a hasty retreat, leaving Krancke effectively blind because of the previous destruction of his coastal radar stations. Yet while alarm continued to grow along the Atlantic Wall itself, this was not mirrored at OKW, where demands that Panzer Group West should be

Below: John Hamilton's painting of the D-Day naval bombardment showing the battleships *Ramillies* and *Warspite* and the monitor *Roberts*. *Imperial War Museum Collection LD7451. By kind permission of Mrs Betty Hamilton*

committed to the invasion area were met by a refusal to disturb the sleeping Hitler. Not until 10.00 was permission given for a limited move by two panzer divisions in the general direction of the fighting, but by then any movement behind the front immediately attracted swarms of Allied fighter-bombers.

Meanwhile, as the last of the American heavy bombers droned away, the shaken defenders emerged to peer through their observation slits. To their horror, they saw a horizon filled with landing-craft of every type, closing the shore slowly but relentlessly. In the lead, here and there, could be seen what appeared to be unmanned ships' whalers which gave no indication that below each low freeboard was a Sherman ready for action.

Sea conditions on 6 June were never less than difficult. Off Utah, where the assault was made by US 4th Division, 30 DDs were launched from 3,000 yards out and, because of the lee provided by the Cherbourg peninsula, all but one reached the shore safely to suppress the fire of the local defences. The enemy, already unsettled by the presence of airborne troops in their rear, began shredding away so that by mid-morning 4th Division were in possession of a landing area 4,000 yards wide and had advanced four miles inland, linking up with 101st Airborne Division later in the day.

Across the Vire, a very different situation prevailed on Omaha Beach, the objective of US 29th and 1st Divisions. There 29 DDs had been launched from 6,000 yards out and all but two had been swamped by heavy seas and gone to the bottom. By a further and unexpected stroke of ill-luck, the German 352nd Division was holding an anti-invasion exercise

in the area, so that when the virtually unsupported infantry left their landing-craft they ran straight into the teeth of a withering fire which stopped them dead at the water's edge with a rising tide at their back. There had been tactical mistakes, too, including the launch of the landing-craft so far out, the decision to assault the enemy strong-points head-on rather than land between them, and the restriction of the naval bombardment to 40 minutes. Soon the 4-mile stretch of shallows became strewn with bodies, smashed equipment and wrecked landing-craft amid which survivors scrabbled for cover in the sand with their entrenching tools and new arrivals simply added to the chaos and confusion. General Bradley, commanding US First Army, was giving serious consideration to abandoning the landing and diverting his follow-up waves to Utah when, at 07.30, a group of eight American and three British destroyers, seeing how matters stood ashore, closed to within 1,000 yards and subjected the enemy to a sustained point-blank battering. This eased the situation sufficiently for small, self-sacrificial and locally inspired groups of infantrymen to fight their way through the obstacles and finally storm the beach exits. During the afternoon the situation was sufficiently brought under control for reinforcements to be landed, including the third US DD battalion, which came in by LCT. By nightfall the beachhead was apparently secure, although it was nowhere more than two miles in depth and had been bought at the cost of 3,000 casualties, approximately 30 per cent of the total Allied loss during the day.

In overall terms, the landings by British 50th Division on Gold, Canadian 3rd Division on Juno and British 3rd Division on Sword Beaches went according to plan. As always, for the fighting troops most closely involved, the devil lay in the detail. The major problems arose in connection with the launching of DDs in the prevailing conditions. Off Sword, for example, A Squadron of Canadian 1st Hussars launched ten tanks from between 1,500 and 2,000 yards out, of which seven touched down.

These quickly eliminated strong points containing two 75mm guns, one 50mm gun and six machine-guns, after which a large party of the enemy came forward to surrender. Nearby, the regiment's B Squadron launched nineteen DDs from 4,000 yards, of which fourteen touched down. The best performance of the day, however, was put up by 13th/18th Hussars who launched 34 tanks some 5,000 yards off Sword and came in with 31. Elsewhere conditions were so dangerous that launching was never contemplated, the DDs landing from their LCTs after the arrival of 79th Armoured Division's breaching teams.

This was, of course, the reverse of what had been planned, but the breaching teams had no option but to deal with the situations confronting them. Two examples will suffice, both taken from Nan Sector, Juno Beach. No 1 Team touched down on a rising tide in an area that was rapidly becoming crowded with infantry. The leading Crab flailed a path to the sea wall against which an AVRE laid its small box girder bridge. The first AVRE across struck a mine not far beyond and blocked the intended exit. Nearby, however, a section of sea wall had been partially blown down by the naval bombardment and two Crabs not only succeeded in flailing their way to the gap but also crawled their way through it to the lateral road beyond, which they proceeded to clear. Two fascine AVREs then advanced across the road and dropped their bundles into an anti-tank ditch. The damaged AVRE was pushed aside by an armoured bulldozer, the driver of which was killed almost immediately by a mine. Finally the gap through the minefield was completed by hand, thereby creating a second beach exit.

No 2 Team touched down 300 yards east of its intended landing point. As they emerged from the LCT, the AVREs were engaged by a 50mm anti-tank gun firing from the west. That carrying the small box girder bridge was knocked out and the commander of another vehicle was killed before the remainder silenced the emplacement with their petards. The sea wall, 12 feet high, was now only 50 yards from

Above: Hitler's Atlantic Wall. This anti-tank gun emplacement, sited to deliver flanking fire along the beach, was neutralised during the landing. *IWM Meg A23995*

the water's edge and the team's Crabs flailed their way up to it. Having lost his SBG bridge, the team commander directed the AVREs to blast a gap in the wall with their petards. This they did, although it was too narrow, steep and soft for the passage of vehicles. The infantry then drew his attention to a ramp blocked with a gate-like girder construction known as Element C, which was blown apart. The Crabs then flailed up the ramp, followed by a fascine AVRE which filled the anti-tank ditch beyond, and the beach exit was complete.

It had never been envisaged that all of 79th Armoured Division's breaching teams would be able to clear lanes through the defences, but sufficient margin for safety had been left for the momentum of the attack to be maintained and enable the assault divisions to start moving inland with their supporting armour and anti-tank guns. Altogether, the division lost twelve out of 50 Crabs, and 22 out of 120 AVREs. Its personnel casualties amounted to only 169

killed, wounded and missing which, given the nature of its task, was astounding.

Although driven back into the hinterland to a depth of between seven and nine miles, the enemy continued to offer fierce if disjointed resistance, but it was not until mid-afternoon that the Germans mounted their only major counter-attack of the day. Lieutenant-General Edgar Feuchtinger, commanding 21st Panzer Division, was ordered to advance north and restore the broken front between Caen and Bayeux. The division advanced in two columns which were soon detected, coming under heavy air attack and naval gunfire. Even before its leading elements had worked their way through Caen losses had begun to mount and at 16.00 its advance was halted by the British 3rd Division's anti-tank gun screen. Feuchtinger shifted the axis of his attack, but was again foiled by artillery fire and hull-down tanks. By the time the division had withdrawn and gone into laager it was down to 70 battle-worthy tanks. On the other hand its counter-attack had prevented the capture of Caen that

Left: Part of the 6th Airborne Division landing by glider to secure the eastern flank of the beachhead. *Illustrated London News*

and Canadians, which was considered incredibly light for what had been achieved.

There was, too, another price that would have to be paid, for while the Normandy beaches had suited the Allied invasion requirements much of the hinterland consisted of *bocage* country which, with its characteristic small fields and sunken lanes bounded by hedge-topped banks, was ideal defensive terrain unsuited to armour. Fierce attritional fighting saw casualties mount steeply on both sides, although for the Germans, starved of reinforcements, penned within range of Allied naval gunfire by Hitler's orders to hold their positions to the last man, and utterly dominated by Allied air power, the situation was much worse. The story of the Normandy campaign, ending with the encirclement and destruction of the German armies during August, has been told many times and in many places. Its conclusion marked a defining moment, not simply because the destruction of the Third Reich had become a certainty, but because as more and more American armies reached the Continent, the leadership of the Western world passed quietly and almost without notice from Great Britain to the USA. None of this would have been possible without Operation Overlord, one of the greatest events of modern times and the largest undertaking in military history.

Commentary 11 – Doomsday Machines

Shortly before the outbreak of the First World War, A. Hilliard Atteridge concluded his history of land warfare by writing this:

'It may safely be said that the development of aerial navigation and the transmission of orders and information by wireless telegraphy and telephony will result in a great revolution in the methods of the battlefield. But there may be other surprises in store for the soldiers

day and this was a serious disappointment for the Allies.

By midnight on 6 June the process of linking the beachheads had begun and most of the airborne troops had been relieved. Some 57,000 American and 75,000 British and Canadian troops had been put ashore; and on the British sector alone 950 fighting vehicles, 5,000 wheeled vehicles, 240 field guns, 280 anti-tank guns and 4,000 tons of stores had been landed. The cost in killed, wounded and missing had been about 6,000 Americans and 4,200 British

of coming wars. We have seen how again and again scientific research and ingenious invention have realised things that were once counted as demonstrably impossible of attainment. Just now more than one student of the later developments of electricity is busy with schemes for new applications of what is popularly known as "wireless electricity" to warfare, and the claim has already been made that it is possible to explode from a distance the materials of a magazine, the charges in a gun limber or in an enemy's gun, the cartridges on the infantry soldier's belt or bandolier. It would be rashness to assert that this is impossible. But its accomplishment might well make the use of explosives an impossibility in war. Such an event would have the strangest results. For once the latest progress would necessitate a long retrogression. It would reverse the course of military history, and bring back to the battlefield the open lines of archers and cross-bowmen, the heavily armoured horsemen, the serried ranks of pikemen or men-at-arms like the Roman legionary and the Greek phalangist. It would be a case of "the wheel turning full circle" and bringing back the warfare of earlier centuries.

'Or there may be another and still more remarkable development. How many of the wild imaginations of romance have in our own time become sober realities? Our growing mastery over the transformation, concentration and transmission of energy may some day result in an inventor finding the means thus to bring into the region of practical realisation some weapon like Mr H. G. Wells' imaginary heat ray – the ray of all-consuming fire that could be turned on the selected target, shrivelling up and destroying all it touched. Such a terror may some day close the long record of military history by making war impossible.'

Much of what Mr Atteridge predicted already existed in one form or another and would become apparent within months of his laying down his pen. Other aspects took longer to materialise but were less fanciful than they may have appeared at the time. Radar, in fact, evolved from experiments designed to produce

a 'death ray', and lasers have many military uses, including accurate range-finding, as well as in space weaponry; no doubt someone, somewhere, is still tinkering with the idea of exploding an enemy's ammunition supply by remote control.

We are, however, getting some way ahead of ourselves. Since the Second World War ended there have been surprisingly few wars involving direct conflict between regular armed forces, and most of these, including the Korean War, the short wars between India and Pakistan and the wars between Israel and her Arab neighbours, have tended to reinforce lessons already learned. Indeed, the protracted war between Iraq and Iran during the 1980s revealed a tendency towards regression. Neither army was strong enough to inflict a decisive defeat on the other and neither seemed capable of securing a strategic objective that would cause the other to sue for peace. Attempts to break the stalemate included the use of chemical weapons by Iraq, while the Iranians exploited political and religious fervour among their larger population by mounting horrific 'human wave' attacks which predictably failed in the teeth of concentrated machine-gun and artillery fire. The war cost more than one million lives and ended with both sides in approximately the same positions they held when it began. In other areas, the so-called Cold War has involved regular forces either in preparing for a battle of mass destruction between NATO and the Warsaw Pact in central Europe, or in protracted guerrilla and counter-insurgency operations in various parts of the world, including most notably the 30-year conflict in Vietnam. Only in the Gulf War of 1991–2, during which a coalition army led by the USA on behalf of the United Nations liberated Kuwait from Iraqi occupation, did it become possible to see the form that full-scale modern warfare might take. This reflected the fact that since 1945 weapon technology has expanded at a rate many times faster than that of all previous centuries put together. In the space available it is manifestly impossible to mention more than the principal avenues of advance.

Many modern weapon systems have their roots in the Second World War, the most obvious being thermo-nuclear devices. The first and only use of these weapons was against Japan in 1945, it being considered that, given the fanatical nature of Japanese resistance thus far, an invasion of the home islands could cost one million Allied casualties. Producing as they did terrible effects of widespread devastation, ghastly burns and terminal radiation sickness, they did procure an early end to the war, but their legacy was to be a balance of terror between opposed ideologies, with the ever-present risk that such weapons of mass destruction might find their way into the armoury of a deranged dictator.

In 1944 Hitler had begun to bombard south-eastern England with flying-bombs and rockets carrying a high-explosive payload. Their effect was insufficient to influence the course of the war, but they did point the way to the future. In the post-war years rocket technology advanced apace, resulting in huge missiles capable of delivering nuclear payloads between continents, putting observation and communication satellites into orbit around the earth, or reaching the moon. When their launching sites became obvious targets, submarines were designed to fire batteries of nuclear missiles from secret locations deep in the world's oceans. For battlefield use, transportable nuclear missiles and heavy guns capable of firing nuclear shells were developed.

During the Second World War the Japanese made occasional, and fairly discrete, use of a frangible glass grenade containing hydrogen cyanide, intended to incapacitate Allied tank crews when employed at close quarters. As far as I am aware, no other battlefield use of chemical or biological weapons took place during the war although belligerents did possess stocks for retaliatory purposes, should the need ever have arisen. The threat remains however, and of course it is a simple matter to fill a missile warhead, bomb or shell with a chemical or biological warfare agent; the dictator Saddam Hussein has used gas against the Iranian Army and his rebellious subjects on several occasions.

The nuclear, biological and chemical (NBC) threat has conditioned the way armies operate. Armour plate does provide some protection against radiation and if an armoured vehicle is fitted with an over-pressure system the danger from chemical and biological weapons is reduced as well. Over the years therefore, all first-class armies have become heavily mechanised, with tanks, armoured personnel carriers, self-propelled guns and other armoured vehicles assuming greater importance than ever before. Further protection is provided by gas masks, disposable outer clothing and field decontamination centres.

In parallel, printed circuit boards, transistors and the microchip have produced miniaturised computers that have apparently open-ended military applications. These include everything from the programming of missiles, through the instant transfer of data from target acquisition radar to fire control systems, to precise calculation of an enemy's mortar baseplate position. Coupled with sensors, computerised fire control systems now produce frighteningly accurate results.

The past half-century has also seen the rocket-driven missile achieve a dominant position in all forms of warfare. Missiles exist for every purpose – air-to-air, air-to-surface, surface-to-air, ground-to-ground, anti-ship, anti-submarine, anti-tank and anti-missile. Depending upon the size and role of the missile, guidance is effected by various means, including pre-programming, radio, radar, command wire, infra-red homing and, in the case of anti-submarine missiles, acoustic homing.

Another development which has revolutionised warfare in general is that of the helicopter, which was first used in any numbers by the US Army for casualty evacuation during the Korean War. Shortly after, the invention of the turboshaft engine provided an enormous improvement in the ratio of power to weight. This not only enabled bigger helicopters to be built, but also broadened the scope of their use to the point that no country dare ignore its helicopter arm, which adds what might be described as a fourth dimension to the land and sea battle.

In the context of the land battle the majority of combat helicopters fall into three main types: attack, assault troop carrier, and supply. The attack helicopter, or gunship, carries a wide variety of weapons for the close support of ground troops, including cannon, machine-guns, rockets and anti-tank guided weapons (ATGW). The assault troop carrier can carry one or more fully equipped infantry sections, dropping them within easy striking distance of their objective and then, if required, lifting them out when their mission has been completed. The supply helicopter is designed for the bulk forward delivery of ammunition and stores but can also double as a troop carrier and 'flying crane' capable of lifting field artillery and vehicles into the combat zone. Helicopter roles on the battlefield include overall surveillance, concentration of superior forces at the point of contact, destruction of the enemy's armour, deep penetration of the enemy's rear areas, the insertion of special forces, interdiction of his transport and supply elements, and disruption of his electronic equipment by jamming.

The helicopter introduced the phrase air mobility to the military vocabulary. As air mobility enables formations to be landed accurately and together, a situation often denied by circumstances to airborne operations, the role of parachute troops has tended to decline. In Vietnam the US Army, faced with a guerrilla war in which the terms front, flank and rear had no meaning, employed the 1st Cavalry Division (Airmobile), which had no fewer than 428 rotorcraft and a strength of 16,000 men. Reaching the war zone in August 1965, the division was in action almost continuously, inflicting hitherto unheard-of casualties on its elusive Communist opponents. In appropriate circumstances, therefore, air mobile formations actually possess a flexibility exceeding that of armoured formations, and the concept has been adopted by all major armies.

The naval applications of the helicopter centre largely around anti-submarine warfare, extending the fleet's defensive zone by many miles and introducing an offensive capability. Hovering above the waves, the helicopter can lower sensitive sonar devices into the water, searching for the submarine's distinctive vocabulary. Once an enemy submarine has been located depth-charges can be dropped with accuracy or a homing torpedo released. For use against surface targets naval helicopters are armed with cannon, machine-guns, rockets and guided air-to-surface missiles. Other uses at sea include the transfer of stores and personnel from ship to ship or from ship to shore.

Since 1945 the shape of navies has undergone numerous radical alterations. With the exception of one or two retained by the US Navy for bombardment purposes, the battleship has vanished from the world's oceans. The new capital ship is the fleet carrier, displacing 90,000 tons and more, capable of launching destructive air strikes over long distances. Equally important, though for different reasons, is the nuclear-powered submarine, driven by a reactor which provides not only a submerged endurance undreamed of in 1939–45, but also an underwater speed comparable to the majority of surface warships. Of the two types of submarine in service one, armed with long-range nuclear missiles, serves as a permanent strategic deterrent. The other, the hunter-killer, employs conventional high-speed or long-range guided torpedoes. Using a variety of underwater detection devices to hunt down and kill its prey from a distance, it can become the scourge of surface units and of its own kind. Similar devices are used to confuse the enemy's response, and the great depths to which these craft can dive provides some measure of security in itself.

For other classes of warship the gun, now fully automated and capable of firing a round every few seconds, has become a secondary weapon, retained for bombardment purposes. The warship's principal armament now consists of a balanced mix of missiles for which early warning, target acquisition and guidance radar scanners are mounted as high as possible to provide the necessary wide horizon. In such a complex electronic environment command in action is exercised not from the bridge but from a control room deep within the interior. As armour plate provides no defence against the shaped charge of a missile warhead, its use in warship construction has long been abandoned. A strike by a large surface-skimming anti-ship missile such as the French Exocet can therefore inflict serious if not fatal damage. Defence against such weapons is provided by anti-missile missiles, but at closer ranges the Vulcan/Phalanx six-barrelled machine- gun, linked to guidance radar and operating on the Gatling principle with an output of 6,000 rounds per minute, offers the best defence.

Developments in land warfare have largely stemmed from the 45-year confrontation between the Warsaw Pact and NATO in Europe. The former, dominated by the Soviet Union, possessed the largest tank fleet in history, training its tank and motor rifle divisions exclusively for an offensive against the West. On the debit side, its command and control system continued to lack the flexibility found in NATO armies and in technical terms its equipment was a half-generation behind Western designs. The NATO forces, on the other hand, while smaller and structured for a defence which would include punishing counter-attacks in the German tradition, were much the better equipped with anti-tank weapons at every level.

Naturally, such a sustained stand-off accelerated the evolutionary process of weapon development. The issue of semi- and fully-automatic assault rifles to the infantry, the giant strides made in artillery weapons and ammunition, and the installation of computerised fire control systems in main battle tanks, has produced a leap in firepower unimaginable to the veteran of the Second World War. The contest between those who design tanks and those who would destroy them has been continuous. An alternative to high-velocity shot penetrating the interior of the vehicle, and also to shaped charge ammunition, is provided by the HESH (High-Explosive Squash-Head) round. This has a 'soft' outer casing which

pancakes on impact, setting up vibrations within the armour; a micro-second later the main charge detonates, blasting jagged scabs of metal off the inner face of the armour to fly round the interior of the vehicle. When, during the Arab–Israeli War of 1973, shaped charge ATGWs were first deployed *en masse*, taking a fearful toll of the Israeli armour, there were predictions that the tank's days were numbered. Shortly afterwards, however, a new type of armour appeared, incorporating a ceramic layer which absorbed and dispersed the intensely hot jet of gas produced by the explosion of a shaped charge round. To this was later added so-called reactive armour, which explodes when struck, causing further dispersion. As far as the main battle tank's immensely thick frontal and, to a lesser extent, side armour is concerned, the threat has been countered. However, scientists immediately began designing weapon systems intended to penetrate the tank's much thinner top armour. These include artillery or mortar rounds that eject disc-shaped sub-munitions known as explosively formed projectiles. The discs descend slowly by parachute or spinning vane until their sensors locate the target vehicle. A charge is then automatically fired forging the disc into a ballistic bolt that is punched at high velocity through the turret roof or engine deck of the tank. In the short term one answer is to strengthen the armour in these areas although this adds to the tank's already considerable weight, but longer term solutions may lie with a fully automated turret and fewer crew housed separately within the hull below, or even unmanned robotic tanks.

The tasks of combat engineers remain unchanged. In the attack these include opening the route, improving roads, building bridges, breaching minefields and destroying obstacles; in defence, the engineers prepare positions, construct fortifications and obstacles, lay minefields, destroy approach roads and demolish bridges. Their techniques and much of their equipment have evolved from methods employed during the Second World War, especially by British 79th Armoured Division, which, as we have seen, used a variety of specially designed armoured vehicles to deal with different problems including bridgelayers, fascine carriers, mine-clearing and demolition devices, to name but a few.

There have been considerable advances in mine warfare. Minefields can still be laid by hand, but the most common method involves a trailer-mounted plough cutting a furrow; mines then pass down a conveyor belt into the furrow and are covered by disks at the rear of the trailer, while trailing chains smooth over the disturbed earth. 'Instant' minefields can be produced with smaller mines fired by carrier rocket up to nineteen miles behind the enemy's front, or more locally from helicopter- or vehicle-mounted projectors. Lanes through minefields can be cleared by a number of methods developed during the Second World War, including detonation by a heavy roller or flailing by chains attached to a rotating drum, or lifting and turning by means of a plough, all of which are attached to specially designed armoured vehicles. Another method involves projecting an explosive-filled hose across the minefield then firing it to detonate every mine in its path. In the final analysis, should none of these devices be available, resort is made to the dangerous and time-consuming method of prodding by hand.

In addition to laid anti-personnel or anti-tank mines, there are also free-standing mines of the Claymore type, sited to cover an obvious approach; when activated, these shred attackers with hundreds of ball-bearings, fired at high-velocity. Soldiers detest anti-personnel mines in their various forms because of their capacity to maim rather than kill. Modern mines, furthermore, are small and, being made largely from plastic material, are difficult to detect. The convention in first-class armies is that minefields should be mapped and marked, but in the sort of Third World guerrilla wars that have been waged in recent years insurgents and government forces have created unmarked minefields wherever they feel inclined, with horrific consequences for the civilian population. In the Falklands War, too,

the Argentine Army scattered thousands of mines without keeping proper records. It is understandable, therefore, that public attitudes have hardened against anti-personnel mines, though whether the international campaign to ban their use will succeed is another matter.

In the light of all the above, survival probability for men and machines on the modern battlefield is lower than ever before although many imponderables remain, such as the standard of training and the quality of the opposition. For this reason much training and many operations take place during the hours of darkness. Even this provides only limited protection because night vision aids, used on a small scale during the Second World War, now include a wide range of active and passive scanning devices.

In the air, too, the story of the past fifty years has largely been one of evolution. The jet engine was in use before the end of the Second World War and subsequent aircraft simply reflect a continuous process of improvement, with one exception. The realisation that in a conflict between NATO and the Warsaw Pact airfield runways would become cratered and unusable has led to the VSTOL (Vertical/Short Take-Off and Landing) concept, of which the Harrier is the most famous example, the thrust being vectored downwards until the aircraft is airborne. This capability enables VSTOL aircraft to be dispersed and operate from forest clearings or other suitable locations away from obvious target airfields.

It is in the areas of weaponry and electronics that air warfare has progressed most. The range of sophisticated weaponry available to modern combat aircraft is bewildering. It includes conventional bombs, bombs which fly down an enemy's radar beam or into a 'basket' of radar reflections from a target indicated by another aircraft, bombs designed to crater runways or penetrate 'hardened' concrete hangars and bunkers, cluster bombs packed with explosive sub-munitions, air-to-air and air-to-ground missiles, cannon and high-output Gatling-type machine-guns. Electronic systems include navigational aids, communication transceivers, radar including IFF (Identification Friend or Foe), enemy surface-to-air missile launch warning, enemy radio and radar jamming, plus a counter-measures pod releasing expendable radar jammers, chaff bundles consisting of thin metal foil which confuse radar-guided missiles, and infra-red flares to decoy heat-seeking missiles.

While modern aircraft fly faster and hit harder than their Second World War counterparts, air forces still perform the same roles, including obtaining air superiority and neutralising an enemy's anti-aircraft defences, close air support of friendly ground forces, co-ordinated when appropriate with helicopter units, battlefield interdiction in the rear areas of the combat zone, interdiction of an enemy's lines of communication, and strategic bombing. One important difference, however, is that while Second World War air operations remained within theatre, the Cold War has made them global, with rapid deployment the keynote. Thus in-flight re-fuelling from tankers is commonplace and giant transports regularly lift ground troops, their equipment and supplies over very long distances into threatened areas.

Because of the highly skilled nature of their task, and the heavy expense involved in their training, the selection of aircrew is a rigorous process from which, out of 1,500 candidates, only 75 can expect to qualify. Aircrew are therefore every air force's major asset and, should they be forced to bail out in enemy territory, every possible effort is made to rescue them.

As modern warfare is so complex and prohibitively expensive, most nations have taken advantage of the reduction in world tension following the collapse of the Soviet Union to re-structure their armed forces on a smaller, more professional basis. Equipment of every kind is costly, and so is the training of personnel in every branch of service, despite the introduction of realistic simulators. The sort of protracted global conflict which has characterised so much of the 20th century is considered unlikely in the foreseeable future, but few sciences are as fallible as the prediction

of wars, or their nature. Like hurricanes, wars arise suddenly and from nowhere; in the months preceding them, few could have foretold that three-dimensional wars would be fought over the Falkland Islands or Kuwait. The question therefore arises, what happens when precious equipment and highly trained personnel, both irreplaceable in the short term, have been expended? Then, as Hilliard Atteridge implied more than 80 years ago, some form of regression will take place, although it will be nothing like as dramatic as he suggested. Given the truth of the old saying that if one wants peace one should prepare for war, the key to the problem would seem to lie in the creation of adequate reserves, a point apparently unintelligible to the majority of politicians.

KUWAIT, 24–28 FEBRUARY 1991

Eight years of inconclusive war with Iran had left the Iraqi treasury exhausted and indebted to foreign powers to the tune of $65,000 million. It had also frustrated the ambitions of Saddam Hussein, dictator of Iraq, to be seen as an all-powerful warrior monarch in the mould of the Great Kings who had once ruled his land. Casting his eyes on Iraq's small but wealthy neighbour Kuwait, he decided that by adding it to his domains his problems would be solved at a stroke, for Kuwaiti foreign investments alone amounted to $2,000,000 million, the income from which would pay his debts and return Iraq to solvency. At 02.00 on 2 August 1990, the Iraqi Army rolled across the border in such overwhelming strength that the Kuwaiti Defence Force could only fight a rearguard action and withdraw into Saudi Arabia.

In the opinion of those best qualified to know, Saddam was neither mad nor unbalanced. He did, nevertheless, possess a psyche based on hero-worship of Nebuchadnezzar, wielding absolute power over his subjects, brooking no opposition to the point where even members of his inner cabinet could be shot on the spot for expressing a contrary opinion. Understandably the remainder chose to flatter his belief that he was a great conqueror. To this end his scientists worked to produce NBC weapons of mass destruction, missile delivery systems and even the largest gun in the world, while his generals received all the conventional weapons they wanted. For all that, his conduct of the coming war, and that of his Revolutionary Command Council, was unbelievably amateur, relying upon hugely destructive gestures such as the release of oil into the Persian Gulf or the torching of Kuwaiti oilfields as demonstrations of naked power.

The invasion of Kuwait was immediately condemned both by the United Nations and the Arab League. Saddam, apparently unperturbed, immediately embarked on a protracted game of diplomatic brinkmanship, in which he had few equals. On 29 November the UN Security Council passed Resolution 678, authorising all necessary means to ensure an Iraqi withdrawal from Kuwait. Meanwhile, at the request of Saudi Arabia, a Coalition of nations, led by the USA and Great Britain, had dispatched contingents to safeguard the Gulf area against further acts of Iraqi aggression, most of the troops arriving by air while much of their heavy equipment followed by sea. Known as *Desert Shield*, this operation developed into a steady build-up which in due course would permit active implementation of Resolution 678.

The task was not to be under-estimated, for although the Iraqi Army had not especially distinguished itself during the war with Iran, and indeed displayed very little aptitude for mechanised operations, it was still the fourth largest army in the world and had been lavishly equipped by the former Soviet Union. Its first-line strength totalled more than 500,000 men, plus 480,000 reservists available for immediate recall. Equipment included some 5,500 main battle tanks, 6,000 APCs, about 4,000 artillery pieces of various types and perhaps 800 surface-to-surface missiles. These assets furnished seven corps containing a total of six regular and one reserve armoured divisions, three mechanised infantry divisions, ten motorised infantry divisions, seventeen regular and fourteen reserve infantry divisions, one naval infantry and one special forces division, an air assault brigade, twenty independent infantry brigades plus, of course, the Republican Guard, which, being better paid and equipped than the rest of the Army, formed the basis of Saddam's power. The Guard had two armoured, two mechanised and three motorised infantry divisions and was referred to with a curious degree of respect by Western media commentators, although in the final analysis its members proved to be rather ordinary soldiers. The Iraqi Air Force numbered about 700 combat aircraft, the great majority being Soviet in origin, and if handled properly had the potential to inflict damaging losses on the Coalition forces. On the other hand, Saddam's tiny navy, consisting of five frigates, six corvettes, missile craft and light forces, was in no position to challenge the armada of Coalition warships assembling in the Gulf.

When complete, the Coalition army, commanded by General H. Norman Schwarzkopf, US Army, would number some 463,000 men. It would include 315,000 Americans, 40,000 Saudis, over 30,000 British, 30,000 Egyptians, 12,000 Syrians, 10,000 French, 10,000 men from the Gulf States of Kuwait, Qatar, Bahrain, Oman and the United Arab Emirates, 8,000 Pakistanis, 6,000 Bangladeshis, 1,200 Moroccans, 500 each from Senegal and Niger, and 300 Czechs. It had more than 3,600 main battle tanks, of which the most important types were the US Marine Corps' M60, the US Army's M1A1 Abrams, the British Challenger and the French AMX30, plus APCs, Infantry Fighting Vehicles (IFVs), artillery and assault engineering assets in proportion.

During the Coalition build-up Saddam could think of nothing more imaginative than stuffing as many divisions as possible into Kuwait until 42 were present in what would become the battle zone. Of these, six were retained along the coast to counter the threat of a landing by a powerful US Marine Corps amphibious task force lying in the Gulf, accompanied by the battleships USSs *Missouri* and

Above: Much of the Iraqi Army's equipment was supplied by the former Soviet Union. Most armoured formations were equipped with elderly T54/55 tanks, as seen here, more modern designs being reserved for the Republican Guard. *Novosti Press Agency*

Wisconsin. The reminder simply dug in to await the inevitable assault. Defence works along the southern frontier of Kuwait consisted of 15-feet-high sand walls, oil-filled flame trenches and extensive minefields. Behind these inter-locked defensive positions were sited in depth, in the Soviet manner. Usually, these were triangular-shaped and enclosed within 10-feet-high sand walls with a barbed-wire perimeter, containing machine-guns, mortars and anti-tank weapons as well as tanks dug in so deeply that their gun barrels swept the ground. Within, the garrisons dug bunkers, some of which were impressively deep and roofed with concrete, although others would barely provide protection against a mortar round. In general, the Iraqi infantry divisions were deployed along the frontier, and the armoured and mechanised formations, including the Republican Guard, were held back in corps or army reserve for the counter-attack role.

One remarkable feature of the war was the manner in which many Western defence analysts over-estimated Iraqi strength and ability. When Saddam promised that anyone attacking Iraq would find himself fighting 'the mother of battles' and 'step into the dark pit of death', he was taken seriously. Because of the earlier war with Iran, the Iraqi Army was described as battle-hardened when, in fact, it was battle-weary and demoralised by Saddam's having handed over to Iran all that had been fought for so that he could embark on the Kuwaiti adventure without threat to his rear. It was estimated that there were half a million Iraqi troops in Kuwait, but we now know that the real figure was in the region of 300,000, giving the Coalition forces a numerical advantage, albeit a lesser one than Schwarzkopf would have liked. Some experts also insisted on giving Iraqi divisions the same fighting and efficiency values as NATO divisions when most of the infantry formations were below half-strength, others were far short of their establishment, and all contained an untrained conscript element. It was predicted, too, that ejecting the Iraqis from Kuwait would cost between 30,000 and 100,000 casualties. In the light of 58,000 American lives having been lost in Vietnam to no apparent purpose, this was a matter for very serious consideration in the USA, where neither the public nor the body politic was likely to take a tolerant view of further heavy losses in a distant quarrel. Furthermore, although Saddam had been warned in no uncertain terms what would happen if he ventured through the NBC threshold, he was unpredictable and precautions had to be taken. Much emphasis was therefore placed upon NBC training and the Coalition troops received a hurriedly prepared programme of inoculations.

By the New Year it had become obvious that, despite intense diplomatic activity, Saddam had no intention whatever of leaving Kuwait. On 17 January 1991, therefore, the Coalition opened its air offensive from airfields in Saudi Arabia and other Gulf states as well as from carriers cruising offshore. Code-named *Desert Storm*, this involved B-52 heavy strategic bombers, low radar profile stealth fighters, Tornados, F-14s, F-15s and F-16s, Jaguars, A-10 tank-busters, Mirages, Harriers and ship-launched Tomahawk cruise missiles which could navigate their way to their programmed target, the intensity of the attack rising at times to 8,000 sorties a day. The first phase, accompanied by expert jamming to blind the enemy's radar, was planned to eliminate the Iraqi Air Force and destroy Iraq's anti-aircraft defences. In fact, little was seen of Saddam's aircraft, most of which remained within their hardened hangars until 26 January when they began a mass exodus to internment in Iran. Nor, save against low-level attack, was the anti-aircraft defence effective, and since its failure revealed Saddam's fallibility to his people its commander was promptly executed. The next phases progressively destroyed the Iraqi command and control apparatus and then set about isolating the enemy army in Kuwait from supplies and reinforcements. 'First, we will cut it off, then we will kill it,' remarked General Colin Powell, Chairman of the US Joint Chiefs of Staff. Bridges across the Tigris and the Euphrates, as well as other elements within the command and logistic infrastructures, were systematically blown apart by 'smart' bombs which thought their way to an indicated target; sadly, their intelligence was sometimes overestimated and civilians were killed, enabling Saddam to pose as the victim of Western aggression against the Arab world. The final and most protracted stage of *Desert Storm* was the sustained pounding of the Iraqi field army in Kuwait. During this, the B-52s made the Republican Guard formations their special target, the impact of their huge bomb-loads making the desert shudder over a wide distance from the target area while the rumble of their

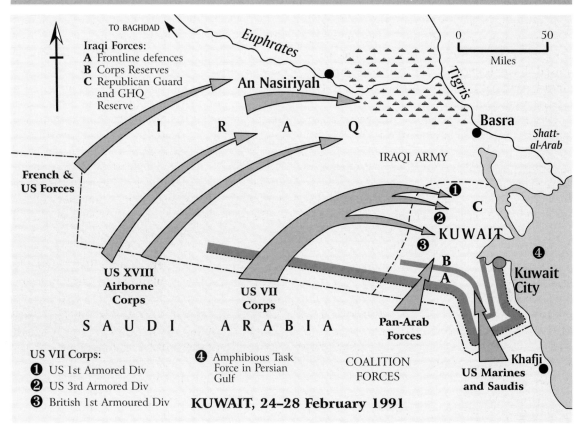

KUWAIT, 24–28 February 1991

Iraqi Forces:
A Frontline defences
B Corps Reserves
C Republican Guard and GHQ Reserve

US VII Corps:
❶ US 1st Armored Div
❷ US 3rd Armored Div
❸ British 1st Armoured Div

❹ Amphibious Task Force in Persian Gulf

COALITION FORCES

multiple explosions could be heard more than 40 miles away. The air offensive was to continue for 38 days without pause, leaving some Iraqi formations incapable of operating while others, shocked and starved into apathy, lost whatever will they might have had to fight. Curiously, less equipment was destroyed than might have been anticipated. One senior Iraqi artillery officer lost only one-fifth of his guns during the air offensive, but of the remaining 80 only seven survived the precise counter-battery fire with which the Coalition opened its ground offensive.

Despite the battering he was receiving from *Desert Storm*, Saddam had some surprises up his sleeve. On 18 January he began to fire Scud long-range surface-to-surface missiles against Israel from mobile launchers, hoping to trigger a response that would immediately alienate the Arab members of the Coalition. Urged to exercise restraint, the Israelis did so, partly at least because of the difficulties involved in tying in

their own operational procedures with the Coalition's air offensive. Simultaneously, more Scuds were fired at targets in Saudi Arabia. The US forces quickly deployed Patriot anti-missile missile batteries to both areas while in the enemy's hinterland British SAS and US Army Special Forces teams, already carrying out clandestine operations, were diverted to locating the Scud launchers and directing air attacks against them. In the event, though it drew off a proportion of the Coalition's air power, the Scud bombardment produced few practical results; of 86 launched, 28 missed their targets, 37 were intercepted and the fate of eight remains unknown.

A further surprise awaited the Coalition on 29 January when three Iraqi mechanised infantry brigades, supported by a small and abortive amphibious operation, crossed the Saudi frontier. All three columns suffered heavy losses although one did penetrate as far as the deserted town of Khafji, only to be flung

305

out on 1 February by a joint Qatari, Saudi and US Marine counter-attack. The fate of this limited offensive did little to restore flagging Iraqi morale, but the probability is that Saddam was influenced by the impact on American public opinion of the Tet Offensive in Vietnam and was seeking a much wider audience. Indeed, comparable opinions were expressed to the effect that, if, after the pounding the Iraqis had received, they were still capable of mounting offensive operations, they were evidently as tough and battle-hardened as their own propaganda suggested. Those more closely associated with what had taken place described the Iraqis' performance as poor and their motivation low.

Meanwhile Schwarzkopf was laying his plans for the Coalition's ground offensive, which would be code-named *Desert Sword*. Aged 56, Schwarzkopf had previously served two combat tours in Vietnam and was a former commander of the American Rapid Deploy-

ment Force. He had familiarised himself with the problems of desert warfare and his planning reflected his knowledge of military history. Like Hannibal at Cannae, therefore, he deployed the disparate elements of his army where their equipment and national characteristics could be put to best use; like Montgomery at Second Alamein he faced a break-in, break-through and break-out battle, the details of which were examined in minute detail; but, most of all, like Allenby at Megiddo, he planned a battle which would annihilate the enemy army within hours.

Envisaging a hard, slogging fight up the coast towards Kuwait city, Schwarzkopf allocated this sector to Lieutenant General Walter Boomer's US Marine Corps, which included 1st and 2nd Marine Divisions and 1st Brigade, US 2nd Armored Division. The Marines would act as the iron fist of the Arab contingents which, under Saudi command, were deployed along the Kuwaiti frontier, including Syrian 9th

Left: A Challenger tank of the 14th/20th King's Hussars. *IWM Neg GLF1419 Crown Copyright*

ipated counter-attack by the Republican Guard. Finally, on the left of the Coalition's 270-mile front, was Lieutenant General Gary E. Luck's US XVIII Airborne Corps, consisting of French 6th Light Armoured Division, US 82nd Airborne, 101st Airborne (Air Assault) and 24th Infantry (Mechanised) Divisions, plus 3rd Armored Cavalry Regiment.

As for the frontier defences so laboriously constructed by Saddam's troops, these were nothing like as formidable as those of the Atlantic Wall, nor were they covered by fire to anything like the same extent. There were, too, plenty of armoured assault engineering vehicles to deal with them, including combat engineer tractors to break through the sand ramparts, bridgelayers to span the flame trenches once their contents had been burned off by napalm strikes, and rocket-launched Giant Viper explosive hoses, flails and ploughs to gap the minefields.

The striking similarities between Schwarzkopf's plan and Allenby's for Megiddo were extended in a manner which Allenby would certainly have approved. In essence, the advance of the Marines and the Arab contingents across the frontier into Kuwait was intended to tie down the Iraqis in an aggressive holding action. Simultaneously VII Corps would advance north into Iraq and then wheel eastwards across the Wadi al Batin into Kuwait, taking the defenders in rear as it headed for the coast. Within the corps' envelopment an inner pincer would be formed as the British held off the Republican Guard, which would be caught between the hammer and the anvil as the American armour, wheeling further north, smashed into its rear. Concurrently, XVIII Airborne Corps would use all its mobility assets to strike deep into Iraq, establishing a blocking position in the Euphrates valley, thereby cutting off the enemy army in Kuwait and ensuring its destruction. The plan was materially assisted by Iraqi preoccupation

Armoured Division, Egyptian 4th Armoured and 3rd Mechanised Divisions, one armoured and four mechanised Saudi brigades, three Kuwaiti mechanised brigades, and one mechanised brigade each from Oman and Qatar/United Arab Emirates. Kuwait's western frontier was delineated by the Wadi al Batin, running approximately from south to north, but beyond this Saudi Arabia shared a common boundary with Iraq. Behind this Schwarzkopf deployed Lieutenant General John Y. Yeosock's US Third Army, consisting of two corps. On the right and prolonging the line of the Arab contingents was US VII Corps, commanded by Lieutenant General Frederick Franks. This consisted of US 1st and 3rd Armored, 1st Armored Cavalry and 1st Infantry Divisions, 2nd Armored Cavalry Regiment and British 1st Armoured Division, the last having been moved from the coast when it was appreciated that VIII Corps would require a hard-slogging formation to hold off the antic-

with the 17,000-strong Marine amphibious force lying offshore in the Gulf, and by Saddam's belief that the Coalition's ground offensive would be confined to Kuwaiti territory. This was a curious decision to have reached, given that the Allied air forces were ranging at will across Iraq, and the result was that very few formations were detailed to defend the common Saudi–Iraqi frontier. While he appreciated that Saddam was virtually operating blind, Schwarzkopf avoided raising his suspicions by delaying US Third Army's movement into its attack assembly areas as long as possible and maintaining a full flow of dummy radio traffic from its original positions.

By the fourth week of February *Desert Storm* had done all that could be expected of it without apparently influencing Saddam on the question of Kuwait and in the interest of preserving Coalition solidarity it was decided to mount the ground offensive. Preliminary probes across the lines resulted in prisoners being taken while the scale of desertions clearly indicated that the Iraqi army was ready for plucking.

The offensive began at 04.00 on 24 February. On the right the Marines and Arab contingents made unexpectedly good progress towards Kuwait City, overrunning several infantry divisions which had no intention of offering serious resistance. So many Iraqis were coming forward to surrender, in fact, that the need to marshal and administer them almost became a threat to progress in itself. Overhead, air support was continuous, obliterating any attempt by the enemy's armour to intervene. One A-10 tank-buster aircraft, for example, was credited with the destruction of 23 tanks in a single day, while some of the war's most graphic footage, taken from an AH-64A Apache anti-tank helicopter, shows a halted column of Iraqi tanks being destroyed in steady succession by missiles the source of which remained a mystery to their crews.

On the Coalition's left, XVIII Airborne Corps, delayed briefly by bad weather, began its deep thrust into Iraq at 07.30. In the largest airmobile operation in history, 101st Airborne lifted off in more than 300 helicopters and flew 70 miles north to establish a forward operating base within striking distance of the Euphrates valley. Simultaneously, French 6th Light Armoured Division, reinforced by a motorised brigade of 82nd Airborne, moved forward on the extreme left, covering 25 miles in the first twelve hours and routing an infantry division on the way.

By mid-morning Schwarzkopf had decided to accelerate the timings of the offensive, partly because progress was so good and casualties minimal, and partly because reports from Kuwait City suggested that the Iraqis were engaged in a farewell round of atrocities. The remainder of XVIII Airborne Corps was therefore set in motion to the north and VII Corps, 140,000 men and 1,300 tanks strong, began its break-in battle.

The turning movement by VII Corps, known as *Desert Sabre*, began with US 1st Infantry Division securing breaches in the frontier defences between 12.00 and 13.00, brushing aside in the process the enemy's 26th and 48th Infantry Divisions. The 2nd Armored Cavalry Regiment passed through the gap to provide a screen, followed that night by British 1st Armoured Division, US 1st and 3rd Armored Divisions having already passed through gaps farther west during the afternoon.

Despite the collapse of their frontier defences, some Iraqi commanders did attempt counter-attacks with their armoured reserves the following morning. Near Al-Jaber airfield the US 2nd Marine Division, 1st Armored Brigade and their supporting ground-attack aircraft beat off a local counter-stroke and inflicted heavy losses, while Iraqi armour squaring up to 1st Marine Division in the region of the Al-Burgan oilfield were treated to a 'time on target' divisional artillery concentration in which all guns landed their first shells at precisely the same moment. Those that survived the shock were chased northwards so that by nightfall on 25 February the Marines and some of the Arab formations were just ten miles short of Kuwait City.

On the left of the offensive French 6th Light Armoured Division, having advanced as far as As-Salman airfield, some 70 miles inside Iraq, paused to form an operational flank guard. The 101st Airborne had continued its air-assault advance overnight, cutting the Baghdad–Basra highway between An-Nasiriya and As-Samara and consolidating a blocking position. Elsewhere in XVIII Airborne Corps, 24th Infantry Division (Mechanised) had advanced 60 miles without encountering the slightest opposition and was also entering the Euphrates valley. During the afternoon and night of 25 February British 1st Armoured Division, commanded by Major-General Rupert Smith, wheeled right to provide an inner flank guard while the rest of VII Corps continued its advance to the north.

For the Iraqi commanders, whether in Baghdad or Kuwait, events were moving too quickly for them to exercise effective control. Many of their orders were issued to formations which had ceased to exist or were disintegrating under attack. Nor did the intervention of sandstorms provide any respite, for the Coalition's satellite navigation systems provided pinpoint locating and the pace of operations never slackened. The battlefield itself resembled a *Götterdämmerung* in which the midday sun was obscured by the smoke from hundreds of blazing oil wells, supplemented by burning Iraqi vehicles. Across this dreary landscape were already trudging more than 25,000 prisoners heading for their compounds in columns, and smaller groups seeking a captor.

During the late afternoon, and on through the night into 26 February, British 1st Armoured Division became engaged with the Iraqi 12th Armoured Division, still dug-in and acting as corps reserve behind the already mauled 26th Infantry Division. Both sides had night-fighting equipment, but the British and Americans, having spent so long preparing for a war in Europe, were technically a full generation ahead of their opponents, being equipped with thermal image gunsights, laser range-finders and fire-control computers, while in themselves the Iraqis' elderly T55s and T62s were no match for modern Challenger and Abrams, especially at long range. Shooting steadily and accurately, the British destroyed the hapless 12th Armoured Division where it stood, then eliminated elements of 17th and

Below: British infantry deploy from their Warrior IFV. *IWM Neg GLF1407 Crown Copyright*

52nd Armoured Divisions as their battle groups forged east towards their next phase line, accounting for an estimated total of 300 fighting vehicles.

The inner pincer of VII Corps was now closing rapidly and inexorably around the enemy flank. The US 1st Infantry Division came into line on the British left while, screened by 2nd Armored Cavalry, US 1st and 3rd Armored Divisions continued to push north, frustrated more by refuelling requirements than the fragmented resistance they were encountering. By evening, however, they too had swung east and made their first contacts with the Republican Guard.

Meanwhile, XVIII Airborne Corps had consolidated its hold on the Euphrates valley. During the evening, US 24th Infantry Division, reaching the Baghdad–Basra road between Jabilah and Talil airfields, swung east towards Basra. Shortly afterwards, an Iraqi armoured brigade, evidently belonging to the Republican Guard since it was equipped with modern T72 tanks, was wiped out as it attempted to flee in the direction of Baghdad.

Throughout 27 February the Marine and Arab formations south and south-west of Kuwait City fought their way through the last of the prepared defences. Within the city, where armed resistance fighters had surfaced, Iraqi soldiers continued to murder civilians and loot to the bitter end. They then seized any transport available and fled north along the road to Basra, only to be pounced upon by the Coalition's air power. The result was a tangle of human and mechanical wreckage reminiscent of the Falaise pocket at the end of the Normandy campaign or the Mitla Pass during the Six Day War.

This day might also have seen the largest tank battle in history, had not so much of the Iraqi armour already been destroyed. Far from delivering a decisive counter-stroke, the Republican Guard allowed itself to penned in the north-eastern corner of Kuwait where it was attacked by US 1st and 3rd Armored, 24th Infantry and 101st Airborne Divisions while British 1st Armoured Division closed in

to the south. Confronted for the first time in their history by a first-class army with technically superior weapons and attacked simultaneously in three dimensions from unexpected directions, the Guard's divisions were cut to pieces. So one-sided was the fighting that at one phase 3rd Armored Division dispensed with its air support to reduce the risk of battlefield accidents.

Nevertheless the Guard, or at least parts of it, eluded destruction. Saddam, publicly humiliated yet desperate to survive, intimated that he was willing to accept the relevant UN Resolutions unconditionally and at 08.00 on 28 February, after 100 hours of fighting, a ceasefire was imposed by US President George Bush. The wisdom of this decision has been questioned ever since. It permitted some 20,000 Iraqi troops with approximately 700 tanks and 1,400 APCs to escape from the trap into Iraq, where they were immediately used by Saddam to put down risings among his countrymen.

This sour note apart, General Norman Schwarzkopf's victory was as complete and as masterly as any in history. Forty of the 42 Iraqi divisions in Kuwait had been swept from the board; between 40,000 and 60,000 Iraqis had been killed; 80,000 had been taken prisoner and a similar if not larger number may simply have deserted; more than 3,000 tanks, 2,400 APCs and 3,000 artillery weapons had been destroyed or captured. Coalition casualties amounted to 166 killed and 207 wounded. Of the former, 28 died in a Scud attack on Dharhan air base and a high proportion of the rest, including nine of the sixteen British soldiers killed, fell to 'friendly fire' battlefield accidents.

Perhaps the last rueful comment on the 'mother of battles' should be left to the captured Iraqi senior officer who remarked that it had been fought on the one hand by an army much of which had spent 40 years preparing for the Third World War, and on the other by an army which had reverted to the methods of the First World War, minus air cover. For good or ill, the story of battlefield technology continues to evolve.

BIBLIOGRAPHY

This list is offered to readers who wish to extend their knowledge of the conduct of war at different periods, battles, important incidents therein, and weapon technology. It is far from being exhaustive, but most of the books listed contain bibliographies that will lead the reader deeper into his areas of interest.

Anglesey, The Marquess of. *A History of the British Cavalry*, vol. V, *1914–19, Egypt, Palestine and Syria*. Leo Cooper, London, 1994

Atteridge, A. Hilliard. *Famous Land Fights*. Methuen, London, 1914

Belchem, Major-General David. *Victory in Normandy*. Chatto & Windus, London, 1981

Bennett, Geoffrey. *The Battle of Jutland*. Batsford, London, 1964

– *Naval Battles of the First World War*. Pan Books, London, 1974

Blond, Georges, trans. Marshall May. *La Grande Armée*, Arms and Armour Press, London, 1995

Bowyer, Chaz. *History of the RAF*. Bison, London, 1979

Brown, David. *Carrier Fighters*. Macdonald and Jane's. London, 1975

Brown, David, Shores, Christopher and Macksey, Kenneth. *The Guinness History of Air Warfare*. Guinness, London, 1976

Caesar, Julius. trans. S. A. Handford. *The Conquest of Gaul*. Penguin Books, London, 1956

Carver, Field Marshal Lord. *El Alamein*. Batsford, 1962

Chandler, David. *Austerlitz – Battle of the Emperors*. Osprey, London, 1990

– (ed.). *Great Battles of the British Army*. Arms and Armour Press, London, 1991

Clowes, William Laird. *The Royal Navy*, vol. V, Chatham Publishing, London, 1997

Cottrell, Leonard. *Enemy of Rome*. Pan Books, London, 1962

– *The Great Invasion*. Pan Books, London, 1961

Creasy, Sir Edward. *The Fifteen Decisive Battles of the World*. Dent, London, 1952

Cross, Robin (ed.) *The Guinness Encyclopedia of Warfare*. Guinness, London, 1991

Davies, David. *Fighting Ships – Ships of the Line 1793–1815*. Constable, London, 1996

Dodds, Glen Lyndon. *Battles in Britain 1066–1746*. Arms and Armour Press, London, 1996

Duffy, Christopher. *Fire and Stone – The Science of Fortress Warfare 1660–1860*. David and Charles, Newton Abbott, 1976

Elliott-Wright, Philipp. *Gravelotte–St Privat 1870*. Osprey, London, 1993

Ellis, John. *The Social History of the Machine-Gun*. Pimlico, London, 1976

Ellis, Major L. F., *et al. Victory in the West*, vol. I, *The Battle of Normandy*. HMSO, London, 1962

Emerson, Barbara. *The Black Prince*. Weidenfeld & Nicolson, London, 1976

Falls, Cyril. *Armageddon 1918*. Weidenfeld & Nicolson, London, 1964

Farrar-Hockley, A. H. *The Somme*. Batsford Books, London, 1964

Featherstone, Donald. *Bowmen of England*. Jarrolds, London, 1967

Frere-Cook, Gervis, and Macksey, Kenneth. *The Guinness History of Sea Warfare*. Guinness, London, 1975

Friedman, Colonel Richard S., *et al. Advanced Technology Warfare*. Salamander, London, 1985

Fuller, J. F. C., ed. John Terraine. *The Decisive Battles of the Western World*, vols I and II, Granada, London, 1970

Gaujac, Colonel Paul, *et al. Sedan 1940*. Service

Historique de l'Armée de Terre, Vincennes, 1990

Godden, John (ed.). *Harrier – Ski-Jump to Victory*. Brassey's, London, 1983

Griffith, Paddy. *The Ultimate Weaponry*. Guild, London, 1991

Gudgin, Peter. *Armour 2000*. Arms and Armour Press. London, 1990

Gunston, Bill (ed.). *The Encyclopedia of World Air Power*. Hamlyn, London, 1980

– *Military Helicopters*. Salamander, London, 1981

Hackett, General Sir John (ed.). *Warfare in the Ancient World*. Sidgwick & Jackson, London, 1989

Hamilton-Williams, David. *The Fall of Napoleon – The Final Betrayal*. Arms and Armour Press, London, 1994

– *Waterloo – New Perspectives*. Arms and Armour Press, London, 1994

Haythornthwaite, Philip J. *The Armies of Wellington*. Arms and Armour Press, London, 1994

– *The World War One Source Book*. Arms and Armour Press, London, 1992

– *The Napoleonic Source Book*. Arms and Armour Press, London, 1990

Hibbert, Christopher. *Agincourt*. Batsford, London, 1964

Hobart, F. W. A., *Pictorial History of the Machine-Gun*. Ian Allan, Shepperton, 1971

– *Fortress – A History of Military Defence*. Purnell, London, 1975

Hogg, Ian V. *A History of Artillery*. Hamlyn, London, 1974

– *Illustrated Encyclopedia of Artillery*. Guild, London, 1987

Holder, P. A. *The Roman Army in Britain*. Batsford Books, London, 1982

Holmes, Richard (ed.). *The World Atlas of Warfare*. Guild, London, 1988

Hooton, E. R. *Eagle in Flames – The Fall of the Luftwaffe*. Arms and Armour Press, London, 1997

Horne, Alistair. *To Lose a Battle – France 1940*. Penguin Books, London, 1979

Howard, Michael. *The Franco-Prussian War*. Routledge, London, 1988

Howarth, David. *Waterloo – A Near Run Thing*. Fontana, 1972

Hughes, Major-General B. P. *Firepower – Weapon Effectiveness on the Battlefield*. Arms and Armour Press. London, 1974

Ito, Masanori. *The End of the Imperial Japanese Navy*. Jove, New York, 1986

Johnson, Air Vice-Marshal J. E. *Full Circle – The Story of Air Fighting*. Chatto & Windus, London, 1964

Johnson, J. H. *Stalemate! – The Great Trench Warfare Battles of 1915–1917*. Arms and Armour Press, London, 1995

– *1918 – The Unexpected Victory*. Arms and Armour Press, London, 1997

Josephus, Flavius, trans. G. A. Williamson. *The Jewish War*, Penguin Books, London, 1960

Jukes, Geoffrey. *Stalingrad – The Turning-Point*. Macdonald, London, 1968

Katcher, Philip. *The American Civil War Source Book*. Arms and Armour Press, London, 1992

Kennedy, Frances H., (ed.) *The Civil War Battlefield Guide*. Houghton Mifflin, Boston, 1990

Kieser, Egbert, trans. Helmut Bögler. *Hitler on the Doorstep – Operation Sea Lion: The German Plan to Invade Britain 1940*. Arms and Armour Press, London, 1997

Laffin, John. *Jackboot – The Story of the German Soldier*. Cassell, London, 1965

Larionov, V., *et al.*, trans. William Biley. *World War II – Decisive Battles of the Soviet Army*. Progress Publishers, Moscow, 1984

Lavery, Brian. *Nelson's Navy – The Ships, Men and Organisation 1793–1815*. Conway Maritime Press, London, 1989

Lewis, Michael. *The Spanish Armada*. Batsford Books, London, 1960

Lord, Walter. *Incredible Victory, The Battle of Midway*. Pocket Books, New York, 1968

Lucas Phillips, C. E. *Alamein*. William Heinemann, London, 1962

Lyon, David. *Sea Battles in Close-Up: The Age of Nelson*. Ian Allan, Shepperton, in association with the National Maritime Museum, Greenwich, 1996

Lyon, Hugh. *Modern Warships*. Salamander, 1980

McCarthy, Chris. *The Somme – The Day by Day*

Account. Arms and Armour Press, London, 1993

McElwee, William. *The Art of War – Waterloo to Mons*. Weidenfeld & Nicolson, London, 1974

McKee, Alexander. *From Merciless Invaders – An Eye-Witness Account of the Spanish Armada*. Souvenir Press, London, 1963

Macintyre, Donald. *Aircraft Carrier – The Majestic Weapon*. Macdonald, London, 1968

Macksey, Kenneth. *The Guinness History of Land Warfare*. Guinness, London, 1973

Manstein, Field Marshal Erich von, ed. and trans. by A. G. Powell. *Lost Victories*. Arms and Armour Press, London, 1982

Marshall, S. L. A. *Night Drop – The American Airborne Invasion of Normandy*. Jove, New York, 1986

Mattingly, Garrett. *The Defeat of the Spanish Armada*. Pelican Books, London, 1965

Messenger, Charles. *Trench Fighting 1914–18*. Pan Books, London, 1972

Moltke, Field Marshal Helmuth von. *The Franco-German War of 1870–71*. Greenhill Books, London, 1992

Montgomery of Alamein, Field Marshal Viscount. *A History of Warfare*. George Rainbird Ltd, London, 1968

Nicolle, David. *Medieval Warfare Source Book*. Arms and Armour Press, London, 1995

Nofi, Albert A. *The Gettysburg Campaign*. Combined Books, Conshohocken, Pennsylvania, 1996

Padfield, Peter. *The Battleship Era*. Granada, London, 1972

Pericoli, Ugo. *1815 – The Armies at Waterloo*. Sphere, London, 1973

Perrett, Bryan. *A History of Blitzkrieg*. Robert Hale, London, 1983, Stein & Day, New York, 1983, Jove, New York, 1989

– *Knights of the Black Cross – Hitler's Panzerwaffe and Its Leaders*. Robert Hale, London, 1986, Wordsworth, Ware, 1989, St Martin's Press, New York, 1986, Dorset, New York, 1994

– *Desert Warfare*. Patrick Stephens, Wellingborough. 1988

– *Last Stand! Famous Battles Against the Odds*. Arms and Armour Press, London, 1991

– *At All Costs! Stories of Impossible Victories*. Arms and Armour Press, London, 1993

– *Seize and Hold – Master Strokes on the Battlefield*. Arms and Armour Press, London, 1994

– *Iron Fist – Classic Armoured Warfare Case Studies*. Arms and Armour Press, London, 1995

– *Against All Odds – More Dramatic 'Last Stand' Actions*. Arms and Armour Press, London, 1995

– *Megiddo 1918*. Osprey, Oxfordshire, 1999

Pfanz, Harry W. *Gettysburg – The Second Day*. University of North Carolina Press, Chapel Hill, 1987

Pimlott, John, and Badsey, Stephen (eds.). *The Gulf War Assessed*. Arms and Armour Press, London, 1992

Pitt, Barrie. *1918 – The Last Act*. Cassell, London, 1962

Rogers, Colonel H. C. B. *Napoleon's Army*. Ian Allan, Shepperton, 1974

Shores, Christopher. *Ground Attack Aircraft of World War II*. Macdonald and Jane's, London, 1977

Smith, Peter C. *Impact! The Dive-Bomber Pilots Speak*. William Kimber, London, 1981

Smurthwaite, David. *The Ordnance Survey Complete Guide to the Battlefields of Britain*. Webb & Bower, Exeter, 1989

Suskind, Richard. *The Crusades*. Ballantine, New York, 1962

Tacitus, Cornelius, trans. Michael Grant. *The Annals of Imperial Rome*. Penguin Books, London, 1959

– trans. H. Mattingly *On Britain and Germany*. Penguin Books, London, 1954

Terraine, John. *The Smoke and the Fire – Myths and Anti-Myths of War 1861–1945*. Sidgwick & Jackson, London, 1980

– *White Heat – The New Warfare 1914–18*. Sidgwick & Jackson, 1982

Tilberg, Frederick. *Gettysburg*. National Parks Service, Washington, DC, 1962

Turner, John Frayn. *D-Day Invasion 1944*. Corgi, London, 1974

Webster, Graham, and Dudley, Donald R. *The Roman Conquest of Britain*. Pan Books, London, 1973

Williams, John. *France, Summer 1940.* Macdonald, London, 1969

Wise, Terence. *The Wars of the Crusades 1096–1291.* Osprey, London, 1978

Wood, Tony, and Gunston, Bill. *Hitler's Luftwaffe.* Salamander, London, 1977

Xenophon, trans. Rex Warner. *The Persian Expedition.* Penguin Books, London, 1952

Zhukov, Marshal Georgi, *et al. Battles Hitler Lost – and The Soviet Marshals Who Won Them.* Jove, New York, 1988

INDEX